California Historical Landmarks

Office of Historic Preservation

CALIFORNIA STATE PARKS

State of California—The Resources Agency
California State Parks
P.O. Box 942896
Sacramento, CA 94296-0001

Marketing and Merchandising
Managing Editor - Linda McDonald
Cover Illustration - Audi Stanton
Editing - Carol Cullens

Project Coordinator and Assistant Executive Secretary for the State Historical Resources Commission:
Sandra J. Elder

Cartography:
Allen Clark

Printed in the United States of America

ISBN: 0-941925-19-6

Front Cover: Marshall Monument (Landmark No. 143) commemorating James Marshall, whose discovery of gold in the tailrace of Sutter's Mill on January 24, 1848 led to the Gold Rush of 1849. The statue of Marshall is pointing to the Gold Discovery Site (Landmark No. 530) near Sutter's Mill. In keeping with the themes of the Sesquicentennial Commemoration, this edition includes the following symbol for Gold Rush related landmarks.

150 Years
A Sesquicentennial

In the year 2000, the state of California will turn 150 years old. To mark this historic event, the California Gold Discovery to Statehood Sesqui-centennial Commemoration will be a massive, statewide celebration taking place in 1998, 1999, and 2000. During these three years, Californians and people from throughout the world will commemorate the 150th anniversaries of gold discovery, the Gold Rush, and California's statehood. The Sesquicentennial will demonstrate to the nation and the world that the diversity of California's proud cultures and natural resources makes our state unlike any other place on earth.

Each year of the commemoration will revolve around a specific theme. The theme for 1998, California's Golden Discoveries, begins with James Marshall's gold discovery and commemorates our state's other "golden discoveries" such as the wine and citrus industries, agriculture, oil, and Hollywood. In 1999, the theme of California's Rich Heritage will celebrate the diversity of cultures and heritages that came to this state as a result of the Gold Rush. Reenactments will highlight the forms of transportation these early pioneers used. Finally, entering the new millennium in the year 2000, the theme of California's Vision and Statehood will focus on social elements that consolidated and gave strength to California's growing communities.

Californians are planning events and programs at many sites where our state's history was made. From Placerita Canyon in Santa Clarita, site of the first commercial gold discovery, to Sutter's Mill in Coloma, where James Marshall's discovery of gold in 1848 triggered the Gold Rush; from Beckwourth Pass in Plumas County, the lowest pass in the Sierras, discovered in 1851 by African-American trailblazer Jim Beckwourth, to the Old Harmony Borax Works in Death Valley, legendary for its 20-Mule Team wagons; from Colton Hall in Monterey where the California Constitution was signed in 1849, to the site of the first state capitol in San Jose; California's myriad historic landmarks are waiting to be discovered by travellers and residents alike.

Through the Sesquicentennial, people will learn about our state's past, experience its present, and dream of our future. So take the time to visit these landmarks locally and throughout the state. By learning and understanding California's history, we can all help to make this a commemoration and a celebration that will be remembered for generations to come.

Table of Contents

NOTE ON LANDMARK SYMBOLS:

 Landmark for which state plaque has been placed

 Missing state plaque

 Private plaque

 Missing private plaque

 Gold Rush related landmark

Foreword

T he Mission of the California Department of Parks and Recreation is to
provide for the health, inspiration, and education of the people of California
by helping to preserve the state's extraordinary biological diversity,
protecting its most valued natural and cultural resources and creating opportunities
for high-quality outdoor recreation.

It is with great pleasure that I present the 1996 edition of California
Historical Landmarks. I know that there are many readers of this guidebook
who enjoy using it while traveling the highways and byways of our beautiful
state. Each year, more people discover the treasure of information within this
volume. And each year, more landmarks are added to the register as we strive
to preserve the best of California for future generations.

This edition is particularly significant in that it was designed in conjunc-
tion with the commemoration of the 150th anniversary in 1998 of the gold
discovery by James Marshall at Sutter's Mill. Both the mill and Marshall's
Monument depicted on the cover are historical landmarks located within
Marshall Gold Discovery State Historic Park. In addition, the landmarks that
reflect the history of the Gold Rush are annotated in this edition with a pick,
pan and shovel symbol.

In keeping with our mission to inspire and educate the people of
California about our most precious cultural resources, we offer you the most
current information available on over 1,070 California Registered Historical
Landmarks that are yours to explore, understand, and enjoy.

Donald Murphy, Director
California State Parks

Map of California by Counties

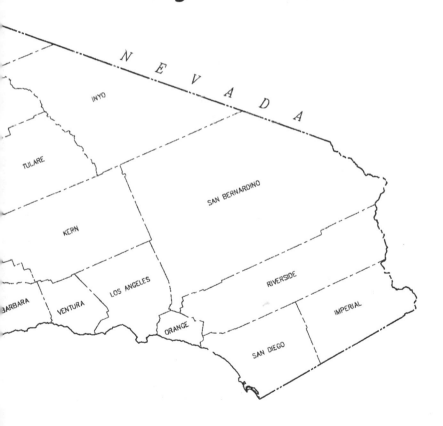

About This Book

This guidebook lists each landmark and gives a brief description of its significance. The landmarks are numbered in the order that they were registered by the State Historical Resources Commission and the Director of California State Parks. In this guidebook, the landmarks are listed by county. A numerical listing and an alphabetical listing are included at the end of this book.

The state historic parks of California are administered by the California State Parks and staffed by rangers, historians, and guides who protect and interpret state park areas for the public. A list of state historic parks and state parks with significant historical resources appears at the beginning of each county chapter.

Historical Landmarks are sites, buildings, features, or events that are of statewide significance and have anthropological, cultural, military, political, architectural, economic, scientific or technical, religious, experimental, or other value. The specific standards now in use were first applied in the designation of Landmark number 770.

State historical landmarks are recommended by the State Historical Resources Commission, to the Director of California State Parks for official designation. The nine-member commission is appointed by the governor and also reviews nominations for listing on the National Register of Historic Places, a federal program that is maintained by the National Park Service.

If a site is primarily of local interest, it may meet the criteria for the California Point of Historical Interest Program. It must: be the first, last, only, or most significant of a type in the county or local area; have the approval of the chairperson of the Board of Supervisors or the City/Town Council; be recommended by the State Historical Resources Commission; and be officially registered by the Director of California State Parks.

For more information about these and other historical preservation programs, write to the State Historical Resources Commission, P.O. Box 942896, Sacramento, California, 94296-0001.

Introduction

T his twelfth edition of *California Historical Landmarks* contains 1020 official landmarks plus fifty satellite and thematic registrations, making a total of 1070. As California moves into the twenty-first century, the landmark program will undoubtedly continue to evolve in response to changing needs.

In order to understand the progress of the landmark program, it is important to reflect on its history. Official recognition of historical sites began in Los Angeles in 1895 with the formation of the Landmarks Club. Charles Lummis had the foresight to institute this organization, which was dedicated to the preservation of historical sites throughout California, starting with the Spanish missions. In 1902, the California Historical Landmarks League was incorporated in San Francisco for similar purposes. This group further sought to "place in appropriate places memorial tablets commemorative of historic places and events."

The landmark program became official in 1931, when legislation required the director of the Department of Natural Resources "to register and mark buildings of historical interest or landmarks." The Natural Resources director delegated the California State Chamber of Commerce to administer the program. The chamber formed a committee to evaluate potential sites. The committee included some of the most prestigious historians of the time: Aubrey Drury, Francis Farquhar, Carl I. Wheat, Herbert Bolton, DeWitt V. Hutchings, Senator Leroy A. Wright, and Lawrence Hill.

The first twenty landmarks were officially designated on June 1, 1932. The emphasis was on well-known places and events in California History, especially missions, early settlements, battles, and the gold rush. By the end of the program's first year, a total of 78 historical landmarks had been registered.

Many early markers were placed through the efforts of such groups as the Native Sons of the Golden West, Native Daughters of the Golden West, and Daughters of the American Revolution. These and other historically motivated organizations carried on a marking program until 1948, the centennial year of the gold discovery, when the State Legislature set up the California Centennial Commission.

This early program was ambitious, but not without its quirks. Landmarks were registered without criteria; documentation requirements were minimal, and some properties were registered simply on the basis of hearsay or local legend.

To assure greater integrity and credibility, Governor Earl Warren created the California Historical Landmarks Advisory Committee in May 1949. In 1962 the Committee adopted registration criteria. Strict adherence to these criteria has lent dignity and integrity to the landmark program. Today, the basic criteria is still used in reviewing the merits of a landmark application:

1. The site must be of statewide historical importance to California.
2. The site must be the first, last, only, or most significant of a type in a large geographical region.

In 1970, the Committee added to the established criteria significant architectural landmarks, such as prototypes or outstanding examples of a period, style, architectural movement, or method of construction. The most notable works, or a region's best surviving work by a pioneer architect, designer, or master builder, would also qualify as an architectural landmark.

Legislation in 1974 changed the California Historical Landmarks Advisory Committee to the State Historical Resources Commission. The Commission has adopted a policy for marking satellite or thematic landmarks that are related to an existing California Registered Historical Landmark. Satellite landmarks are related sites that have the same number as the first application, but with the addition of a hyphen and the number "1." Thus the 1844 Fremont Expedition in California (San Joaquin County) is No. 995, while the second request (Mono County) is registered as No. 995-1.

A few landmarks are related to one another by a theme (thematic landmark) that identifies their historical, social, or architectural significance, but are not landmark sites integrally identified with, and contiguous with one another. Examples include Native American Ceremonial Roundhouses (No. 1001), Twentieth Century Folk Art Environments (No. 939), Japanese American Temporary Detention Camps (No. 934), and Light Stations of California (No. 951).

The California Register of Historical Resources, enacted in 1992, is a related program acting as an authoritative guide to be used by state and local agencies, private groups, and citizens to identify the state's historical resources. The California Register program encourages public recognition of resources of architectural, historical, archeological, and cultural significance;

identifies historical resources for state and local planning purposes; and defines threshold eligibility for state historic preservation grant funding. Currently the California Register consists of resources that are listed automatically by statutes through the California Register enabling legislation (AB 2881). The California Register includes properties listed in, or formally determined eligible for, the National Register of Historic Places and California Registered Landmarks from No. 770 onward. Landmarks from No. 1 through No. 769 and California Points of Historical Interest will be evaluated and recommended to the State Historical Resources Commission for inclusion in the California Register when criteria for evaluating properties for listing are adopted.

Sandra J. Elder
Assistant Executive Secretary
State Historical Resources Commission

Post Mile Designations California Highway System

Many California historical landmarks and their plaques can be located by referring to their post mile designations. Such designations are easily visible to highway users on those little white, paddle-shaped signs that line state highways. Post mile designations have also been used in the locator descriptions in this book.

Post mile designations were set up by the California Department of Transportation many years ago for highway planning, management, and maintenance purposes. They are still in use today and are also used by law enforcement personnel to record accident information and assist disabled vehicles requiring such assistance as towing.

Post mile signs include mileage within a particular county, running from south to north and usually from west to east. For example, post mile designations along U.S. Highway 395 in Inyo County start with 0.0 at the southern county line and increase to the north. The post mile sign illustrated here indicates that the traveller is on Highway 80 in Placer County, eight miles east of the county line. PMP = Post Mile Post.

Post miles are denoted in tenths of a mile with signs posted at strategic spots along the road such as intersections and bridges, and at the even post mile locations such as P.M. 5.0, 10.0, 20.0, etc. Within any given post mile length, there may actually be more or less than an exact mile of distance. When this is true, an "R" designation is used (R 11.3, for example. This indicates that some kind of realignment has taken place within the original post mile limit established for the highway. This allows flexibility when highways undergo minor changes and precludes redesignating the entire route within the county.

Alameda County

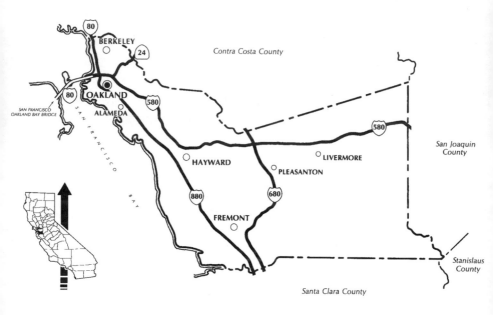

Alameda
Est. 1853

A lameda County was named for El Arroyo de la Alameda (Alameda Creek), which was lined with silver-barked sycamore trees and willow. The word Alameda means "a place where poplar trees grow." The county makes up an important section of the "East Bay" area and borders San Francisco Bay. Historical highlights include Native American shell mounds, early Spanish and Mexican land grants, and historic agricultural sites such as vineyards and wineries.

NO. 45 🔔
SITE OF COLLEGE OF CALIFORNIA

The University of California, chartered March 23, 1868, used buildings of the former College of California between Franklin and Harrison and 12th and 14th Streets from 1869 to 1873. Henry Durant, who founded the Contra Costa Academy in June 1853, was elected first university president in June 1870. The university moved to its present site in Berkeley in September 1873.

NE corner of 13th and Franklin Sts, Oakland

NO. 46 🔔
VALLEJO FLOUR MILL

In 1853, José de Jesús Vallejo, brother of General M. G. Vallejo, built a flour mill here, on his Rancho Arroyo de la Alameda. Niles was once called "Vallejo Mills." The stone aqueduct built to carry water for the mill parallels Niles Canyon Road.

Vallejo Mill Historical Park, NE corner Niles Canyon Rd and Mission Blvd (Hwy 238), Fremont

NO. 107 ☐
JOAQUIN MILLER HOME

Joaquin Miller, "Poet of the Sierras," resided on these acres, which he called "The Hights," from 1886 to 1913. In this building, The Abby, he wrote *Columbus* and other poems. He planted the surrounding trees and he personally built, on the eminence to the north, the funeral pyre and the monuments dedicated to Moses, General John C. Frémont, and Robert Browning. "The Hights" was purchased by the City of Oakland in 1919.

Joaquin Miller Park, NW corner of Joaquin Miller Rd and Sanborn Dr, Oakland

NO. 241 ☐
LIVERMORE MEMORIAL MONUMENT

Robert Livermore, first settler of Livermore Valley, was born in England in 1799. He arrived in Monterey in 1822 and married Josefa Higuera y Fuentes in 1830. On his Rancho las Positas, where he settled in 1835, "Next to the mission fathers, he was the first man to engage himself in the culture of grapes, fruit, and grain." He died in 1858. The Livermore hacienda was a short distance north of this spot.

Portola Park, Portola Ave and N Livermore Ave, Livermore

NO. 246 🔔
RANCHO SAN ANTONIO (PERALTA GRANT)

Governor Pablo de Sola, last Spanish governor of California, recognized the forty years' service of Don Luís María Peralta by awarding him the 43,000-acre San Antonio Grant on August 3, 1820. From this point northward, the grant embraced the sites of the cities of San Leandro, Oakland, Alameda, Emeryville, Piedmont, Berkeley, and Albany.

In city park at NW corner of E 14th and Hays Sts, San Leandro (southern boundary of rancho)

NO. 279
ESTUDILLO HOME

Site of the last home, built about 1850, of José Joaquín Estudillo, grantee of Rancho San Leandro, and his wife, Juana Martínez de Estudillo. The family founded San Leandro, built a hotel, and donated several lots, including the original site of St. Leander's Church, to the city.

550 W Estudillo Ave, San Leandro

NO. 285 🔔
PERALTA HOME

The first brick house built in Alameda County, the Peralta home was constructed in 1860 by W. P. Toler for Ignacio Peralta, early San Leandro Spanish settler. His father, Don Luís María Peralta, received the land grant from Spanish Governor Don Pablo Vicente de Solá on October 20, 1820.

561 Lafayette at Leo Ave, San Leandro

NO. 299
CAMINO OF RANCHO SAN ANTONIO

The Camino of Rancho San Antonio ran from Mission San Jose to Fruitvale, and later to San Pablo by way of Oakland and El Cerrito. The word *camino* means trail, road, highway, or line of communication that is in general public or private use.

SW corner of Oakland and Santa Clara Aves, Oakland

NO. 334 ☐
MISSION SAN JOSÉ

On June 9, 1797, troops under Sergeant Pedro Amador, accompanied by Father Fermín Lasuén, set out from Santa Clara for the spot that the natives called Oroysom in the valley of San Jose. The following day a temporary chapel was erected, and on June 11, the father presidente "raised and blessed the cross. In a shelter of boughs he celebrated holy mass." On the 28th Fathers Isidoro Barcenilla and Agustín Merino arrived to take charge of the new mission. The mission, except part of the padre's quarters, was completely destroyed in the earthquake of 1868.

Mission Blvd at Washington Blvd, Fremont

NO. 335

SITE OF SHELL MOUND

It is said that the Indians who came to this site camped just above the shoreline. The shells they threw aside from their catches of shellfish eventually covered some hundreds of thousands of square feet, marked by several cones. When the University of California excavated this site in the 1920s, they found that the mound consisted mostly of clam, mussel, and oyster shells, with a plentiful mixture of cockleshells.

4600 block of Shell Mound St, Emeryville

NO. 440 🔔

ALAMEDA TERMINAL OF THE FIRST TRANSCONTINENTAL RAILROAD

With the Pacific Railroad Act of 1862 authorizing construction of a railroad and telegraph line, the first concentration of activity was east of Sacramento. Subsequently the line was opened from Sacramento to San Jose. During June 1869 construction was started near Niles, and by August a temporary connection had been made at San Leandro with the San Francisco and Alameda Railroad. On September 6, 1869, the first Central Pacific train reached San Francisco Bay at Alameda.

NW corner of Lincoln Ave and Webster St, Alameda

NO. 503 🔔

SITE OF FIRST COUNTY COURTHOUSE

This is the site of Alameda County's first courthouse where county government began on June 6, 1853. Officials met in a two-story wooden building erected by Henry C. Smith and A. M. Church as a merchandise store. The seat of government moved to San Leandro in 1856, following an election in December 1854.

30977 Union City Blvd and Smith St, Alvarado District, Union City

NO. 510

FRANCISCO SOLANO ALVISO ADOBE

This building, erected in 1844-46 by Francisco Solano Alviso, was the first adobe house to be built in the Pleasanton Valley. It was originally called *Alisal*—The Sycamores. Following the Battle of Sunol Canyon, General John C. Frémont withdrew to this building, which became his headquarters for several days.

3459 Foothill Rd, 3 mi south of Dublin

NO. 586 🔔

CRESTA BLANCA WINERY

Here Charles A. Wetmore planted his vineyard in 1882. The Cresta Blanca wine he made from its fruit won for California the first International Award, the highest honor at the 1889 Paris Exposition, first bringing assurance to California wine growers that they could grow wines comparable to the finest in the world.

5050 Arroyo Rd across from Veterans Hospital, S of Livermore

NO. 641 🔔

CONCANNON VINEYARD

Here, in 1883, James Concannon founded the Concannon Vineyard. The quality it achieved in sacramental and commercial wines helped establish Livermore Valley as one of America's select wine-growing districts. Grape cuttings from this vineyard were introduced to Mexico between 1889 and 1904 for the improvement of its commercial viticulture.

4590 Tesla Rd at S Livermore Ave, 2 mi SE of Livermore

NO. 642 🔔

LELAND STANFORD WINERY

This winery was founded in 1869 by Leland Stanford — railroad builder, Governor of California, United States Senator, and founder of Stanford University. The vineyard, planted by his brother Josiah Stanford, helped to prove that wines equal to any in the world could be produced in California. The restored buildings and winery are now occupied and operated by Weibel Champagne Vineyards.

From I-680 take Mission Blvd N 0.5 mi to Stanford Ave, turn E to winery in Mission San Jose District, Fremont

NO. 676 ☐

SITE OF SAINT MARY'S COLLEGE

Site of Saint Mary's College, "The Old Brick Pile," 1899-1928. Plaque placed by Saint Mary's College Alumni, April 25, 1959.

3093 Broadway and Hawthorne, Oakland

NO. 694 🔔

CHURCH OF ST. JAMES THE APOSTLE

This church, founded under authority of Bishop Kip, first Episcopal Bishop for California, has given uninterrupted service to this community since June 27, 1858.

1540-12th Ave at Foothill Blvd, Oakland

NO. 768 🔔

SITE OF NATION'S FIRST SUCCESSFUL BEET SUGAR FACTORY

E. H. Dyer, "father of the American beet sugar industry," built the factory in 1870 on a corner of his farm. It began to process sugar beets on November 15, 1870, and produced 293 tons of sugar during its first operating season. The plant has since been completely rebuilt on the original site.

30849 Dyer St, Union City

NO. 776 🔔

SITE OF FIRST PUBLIC SCHOOL IN CASTRO VALLEY

This site was part of the original Don Castro Land Grant. In 1866 pioneer settler Josiah Grover Brickell donated it for "educational purposes only" and paid the salary of the teacher, who taught children in the one-room schoolhouse by day, and farmhands by candlelight at night.

19200 Redwood Rd, between James and Alma, Castro Valley

NO. 824 🔔
SAN LEANDRO OYSTER BEDS

During the 1890s the oyster industry thrived until it became the single most important fishery in the state. Moses Wicks is supposed to have been the first to bring seed oysters around the horn and implant them in the San Leandro beds. The oyster industry in San Francisco Bay was at its height around the turn of the century; it reached a secondary peak by 1911 and then faded away because of polluted conditions of the bay.

San Leandro Marina, S end of N Dike Rd, San Leandro

NO. 849
MILLS HALL

When Mills Seminary, forerunner of Hue college, transferred its operations to Oakland from Benicia in 1871, it moved into a long, four-story building with a high central observatory. The mansarded structure, which provided homes for faculty and students as well as classrooms and dining halls, long was considered the most beautiful educational building in the state.

Mills College, 5000 MacArthur at Pierson St, Oakland

NO. 884 🔔
PARAMOUNT THEATRE

This is the "Art Deco," or "Moderne" style of movie palace built during the rise of the motion picture industry. The Paramount, which opened on December 16, 1931, is the most ambitious theatre design of architect Timothy L. Pflueger. Restored in 1973, it has retained an exceptional unity of style.

2025 Broadway, Oakland; plaque located at 475-21st St

NO. 896 🔔
FIRST UNITARIAN CHURCH OF OAKLAND

Designed in 1889 by Walter J. Mathews, this solid masonry Romanesque church departed radically from California's traditional Gothic wood frame construction. Noted for its world famous stained glass windows produced by Goodhue of Boston, and for arching redwood spans, the widest at that time west of the Rockies, the church remains a significant cultural and architectural landmark.

685 14th St at Castro St, Oakland

NO. 908 🔔
BERKELEY CITY CLUB

The Berkeley City Club was organized by women in 1927, to contribute to social, civic, and cultural progress. The building, constructed in 1929, is one of the outstanding works of noted California architect Julia Morgan, whose interpretation of Moorish and Gothic elements created a landmark of California design.

2315 Durant Ave, Berkeley

NO. 925
PERALTA HACIENDA SITE

One of California's original Spanish colonists, Luís Peralta received the first and largest Mexican land grant. His hacienda was the nucleus of the Rancho de San Antonio, which covered the sites of seven present-day East Bay cities and reached to the Contra Costa frontier. The rancho's first permanent adobe was located here, and the 1870 Italianate frame house is one of two remaining Peralta buildings.

2465 34th Ave and Paxton St, Oakland

NO. 946 🔔

UNIVERSITY OF CALIFORNIA, BERKELEY CAMPUS

These landmarks form the historic core of the first University of California campus, opened in 1873: Founders' Rock, University House, Faculty Club and Glade, Hearst Greek Theatre, Hearst Memorial Mining Building, Doe Library, Sather Tower and Esplanade, Sather Gate and Bridge, Hearst Gymnasium, California, Durant, Wellman, Hilgard, Giannini, Wheeler, North Gate and South Halls.

University Ave, Berkeley

NO. 954

CROLL BUILDING

This building is closely associated with sporting events significant to the history of the City of Alameda, the San Francisco Bay area and the State of California. Croll's is important in the early development of boxing during the Golden Age of Boxing in California, a period of great California champions such as Jim Corbett and James Jeffries. From the 1890s to about 1910, Croll housed many of the best boxers in America in his hotel.

1400 Webster St, Alameda

NO. 957 🔔

WENTE BROS. WINERY

Here the first Wente vineyard of 47 acres was established by C. H. Wente in 1883. In 1935 his sons, Ernest and Herman, introduced California's first varietal wine label, Sauvignon Blanc. The efforts of the Wente family have helped establish the Livermore Valley as one of the premier wine-growing areas of California. In their centennial year, Wente Bros. is the oldest continuously operating, family-owned winery in California.

5565 Tesla Rd, Livermore

NO. 962 🔔

SITE OF BLOSSOM ROCK NAVIGATION TREES

Until at least 1851, redwood trees on this site were used as landmarks to avoid striking the treacherous submerged Blossom Rock, in San Francisco Bay, west of Yerba Buena island. Although by 1855 the original stems had been logged, today's trees are sprouts from their stumps.

Madrone Picnic Area, Thomas J. Roberts Recreation Area, Redwood Regional Park, 11500 Skyline Blvd, Oakland

NO. 968 🔔

SITE OF THE CHINA CLIPPER FLIGHT DEPARTURE

Pan American World Airways' fabled China Clipper (Martin M/130 Flying Boat) left Alameda Marina on November 22, 1935. Under the command of Captain Edwin C. Musick, the flight would reach Manila via Honolulu, Midway, Wake, and Guam. The inauguration of ocean airmail service and commercial airflight across the Pacific was a significant event for both California and the world.

Naval Air Station Mall, in front of Building No. 1, Alameda Naval Air Station, Alameda (contact Staff Civil Engineer's Office , 510/263-3712, for permission to see plaque–3 weekdays only)

NO. 970🔔

RAINBOW TROUT SPECIES IDENTIFIED

The naming of the Rainbow Trout species was based on fish taken from the San Leandro Creek drainage. In 1855, Dr. W. P. Gibbons, founder of the California Academy of Sciences, was given three specimens obtained from the creek. He described and assigned them the scientific name *Salmo iridia*. Rainbow Trout are now worldwide in distribution and are a highly prized game fish.

50 yards past Redwood Gate entrance kiosk, Redwood Regional Park, Oakland

NO. 986🔔

PIEDMONT WAY

Piedmont Way was conceived in 1865 by Frederick Law Olmsted, America's foremost landscape architect. As the centerpiece of a gracious residential community close beside the College of California, Olmsted envisioned a roadway that would follow the natural contours of the land and be sheltered from sun and wind by "an overarching bowery of foliage." This curvilinear, tree-lined parkway was Olmsted's first residential street design. It has served as the model for similar parkways across the nation.

Piedmont Ave between Gayley Rd and Dwight Way, Berkeley

Landmark No. 968

Alpine County

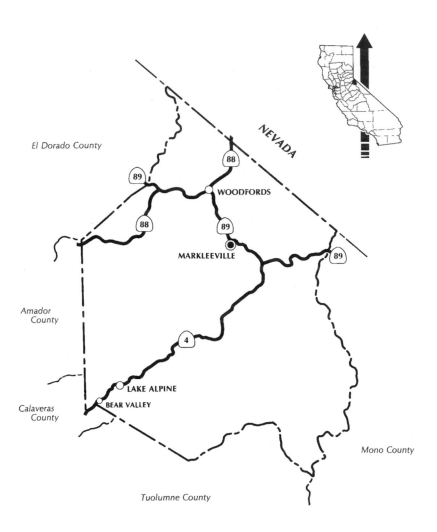

Alpine
Est. 1864

Iigh in the Sierra along the Nevada border, Alpine County is sparsely populated. In 1844, John C. Fremont's expedition, accompanied by Kit Carson, passed through the area and over today's Carson Pass. The Overland Emigrant Trail passed through this county, and is marked today by yellow painted iron markers and plaques.

NO. 240
MARKLEE'S CABIN SITE

Jacob J. Marklee recorded his land claim of 160 acres on June 23, 1862, in Douglas County, Nevada, but after the boundary survey his claim was in California. During the rush to the Comstock Lode, the town of Markleeville was built upon Marklee's land; the Alpine County Courthouse now occupies the site of his cabin.

County Courthouse, Markleeville

NO. 315 □
KIT CARSON MARKER

On this spot, the summit of the Kit Carson Pass, stood the Kit Carson Tree on which the famous scout Kit Carson inscribed his name in 1844 when he guided the then Captain John C. Frémont, head of a government exploring expedition, over the Sierra Nevada. The original inscription was cut from the tree in 1888 and is now in Sutter's Fort, Sacramento.

On State Hwy 88 (P.M. 5.2), 14.5 mi W of Woodfords

NO. 318 □
EBBETTS PASS ROUTE

The Emigrant Trail through Ebbetts Pass, discovered by and named after "Major" John Ebbetts, was opened up in the early 1850s, but no wagon road went that way until 1864, when a toll road, under the name of Carson Valley and Big Tree Road, was completed to help open up the Comstock Lode in Nevada.

Ebbetts Pass on Hwy 4 (P.M. 18.5), 18 mi SW of Markleeville

NO. 378 □
MEMORIAL TO PIONEER ODD FELLOWS

On some large rocks near Carson Pass, a group of pioneers inscribed their names and the emblem of the Independent Order of Odd Fellows in 1849.

On State Hwy 88 (P.M. 5.3), 14.4 mi W of Woodfords

NO. 661 🔔

OLD EMIGRANT ROAD

Here the Old Emigrant Road of 1848 swung down across the meadow now covered by Caples Lake (Twin Lakes) and climbed along the ridge at the right to the gap at the head of the valley. From this summit (9,460 feet) it descended to Placerville. This rough and circuitous section became obsolete in 1863 when a better route was blasted out of the face of the cliff at Carson Spur.

Lake Caples, on State Hwy 88 (P.M. 2.4), 173 mi W of Woodfords

NO. 805 ☐

PONY EXPRESS REMOUNT STATION AT WOODFORDS

Woodfords became a remount station of the Pony Express on April 4, 1860, when Warren Upson scaled the mountains in a blinding snowstorm and made his way down the eastern slope of the Sierra on his way to Carson City. Five weeks later the Pony Express was rerouted by way of Echo Summit and Luther Pass.

On Hwy 89, 0.1 mi N of intersection of State Hwy 4 and Old Pony Express Rd, Woodfords

Landmark No. 661

Landmark No. 315

Landmark No. 378

Landmark No. 805

Amador County

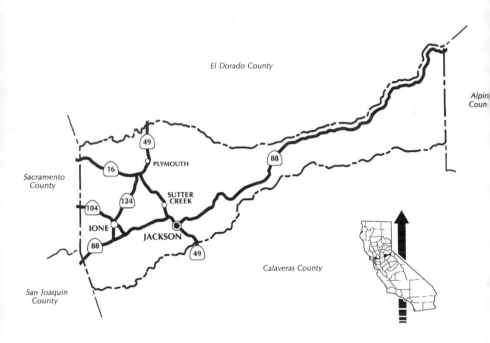

El Dorado County

Alpin
Coun

Sacramento
County

PLYMOUTH

49

16

88

SUTTER
CREEK

124

104

IONE

88

JACKSON

49

Calaveras County

San Joaquin
County

Indian Grinding Rock State Historic Park - Miwok Indian
village site. Located 2 1/4 miles SW of Volcano.

Amador
Est. 1854

The eastern slope of Amador County begins at Kirkwood's historic stage stop. The relatively narrow county is aligned between the Mokelumne and Cosumnes rivers and roughly follows an important emigrant trail route. Gold rush camps and boomtowns abound in the history of the area.

NO. 28 □
MAIDEN'S GRAVE

It is said that in 1850 a young girl, Rachel Melton, native of Iowa, was accompanying her parents on a journey West via covered wagon train when she became violently ill. Camp was made and every effort was made to cure her, as she was the joy of the party, but she passed away and was buried on this spot.

On State Hwy 88 (P.M. 61.3), 10.5 mi W of Kirkwood

NO. 29 🔔 ⚒
VOLCANO

The spot was discovered in 1848 by Colonel Stevenson's men, who mined Soldiers Gulch in 1849. By 1853 the flats and gulches swarmed with men who named them picturesquely. Hydraulic operations, begun in 1855, brought thousands of fortune seekers to form a town of 17 hotels, a library, a theater, and courts of quick justice. During the Civil War, Volcano's gold served the Union; Volcano Blues smuggled the cannon "Old Abe" in by hearse to quell rebels.

Intersection of Main and Consolation Sts, Volcano

NO. 30 ⚒
LANCHA PLANA

Lancha Plana (Flat Boat) was well settled by 1850 due to the hydraulic mining operations in the extensive gravel beds along the Mokelumne River. The Amador Dispatch newspaper was born here in 1856. Poverty Bar, Camp Opra, Copper Center, and Put's Bar were "suburbs" of the larger town.

North shore of Camanche Reservoir, 1 mi W of County Line Bridge on Lancha Plana Buena Vista Rd, 6.0 mi S of Buena Vista

NO. 31 🔔 ⚒
DRYTOWN

Founded in 1848, this is the oldest town and first in which gold was discovered in Amador County. Its venerable town hall and other picturesque structures remain. The town was not "dry," as the name implies–it once contained 26 saloons.

On State Hwy 49 (P.M. 13. 7), 0.2 mi N of Drytown

NO. 34 □
PIONEER HALL

The Order of Native Daughters of the Golden West was organized on these premises, the site of the Pioneer Hall, on September 11, 1886.

113 Main St, Jackson

NO. 35

OLETA "OLD FIDDLETOWN"

Settled by Missourians in 1849, Fiddletown was a trading center for American, Loafer, and French Flats, Lone Hill, and other rich mining camps. Called Fiddletown because residents "were always fiddling," the settlement became Oleta in 1878 but the original name was later restored. Bret Harte added to the community's fame in "An Episode of Fiddletown."

South side of street from Dr. Yee's Chinese Herb Shop, Fiddletown

NO. 36

MIDDLE BAR

Site of gold rush town on the Mokelumne River, now inundated by Pardee Reservoir at certain times of the year.

2.8 mi S of State Hwy 49 (P.M. 2.5) on Middle Bar Rd at Mokelumne River, 4.5 mi S of Jackson

NO. 37

CLINTON

Clinton was the center of a placer mining community during the 1850s and of quartz mining as late as the 1880s. This town once decided Amador County elections as its votes were always counted last.

Intersection of E Clinton and Clinton Rd, 1.0 mi SE of State Hwy 88, 3.2 mi SW of Pine Grove

NO. 38

IRISHTOWN

This was an important stopping place for emigrants on their way to the southern mines. The first white settlers on this spot found it a "city of wigwams," and hundreds of mortars in the rocks testify that this was a favorite Indian camping ground.

On State Hwy 88 (P.M. 20.8) at Pine Grove Wieland Rd, 2.2 mi SW of Pine Grove

NO. 39

BUTTE STORE

This is the only structure remaining of Butte City, prosperous mining town of the 1850s. As early as 1854 Xavier Benoist was conducting a store and bakery in this building. Later Ginocchio had a merchandise business here.

On State Hwy 49 (P.M. 1.4), 2.6 mi S of Jackson

NO. 40 ☐

KIRKWOOD'S

Resort, stage station, and post office were originally built by Zack Kirkwood in 1864. When Alpine County was formed from Amador County, the division left the barn and milkhouse in Alpine, while the Alpine-El Dorado line went directly through the barroom of the inn.

On State Hwy 88 (P.M. 71.8), Kirkwood

NO. 41

BIG BAR

The Mokelumne River was mined at this point in 1848. Established in 1849, the Whale Boat Ferry operated until the first bridge was built, about 1852.

On State Hwy 49 (P.M.. 0.0) at county line. 4.0 mi S of Jackson

NO. 118

JACKSON GATE

Jackson Gate, on the north fork of Jackson Creek, takes its name from a fissure in a reef of rock that crosses the creek. In 1850 about 500 miners worked here and the first mining ditch in the county was dug here; its water sold for $1 per inch.

On N Main St, 1.3 mi NE of Jackson

NO. 322

SUTTER CREEK

This town was named after John A. Sutter, who came to the region in 1846, and was the first to mine the locality in 1848. There was little activity at Sutter Creek until 1851, when quartz gold was discovered. In 1932 the Central Eureka mine, discovered in 1869, had reached the 2,300-foot level. By 1939, it was the best-paying mine at Sutter Creek.

Veteran's Memorial Hall, Main and Badger Sts, Sutter Creek

NO. 470

PLYMOUTH TRADING POST

This building, constructed entirely of brick, was built by Joe Williams in 1857. In 1873 the many small mines of the area were combined to become Plymouth Consolidated, and this building became the new company's office and commissary.

On Main St, between Mill and Mineral Sts, next to Wells Fargo Bank, Plymouth

NO. 506

THE COMMUNITY METHODIST CHURCH OF IONE

The cornerstone was laid in 1862 and the church, constructed of locally fired brick, was completed in 1866. Dedicated as the Ione City Centenary Church and later popularly known as the Cathedral of the Mother Lode, this church was the first to serve the people in the area.

150 W Marlette, Ione

NO. 662

OLD EMIGRANT ROAD

Here the Old Emigrant Road began a long loop around the Silver Lake basin, reaching an elevation of 9,640 feet at one place. This difficult portion of the road was used by thousands of vehicles from 1848 to 1863, when it was superseded by a route approximating the present highway.

On State Hwy 88 (P.M. 63.1) at Mud Lake Rd, 8. 7 mi W of Kirkwood

NO. 715 ⟨M⟩

SITE OF FIRST AMATEUR ASTRONOMICAL OBSERVATORY OF RECORD IN CALIFORNIA

On the knoll behind this marker George Madeira built the first amateur astronomical observatory of record in California. It was there that he discovered the Great Comet of 1861 with a three-inch refractor telescope.

Volcano

NO. 762 ⟨🔔⟩

D'AGOSTINI WINERY

D'Agostini Winery was started in 1856 by Adam Uhlinger, a Swiss immigrant. The original wine cellar, with walls made from rock quarried from nearby hills, hand-hewn beams, and oak casks, is part of the present winery; some of its original vines are still in production.

On Plymouth-Shenandoah Rd, 72 mi NE of Plymouth

NO. 786 ⟨🔔⟩ ⟨⚒⟩

ARGONAUT AND KENNEDY MINES

Argonaut Mine, discovered 1850, and Kennedy Mine, discovered 1856, played dramatic roles in the economic development of California, producing $105,268,760 in gold. Kennedy Mine has a vertical shaft of 5,912 feet, the deepest in the United States. The Argonaut was the scene of the Mother Lode's most tragic mine disaster—on August 27, 1922, 48 miners were trapped in a fire at the 3,500-foot level; few survived. Both mines closed in 1942.

W roadside rest, State Hwy 49 (P.M. 5.6), 1.6 mi N of Jackson

NO. 788 ⟨🔔⟩

D. STEWART CO. STORE

This general merchandise store built by Daniel Stewart in 1856 was the first building erected in Ione Valley from nearby Muletown brick. Once known as "Bed-Bug" and "Freeze Out," Ione was an important supply center on the main road to the Mother Lode and Southern Mines.

18 E Main St, Ione

NO. 865 ⟨🔔⟩

SITE OF JACKSON'S PIONEER JEWISH SYNAGOGUE

On September 18, 1857, Congregation B'nai Israel of Jackson dedicated on this site the first synagogue in the Mother Lode. High holy day worship continued until 1869 when the larger Masonic Hall was used to accommodate the congregation. The wooden structure then served as a schoolhouse until 1888. Relocated onto a nearby lot, it became a private dwelling, and was razed in 1948.

SE corner of Church and Main Sts, Jackson

NO. 867 ⟨🔔⟩

PRESTON CASTLE

The "Castle," built in 1890-1894, is the most significant example of Romanesque Revival architecture in the Mother Lode. It was built to house the Preston School of Industry, established by the State Legislature as a progressive action toward rehabilitating, rather than simply imprisoning, juvenile offenders. Doors of the 120-room "Castle" closed in 1960 after new facilities were completed.

Preston School of Industry, Waterman Rd; plaque located 0.9 miles N of site on State Hwy 104 (P.M. 4.3), 1 mi N of Ione

NO. 1001 🔔

CALIFORNIA NATIVE AMERICAN CEREMONIAL ROUNDHOUSES (THEMATIC), CHAW SE' ROUNDHOUSE

In a village, the roundhouse served as the center of ceremonial and social life. Constructed in 1974, the Chaw se' roundhouse continues this tradition. With its door facing the east, towards the rising sun, four large oaks are the focal point of this sixty-foot-in-diameter structure. Today ceremonial roundhouses are the most significant architectural manifestation of the continuing Mistook spiritual heritage.

Chaw Se Indian Grinding Rock State Historic Park., 14881 Pine Grove/Volcano Rd, Pine Grove

NO. 1007 🔔

KNIGHT FOUNDRY

Knight Foundry was established in 1873 to supply heavy equipment and repair facilities to the gold mines and timber industry of the Mother Lode. Samuel N. Knight developed a high speed, cast iron water wheel which was a forerunner of the Pelton Wheel design. Knight Wheels were used in some of the first hydroelectric plants in California, Utah, and Oregon. This site is the last water powered foundry and machine shop in California. A 42-inch Knight Wheel drives the main line shaft, with smaller water motors powering other machines.

81 Eureka St, Sutter Creek

Landmark No. 1007

Butte County

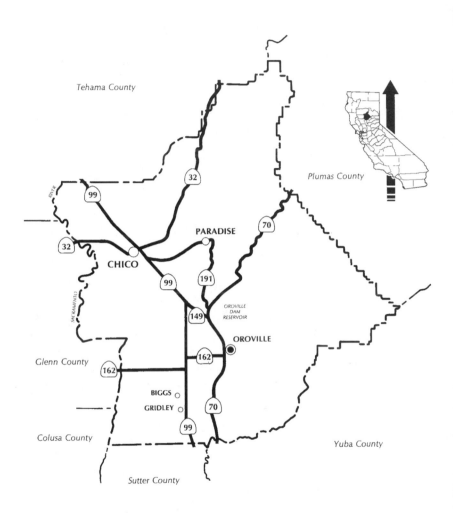

Bidwell Mansion State Historic Park - Home of California pioneer John Bidwell. Located in Chico.

Butte
Est. 1850

Highlights of Butte County history include John Bidwell's establishment of Rancho Chico and Bidwell Bar, and the discovery of Ishi, the last Yahi Indian. This county progressed swiftly from a collection of mining towns into a trendsetter for California agriculture.

NO. 313 ☐

HOOKER OAK

In 1887 Annie E. K. Bidwell named this huge oak after English botanist Sir Joseph Hooker. When it fell during a windstorm in 1977, it was estimated to be over a thousand years old; it was nearly a hundred feet tall and 29 feet in circumference eight feet from the ground. The largest branch measured 111 feet from trunk to tip; circumference of outside branches was nearly five hundred feet.

Bidwell Park, Hooker Oak Recreation Area, Manzanita Ave between Vallombrosa and Hooker Oak Ave, Chico

NO. 314 ☐

OLD SUSPENSION BRIDGE

The Mother Orange Tree of Butte County was planted at this spot by Judge Joseph Lewis in 1856. The Bidwell Bar Bridge, first suspension bridge of California, was transported from New York via Cape Horn 1853 and was completed 1856. Its site is now inundated by Oroville Reservoir.

Lake Oroville State Recreation Area, Bidwell Canyon, Bidwell Canyon Rd, Oroville

NO. 329 🔔

RANCHO CHICO AND BIDWELL ADOBE

The 26,000-acre Rancho Chico was purchased in 1845-50 by John Bidwell. In 1865 he began construction of the mansion, which in time became the social and cultural center of the upper Sacramento Valley. It was through his advancement of agriculture, however, that Bidwell made his greatest contribution. Plants from all over the world were introduced to Rancho Chico to open the door to California's present agricultural treasure house.

Bidwell Mansion State Historic Park, 525 The Esplanade, Chico

NO. 330 ☐

BIDWELL'S BAR

From 1853 to 1856 Bidwell's Bar served as the second county seat of Butte County. The site of the courthouse, now inundated by Oroville Reservoir, is 120 yards west of this small monument.

Lake Oroville State Recreation Area, Bidwell Canyon, Bidwell Canyon Rd, Oroville

NO. 770

CHINESE TEMPLE

Dedicated in the spring of 1863, this building served as a temple of worship for 10,000 Chinese then living here. Funds for its erection and furnishings were provided by the Emperor and Empress of China; local Chinese labor built the structure. The building was deeded to the City of Oroville in 1935 by the Chinese residents.

1500 Broderick St, Oroville

NO. 771

DOGTOWN NUGGET DISCOVERY SITE

The Dogtown nugget was discovered April 12, 1859 at the Willard Claim, a hydraulic mine in the Feather River Canyon northeast of the town.

0.3 mi N of Pentz-Magalia Rd on Skyway, Magalia

NO. 807

OREGON CITY

Entering California over the Applegate and Lassen Trails, a party of Oregonians arrived here in autumn of 1848 to establish Oregon City. Little more than a year later their captain, Peter H. Burnett, became the first civil Governor of California. For a time, Oregon City prospered as a gold mining and supply center; then it declined into virtual oblivion.

Diggins Dr between Oroville and Cherokee

NO. 809

DISCOVERY SITE OF THE LAST YAHI INDIAN

Ishi, a Yahi Yana Indian, was the last of his people. Prior to European contact, the Yana population numbered approximately 3,000. In 1865 Ishi and his family were the victims of the Three Knolls Massacre, from which approximately 30 Yahi survived. The remaining Yahi escaped but were forced into hiding after cattlemen killed about half of the survivors. Eventually all of Ishi's companions died, and he was discovered by a group of butchers in their corral at Oroville, August 29, 1911. Alfred L. Kroeber and T. T. Waterman, anthropologists at the University of California, Berkeley, brought Ishi to San Francisco where he helped them reconstruct Yahi culture. He identified material items and showed how they were made. Ishi's death in 1916 marked the end of an era in California.

2547 Oroville-Quincy Hwy at Oak Ave, Oroville

NO. 840-2

CHICO FORESTRY STATION AND NURSERY

In 1888, the State Board of Forestry established an experimental forestry station and nursery. It and the Santa Monica station established in 1887 were the first such stations in the Nation. Exotic and native trees were tested and produced for scientific and conservation purposes. The station was operated by the Board of Forestry until 1893.

Bidwell Nature Center, Cedar Grove Picnic Area, Cedar Grove and E 8th, Bidwell Park, Chico

Landmark No. 840-?

Landmark No. 770

Calaveras County

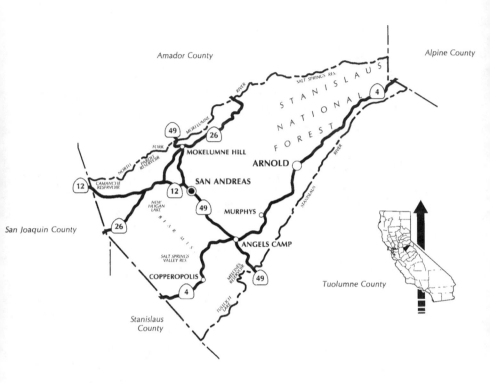

Amador County

Alpine County

San Joaquin County

Tuolumne County

Stanislaus County

STANISLAUS NATIONAL FOREST

SALT SPRINGS RES.

RIVER

MOKELUMNE

49

26

MOKELUMNE HILL

ARNOLD

SAN ANDREAS

MURPHYS

49

ANGELS CAMP

COPPEROPOLIS

4

49

12

12

26

4

NORTH FORK

PARDEE RESERVOIR

CAMANCHE RESERVOIR

NEW HOGAN LAKE

BEAR MTS.

SALT SPRINGS VALLEY RES.

MELONES RESERVOIR

TULLOCH LAKE

STANISLAUS

RIVER

Calaveras
Est. 1850

Locale of Mark Twain's "Jumping Frog" fame, Calaveras County is rich with Gold Rush history and folklore. Remnants of early railroading and Mexican culture add to the charm of this area of the Sierra and foothills.

NO. 41

BIG BAR

The Mokelumne River was mined at this point in 1848. Established in 1849, the Whale Boat Ferry operated until the first bridge was built, about 1852.

On State Hwy 49 (P.M. 0.0) at county line, 4.0 mi S of Jackson

NO. 251

VALLEY SPRINGS

in 1885 the San Joaquin and Sierra Nevada Railroad Company completed a narrow-gauge railroad from Brack's Landing to Valley Springs. The line eventually became the property of Southern Pacific Company, and a standard-gauge line into Valley Springs was substituted.

At intersection of State Hwys 12 and 26, Valley Springs

NO. 252 ☐

SAN ANDREAS

Settled by Mexicans in 1848 and named after the Catholic parish St. Andres, the town has been a noted mining camp since early days. Gold from the surrounding ancient river channels and placer mines contributed greatly to the success of the Union during the Civil War. The first newspaper was published here on September 24, 1846. Destroyed by fire June 4, 1858, and in 1863, San Andreas became the seat of Calaveras County in 1866. It was said to be a rendezvous for Joaquin Murieta; notorious stage robber Black Bart was tried here and sent to prison.

NW corner of State Hwy 49 and Main St, San Andreas

NO. 253 ☐

SANDY GULCH

This monument was erected to the memory of pioneers of Sandy Gulch, 1849 trading center for miners of northeastern Calaveras County. The settlement, in an area that was home to many Miwok Indians, was named after the gulch where William and Dan Carsner found large nuggets of gold embedded in the coarse sands. Water for mining was brought from the middle fork of the Mokelumne River through Sandy Gulch and Kadish Ditches; quartz mining began in the early 1850s, and the first custom stamp mill in the district was located at the head of Sandy Gulch. School and election precincts were established early, and one of California's many Hangman's Trees stood near the center of town.

On State Hwy 26 (P.M. 32.3), 2.1 mi W of West Point

NO. 254 🔔/⚒

CAMANCHE

Once called Limerick, the town became Camanche (after Camanche, Iowa) in 1849. Rich mining at nearby Cat Camp, Poverty Bar, and Sand Hill brought its population to a peak of 1,500. Mokelumne River water was brought in by Lancha Plana and Poverty Bar Ditch. A fire on June 21, 1873 destroyed Camanche's large Chinatown. Buhach, an insect powder made from a plant, was manufactured on the nearby Hill Ranch. Camanche is now inundated by Camanche Reservoir.

South Camanche Shore Park, picnic area near south entrance, Camanche Parkway South, 3.0 mi NW of Burson

NO. 255 🔔/⚒

CALAVERITAS

Calaveritas, settled in 1849 by Mexicans, was a flourishing mining town complete with stores, saloons, gambling houses, and fandango halls, the latter two said to be frequented by Joaquin Murieta. The town was destroyed by fire in 1858.

On Calaveras Rd at Costa Rd, 4.5 mi SE of San Andreas

NO. 256 Ⓜ

I.O.O.F. HALL, MOKELUMNE HILL

This is said to be California's first three-story building to be erected outside the coastal towns. The original building was erected in 1854 as a two-story building; a third story to be used for lodge purposes was added later.

NE corner of Main and Center Sts, Mokelumne

NO. 257 🔔/⚒

CAMPO SECO

Campo Seco was settled in 1849 by Mexicans who worked placers in Oregon Gulch. The largest living cork oak tree in California was planted here in 1858. The iron doors of the ruined Adams Express Building were still standing in 1950.

Intersection of Campo Seco and Penn Mine Rds, Campo Seco

NO. 258 🔔/⚒

FOURTH CROSSING

Located on the Stockton-Murphys Road at a crossing of the Calaveras River, this early mining settlement, once called Foremans, was famous in the 1850s for its rich placer ores. Later, as an important stage and freighting depot, it served the southern mines until after the turn of the century.

On State Hwy 49 (P.M. 14.0) at San Antonio Creek, 5 mi S of San Andreas

NO. 261

CONGREGATIONAL CHURCH

The Congregational Church in Mokelumne Hill was organized August 28, 1853. The church building, erected in 1856, is the oldest Congregational Church building in the state.

NE corner of Main and Church Sts, Mokelumne Hill

NO. 262

MILTON

Completion of the Southern Pacific Railroad in 1871 marked the birth of the town of Milton. Named after Milton Latham, one of the railroad construction engineers, this town was the first in Calaveras County to have a railroad. Freight and passengers continued their journeys to other parts of Calaveras County by wagon and stagecoach.

15 mi NW of Copperopolis via Rock Creek Rd, County Road J14, and Milton

NO. 263
STONE CORRAL

Stone Corral, consisting of a hotel, barns, and the large corrals for which it was named, was one of the stopping places on the road from the mines to Stockton.

Stone Corral Ranch, on State Hwy 26 (P.M. 0.8), 9.5 mi SW of Valley Springs

NO. 264 ☐
DOUBLE SPRINGS

Founded February 18, 1850, Double Springs was once the seat of Calaveras County. The old courthouse, said to be constructed of lumber brought from China, is still standing, but not on its original site.

On Double Springs Rd, 3.6 mi E of Valley Springs

NO. 265 🔔/🚫
CHILI GULCH

This five-mile gulch was the richest placer mining section in Calaveras County. It received its name from Chileans who worked it in 1848 and 1849, and was the scene of the so-called Chilean War. The largest known quartz crystals were recovered from a mine on the south side of the gulch.

On State Hwy 49 (P.M. 26.4), 1.4 mi S of Mokelumne Hill

NO. 266 🚫
JENNY LIND

Jenny Lind, located on the north bank of the Calaveras River, was a placer mining town as early as 1849. Most of the placer mining was done along the hillsides above the river; later the river was mined with dredgers. In 1864 the population was said to be 400, half of them Chinese.

On Milton Rd, County Road J1 4, 8 mi SW of Valley Springs

NO. 267 🔔
MITCHLER HOTEL

This is one of the oldest hotels still operating in California. First called the Sperry and Perry Hotel, it was opened by James L. Sperry and John Perry on August 20, 1856. Henry Atwood was its proprietor in 1881; later, ownership passed to Harvey Blood. Renamed the Mitchler Hotel in 1882, and the Murphys Hotel in 1945 by the McKimins family, it was bought by a College of the Pacific group in 1963.

457 Main at Algiers St, Murphys

NO. 268 🔔
WEST POINT

West Point was named by scout Kit Carson, who was searching for a pass over the Sierra. One emigrant road forked by Big Meadows; its north branch came directly to West Point, which was a thriving trading post prior to the gold discovery. Bret Harte, famous author, lived here for a time.

Intersection of State Hwy 26 (P.M. 34.4) and Main St, West Point

NO. 269 ☐ 🏷

MOKELUMNE HILL

Mokelumne is an Indian word, first applied to the nearby river. Earliest settlement was at Happy Valley by French trappers. Gold was discovered by discharged members of Stevenson's Regiment in 1848. Mokelumne Hill was the center of the richest placer mining section of Calaveras County and one of the principal mining towns of California. Corral Flat produced over thirty millions in gold. Sixteen feet square constituted a claim. The so-called "French War" for possession of gold mines occurred in 1851. "Calaveras Chronicle" was established in 1850. Fights between grizzly bears and bulls amused early residents. The town was destroyed by fires in 1854, 1864, and 1874. County seat of Calaveras County from 1853 to 1866.

SW corner of Main and Center Sts, Mokelumne Hill

NO. 271

PIONEER CEMETERY

This pioneer cemetery was said to have been established in 1851. Most of the graves are unmarked; stones appeared over only three of them in 1936. This cemetery is located almost opposite where the town of North Branch originally stood, before the site was mined for gold.

On State Hwy 12 (P.M. 176), 0.7 mi W of junction with State Hwy 49, 1.8 mi W of San Andreas

NO. 272 🔔 🏷

DOUGLAS FLAT

Douglas Flat was a roaring mining camp of the early 1850s. In 1857 the Harper and Lone Star Claims produced $130,000 worth of gold. The so-called Central Hill Channel, an ancient river deposit from which vast quantities of gold have been taken, is located here.

On State Hwy 4 (P.M. 275), Douglas Flat

NO. 273 🏷

VALLECITO

This mining camp of the early 1850s was almost totally destroyed by fire on August 28, 1859. Nearby is Moaning Cave, which the Indians used as a burial ground.

On State Hwy 4 (P.M. 25.6), Vallecito

NO. 274 🔔 🏷

CARSON HILL

Gold was discovered in the creek just below here in 1848 by James H. Carson, whose name was given to the creek, hill, and town. In November 1854 the largest gold nugget in California, weighing 195 pounds troy, was found. It was worth $43,000 at that time.

On State Hwy 4 (P.M. 3.3), 3.7 mi S of Angels Camp on Hwy 49

NO. 275 ☐ 🏷

MURPHYS

One of the principal mining communities in Calaveras County, Murphys was named for the discoverer of gold on the flat in 1849. The objective of many immigrants coming over the Sierras by Ebbetts Pass, Murphys Flat and surrounding mines produced 20,000,000 dollars in gold. Early regulations restricted claims to 8 ft. square. A suspension flume conveying water across Murphys Creek and drainage race draining the flat were two outstanding accomplishments of early day miners. The business portion of town was destroyed by fire August 20, 1859. Joaquin Murieta bandit, is said to have begun his murderous career here. Calaveras Light Guards recruiting for Civil War, organized here on May 4, 1861.

Intersection of Main and Jones Sts, Murphys

NO. 276 🔔
ROBINSON'S FERRY

In 1848 John W. Robinson and Stephen Mead established ferry transport for freight, animals and persons across river. In 1856 Harvey Wood purchased interest and later acquired property which was maintained by Wood Family until 1911. Charges were 50 cents for each passenger, horse, jenny or other animal.

Vista point on State Hwy 49 (P.M. 0.6), 5.4 mi S of Angels Camp

NO. 280 🏹
GLENCOE (MOSQUITO GULCH)

Glencoe was formerly called Mosquito Gulch. The business portion of the town was on the north side of Mosquito Gulch, but not one of the old buildings remains. The mines were first worked by the Mexicans in the early 1850s; quartz mining predominated but there was some placer mining.

On State Hwy 26 (P.M. 26.2), Glencoe

NO. 281 🔔 🏹
O'BYRNE FERRY

In 1852 a chain cable bridge replaced the ferries that once crossed here, to be supplanted in its turn by a covered truss structure in 1862. Some writers claimed this was the locale of Bret Harte's Poker Flat. In late '49 there was a large camp here, with miners washing gold out on both banks of the Stanislaus River.

On County Hwy 48 (P.M. 0.3), O'Byrne Ferry Rd, 71 mi SE of Copperopolis

NO. 282 ☐
EL DORADO

Patented as a townsite in 1872, this early town derived its name from a sawmill located here. Mountain Ranch, the post office established in 1856, was moved to El Dorado in 1868, so El Dorado became known as Mountain Ranch. The bell was used in the local school from 1885 to 1953. Established as Cave City School District in 1855, this school joined with the Banner District in 1946 to become the El Dorado Union Elementary School District.

NW corner of Mountain Ranch Rd and Whiskey Slide Rd, Mountain Ranch

NO. 284 🏹
JESUS MARIA

The town, center of a large placer mining section, was named for a Mexican who raised vegetables and melons for the miners. It was settled in the early 1850s with a large population of Mexicans, French, Chileans, and Italians.

On Jesus Maria Rd, County Road 27 (P.M. 10.2), 4.9 mi SE of Mokelumne Hill

NO. 286

RAIL ROAD FLAT

This historic mining town, elevation 2,600 feet, was named after primitive mule-drawn ore cars used here. It was the site of an Indian council as well as the center of rich placer and quartz mining. Its largest producer was the Petticoat Mine. The post office was established in 1857, and the Edwin Taylor store built in 1867. The town's population was decimated in 1880 by black fever.

NE of intersection of Rail Road (County Road 13) and Summit Level Rds, 0.5 mi W of post office, Rail Road Flat

NO. 287

ANGELS CAMP

Founded in 1849 by George Angel, who established a mining camp and trading store 200 feet below this marker, this was in a rich gravel mining area that was also one of the richest quartz mining sections of the Mother Lode–production records reached over $100 million for Angels Camp and vicinity. Prominent in early-day California history, it was said to be frequented by Joaquin Murieta, Black Bart, and other early-day bandits, and was the locale of Mark Twain's famous story, The Jumping Frog of Calaveras County.

NE corner of Main St and Birds Way, Angels Camp

NO. 288

ALTAVILLE

The history of Altaville is closely identified with that of Angels Camp. Altaville has been the foundry town of Calaveras County since D. D. Demerest established a foundry there in 1854. Most of the stamp mills and a large part of the mining machinery erected in Calaveras and Tuolumne Counties were built at the Altaville Foundry. A brick schoolhouse was built at Altaville in 1858 and the townsite was established in 1873.

Intersection of State Hwys 49 and 4, Altaville

NO. 295

PALOMA

Gwin Mine, Paloma, and Lower Rich Gulch were mined for placer gold in 1849, and quartz was discovered by J. Alexander in 1851. Property here was acquired by Wm. M. Gwin, California's first U.S. Senator, in 1851. After yielding millions of dollars in gold, the Gwin Mine closed in 1908.

Intersection of Paloma Rd and Edster St, 5 mi SW of Mokelumne Hill

NO. 296

COPPEROPOLIS

W. K. Reed and Thomas McCarty discovered copper here in 1860. The mines were utilized during the Civil War, when they were the principal copper producing section of the United States, and World Wars I and II.

State Dept of Forestry Station, 375 Main St, Copperopolis

NO. 370☐ 🔍

VALLECITO BELL MONUMENT

Named "Little Valley" by Mexicans, Vallecito was one of California's important early-day mining towns. Gold was discovered here by the Murphy brothers in 1849, and it was originally called "Murphy's old diggings." This bell, cast at Troy, New York in 1853, was brought around the horn. It was purchased from the ship with funds contributed by early-day residents and brought to Vallecito to be erected in a large oak tree in 1854. It was used to call the people together until February 16, 1939, when a severe wind blew the old tree down.

Intersection of Church St and Cemetery Ln, Vallecito

NO. 465🔔 🔍

OLD MINING CAMP OF BROWNSVILLE

A thriving mining camp on rich Pennsylvania Gulch in the 1850s and 1860s, the camp was named for Alfred Brown, former owner of Table Mountain Ranch. Laws of the Brownsville mining district provided that each miner could own one wet and one dry claim, not to exceed 150 square feet each.

On Pennsylvania Gulch Rd, 0.9 mi SW of Murphys

NO. 466🔔

THE PETER L. TRAVER BUILDING

Constructed by Peter L. Traver in 1856, this is the oldest stone building in Murphys. Its iron shutters and sand on the roof protected it from the fires of 1859, 1874, and 1893. It served as a general store, a Wells Fargo office, and later a garage.

470 Main St, Murphys

NO. 499🔔

RED BRICK GRAMMAR SCHOOL

This brick building, erected in 1848 with funds raised by a dance in the Billiard Saloon of the N.R. Prince Building (which still stands, 1955) is one of the oldest schools of California. It was in use until 1950, when it was replaced by the Mark Twain Elementary School in Altaville.

Division of Forestry Station, 125 N Main St, Altaville

NO. 663🔔

COURTHOUSE OF CALAVERAS COUNTY, 1852-1866, AND LEGER HOTEL

A portion of this building served as the Calaveras County Courthouse from 1852 to 1866, when the county seat was removed to San Andreas. George W. Leger then acquired the court building and made it a part of his adjoining hotel, which has been in operation since early gold mining days; it was known as the Grand Hotel in 1874 when fire damaged it and destroyed its dance hall. Restored in 1879, it has since been known as the Leger Hotel.

SE corner of Main and Lafayette Sts, Mokelumne Hill

NO. 734 🔔

ANGELS HOTEL

The canvas hotel that C. C. Lake erected here in 1851 was replaced by a one-story wooden structure, and then in 1855 by one of stone; a second story was added in 1857. It was here that Samuel Clemens first heard the yarn that was later to bring him fame as Mark Twain, author of The Jumping Frog of Calaveras County.

NE corner of Main St and Bird Way, Angels Camp

NO. 735 🔔

PRINCE-GARIBARDI BUILDING

This structure was erected in 1852 by B. R. Prince and G. Garibardi for a general merchandise business. Improved in 1857 with living quarters on the second floor, it is still used for living and warehouse purposes.

298 S Main St, near Hwy 4 junction, Altaville

NO. 769 ☐

BIRTHPLACE OF ARCHIE STEVENOT

The Stevenot family established the borax industry in California; Archie Stevenot was proclaimed "Mr. Mother Lode" by resolution of the 1961 session of the State Legislature. Not only he but his father and grandfather lent fame to the Carson Hill region of California.

On State Hwy 4 (P.M. 3.3), 3.7 mi S of Angels Camp

NO. 956

CALIFORNIA CAVERNS AT CAVE CITY

The historical significance of California Caverns is well established as a major cavern system and as one of the earliest officially recorded caves (1850) in the Mother Lode region of California. The early commercial enterprise associated with California Caverns is evidenced by the historical documents verifying organized tourist activities as early as 1854. Although one of numerous caves in the Mother Lode region, California Caverns claims the distinction of having the most extensive system of caverns and passageways.

Cave City Rd, approx 4 mi from Mountain Ranch Rd via Michel Rd, 11 mi E of Hwy 49 in San Andreas

Landmark No. 769

Landmark No. 645

Colusa County

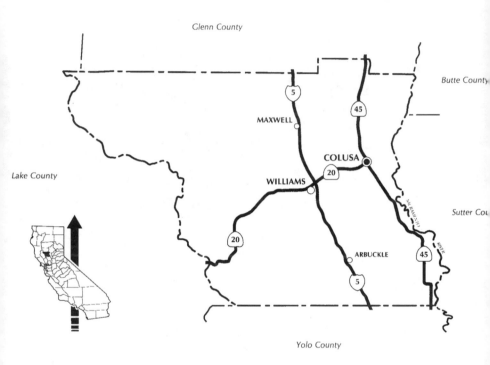

Colusa
Est. 1850

R ich agricultural soil prompted early settlement of this county west of the Sacramento River. The town of Colusa was built on an early village site of the Ko-ru-si Indians, from whom the town and county name was derived.

NO. 238 □

SWIFT'S STONE CORRAL

The original owner and builder of this stone corral was Granville P. Swift, a native of Kentucky. In 1847 Swift began ranching in Stone Creek Valley in Colusa County. In 1850 he and his partner Frank Sears needed a corral and, as there was no timber in the surrounding country, they built one from the flat stones that were scattered over the area.

1,000 ft S of Maxwell-Sites Rd, 6.4 mi W of Maxwell

NO. 736 🔔

LETTS VALLEY

This valley was settled in 1855 by Jack and David Lett. The present lake spillway is the site of a tunnel that they built to facilitate drainage. The brothers were killed in 1877 in an attempt to prevent squatters from settling on their land.

Letts Lake Campground, Fouts Springs Rd (18N01), 18.5 mi SW of Stonyford

NO. 890 🔔

COLUSA COUNTY COURTHOUSE

Erected in 1861, this Federal/Classic Revival style building is the oldest remaining courthouse in the Sacramento Valley. The "Southern" style reflects the county's heritage and states' rights sympathies during the Civil War. In its early years, the courthouse also served as a center for cultural, social, and religious activities.

547 Market and 6th Sts, Colusa

Contra Costa County

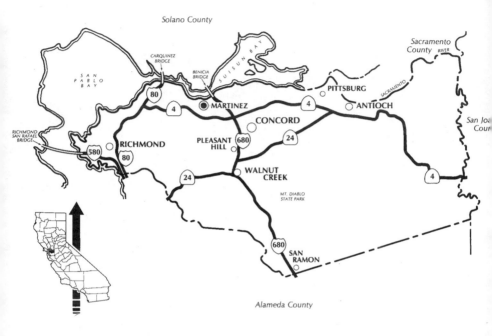

Contra Costa
Est. 1850

Mount Diablo is the most prominent geological feature of this East Bay county. Historically, Contra Costa has been home to prominent Californios — long-term residents of Spanish and Mexican descent who owned rancheros and settled in the romantic Mexican Era of California History.

NO. 312🔔
JOHN MUIR HOME

This is the ranch home of John Muir, 1838-1914, explorer, naturalist, author and foremost advocate of forest protection and of national parks. The John Muir Trail through the high Sierra, Muir Woods National Monument, and Muir Glacier in Alaska are named for him.

John Muir National Historic Site, 4202 Alhambra Ave, Martinez

NO. 356
CASTRO HOME

The El Cerrito adobe, as it was known because it was built near the north bank of El Cerrito Creek, was one of the adobes built by the Castro family on Rancho San Pablo. It was destroyed by fire in April 1956.

El Cerrito Plaza, 9800 San Pablo Ave, El Cerrito

NO. 455🔔
DON FERNANDO PACHECO ADOBE

One-quarter mile north of this spot is the site of the adobe house constructed in 1843 by Don Fernando Pacheco. Reconstructed in 1941, it is preserved as a memento of the historic past of Contra Costa County.

Contra Costa Horseman's Association, 3119 Grant St; State plaque located at NE corner of Grant and Solano Way, Concord

NO. 509 ☐
JOAQUÍN MORAGA ADOBE

In 1835 Don Joaquín Moraga, with his cousin Don Juan Bernal, was awarded this grant which they called Rancho Laguna de los Palos Colorados; the adobe was completed in 1841. Don Joaquín was the grandson of José Joaquín Moraga, founder and first commandante of the Presidio of San Francisco.

24 Adobe Ln, Orinda (private residence)

NO. 511🔔
VICENTE MARTÍNEZ ADOBE

In 1849 Vicente J. Martínez built this adobe on Rancho Pinole, which had been granted to Ignacio Martínez in 1836. In 1853, Vicente sold the adobe to Edward Franklin, after whom the canyon in which the adobe was located was named, and the adobe was known as the Franklin Canyon Adobe.

Alhambra Ave and Hwy 4, Martinez

NO. 512 🔔
ALVARADO ADOBE

Site of adobe house, grape arbor, and gardens built in 1842 by Jesús María Castro for his mother, Dona Gabriéla Berryessa de Castro, widow of Francisco María Castro who had been granted Rancho (Cuchiyunes) San Pablo in 1823. When Dona Gabriéla died in 1851, the adobe became the property of her daughter, Martina Castro de Alvarado, wife of Juan Bautista Alvarado, who was Governor of California from 1836 to 1842.

Civic Center, Alvarado Square, NW corner of San Pablo Blvd and Church Ln, San Pablo

NO. 515 ☐
DON SALVIO PACHECO ADOBE

In 1834 Don Salvio Pacheco was awarded a grant called Monte del Diablo and on June 24, 1835 completed this two-story adobe, the first building to be erected in this valley. Don Salvio gave the land surrounding this adobe to the refugees of the earthquake-flood of 1868, and the community became known as Concord.

1870 Adobe St at Salvio St, Concord

NO. 722 🔔
SITE OF THE MURDER OF DR. JOHN MARSH

Dr. Marsh, who practiced medicine throughout the state from his home near Brentwood, purchased Rancho Meganos in 1837. On his way home from Martinez, he was murdered here by ruffians on September 24, 1856.

Across street from 4575 Pacheco Blvd, Martinez

NO. 731 🔔
"THE OLD HOMESTEAD"

This was the first American home in Crockett, located on an earlier Indian village near the Carquinez Straits. Constructed in 1867 by Thomas Edwards, Sr., on land purchased in 1866 from Judge J. B. Crockett, its timbers, some of them brought around the Horn, have been well preserved.

993 Loring Ave at Ralph Ave, Crockett

NO. 853 🔔
CAPTAIN PEDRO FAGES TRAIL

In 1772 Fages, commandante at Monterey, vainly looked for a way across San Francisco Bay. With Franciscan missionary Juan Crespí, 14 soldiers, a muleteer, and an Indian servant, he trekked along Carquinez Strait, thence eastward nearly to Antioch before turning back. These, the first white men to explore what became Contra Costa County, passed this point and camped near Danville on March 31, 1772.

856 Danville Blvd at El Portal, Danville

NO. 905 🔔
MOUNT DIABLO

Mount Diablo had been a home with spiritual significance to the Costanoan Indians for at least 500 years when Spanish explorers viewed the mountain in 1772. In 1851 Mount Diablo was selected as the initial point for land surveys of Northern California and Nevada, with the Mount Diablo Base and Meridian Lines originating at its peak. Due to the mountain's variations in wind, rainfall, and temperature, it is also a preserve for a wide variety of plant and animal life.

Mount Diablo State Park, on summit, 4.5 mi E of ranger station, 14 mi E of Danville

NO. 932

MOUNT DIABLO COAL FIELD

This was the largest coal-mining district in California from 1860 to 1914, with five towns—Nortonville, Somersville, Stewartsville, Judsonville, and West Hartley–near twelve major mines. Today the towns are gone, their buildings moved to other communities after the mines closed; the East Bay Regional Park District is preserving mine openings, tailings, railroad beds, and a pioneer cemetery.

Black Diamond Mines Regional Park, from State Hwy 4 take Somersville Rd 3.9 mi S, Antioch

NO. 951

LIGHT STATIONS OF CALIFORNIA (THEMATIC), EAST BROTHER LIGHT STATION

East Brother is the oldest wood-frame lighthouse on the West Coast stilll fully operational and still in its historic configuration with functioning equipment. It was one of a group of twelve lighthouses similar but unique in design, built in California during the early 1870's. At the time it was built, it provided both a light and roof signal to guide boats ferrying mail, passengers, and freight between San Francisco and various island ports.

Off Point San Pablo, in Straits of San Pablo, connecting San Francisco and San Pablo Bays

NO. 1002-1

SITE OF GIANT POWDER COMPANY (POINT PINOLE)

Pt. Pinole is the last site of the Giant Powder Company, the first company in America to produce dynamite. Following devastating explosions at their san Francisco and Berkeley sites, the business moved to this isolated location in 1892. Incorporating the established Croatian community of Sobrente, the company town of Giant quickly grew into one of the North Bay's industrial centers. Explosives were produced here until 1960 and were essential to mining, dam and other construction projects throughout the Western Hemisphere.

Giant and Atlas Rds, Richmond

Del Norte County

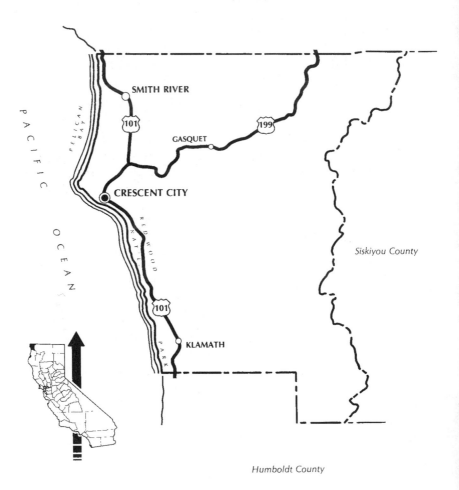

OREGON

PACIFIC OCEAN

PELICAN BAY

SMITH RIVER

101

199

GASQUET

CRESCENT CITY

REDWOOD NAT'L

Siskiyou County

101

KLAMATH

PARK

Humboldt County

Del Norte
Est. 1857

California's most northwestern county is appropriately named with the Spanish words for "of the north." This coastal region's history is marked with historic lighthouses, shipwrecks and military presence established to protect the interests of early settlers on Native American lands.

NO. 497 🔔
S.S. EMIDIO

Nearby are portions of the hull of the General Petroleum Corporation tanker S.S. Emidio, which on December 20, 1941 became the first casualty of the Imperial Japanese Navy's submarine force action on California's Pacific Coast. The ship was attacked some 200 miles north of San Francisco and five crewmen were killed. Abandoned, the vessel drifted north and broke up on the rocks off Crescent City. The bow drifted into the harbor, where it lay near this marker until salvaged in 1950.

Beach Front Park and Picnic Area, SW corner of Front and H Sts, Crescent City

NO. 541 🔔
BROTHER JONATHAN CEMETERY

This memorial is dedicated to those who lost their lives in the wreck of the Pacific Mail steamer Brother Jonathan at point St. George's Reef, July 30, 1865.

Located in park at Brother Johnathan Vista Point, SE corner 9th St and Pebble Beach Dr, Crescent City

NO. 544 🔔
FORT TER-WER

Site of Fort Ter-Wer, United States military post established October 12, 1857 by First Lieutenant George Crook and the men of Company D to keep peace between the Indians and whites. The fort was destroyed by a flood in December 1861, and abandoned June 10, 1862.

From Hwy 101 take Ter-Wer Valley exit (Hwy 169), go 3.4 mi to end of road, turn right on Ter-Wer Riffle Rd. Site at intersection of Ter-Wer Riffle and Klamath Glen Rds, Klamath

NO. 545 🔔
CAMP LINCOLN

A United States military post was established here September 12, 1862 by the men of Company G, 2nd Regiment, Infantry, California Volunteers, to keep peace between the Indians and the miners and settlers of northwestern California. It was abandoned in May 1870. Commanding officer's quarters and one barracks remain at the date of dedication of this site (1962).

Take Hwy 199 E to Kings Valley Rd, go 1.2 mi NE to site, Crescent City

NO. 645 🔔

CRESCENT CITY PLANK AND TURNPIKE ROAD

This was the route of the Crescent City Turnpike, constructed in 1858. Following the present Elk Valley Road to Old Camp Lincoln, it then crossed the ridge, forded Smith River to Low Divide, and continued to Jacksonville, Oregon by way of various gold camps.

Take Hwy 199 to Parkway Dr, go 1,000 ft to SE corner of Parkway Dr and Elk Valley Rd, Crescent City

NO. 649 🔔

SITE OF OLD INDIAN VILLAGE AT PEBBLE BEACH, CRESCENT CITY

At the time of white contact the principal villages of the native Tolowa Indians of northern Del Norte County were located at Battery Point in Crescent City (Ta'atun), Pebble Beach (Meslteltun), south of Point St. George (Tatintun), and north of Point St. George (Tawiatun). The major villages were almost completely independent economic units.

1886 Pebble Beach Dr, 500 ft S of Pacific Ave, Crescent City

NO. 951 🔔

BATTERY POINT LIGHTHOUSE

The Battery Point Lighthouse is one of the first lighthouses on the California coast. Rugged mountains and unbridged rivers meant coastal travel was essential for the economic survival of this region. In 1855 Congress appropriated $15,000 for the construction of the light station, which was completed in 1856 by the U.S. Lighthouse Service. Theophilis Magruder was the station's first keeper; Wayne Philand was its last before automation in 1953.

Battery Pt Island, end of A St, Crescent City

Landmark No. 645

Landmark No. 968

El Dorado County

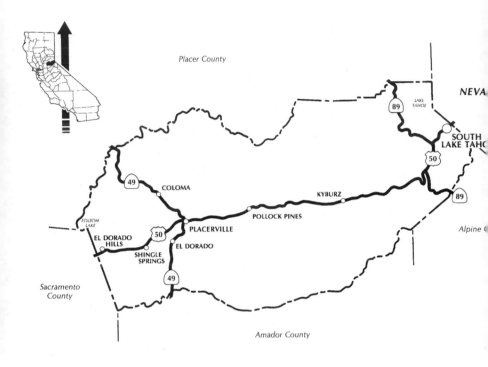

Emerald Bay State Park - Features Vikingsholm, patterned after a Norse fortress circa 800 AD. Located 22 miles S of Tahoe City on Highway 89.

Marshall Gold Discovery State Historic Park - Site of California gold discovery, 1848. Located in Coloma.

El Dorado
Est. 1850

Stretching from oak-studded foothills to the western shore of Lake Tahoe, El Dorado County is probably best known for the 1848 gold discovery at Coloma. "Old Hangtown" sprang up during the Gold Rush and was later renamed Placerville. The county name comes from the mythical land rich in gold sought by Spanish explorers.

NO. 141 ☐

HANGMAN'S TREE

In the days of 1849, when this city was called Hangtown, vigilantes executed many men for various crimes. This was the site of Hay Yard, on which stood the "Hangman's Tree." The stump of the tree is under the building on which the plaque is placed.

305 Main St. Placerville

NO. 142 ☐

STUDEBAKER'S SHOP (SITE OF)

This shop was built in the early 1850s. The front part housed a blacksmith shop operated by Ollis and Hinds, and John Mohler Studebaker rented a part of the rear. Here he had a bench and sort of woodworking shop where he repaired and worked on wagon wheels and the like. A little later he began to make wheelbarrows for the miners' use. He became engaged in the making of ammunition wagons for the Union Army; from that grew his extensive wagon and carriage business and, eventually, the automobile business.

543 Main St, Placerville

NO. 143 ☐

MARSHALL MONUMENT

In 1887 the State of California purchased the site for a monument to commemorate James Marshall, who in 1848 discovered gold near Coloma. Marshall's discovery started the "gold rush," that westward trek of Argonauts that marked a turning point in California history. The figure of Marshall atop the monument is pointing to the place of discovery on the South Fork of the American River.

Marshall Gold Discovery State Historic Park, Coloma

NO. 319

MARSHALL'S BLACKSMITH SHOP

Marshall's blacksmith shop, located on the Gray Eagle Mine property, was built in 1872-73. Marshall not only was a smithy but also a qualified carpenter.

On State Hwy 193 (P.M. 21.1), Kelsey

NO. 456 🔔/⛏

SHINGLE SPRINGS

The Boston-Newton Joint Stock Association, which left Boston April 16 and arrived at Sutter's Fort September 27 after a remarkable journey across the continent, camped here on September 26, 1849. A rich store of written records preserved by these pioneers has left a fascinating picture of the gold rush.

Mother Lode Dr near post office, Shingle Springs

NO. 475 🔔/⛏

OLD DRY DIGGINS—OLD HANGTOWN—PLACERVILLE

This rich mining camp was established on the banks of Hangtown Creek in the spring of 1848. Millions in gold were taken from its ravines and hills, and it served as a supply center for mining camps and transportation terminus for the famous Comstock Lode. John M. Studebaker, Mark Hopkins, Leland Stanford, Phillip Armour, and Edwin Markham were among well-known men who contributed to Placerville's history, as did John A. "Snowshoe" Thompson, who carried from 60 to 80 pounds of mail on skis from Placerville over the Sierra to Carson Valley during winter months.

NE corner of Bedford and Main, Placerville

NO. 484 🔔/⛏

GEORGETOWN

Founded August 7, 1849, by George Phipps and party, Georgetown was nicknamed Growlersburg because of the heavy nuggets that "growled" in the miners' pans. After the disastrous fire of 1852 the old town was moved from the canyon in lower Main Street to its present site, and, unique in early-day planning, Main Street was laid out 100 feet wide, with side streets 60 feet. The hub of an immensely rich gold mining area, Georgetown had a population of about three thousand in 1854-56.

Mounted on wall in front of fire station, Main St, Georgetown

NO. 486 🔔/⛏

EL DORADO (ORIGINALLY "MUD SPRINGS")

El Dorado, "The Gilded One," was first known as Mud Springs from the boggy quagmire the cattle and horses made of a nearby watering place. Originally an important camp on the old Carson Emigrant Trail, by 1849-50 it had become the center of a mining district and the crossroads for freight and stage lines. At the height of the rush its large gold production supported a population of several thousand.

N side of intersection of Pleasant Valley Rd and Church St, El Dorado

NO. 487 🔔/⛏

DIAMOND SPRINGS

This town, settled in 1848, derived its name from its crystal clear springs. Among the richest spots in this vicinity, its diggings produced a 25-pound nugget, one of the largest ever found in El Dorado County. Its most thriving period was in 1851 and, through its lumber, lime production, and agriculture, Diamond Springs has retained some of its early importance.

NW corner of Hwy 49 at China Garden Rd, Diamond Springs

NO. 521 🔔 ⨯

GREENWOOD

John Greenwood, a trapper and guide who came to California in 1844, established a trading post here in 1849. The gold rush town of Greenwood boasted a theater, four hotels, 14 stores, a brewery, and four saloons. Among its illustrious citizens was John A. Stone, California songwriter, who was buried here in 1863.

SW corner of the intersection of State Hwy 193 and Greenwood St, Greenwood

NO. 530 ☐ ⨯

GOLD DISCOVERY SITE

This monument marks the site of John A. Sutter's sawmill. In its tail-race, on January 24, 1848, James W. Marshall discovered gold and started great rush of Argonauts to California. The Society of California Pioneers definitely located and marked the site in 1924; additional timbers and relics, including the original tail-race unearthed in 1947, were discovered after the property became a state park. The State erected the Marshall Monument overlooking this spot in 1890 through efforts begun in 1886 by the Native Sons of the Golden West.

Marshall Gold Discovery State Historic Park, follow trail from Gold Discovery parking lot to American River, State Hwy 49 (P.M. 23.3), Coloma

NO. 551 🔔

SITE OF CALIFORNIA'S FIRST GRANGE HALL

Pilot Hill Grange No. 1, with 29 charter members–Master, F. D. Brown; Secretary A. J. Bayley–was organized August 10, 1870. The Grange hall, dedicated at this site on November 23, 1889, was built by Alcandor A. Bayley.

On State Hwy 49 (P.M. 31.3), 0.2 mi N of Pilot Hill

NO. 569 ☐ ⨯

MORMON ISLAND

Early in March 1848, W. Sidney, S. Willis, and Wilford Hudson, members of the Mormon Battalion, set out from Sutter's Fort to hunt deer. Stopping on the south fork of the American River, they found gold. They told their story on returning to the fort, and soon about 150 Mormons and other miners flocked to the site, which was named Mormon Island. This was the first major gold strike in California after James W. Marshall's discovery at Coloma. The population of the town in 1853 was more than 2,500. It had four hotels, three dry-goods stores, five general merchandise stores, an express office, and many small shops. The first ball in Sacramento County was held here on December 25, 1849. A fire destroyed the town in 1856, and it was never rebuilt. Its site was inundated by Folsom Lake in 1955.

Folsom Lake State Recreation Area, N side, Dyke 8 picnic area, 3 mi NE of Folsom

NO. 570, 571, 572 🔤

NEGRO HILL, SALMON FALLS, CONDEMNED BAR

These historic mining towns, and other mining camps of the gold rush era now inundated by Folsom Lake, are commemorated by the nearby Mormon Island Memorial Cemetery. Here were reburied the pioneers whose graves were flooded when the lake was formed by Folsom Dam.

Folsom Lake State Recreation Area, Green Valley Rd, 0.1 mi NE of El Dorado-Sacramento County line, 4 mi NE of Folsom

NO. 699 🔔

MORMON TAVERN—OVERLAND PONY EXPRESS ROUTE IN CALIFORNIA

At this site on the old Clarksville-White Rock Emigrant Road was Mormon Tavern. Constructed in 1849, this popular stage stop was enlarged and operated by Franklin Winchell in 1851. It became a remount station of the Central Overland Pony Express and on April 4, 1860, pony rider Sam (Bill) Hamilton changed horses here on the first eastbound trip.

On frontage rd adjacent to State Hwy 50 (P.M. 1.5), take El Dorado Hills Blvd S for 0.5 mi to old White Rd (rd to Clarksville), then NE 0.9 mi, then go W 0.3 mi on PG&E Clarksville Substation Rd to plaque, 0.5 mi W of Clarksville

NO. 700 🔔

EL DORADO—NEVADA HOUSE (MUD SPRINGS) —OVERLAND PONY EXPRESS ROUTE IN CALIFORNIA

Trading post, emigrant stop, and mining camp of the 1850s, this became one of the remount stations of the Central Overland Pony Express. On April 13, 1860, pony rider William (Sam) Hamilton changed horses here at the Nevada House while carrying the first westbound mail of the Pony Express from St. Joseph, Missouri to Sacramento.

SW corner of Pleasant Valley Rd near Church St, El Dorado

NO. 701 🔔

PLACERVILLE—OVERLAND PONY EXPRESS ROUTE IN CALIFORNIA

Gold rush town and western terminus of the Placerville-Carson Road to the Comstock, Placerville was a relay station of the Central Overland Pony Express from April 4, 1860 until June 30, 1861. Here on April 4, 1860, the first eastbound pony rider, William (Sam) Hamilton, changed horses, added an express letter to his mochila, and sped away for Sportsman's Hall. Placerville was the western terminus of the Pony Express from July 1, 1861 until its discontinuance on October 26, 1861.

SW corner of Main and Sacramento, Placerville

NO. 703🔔

PLEASANT GROVE HOUSE — OVERLAND PONY EXPRESS ROUTE IN CALIFORNIA

This was the site of a popular road-house where the ponies of the Central Overland Pony Express were changed from July 1, 1860 to June 30, 1861. From here the route of the pony riders continued westward to Folsom and eastward to Placerville through Rescue, Dry Creek Crossing, and Missouri Flat.

Green Valley Rd (P.M. 5.5), 3.9 mi W of Rescue

NO. 704🔔

SPORTSMAN'S HALL—OVERLAND PONY EXPRESS ROUTE IN CALIFORNIA

This was the site of Sportsman's Hall, also known as Twelve-Mile House, the hotel operated in the latter 1850s and 1860s by John and James Blair. A stopping place for stages and teams of the Comstock, it became a relay station of the Central Overland Pony Express. Here, at 7:40 a.m., April 4, 1860, pony rider William (Sam) Hamilton rode in from Placerville and handed the express mail to Warren Upson, who two minutes later sped on his way eastward.

5622 Old Pony Express Trail, Cedar Grove

NO. 705🔔

MOORE'S (RIVERTON)–OVERLAND PONY EXPRESS ROUTE IN CALIFORNIA

This was the site of a change station of the Pioneer Stage Company in the 1850s and 1860s. During 1860-1861, the Central Overland Pony Express maintained the first pony remount station east of Sportsman's Hall here.

At intersection of US. Hwy 50 and Ice House Rd (P.M. 39.7), 9.0 mi W of Kyburz

NO. 706🔔

WEBSTER'S (SUGAR LOAF HOUSE)–OVERLAND PONY EXPRESS ROUTE IN CALIFORNIA

This was the site of Webster's Sugar Loaf House, well-known stopping place during the Comstock rush. Beginning in April 1860, it was used as a remount station of the Central Overland Pony Express, and in 1861 it became a horse change station for pioneer stage companies and the Overland Mail.

On Hwy 50 (P.M. 48. 0), 1.0 mi W of Kyburz

NO. 707🔔

STRAWBERRY VALLEY HOUSE—OVERLAND PONY EXPRESS ROUTE IN CALIFORNIA

This popular resort and stopping place for stages and teams of the Comstock, established by Swift and Watson in 1856, became a remount station of the Central Overland Pony Express. Here on April 4, 1860, Division Superintendent Bolivar Roberts waited with a string of mules to help pony rider Warren Upson through the snowstorm on Echo Summit.

Strawberry, on Hwy 50 (P.M. 578), 8.7 mi E of Kyburz

NO. 708 🔔

YANK'S STATION—OVERLAND PONY EXPRESS ROUTE IN CALIFORNIA

This was the site of the most eastern re-mount station of the Central Overland Pony Express in California. Established as a trading post on the Placerville-Carson Road in 1851 by Martin Smith, it became a popular hostelry and stage stop operated by Ephraim "Yank" Clement. Pony rider Warren Upson arrived here on the evening of April 28, 1860 and, changing ponies, galloped on to Friday's in Nevada to de-liver his mochila to Bob Haslam for the ride to Genoa. Used as a pony remount station until October 26, 1861, the station was sold to George D. H. Meyers in 1873.

Yank's Station shopping center, SW corner State Hwy 50 and Apache Ave, Meyers

NO. 728

FRIDAY'S STATION—OVERLAND PONY EXPRESS ROUTE IN CALIFORNIA

At this point the riders of the Central Overland Pony Express crossed the Ne-vada-California line. Three-quarters of a mile east of here, at Edgewood in Nevada, are the remains of the most easterly re-mount station of the California Division of the Pony Express. Established about 1858 by Friday Burke and James Small as a stage station on the Placerville-Carson City Road, it became the home station of pony rider Bob Haslam until October 26, 1861 when the Pony Express was suc-ceeded by the Transcontinental Tele-graph.

Stateline, Hwy 50

NO. 747 🔔

COLOMA ROAD—RESCUE

Past this point on the old Coloma Road, running between Sutter's Fort and his sawmill on the American river, James W. Marshall rode with the first gold discov-ered at Coloma on January 24, 1848. Traveled by thousands to and from the diggings, this road became the route of California's earliest stageline, established in 1849 by James E. Birch.

At intersection of Green Valley and Deer Valley Rd, Rescue

NO. 748 🔔

COLOMA ROAD—COLOMA

Here in the valley of the Cul-luh-mah Indians, James W. Marshall discovered gold on January 24, 1848, in the tailrace of Sutter's sawmill. The old Coloma Road, opened in 1847 from Sutter's Fort to Coloma, was used by Marshall to carry the news of the discovery to Captain John A. Sutter. During the gold rush, it was used by thousands of miners going to and from the diggings. In 1849 it became the route of California's first stage line, established by James E. Birch.

Marshall Gold Discovery State Historic Park, in Gold Discovery parking area, State Hwy 49, Coloma

NO. 767 🔔

METHODIST EPISCOPAL CHURCH

Erected in 1851, this is the oldest church building in El Dorado County. Its origi-nal site was on the corner of Cedar Ra-vine and Main Street, Placerville.

1031 Thompson Way near Cedar Ravine St, Placerville

NO. 815 🔔

WAKAMATSU TEA AND SILK FARM COLONY

The agricultural settlement of pioneer Japanese immigrants who arrived at Gold Hill on June 8, 1869–the only tea and silk farm established in California–had a promising outlook but failed tragically in less than two years. This was the initial Japanese-influenced agricultural attempt in California.

Gold Trails Elementary School, 1336 Cold Springs Rd, Gold Hill

Landmark No. 815

Landmark No. 551

Fresno County

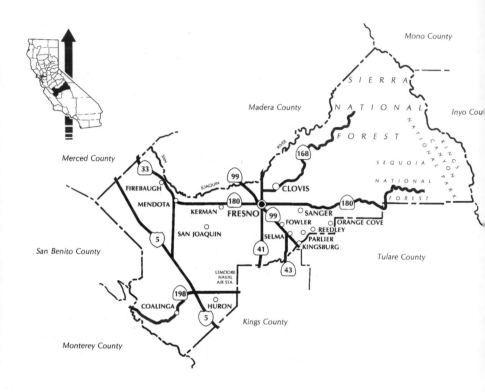

Millerton Lake State Recreation Area - Reconstructed courthouse originally built in 1867. Located 20 miles NE of Fresno.

Fresno
Est. 1856

From casual observation, Fresno County might appear to have been a gathering of quiet, mostly agricultural communities. At the confluence of the San Joaquin River and the Fresno Slough, Spaniards and Mexicans first settled in the San Joaquin Valley. Outlaw's hideouts, the free speech movement, oil discovery and preservation of the giant sequoia are just a few elements of the diverse history of Fresno County.

NO. 344

ARROYO DE CANTUA

This was said to be the headquarters of notorious bandit Joaquin Murieta who made a career of terrorizing mining camps and stage operations. He was killed here July 25, 1853 by a posse of state rangers led by Captain Harry Love.

Site is three large rocks in foothills SW of Cantua Creek Bridge, plaques located on State Hwy 198, 9 mi N of Coalinga

NO. 488

FRESNO CITY

"Fresno City" gradually arose at the head of navigation of the Fresno Slough, and existed from approximately 1855 to 1875; today there are no traces of it left. In 1872, the "City of Fresno," later the county seat, was established about 30 miles to the southwest, on the newly built Central Pacific Railroad.

On Fresno Slough, 0.8 mi N of James Rd, from Tranquillity, then 1.3 mi NW on levee rd (dirt), Tranquillity

NO. 584

FORT MILLER

Now inundated by Millerton Lake, Fort Miller was established in 1852 as a temporary headquarters for the Commissioners during the latter part of the Mariposa Indian War. The peace treaty was signed there April 29, 1851. The first recorded religious services in the Fresno area were performed here on October 21, 1855 by Right Reverend William Ingraham Kip, first Protestant Episcopal Bishop of California. The village of Rootville grew into the town of Millerton and became the first seat of Fresno County in 1856.

South shore of Millerton Lake State Recreation Area, adjacent to Millerton historical courthouse, Friant

NO. 803☐

SITE OF FIRST JUNIOR COLLEGE IN CALIFORNIA

Constructed in 1895, the school was known as Fresno High School from 1895-1921. Established as the first junior college of California in 1910, in 1911 it became a normal school, forerunner to Fresno State College. From 1921 to 1948 it was called Fresno Technical High School, and Fresno Junior College from 1948 to 1959. Plaque placed by the Fresno Tech Alumni Association.

NE corner of intersection of Stanislaus and "O" Sts, Fresno

NO. 873🔔

SITE OF THE FRESNO FREE SPEECH FIGHT OF THE INDUSTRIAL WORKERS OF THE WORLD

At the corner of Mariposa and I Streets, from October 1910 to March 1911, the Industrial Workers of the World fought for the right of free speech in their efforts to organize Fresno's unskilled labor force. This was the first fight for free speech in California, and the first attempt to organize the valley's unskilled workers.

In planter, 100 ft SW of clock tower, Fulton and Mariposa Mall, Fresno

NO. 916🔔

FORESTIERE UNDERGROUND GARDENS

Here, beneath the hot, arid surface of the San Joaquin Valley, Baldasare Forestiere (1879-1946) began in the early 1900s to sculpt a fantastic retreat. Excavating the hardpan by hand, he created a unique complex of underground rooms, passages, and gardens which rambled throughout a ten-acre parcel. His work is being preserved as a living monument to a creative and individualistic spirit unbounded by conventionality.

5021 W Shaw Ave, Fresno

NO. 934🔔

TEMPORARY DETENTION CAMPS FOR JAPANESE AMERICANS—FRESNO ASSEMBLY CENTER

This memorial is dedicated to over 5,000 Americans of Japanese ancestry who were confined at the Fresno Fairgrounds from May to October 1942. This was an early phase of the mass incarceration of over 120,000 Japanese Americans during World War II pursuant to Executive Order 9066. They were detained without charges, trial or establishment of guilt. May such injustice and suffering never recur.

Fresno District Fairgrounds, front of Commerce Bldg, Chance Ave entrance, Fresno

NO. 934

TEMPORARY DETENTION CAMPS FOR JAPANESE AMERICANS— PINEDALE ASSEMBLY CENTER

The temporary detention camps (also known as "assembly centers") represent the first phase of the mass incarceration of 97,785 Californians of Japanese ancestry during World War II. Pursuant to Executive Order 9066 signed by President Franklin D. Roosevelt on February 19, 1942, thirteen makeshift detention facilities were constructed at various California racetracks, fairgrounds, and labor camps. These facilities were intended to confine Japanese Americans until more permanent concentration camps, such as those at Manzanar and Tule Lake in California, could be built in isolated areas of the country. Beginning on March 30, 1942, all native-born Americans and long-time legal residents of Japanese ancestry living in California were ordered to surrender themselves for detention.

Pinedale

Landmark No. 803

Glenn County

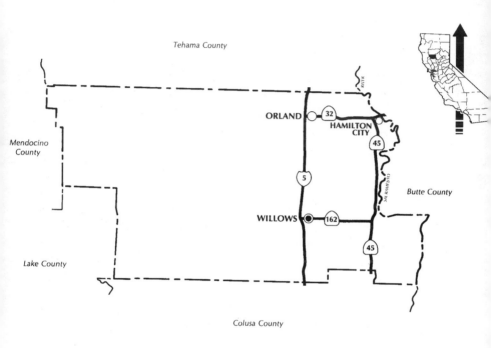

Tehama County

ORLAND

HAMILTON CITY

32

45

5

Mendocino County

Butte County

WILLOWS 162

45

Lake County

Colusa County

Glenn
Est. 1891

Glenn County is named for Dr. Hugh James Glen, who came to California in 1849 to stake a gold claim. After having been a dentist in Missouri, he turned to wheat farming on his 55,000 acres of property near the town of Jacinto.

NO. 345 ☐

GRANVILLE P. SWIFT ADOBE

Granville P. Swift crossed the plains to Oregon in 1843 and entered California with the Kelsey party in 1844. In 1849, in partnership with Frank Sears, he purchased the cattle and brand of the Larkin grant from J. S. Williams. Swift soon had droves of cattle herded by Indian vaqueros, and rodeos were held annually at this adobe site.

Old Hwy 99 W at Hambright Creek, 1.0 mi N of Orland

NO. 831 ☐

SITE OF FIRST POSTED WATER NOTICE BY WILL S. GREEN

Coming via Panama, William Semple Green (1832-1905) arrived in San Francisco on October 10, 1849 and in Colusa County on July 6, 1850. He was a ferryboat captain, mail carrier, surveyor, editor, writer, legislator, Surveyor General of the United States, California State Treasurer, irrigationist, and friend of man. On December 18, 1883, on an oak tree on the west bank of the Sacramento River immediately east of this spot, he posted the first water notice, stating that 500,000 miner's inches of river water was being diverted for irrigation of lands on the west side of the Sacramento Valley.

NE corner Cutler and 1st Aves, 3.7 mi N of Hamilton City

Humboldt County

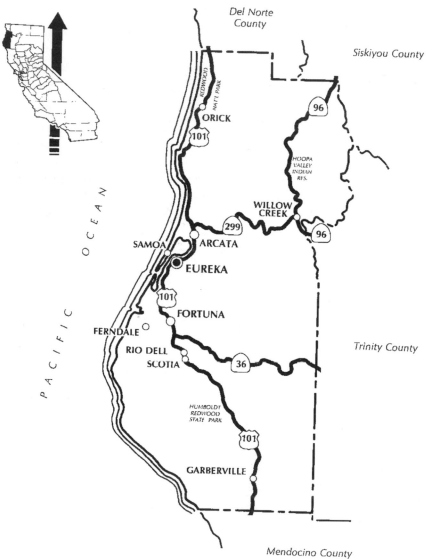

Del Norte
County

Siskiyou County

REDWOOD NAT'L PARK

ORICK

101

96

HOOPA
VALLEY
INDIAN
RES.

WILLOW
CREEK

299

96

SAMOA   ARCATA

EUREKA

101

FORTUNA

FERNDALE

RIO DELL

SCOTIA

36

HUMBOLDT
REDWOOD
STATE PARK

101

GARBERVILLE

Trinity County

Mendocino County

PACIFIC OCEAN

Fort Humboldt State Historic Park - U.S. military post,
1850s. Located at 3431 Fort Avenue, Eureka.

Humboldt
Est. 1853

Also known as the "Redwood Empire," Humboldt County on California's rugged north coast offers many attractions for visitors. Victorian homes constructed of durable redwood give an historical flavor to towns and cities. The fishing and logging industries have left their mark, along with the remnants of early conflict between settlers and Native Americans.

NO. 146 □
TRINIDAD HEAD

On June 11, 1775, Bruno de Hezeta, commandant of an expedition up the northwest coast, marched with his men and two Franciscan fathers from the shore of the bay to the summit of Trinidad Head. Here they erected a cross and took possession in the name of Charles III of Spain.

1.5 mi W of Hwy 101, Trinidad, USCG Station

NO. 154 🔔
FORT HUMBOLDT

By the early 1850s, newly arrived white settlers had moved into the Humboldt Bay area, causing conflict with the native inhabitants. To protect both Indians and settlers, Fort Humboldt was established in 1853 and operated until 1866. It became a focal point in the violent struggle between two cultures. Many Native Americans were assembled here before removal to reservations.

3431 Fort Ave, Eureka

NO. 164
THE OLD ARROW TREE

This site is said to have been used by Indians to commemorate an important peace treaty. In memory of the treaty, each tribe, upon passing, was supposed to have shot an arrow into the bark.

0.8 mi E of Korbel County Hwy F5L 100 (P.M. 2.2), Korbel

NO. 173 🔔
CENTERVILLE BEACH CROSS

On January 6, 1860 the steamer Northerner, northward bound from San Francisco, struck a hidden rock two miles off Cape Mendocino, and from there drifted to the Centerville Beach. Thirty-three passengers and 32 crew members were saved; the cross was erected by the Ferndale Parlor No. 93, N.D.G.W., in memory of the 17 passengers and 21 crew members who lost their lives in this disaster.

5 mi W of Ferndale on Centerville Rd (P.M. 0.8)

NO. 215 🔔
CAMP CURTIS

Camp Curtis was the headquarters of the Mountain Battalion from 1862 to 1865. There were many military posts established throughout this area for the protection of the white settlers. (Army spells Curtis with one s.)

Take Sunset Ave offramp Hwy 101, go N 0.9 mi on L. K. Wood Blvd frontage Rd, Arcata

NO. 216 🔔
TOWN OF TRINIDAD

Founded April 8, 1850, Trinidad is the oldest town on the Northern California coast. During the 1850s, it served as a vital supply link between ships anchored at Trinidad Bay and miners in the Klamath, Trinity, Salmon River, and Gold Bluff mines. It was the county seat of Klamath County (now disbanded) from 1851 to 1854, but its population declined as Eureka and other area port cities developed.

NW corner of Edwards and Hector Sts, Trinidad

NO. 477 🔔
CITY OF EUREKA

Eureka was founded as a town in 1850 and incorporated as a city in 1874. Located on the remote northwestern coast of California, Eureka was the region's major port of entry by water in the 19th century before the construction of good access by land, and rose to historical prominence as the major social, political, and economic center of the region. "Eureka" is a Greek expression and a popular mining term meaning "I have found it."

NW corner, 3rd and E Sts, old town, Eureka

NO. 543 🔔
CALIFORNIA'S FIRST DRILLED OIL WELLS

California's first drilled oil wells that produced crude to be refined and sold commercially were located on the North Fork of the Mattole River approximately three miles east of here. The old Union Mattole Oil Company made its first shipment of oil from here, to a San Francisco refinery, in June 1865. Many old well heads remain today.

NE corner Mattole Rd and Front St, Petrolia

NO. 783 🔔
JACOBY BUILDING

The basement and first story of this building were constructed in 1857 for Agustus Jacoby, and housed various mercantile firms during its early years as a principal supply point for the Klamath-Trinity mining camp trade. It served occasionally as a refuge in time of the Indian troubles from 1858 through 1864. It was acquired by A. Brizard in 1880.

Eighth and H (plaque at NE corner, structure at SE corner), Arcata

NO. 838 🔔
OLD INDIAN VILLAGE OF TSURAI

Directly below was located the Yurok village of Tsurai. A prehistoric permanent Indian community, it was first located and described by Captains Bodega and Heceta, June 9-19, 1775. The houses were of hand-split redwood planks, designed for defense and protection. The village was occupied until 1916.

SW corner of Ocean and Edwards Sts, Trinidad

NO. 842

ARCATA AND MAD RIVER RAIL—ROAD COMPANY

Incorporated December 15, 1854, as the Union Plank Walk, Rail Track, and Wharf Company, the Arcata and Mad River Rail Road is the oldest line on the north coast. Originally using a horse-drawn car, the railroad served as a link between Humboldt Bay and the Trinity River mines. Later, locomotives were added as the line grew to serve the red-wood industry.

330 Railroad Ave, NW corner Hatchery Rd and Railroad Ave, Blue Lake

NO. 882

HUMBOLDT HARBOR HISTORICAL DISTRICT

Captain Jonathan Winship made the first recorded entry into Humboldt Bay by sea in June 1806, and Josiah Gregg's party visited the bay in 1849. By 1850 the Laura Virginia Association had founded Humboldt City, Union (Arcata), Bucksport, and Eureka; in subsequent years, the bay became a major North Coast lumber port and shipbuilding center.

Harold Larsen Vista Pt, Humboldt Hill Rd off Hwy 101 (P.M. 73.7), Eureka

NO. 883

FERNDALE

This pioneer agricultural community, settled in 1852, helped feed the booming population of mid-century San Francisco. Long known as "cream city," Ferndale made innovative and lasting contributions to the dairy industry. Local creameries, and the town's role as a transportation and shipping center in the late 19th and early 20th centuries, fostered prosperity that produced Ferndale's outstanding Victorian-Gothic residential and false-front commercial architecture.

Ferndale City Hall Park, intersection of Main and Herbert Sts, Ferndale

Landmark No. 477

Imperial County

Riverside County

SALTON SEA

PALO VERDE

86

SALTON
CITY

MILITARY

NILAND

RESERVATION

CALIPATRIA

78

ARIZONA

San Diego
County

111

SAND

MILITARY

WESTMORLAND

RESERVATION

BRAWLEY

86

HILLS

IMPERIAL

EL CENTRO

HOLTVILLE

OCOTILLO

8

8

WINTERHAVEN

111

CALEXICO

MEXICALI

MEXICO

Anza-Borrego Desert State Park - Pioneer trail and early stage
route. Located 65 miles NE of San Diego.

Imperial
Est. 1907

The newest of California's 58 counties, Imperial County is made up of an area known as the "Imperial Valley." In 1540, Europeans made their first sighting of Alta California here. From that time on, overland routes from Mexico were established, leaving their mark on the fragile desert landscape. The county also offers many prehistoric and geologic wonders to explore.

NO. 182

TUMCO MINES

Pete Walters of Ogilby discovered the first gold vein at Gold Rock on January 6, 1884. From his Little Mary Claim began a gold camp which reached its peak development between 1893 and 1899 as Hedges, with 3,200 residents. Nearly closed, 1900-10, it was reopened as Tumco, 1910-13, and worked intermittently until 1941. Tumco has long been a California ghost town.

On Gold Rock Ranch Rd, 1.0 mi E of County Hwy S34, 9.0 mi N of I-8, 4.5 mi NE of Ogilby

NO. 193

PICACHO MINES

Opened by placer miners after 1852, the gold mines expanded into hard rock quarrying by 1872. Picacho employed 700 miners at its peak from 1895 to 1900. Mill accidents, low ore quality, and the loss of cheap river transport with the building of Laguna Dam led to numerous periods of inactivity. With ores far from worked out, the Picacho Mines, using modern techniques, again resumed operations in 1984.

On Picacho Rd, 18.2 mi N of Winterhaven

NO. 194

MOUNTAIN SPRINGS STATION

In 1862-70, about a mile north of here Peter Larkin and Joe Stancliff used a stone house as a store from which ox teams pulled wagons up a 30% grade. The San Diego and Fort Yuma Turnpike Co. used the site as a toll road station until 1876. The crumbling house was replaced in 1917 by another still visible to its east. But road changes, beginning in 1878 and culminating in today's highway, have left the older stone house ruins inaccessible.

Site is 200 ft W of westbound lane, I-8 (P.M. 2.3), just N of Mountain Springs Rd, 2.3 mi E of county line, Mountain Springs

Plaque is located adjacent to Desert View Tower, approximately 100 yards distant from the Desert View Tower landmark plaque, old State Hwy 80, 1 mi N of the I-8 and In-Ko-Pah Park Rd interchange, 7 mi NE of Jacumba

NO. 350 🔔

MISSION DE LA PURÍSIMA CONCEPCIÓN (SITE OF)

In October 1780, Father Francisco Garcés and companions began Mission La Purísima Concepción. The mission/pueblo site was inadequately supported. Colonists ignored Indian rights, usurped the best lands, and destroyed Indian crops. Completely frustrated and disappointed, the Quechans (Yumas) and their allies destroyed Concepción on July 17-19, 1781.

St. Thomas Indian Mission, Indian Hill on Picacho Rd, Fort Yuma, 1 mi S of Winterhaven

NO. 568 🔔

HERNANDO DE ALARCÓN EXPEDITION

Alarcón's mission was to provide supplies for Francisco Coronado's expedition in search of the fabled Seven Cities of Cibola. The Spaniards led by Hernando de Alarcón ascended the Colorado River by boat from the Gulf of California past this point, thereby becoming the first non-Indians to sight Alta California on September 5, 1540.

On Algondes Rd, State Hwy 186 (P.M. 0.4), 0.5 mi S of I-8, 0.4 mi N of Andrade Border, Andrade

NO. 806 🔔

FORT YUMA

Originally called Camp Calhoun, the site was first used as a U.S. military post in 1849. A fire destroyed the original buildings. By 1855 the barracks had been re-

built. Called Camp Yuma in 1852, it became Fort Yuma after reconstruction. Transferred to the Department of the Interior and the Quechan Indian Tribe in 1884, it became a boarding school operated by the Catholic Church until 1900.

On bank of Colorado River, 350 Picacho Rd, Winterhaven

NO. 808 🔔

CAMP SALVATION

Here, on September 23, 1849, Lieut. Cave J. Couts, Escort Commander, International Boundary Commission, established Camp Salvation. From September till the first of December 1849, it served as a refugee center for distressed emigrants attempting to reach the gold fields over the Southern Emigrant Trail.

Rockwood Plaza, Sixth St E at Heber Ave, Calexico

NO. 845 🔔

PLANK ROAD

This unique plank road, seven miles long, was the only means early motorists had of crossing the treacherous Imperial sand dunes. The 8-by-12-foot sections were moved with a team of horses whenever the shifting sands covered portions of the road. Double sections were placed at intervals to permit vehicles to pass.

Algodones Sand Dunes County Rest Area, S side of I-8 (P.M. 77.4), 18 mi W of Winterhaven

NO. 921 🔔

SITE OF MISSION SAN PEDRO Y SAN PABLO DE BICUNER

To protect the Anza Trail where it forded the Colorado River, the Spanish founded a pueblo and mission nearby on January 7, 1781. Threatened with the loss of their land, the Quechans (Yumas) attacked this strategic settlement on July 17, 1781. The Quechan victory closed this crossing and seriously crippled future communications between upper California and Mexico.

On County Rd 524, 0.2 mi W of intersection of Levee and Mehring Rds, 4.4 mi NE of Bard

NO. 939 🔔

Twentieth Century Folk Art Environments (Thematic) —DESERT TOWER

Bert Vaughn of Jacumba built the stone tower in 1922-23 to commemorate the pioneers and road and railroad builders who opened the area. In the 1930s, W. T. Ratcliffe carved the stone animal figures which lurk in the rocks surrounding the tower, creating a fantasy world of surprise and strange beauty. This remarkable sculptural assemblage is one of California's exceptional Folk Art Environments.

On old State Hwy 80, 1 mi N of I-8 and In-Ko-Pah Park Rd interchange, 7.0 mi NE of Jacumba

NO. 939

Twentieth Century Folk Art Environments (Thematic) — CHARLEY'S WORLD OF LOST ART

Charles Kasling began sculpturing near Andrade in 1967, and his creations now fill a site of approximately two and a half acres. His style, best described as eclectic, was inspired partly by his world travels with the U.S. Navy and partly by the desert terrain.

On dirt rd, 0.5 mi NW of Andrade, 7 mi SW of Winterhaven

NO. 944 🔔

SITE OF FORT ROMUALDO PACHECO

In 1774, Spain opened an overland route from Sonora to California but it was closed by Yuma Indians in 1781. In 1822, Mexico attempted to reopen this route. Lt. Romualdo Pacheco and soldiers built an adobe fort at this site in 1825-26, the only Mexican fort in Alta California. On April 26, 1826, Kumeyaay Indians attacked the fort, killing three soldiers and wounding three others. Pacheco abandoned the fort, removing soldiers to San Diego.

W bank of New River, S of Worthington Rd, 6-1/2 mi due W of City of Imperial

NO. 985 🔔

DESERT TRAINING CENTER, CALIFORNIA-ARIZONA MANEUVER AREA (ESTABLISHED BY MAJOR GENERAL GEORGE S. PATTON, JR.) – CAMP PILOT KNOB

Camp Pilot Knob was a unit of the Desert Training Center, established by General George S. Patton, Jr., to prepare American troops for battle during World War II. It was the largest military training ground ever to exist. At the peak of activity here at Pilot Knob, June–December, 1943, the 85th Infantry Division, and the 36th and 44th Reconnaissance Squadrons of the 11th (Mechanized) Cavalry trained here for roles in the liberation of Europe, 1944-45.

On Sidewinder Rd, 200 yards N of I-8, Town of Felicity

NO. 1008 🔔

YUHA WELL

Known as Santa Rosa de Las Lajas (Flat Rocks), this site was used on March 8, 1774 by the Anza Exploring Expedition, opening the land route from Sonora, Mexico, to Alta California. On December 11 to 15, 1775, the three divisions of Anza's colonizing expedition used this first good watering spot beyond the Colorado River on the way from Sonora to San Francisco.

Eastbound Sunbeam Roadside Rest Area, between Drew and Forrester Rds (P.M. R31.3), on I-8 near Seeley

Landmark No. 939

Landmark No. 806

Landmark No. 845

Inyo-Mono Counties

Alpine County

[395]

● **BRIDGEPORT**

Tuolumne County

Mono County

MONO LAKE

MAMMOTH LAKES

[6]

Madera County

○

_S I E R R A_

Fresno County

NEVADA

_I N Y O   N A T ' L   F O R E S T_

○ **BISHOP**

_O W E N S_

[395]

● **INDEPENDENCE**

_V A L L E Y_

MT. WHITNEY

Inyo County

_N E V A D A_

D E A T H

V A L L E Y

N A T I O N A L

NAVAL WEAPONS CENTER

M O N U M E N T

Tulare County

Kern County

San Bernardino County

Inyo
Est. 1866

I nyo means "dwelling place of a great spirit" in Paiute Indian language. Inyo County has many "greats." Mount Whitney, the highest peak in the continental United States and Death Valley, the lowest spot in the Western Hemisphere are both within Inyo's boundaries. Great earthquakes have left their mark in recent history, changing the course of the Owens River and exposing ancient sedimentary rock.

NO. 208 ☐
SAN FRANCIS RANCH
In 1861, Samuel A. Bishop, his wife, and party left Fort Tejón for the Owens Valley driving 650 head of stock. On August 22, Bishop reached a creek later named for him and southwest of this spot. San Francis Ranch was established there. At the site a peace treaty was signed by the settlers and the chiefs of the Paiute Indians.

3 mi SW of Bishop at intersection of Red Hill Rd and State Hwy 168

NO. 209
SITE OF BEND CITY
Bend City, a population center in the middle 1860s, was designated as the seat of Coso County, but the county was never formed. It was here that the first county bridge across Owens River was constructed. The 1872 earthquake changed the course of Owens River, so the site of Bend City was near an empty ravine instead of on a river bank.

On Mazourka Canyon Rd, 4.6 mi W of Independence

NO. 211
MAYFIELD CANYON BATTLEGROUND
On April 8, 1862, a body of troopers and settlers entered Mayfield Canyon (named for one of the settlers) to fight the Indians supposed to be there. However, the Indians had evacuated the canyon so the group made camp at its mouth. The next day they went up the canyon again, but this time they were forced to retreat to Owens Valley.

Mayfield Canyon, 0.2 mi N of Farmer Wells Meadow Ranger Station, 1.5 mi NW from intersection of Pine Creek Rd and North Round Valley Rd, then 1.5 mi N on Ranger Station Rd to site, 15 mi NW of Bishop

NO. 223 🔔
SITE OF PUTNAM'S CABIN
In August 1861, Charles Putnam built the first cabin for permanent habitation in what is now Inyo County. The building, located 130 feet west of this site, served as a home, trading post, hospital, and "fort" for early settlers, as well as a survival point for travelers. It became the center of the settlement of "Putnam's" which five years later took the name "Independence."

139 Edwards St (Hwy 395), Independence

NO. 229 🔔
MARY AUSTIN'S HOME

Mary Austin, author of *The Land of Little Rain* and other volumes that picture the beauty of Owens Valley, lived in Independence. "But if ever you come beyond the borders as far as the town that lies in a hill dimple at the foot of Kearsarge, never leave it until you have knocked at the door of the brown house under the willow-tree at the end of the village street, and there you shall have such news of the land, of its trails and what is astir in them, as one lover of it can give to another . . ." excerpt from *The Land of Little Rain.*

253 Market St, Independence

NO. 230 ☐
FIRST PERMANENT WHITE HABITATION IN OWENS VALLEY

In August of 1861, A. Van Fleet and three other men drove their cattle into Owens Valley and prepared to stay. A cabin of sod and stone was built at the big bend of the Owens River at the northern end of the valley.

At intersection of State Hwy 6 (P.M. 3.9) and Silver Canyon Rd, 4 mi NE of Bishop

NO. 349 ☐
CAMP INDEPENDENCE (FORT)

At the request of settlers, Colonel George Evans led a military expedition to this site on July 4, 1862. Hence its name "Independence." Indian hostilities ceased and the camp closed. War again broke out in 1865 and the camp was reoccupied as Fort Independence until its abandonment in 1877. This fort made possible the early settlements in the Owens Valley.

500 ft W of intersection of Miller Ln and Salvabell Ln, 3 mi NE of Independence

NO. 441 🔔
BURNED WAGONS POINT

Near this monument, the Jayhawker group of Death Valley '49ers, gold seekers from the Middle West who entered Death Valley in 1849 seeking a short route to the mines of central California, burned their wagons, dried the meat of some oxen and, with surviving animals, struggled westward on foot.

Death Valley National Monument, 100 ft S of State Hwy 190 (P.M. 85.9), Stovepipe Wells

NO. 442 🔔
DEATH VALLEY GATEWAY

Through this natural gateway the Death Valley '49ers, more than 100 emigrants from the Middle West seeking a shortcut to gold fields of central California, entered Death Valley in December 1849. All suffered from thirst and starvation. Seeking an escape from the region, two contingents went southwest from here, while the others proceeded northwest.

Death Valley National Monument, on State Hwy 190 (P.M. 111.8), 1.3 mi SE of Furnace Creek

NO. 443 🔔
VALLEY WELLS

In this area, several groups of midwestern emigrants who had escaped from hazards and privations in Death Valley in 1849 sought to secure water from Searles Lake. They turned northward and westward in despair when they discovered its salty nature, and with great difficulty crossed the Argus and other mountains to reach settlements of Central and Southern California.

Trona Wildrose Rd at Valley Wells Rd, 5.5 mi NE of Trona

NO. 444 🔺
BENNETT-ARCANE LONG CAMP

Near this spot the Bennett-Arcane contingent of the Death Valley '49ers, emigrants from the Middle West seeking a shortcut to California gold fields, were stranded for a month and almost perished from starvation. William Lewis Manley and John Rogers, young members of the party, made a heroic journey on foot to San Fernando and, returning with supplies, led the party to the safety of San Francisquito Rancho near Newhall.

Death Valley National Monument from State Hwy 190 (P.M. 111.8), go approx 16 mi S of intersection of Badwater Rd and Westside Rd, on Westside Rd

NO. 507 ☐
GRAVE OF 1872 EARTHQUAKE VICTIMS

On March 26, 1872, a major earthquake shook Owens Valley, nearly destroying the town of Lone Pine. About fourteen of its victims (the exact number is not known) were interred in a common grave, enclosed by this fence.

200 ft W of State Hwy 395 (P.M. 58. 7), 0.9 mi N of Lone Pine

NO. 537 Ⓜ
COTTONWOOD CHARCOAL KILNS

In June 1873, on Cottonwood Creek directly west of this spot, Colonel Sherman Stevens built a sawmill and a flume that connected with the Los Angeles bullion road. The lumber was used for timbering in the mine and for buildings; the wood turned into charcoal in the kilns was hauled to Steven's Wharf on Owens Lake, where it was put on the steamer *The Bessie Brady*, and hauled across the lake. From there wagons took it up to Cerro Gordo Mine. Since all the wood available around the Cerro Gordo had been burned, this charcoal was necessary to continue production.

1.0 mi E of State Hwy 395 (P.M. 44.5), 70 mi N of Cartago

NO. 752 🔺
FURNACE OF THE OWENS LAKE SILVER-LEAD COMPANY

The Owens Lake Silver-Lead furnace and mill were built here by Colonel Sherman Stevens in 1869 and used until March 1874. James Brady assumed their operation in 1870 for the Silver-Lead Company and built the town of Swansea. During the next few years the output of this furnace and one at Cerro Gordo was around 150 bars of silver, each weighing 83 pounds, every 24 hours.

300 ft W of State Hwy 136 (P.M. 9.5), 3.1 mi NW of Keeler

NO. 773 🔔

OLD HARMONY BORAX WORKS

In 1881 Aaron Winters discovered borax on the marsh near this point. He later sold his holdings to W. T. Coleman of San Francisco, who built the Harmony Borax Works in 1882 and commissioned his superintendent, J. W. S. Perry, to design wagons and locate a suitable route to Mojave. The work of gathering the ore (called "cottonball") was done by Chinese workmen. From this point, 20-mule teams transported the processed borax 165 miles to the railroad until 1889.

Death Valley National Monument, on State Hwy 190 (P.M. 109.1), 1.4 mi N of Furnace Creek

NO. 796 🔔

FARLEY'S OLANCHA MILL SITE

In 1860, while working for the Silver Mountain Mining Company in the Coso Mountains, M. H. Farley conceived the idea of building a processing mill on a creek that flowed into Owens Lake. He explored and named Olancha Pass that year, and by December of 1862 had completed the first mill and furnace in the Owens River Valley, on Olancha Creek about one mile west of this marker.

On State Hwy 395 (P.M. 34.1), at Fall Rd, 0.6 mi S of Olancha

NO. 811 🔔

BISHOP CREEK BATTLEGROUND

On April 6, 1862, a battle took place around this site between newly arrived citizens of the Owens River Valley and the original inhabitants of the land, the Paiute and Shoshone Indians. The reason for this battle is lost but brave men on both sides died here for a cause which they held inviolate.

SE corner of the intersection of State Hwy 168 (P.M. 13.0) and Bishop Creek Rd, 5.2 mi SW of Bishop

NO. 826 🔔

OLD STOVEPIPE WELLS

This waterhole, the only one in the sand dune area of Death Valley, was at the junction of the two Indian trails. During the bonanza days of Rhyolite and Skidoo, it was the only known water source on the cross-valley road. When sand obscured the spot, a length of stovepipe was inserted as a marker.

Death Valley National Monument, from State Hwy 190 (P.M. 92.1) go N 2.8 mi on (unpaved) Sand Dunes Access Rd, 6.1 mi E of Stovepipe Wells

NO. 848 🔔

EICHBAUM TOLL ROAD

In 1926, H. W. Eichbaum obtained a franchise for a toll road from Darwin Falls to Stovepipe Wells, the first maintained road into Death Valley from the west. It changed the area's economic base from mining to tourism and brought about the creation of Death Valley National Monument seven years later.

Death Valley National Monument, 100 ft S of State Hwy 190 (P.M. 85.83), Stovepipe Wells

NO. 850 🔔

MANZANAR RELOCATION CENTER

In the early part of World War II, 110,000 persons of Japanese ancestry were interned in relocation centers by Executive Order No. 9066 issued February 19, 1942. Manzanar, the first of ten such concentration camps, was bounded by barbed wire and guard towers. It confined ten thousand persons, the majority of them American citizens. May the injustices and humiliation suffered here as a result of hysteria, racism, and economic exploitation never emerge again.

200 ft W of State Hwy 395 (P.M. 673), 9.6 mi N of Lone Pine

NO. 934

TEMPORARY DETENTION CAMPS FOR JAPANESE AMERICANS— MANZANAR ASSEMBLY CENTER

The temporary detention camps (also known as "assembly centers") represent the first phase of the mass incarceration of 97,785 Californians of Japanese ancestry during World War II. Pursuant to Executive Order 9066 signed by President Franklin D. Roosevelt on February 19, 1942, thirteen makeshift detention facilities were constructed at various California racetracks, fairgrounds, and labor camps. These facilities were intended to confine Japanese Americans until more permanent concentration camps, such as those at Manzanar and Tule Lake in California, could be built in isolated areas of the country. Beginning on March 30, 1942, all native-born Americans and long-time legal residents of Japanese ancestry living in California were ordered to surrender themselves for detention.

Manzanar

NO. 953 ♠

LAWS NARROW GAUGE RAILROAD STATION AND YARD

In 1883, the Carson & Colorado Railroad was built between Mound House (near Carson City, Nevada) through Laws to Keeler, California, a distance of 300 miles. Laws Station was named in honor of Mr. R. J. Laws, Assistant Superintendent of the railroad. Between 1883 and about 1915, this railroad provided the only dependable means of transportation in and out of Owens Valley. Train service was stopped on April 30, 1960.

On Silver Canyon Rd (Inyo County Rd), on old town of Laws, 4 mi NE of Bishop

Kern County

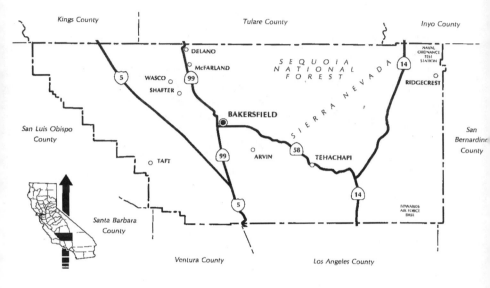

Fort Tejon State Historic Park - Military post to protect Indians. Located 38 miles S of Bakersfield on I-5.

Kern
Est. 1866

Edward M. Kern, a topographer who crossed Walker's Pass, is the namesake of the Kern River and Kern County. This region is known for its important travel routes: the Grapevine, the Butterfield Overland Route, Joseph Walker's route of 1843, Tehachapi, and more.

NO. 97 ☐
OAK CREEK PASS

In 1776, Father Francisco Garcés used the Oak Creek Pass to return to the Mojave after exploring the San Joaquin Valley, as did Frémont in 1844-1845. Until the railroad was built through the Tehachapi Pass in 1876, Oak Creek Pass was the only route used through the Tehachapi Mountains.

On Willow Pass Rd, 4.6 mi S of Tehachapi Blvd, 74 mi SE of Tehachapi

NO. 98 ☐ 🪧
KEYSVILLE

From 1853 until 1870, Keysville was a center of both placer and quartz gold mining. On the knoll just below the townsite may still be seen the outlines of an earthworks fort, built to meet a possible Indian attack in 1863.

On Black Gulch Rd, 2.0 mi S of State Hwy 155 (P.M. 70.0), 3.3 mi W of Lake Isabella

NO. 99 ☐
WALKER'S PASS

Discovered by Joseph R. Walker, American trailblazer, who left the San Joaquin Valley through this pass in 1834. This area was traversed by topographer Edward M. Kern, after whom the Kern River was named, while accompanying the Frémont expedition of 1845. After 1860 it became a mining freight route to Owens Valley.

At summit on State Hwy 178 (P.M. 79.8), 8.4 mi NW of Freeman Jct (State Hwy 14)

NO. 100 ☐ 🪧
HAVILAH

Gold deposits at Havilah were discovered in 1864. Havilah was the county seat between 1866, when Kern County was organized, and 1872, when the government was moved to Bakersfield. Havilah was an active mining center for more than 20 years, and there are still some operating mines in this vicinity.

State plaque in front of Bodfish post office, NE corner of Miller St and Kern River Canyon Rd, Bodfish; private plaque S side of 1866 county courthouse, Caliente-Bodfish Rd (P.M. 279), Havilah

NO. 129 🔔
FORT TEJÓN

This military post was established by the United States Army on June 24, 1854, to suppress stock rustling and protect the Indians in the San Joaquin Valley. Camels for transportation were introduced here in 1858. As regimental headquarters of the First Dragoons, Fort Tejón was an important military, social, and political center; it was abandoned September 11, 1864.

Fort Tejón State Historic Park, on Lebec Rd, 2.8 mi N of Lebec

NO. 130 ☐
WILLOW SPRINGS

Willow Springs was visited by Padre Garcés in 1776 while following the old Horse Thief Trail (later known as Joe Walker Trail); Frémont stopped here in 1844, and the famished Jayhawk Party of 1850 found water here while struggling from Death Valley to Los Angeles. Still later, Willow Springs was a stage station of the Los Angeles-Havilah and Inyo Stage Lines.

From State Hwy 14, go 6.8 mi W on Rosamond Blvd, then N 0.7 mi on Tehachapi Willow Springs Rd, then 0.6 mi NW on Truman-Manly Rd, Rosamond

NO. 132 ☐ 🚫⛏
KERNVILLE

Called Whiskey Flat until 1864, Kernville was founded in 1860 when whiskey dealer Adam Hamilton moved shop here from more temperate Quartzburg, founded earlier that year. Both camps resulted from a discovery by "Lovely" Rogers, who found the Big Blue Ledge while tracking a stray mule from the earlier camp of Keysville.

Old Kernville Cemetery, Wofford Rd, 2.7 mi SE of Kernville

NO. 133 ☐
SEBASTIAN INDIAN RESERVATION

The Sebastian or Tejón Indian Reservation (headquarters ten miles east of here) was established in 1853 by General Edward Fitzgerald Beale as one of several California reservations. The number of Indians quartered here varied from 500 to 2,000. General Beale acquired title to this area under Mexican land grant of 1843. In 1864 the U.S. government transferred the Indians to other reservations.

Grapevine, NE corner of Grapevine Rd and "D" St, 70 mi S of Mettler

NO. 137 ☐
GORDON'S FERRY ON THE KERN RIVER

Gordon's Ferry was an overhead cable-type of ferry operated during the 1850s by Major Gordon. An adobe station house was located on the south bank of the Kern River, just a few yards to the west of this marker, which also served as a station on the Butterfield Overland Mail Route from 1856 to 1860.

SE side of Kern River bridge, on China Loop, 1,000 ft S of Round Mountain Rd, Bakersfield

NO. 277 ☐
GARCÉS CIRCLE

This is the approximate site of the Indian rancheria visited by Franciscan friar Padre Francisco Garcés on May 7, 1776. Padre Garcés named this spot San Miguel de los Noches por el Santa Príncipe.

Center intersection of Chester Ave and 30th St, Bakersfield

NO. 278 ☐

PLACE WHERE FRANCISCO GARCÉS CROSSED THE KERN RIVER

On May 1, 1776, Franciscan friar Francisco Garcés crossed the Kern River one mile north of here. Searching for a shorter route from Sonora, Mexico to Monterey, California, he was the first known explorer to describe this river, which he named Río de San Felipe.

State Hwy 178 (P.M. 10.9) at Rancheria Rd, 11.0 mi E of Bakersfield

NO. 283 ☐

TOP OF GRAPEVINE PASS, WHERE DON PEDRO FAGES PASSED IN 1772

In 1772, Don Pedro Fages passed this site, traveling from San Diego to San Luis Obispo via Cajón Pass, Mojave Desert, Hughes Lake, Antelope Valley, Tejón Pass, Cañada de los Uvas (Grapevine Canyon), and Buena Vista Lake. He left the first written record of exploration in the south San Joaquin Valley.

On Lebec Rd, 0.6 mi N of Lebec

NO. 290 ☐

DISCOVERY WELL OF KERN RIVER OILFIELD

Oil was discovered at 70 feet in 1899, when Tom Means persuaded Roe Elwood and Frank Wiseman, aided by Jonathan, Bert, Jed, and Ken Elwood, George

Wiseman, and John Marlowe, to dig here for oil. On June 1, 1899, 400 feet to the north, Horace and Milton McWhorter drilled this region's first commercial well.

On Round Mountain Rd, 0.7 mi E of China Grade Loop, 7 mi NE of Bakersfield

NO. 291 ☐

FAGES-ZALVIDEA CROSSING

In 1772, Don Pedro Fages, first recorded non-Indian to visit the southern San Joaquin Valley, crossed this spot on his way from San Diego to San Luis Obispo. Near this point crossed Father José María de Zalvidea in 1806, while accompanying the Ruiz expedition in search of mission sites.

On State Hwy 166 (P.M. 19.0), 5.5 mi W of Mettler

NO. 300 ☐

ROSE STATION

From 1853 to 1875 this site, originally a vaquero camp of the Sebastian Indian Reservation, was known as Rancho Canoa (trough). In 1875, Wm. B. Rose built an adobe stage station on the site of the Overland Mail way station established 1858. Rose Station was a stockmen's headquarters, post office, and polling place.

NE corner of Grapevine Rd and "D" St, 70 mi S of Mettler

NO. 371 ☐

OUTERMOST POINT IN THE SOUTH SAN JOAQUIN VALLEY (VISITED BY PADRE GARCÉS IN 1776)

Padre Garcés, first recorded non-Indian to visit this locality, came in April of 1776, seeking a new route from Mexico to California. His epic journey covered more than two thousand miles of uncharted wilderness, opening trails that later became highways and railroads.

Courtyard of Saint Thomas the Apostle Church, 350 E Bear Mountain Blvd, Arvin

NO. 374 ☐

TULAMNIU INDIAN SITE

The old Yokuts village of Tulamniu was named Buena Vista by Spanish Commander Fages in 1772. Fr. Zalvidea again recorded the site in 1806. This village was occupied for several centuries, and in 1933-34 its site was excavated by the Smithsonian Institution.

300 ft SE of Block House #BV4, 1.1 mi N of Buena Vista pumping station, 8 mi E of Taft

NO. 376

CALIFORNIA STANDARD OIL WELL NO. 1

This well was one of the early wells that in 1899 started a new oil field called the McKittrick Field. The well pumped about 150 barrels of oil per day for the first six months; its last production was in April 1929.

McKittrick Field, 400 ft N of Well #CS-54, 0.4 mi N of State Hwy 50 (P.M.. 15.1), 1 mi S of McKittrick

NO. 382 ☐

COLONEL THOMAS BAKER MEMORIAL

In 1863 Colonel Baker, friend to all travelers, came here to found "Bakers Field." His motto was, "Time will justify a man who means to do right." This civic center is his dream come true.

City Hall, SW corner of Truxtun and Chester Aves, Bakersfield

NO. 457 🔔

INDIAN WELLS

After five days' travel from the Argus Range, the Manly-Jayhawker parties of 1849 found their first water at this Indian waterhole on the Joseph R. Walker Trail of 1843. During the 1860s, this was the site of a stage and freight station for traffic between Los Angeles and the Coso and Cerro Gordo Mines.

Indian Wells Lodge, 4.9 mi N of Freeman Jct (Hwys 14 and 178) on Hwy 14 (P.M. 62.6)

NO. 476 🔔

DESERT SPRING

This spring was on an old Indian horse thief trail and later (1834) Joe Walker Trail. The famished Manly-Jayhawk Death Valley parties (1849-50) were revived here after coming from Indian Wells through Last Chance Canyon. This was also a station on the Nadeau Borax Freight Road.

SE corner Pappas Ranch, on Pappas Rd, then walk 1/4 mi W toward trees, 0.5 mi S of Valley Rd, 3.7 mi E of Cantil post office

NO. 485 ☐

LAKEVIEW GUSHER NO. 1

America's most spectacular gusher blew in here on March 14, 1910. Initially 18,000 barrels per day, the flow later reached an uncontrolled peak of 100,000 barrels per day, completely destroying the derrick. This Union Oil Company well produced nine million barrels of oil in 18 months.

Petroleum Club Rd (County Rd 277T, P.M. 1.1) between Kerto and Cadet Rds, 1.5 mi N of Maricopa via Hwy 33

NO. 492 ☐

BUTTONWILLOW TREE

This lone tree, which gave the town of Buttonwillow its name, served as a landmark on an old trans-valley trail. An ancient Yokuts Indian meeting place, it later became the site of settlers' stock rodeos. Miller and Lux established their headquarters and store here about 1885.

On Buttonwillow Dr, 0.5 mi N of State Hwy 58, Buttonwillow

NO. 495 ♠

GLENNVILLE ADOBE

This is Kern County's oldest residence, built before the Civil War by Thomas Fitzgerald as a trading post at the junction of two Indian trails. The present Greenhorn Road follows the east-west trail (later the McFarland Toll Road) to the Kern River mining districts. The town was named in 1857 after James Madison Glenn, an early settler.

Kern Co Fire Dept, Glennville Substation, on State Hwy 155 (P.M. 40.2), Glennville

NO. 498 ☐

McKITTRICK BREA PIT

Located one-eighth mile west of here is an ancient asphaltum seepage in which hundreds of Pleistocene Age (15,000-50,000 years ago) birds and animals were trapped. The site was first explored in 1928 by the University of California; excavation was completed in 1949 by the Los Angeles and Kern County museums.

SW corner of intersection of State Hwy 33 (P.M. 33.5) and State Hwy 58 (P.M. 15.4), 0.5 mi S of McKittrick

NO. 504 ☐

BUENA VISTA REFINERY

Eight miles due west of this marker stood one of California's first commercial oil refineries. Between August 1864 and April 1867, approximately 4,000 gallons of illuminating oil produced there was shipped to San Francisco by the Buena Vista Petroleum Company. Refining operations terminated due to excessive transportation rates.

NE corner State Hwy 22 (P.M. 41.1) and LoKern Rd, 10 mi N of McKittrick

NO. 508 ☐

TEHACHAPI LOOP

From this spot may be seen a portion of the world-renowned Loop completed in 1876 under the direction of William Hood, Southern Pacific railroad engineer. In gaining elevation around the central hill of the Loop, a 4,000-foot train will cross 77 feet above its rear cars in the tunnel below.

On Old State Hwy, 3.2 mi E of Keene exit, 6.5 mi W of Tehachapi

NO. 539 [M]

POSEY STATION OF BUTTERFIELD OVERLAND MAIL LINES

Two and one-half miles east of this point stood the Posey Station on the Butterfield Overland Stage route that ran from St. Louis, Missouri through present-day Kern County to San Francisco during 1858-61, until the outbreak of the Civil War.

NE corner of Bakersfield-Glennville Rd (Ca Rd 365AY, P.M. 8.3) and Round Mountain Rd, 11 mi NE of Bakersfield

NO. 540 🔔

SINKS OF THE TEJÓN, ALSO KNOWN AS ALAMO, STATION OF BUTTERFIELD OVERLAND MAIL LINES

Six miles east of this point was the site of the Butterfield Stage Line station Sinks of Tejón. Operating through present Kern County during 1858-61, this famous line ran from St. Louis, Missouri to San Francisco until the outbreak of the Civil War.

SW corner of intersection of David and Wheeler Ridge Rds, 6.0 mi NE of Mettler

NO. 581 ☐

WELL "2-6"

Near an area of small 40- and 50-barrel wells, it blew in over the derrick top November 27, 1909, with a production of 2,000 barrels a day and started one of the greatest oil booms California ever experienced. Well 2-6 was located as a wildcat, on June 1, 1909 by Fred C. Ripley.

100 ft W of Fellows Fire Station on Broadway, Fellows

NO. 588 [M]

KERN RIVER SLOUGH STATION

Just south of this point stood the Kern River Slough Station on the Butterfield Overland Stage route. Operating through present Kern County during 1858-1861, this famous line ran from St. Louis, Missouri to San Francisco until the outbreak of the Civil War.

On Panama Rd (Co Hwy 244, P.M. 9.0), 3.1 mi W of Lamont

NO. 589 🔔

MOUNTAIN HOUSE

One and one-half miles north of this point stood the Mountain House Station on the route of the Butterfield Stage. Operating through present Kern County during 1858-1861, this famous line ran from St. Louis, Missouri to San Francisco until the outbreak of the Civil War.

Dry Creek, on Bakersfield-Glennville Rds (Co Rd 363AZ, P.M. 19.1), 6.3 mi SW of Woody

NO. 631 ☐

GARCÉS BAPTISMAL SITE

Three miles north of this point was the site of the first recorded Christian baptism in the San Joaquin Valley. On May 23, 1776, Padre Francisco Garcés, earliest non-Indian in this area, baptized an Indian boy whom he called Muchachito at a Yokuts Rancheria in Grizzly Gulch.

On State Hwy 155 (P.M. 18.8), 77 mi W of Woody

NO. 643 🔔

OLD TOWN (TEHACHAPI)

The oldest settlement in Tehachapi Valley, known as "Old Town," was established here during the 1860s. Long an important station on the road between Southern California and the San Joaquin Valley, the community began to decline when residents gradually moved to nearby Greenwich, later renamed Tehachapi, after completion of the Southern Pacific Railroad in 1876.

NE corner of Old Town Rd and Woodford-Tehachapi Rd, 1.3 mi N of State Hwy 202, 2.5 mi W of Tehachapi

NO. 652 🔔

20-MULE-TEAM BORAX TERMINUS

Just west of this point was the Southern Pacific terminus for the 20-mule-team borax wagons that operated between Death Valley and Mojave from 1884 to 1889. The route ran from the Harmony Borax Mining Company works, later acquired by the Pacific Coast Borax Company, to the railroad loading dock in Mojave over 165 miles of mountain and desert trail. A round trip required 20 days. The ore wagons, which hauled a payload of 24 tons, were designed by J. W. S. Perry, Borax Company superintendent in Death Valley, and built in Mojave at a cost of $900 each. New borax discoveries near Barstow ended the Mojave shipments in 1889.

16246 Sierra Hwy (Hwy 14), Mojave

NO. 660 🔔

POINT ON THE JEDEDIAH SMITH TRAIL

About February 1, 1827, Jedediah Strong Smith, first American to reach Mexican California overland, passed near this spot with his party of fur trappers. From San Gabriel Mission, the group was en route north to a land reported teeming with "plenty of Beaver." Smith and his men were trailblazers whose exploits soon led to the American conquest of California.

SE corner of Old Bena and Tower Line Rds, 3.6 mi E of Edison

NO. 671 🔔

SITE OF THE TOWN OF GARLOCK

In 1896, Eugene Garlock constructed a stamp mill near this spot to crush gold ore from the Yellow Aster Mine on Rand Mountain. Known originally as Cow Wells by prospectors and freighters during the 1880s and early 1890s, the town of Garlock continued to thrive until 1898, when water was piped from here to Randsburg and the Kramer-Randsburg rail line was completed.

74 mi W of State Hwy 395 on Garlock Rd, 13.4 mi NE of Cantil post office

NO. 672 ☐

LAVERS CROSSING

In 1854, John C. Reid filed a squatter's claim on this spot; the same year Kern County's first school class was held here. In 1859, David Lavers, with his father and brother, John, built a hotel and stage barn on the old Bull Road. The crossing was the principal community in Linn's Valley until about 1870.

NE corner of White River and Jack Ranch Rds, 1.1 mi W of Glennville

NO. 690

SITE OF THE LAST HOME OF ALEXIS GODEY

Near this site stood the home of Alexis Godey, frontiersman and scout, who lived here from 1883 until his death on January 19, 1889. Born in St. Louis, Missouri in 1818, he acted as guide for John C. Frémont's expedition through the Kern area in 1843-44, and was honored for his services at the Battle of San Pasqual in 1846.

414-19th St W of Union Ave, Bakersfield

NO. 732

SITE OF THE HOME OF ELISHA STEVENS

Near this spot stood the last home of Elisha Stevens, noted American pathfinder and scout. Born in Georgia April 5, 1804, he learned blacksmithing during his youth; then, drifting west, he became a trapper on the upper Missouri for more than two decades. In 1844 he led the 50-member Murphy-Townsend wagon train safely from Council Bluffs, Iowa to Sutter's Fort. During the Mexican War he served as an ordnance mechanic under Commodore Stockton. For a time he lived in Santa Clara County, then settled here on a 38-acre tract, the first permanent settler in the Bakersfield district. He died September 9, 1887 and is buried in Union Cemetery.

NW corner of W Columbus and Isla Verde Sts, Bakersfield

NO. 741

BEALVILLE

Edward Fitzgerald Beale, serving under Commodore Stockton in 1846, established his home here on Rancho le Libre in 1855. He also engaged in mining and became Superintendent of Indian Affairs for California and Nevada, and Minister to Vienna.

On Bealville Rd, 0.9 mi N of State Hwy 58, 1.3 mi S of Caliente

NO. 742

CAMPSITE OF EDWARD M. KERN

Near this spot at the confluence of the north and south forks of the Kern River, the Theodore Talbot party of Captain John C. Frémont's third expedition to the West camped for several weeks during December 1845 and January 1846. Frémont named the river in honor of Edward M. Kern, topographer for the expedition; Kern County was established in 1866.

Entrance to Old Isabella Rd Recreation Area, on State Hwy 178, 2 mi N of the town of Lake Isabella

NO. 757

CALIENTE

Originally known as Allen's Camp after Gabriel Allen, who in the 1870s had a cabin and stock pasture near here, the settlement was named Caliente when railroad construction reached this point in April 1875. The town became a railroad terminal for about 16 months while a force of up to three thousand men, most of them Chinese, labored on the heavy railroad construction on the mountain.

2.3 mi N of Hwy 58 on Bealville Rd, Caliente

NO. 766

FREEMAN JUNCTION

Explorer Joseph R. Walker passed this junction of Indian trails in 1834 after discovering nearby Walker Pass. After their escape from Death Valley, '49er parties split here to go west and south to the California gold fields. Here the bandit Tiburcio Vásquez preyed on stages and freighters traveling between the Kern River mines and Los Angeles and the mines of Bodie and the Panamints.

On State Hwy 178 (P.M. 88.0), 0.2 mi W of junction with State Hwy 14

NO. 923

SITE OF THE FLIGHT OF THE GOSSAMER CONDOR

This plaque at Shafter Airport commemorates the world's first man-powered flight to complete the Kremer Circuit, August 23, 1977. The circuit, a figure eight around two pylons one-half mile apart, was completed in six minutes, twenty-two seconds. The plane was designed by Dr. Paul MacCready, Jr. and flown by Bryan Allen. A cash prize of 50,000 pounds was awarded by the Royal Aeronautical Society, London, England.

Entrance to Shafter Airport, Lerdo Hwy, 5 mi E of Shafter

NO. 938

RAND MINING DISTRICT

The Yellow Aster, or Rand, mine was discovered in April 1895 by Singleton, Burcham, and Mooers. The town of Randsburg quickly developed, followed by the supply town of Johannesburg in 1896. Both names were adopted from the profusion of minerals resembling those of the ranch mining district in South Africa. In 1907, Churchill discovered tungsten in Atolia, used in steel alloy during World War I. In June 1919, Williams and Nosser discovered the famous California Rand Silver Mine at Red Mountain.

Kern Co Desert Museum, Butte Ave, Randsburg

Landmark No. 652

Kings County

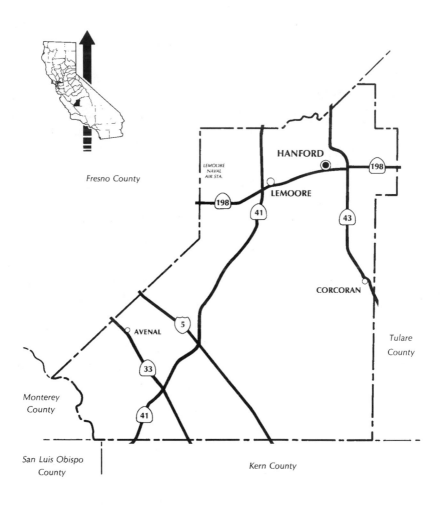

Fresno County

LEMOORE NAVAL AIR STA.

HANFORD

198

LEMOORE

198

41

43

CORCORAN

Tulare County

5

AVENAL

33

Monterey County

41

San Luis Obispo County

Kern County

Kings
Est. 1893

Kings County is named for the Kings river, which originates high in the Sierra, flows through the San Joaquin Valley and ends its natural drainage in Tulare Lake. In a "rain shadow" from the coast ranges to the West, Kings County today depends on a system of irrigation canals.

NO. 206 🔔
EL ADOBE DE LOS ROBLES RANCHO

This restored adobe, second oldest in San Joaquin Valley, was built by Daniel Rhoades, who came to California in 1846 by overland caravan. Rhoades and his brother, John, were among organizers of the first expedition that attempted to rescue the Donner party at Donner Lake. Built in 1856, the adobe has been continuously occupied since.

10036–19-1/2 Ave, SW corner State Hwy 41 and Lacy Blvd, 3 mi N of Lemoore

NO. 245 🔔
LOCATION OF THE FAMOUS MUSSEL SLOUGH TRAGEDY

Here on May 11, 1880, during a dispute over land titles between settlers and railroad, a fight broke out in which seven men–two deputy U.S. marshals and five ranchers lost their lives. The legal struggle over titles was finally settled by a compromise.

5833–14th Ave, between Everett and Elder Aves, 1.5 mi SE of Hardwick

NO. 270 🔔
KINGSTON

Founded in 1856 by L. A. Whitmore, who operated the first ferry to cross the Kings River, Kingston became stopping place for Butterfield stages after 1858. A toll bridge superseded the ferry in 1873. On December 26, 1873, Tiburcio Vásquez and his bandit gang made a bold raid, robbing the entire village.

Kingston Park, Douglas Ave, 4 mi W of 12-3/4 Ave, 1.1 mi SW of Laton

Lake County

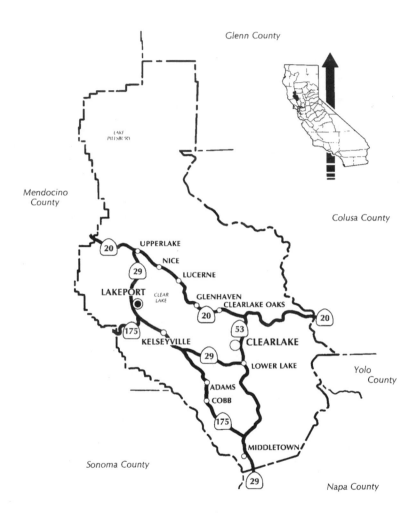

Anderson Marsh State Historic Park -
Native American and pioneer American
ranch site. Located on Highway 53 between
Lower Lake and Clear Lake.

Lake
Est. 1861

Native Americans thrived on the abundant resources of Clear Lake and the surrounding countryside. Conflict arose as settlers moved in to claim the land and its bounty. The Pomo Indian culture is still strong today and known for producing some of the finest basketry in the world.

NO. 426 🔔

SITE OF STONE AND KELSEY HOME

This home was built by Charles Stone and Andy Kelsey on land purchased from Salvador Vallejo. They forced Indians to do the construction work, causing much resentment. Finally, in the fall of 1849, the Indians killed both Stone and Kelsey; their remains are buried beneath this monument.

Intersection of Main St and Bell Hill Rd, Kelseyville

NO. 427 🔔

THE BATTLE OF BLOODY ISLAND

One-fourth mile west is Bloody Island, now a hill surrounded by reclaimed land, where, in 1850, U.S. soldiers nearly annihilated the Indian inhabitants for the murder of two white men. Doubt exists of these Indians' guilt. In 1851 a treaty was negotiated between whites and Indians.

Intersection of State Hwy 20 and Reclamation Rd, 1.7 mi SE of Upper Lake

NO. 428 🔔

SULPHUR BANK MINE

This sulphur mine also became one of the most noted quicksilver producers in world. First worked for sulphur in 1865, in four years it produced a total of 2,000,000 pounds; reopened and developed for quicksilver in 1873, it is credited with total output of 92,400 flasks, and was an important producer in World Wars I and II.

Intersection of State Hwy 20 (P.M. 29.5) and Sulphur Bank Rd, 1.5 mi S of Clearlake Oaks

NO. 429 🔔

LOWER LAKE STONE JAIL

This jail, claimed to be the smallest in the United States, was erected in 1876 of stone locally quarried and reinforced with iron. During the stirring days of the first quicksilver operations of the Sulphur Bank Mine, lasting from 1873 to 1883, obvious need for a jail led to its construction.

0.1 mi S of intersection of State Hwys 29 and 53, 16118 Main St, Lower Lake

NO. 450 🔔

STONE HOUSE

Oldest building in Lake County, the Stone House was erected of stone in 1853-54 by Robert Sterling, whose wife was first non-Indian woman in Coyote Valley. It was rebuilt in 1894 and served as headquarters of the Guenoc land grant and the first store in the valley.

NE corner Hwy 29 and Hidden Valley Rd, 5.3 mi N of Middletown

NO. 467 🔔

ST. HELENA TOLL ROAD AND BULL TRAIL

The old bull trail from Napa Valley to Middletown was built by volunteers in the 1850s. A number of its grades were 35 percent. An official road in 1861, it was abandoned in 1868. The St. Helena Toll Road, completed in 1868, ran between the same points with grades of 12 percent.

NW corner of State Hwy 29 (P.M. 5.5) and Hill Ave, Middletown

NO. 897 🔔

OLD LAKE COUNTY COURTHOUSE

This brick courthouse, constructed by A. P. Pettit in 1870-71, was one of the few buildings in the vicinity to survive the 1906 earthquake with only minor damage. It served Lake County as a seat of government from 1871 until 1968. Precedent-setting trials on water rights were held here, along with the "White Cap" murder trial in 1890.

255 N Main St, Lakeport

Landmark No. 428

Landmark No. 897

Lassen County

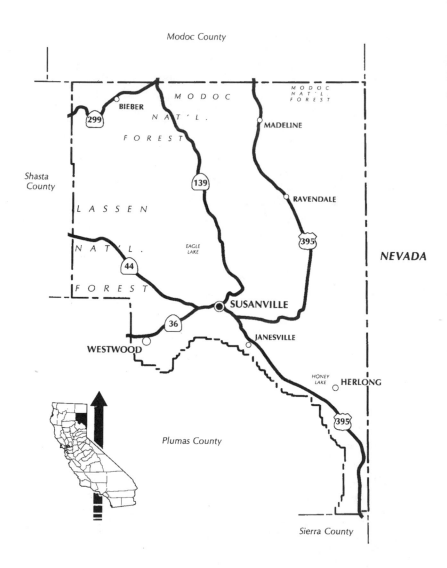

Lassen
Est. 1864

High in the northeastern Sierra is Lassen County, where volcanic activity has shaped the landscape. Peter Lassen, a Danish immigrant, came to Oregon in 1839 and later settled in the northern Sacramento Valley. He returned to Missouri and led a 12-wagon emigrant train along "Lassen Emigrant Trail" in 1848 into California.

NO. 76 ☐

ROOP'S FORT

Built in July 1854 by Isaac N. Roop, Roop House was a stopping place for emigrant trains. It was the locale of the "sagebrush war" fought in 1863 between the citizens of Plumas County and Lassen County.

Memorial Park, N Weatherlow at Nevada St, Susanville

NO. 565 ☐

PETER LASSEN GRAVE

In memory of Peter Lassen, the pioneer who was killed by the Indians April 27, 1859, at 66 years of age.

2550 Wingfield Rd via Richmond Rd, 5 mi SE of Susanville

NO. 675 🔔

NOBLE EMIGRANT TRAIL, SUSANVILLE

This meadow, now a city park, was a welcome stopping place on the Noble Emigrant Trail, pioneered by William H. Nobles in 1851 and first used in 1852.

Here, emigrants en route to the Northern California mines were able to rest, refresh their stock, and obtain needed provisions at Isaac Roop's establishment, from which grew the city of Susanville.

Lassen Memorial Park, S side of Adaline and North Sts, Susanville

NO. 677 🔔

NOBLE EMIGRANT TRAIL

This route was first used in 1852 by emigrants to Northern California seeking to avoid the hardships of the Lassen Trail. It crossed the desert from the Humboldt River in Nevada, passed this point, and proceeded over the mountains to the town of Shasta. Later, 1859-1861, it was known as the Fort Kearney, South Pass and Honey Lake Wagon Road. On October 4, 1850, while hunting for Gold Lake, Peter Lassen and J. G. Bruff saw Honey Lake from this point.

On State Hwy 395 (P.M. 80.5), 76 mi N of Litchfield

NO. 678

LASSEN EMIGRANT TRAIL

Through this draw passed many covered wagons and gold seekers en route to California over the Lassen Trail during 1848-1851. Approaching this location from the north, the trail passed what is now Bogard Ranger Station. Proceeding southward to Big Springs and Big Meadows (now Lake Almanor), it then turned westward to Deer Creek, which it followed generally to Vina in the Sacramento Valley.

Hwy 36 (P.M. 0.3), 2.5 mi W of Westwood

NO. 758 ☐

FORT JANESVILLE

Thoroughly terrified by "The Ormsby Massacre," the people of Honey Lake valley built themselves a stockade for protection from an Indian attack that never materialized.

0.1 mi N of Janesville Elementary School, Main St, Janesville

NO. 763

LASSEN EMIGRANT TRAIL, BIEBER

Peter Lassen opened the Lassen Emigrant Trail in 1848 when he led a 12-wagon emigrant train from Missouri to California. The route, which passed near this place, was extensively traveled during the years 1848-53 by emigrants seeking gold, adventure, and a new life in the west; but because of the hardships of the route and the hostility of the Indians, the trail was little used after 1853.

County of Lassen Library-Historical Museum, NE corner Veterans Ln and Bridge St, Bieber

Landmark No. 678

Landmark No. 76

Landmark No. 758

Los Angeles County

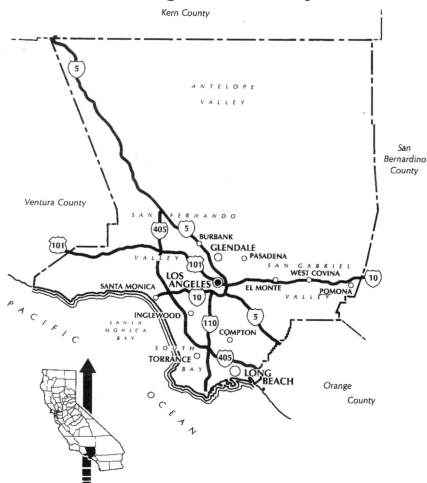

Kern County

ANTELOPE VALLEY

San Bernardino County

Ventura County

SAN FERNANDO VALLEY

405 5 BURBANK
101 GLENDALE
101 PASADENA
LOS ANGELES
SAN GABRIEL
WEST COVINA
10
SANTA MONICA
EL MONTE
POMONA
10 VALLEY
INGLEWOOD
110 5
SANTA MONICA BAY
COMPTON
SOUTH BAY
TORRANCE
405
LONG BEACH

PACIFIC

Orange County

OCEAN

Antelope Valley Indian Museum - Native American artifacts in folk art building. Located 15 miles W of Lancaster.

Los Encinos State Historic Park - Mexican adobe and early-American period buildings. Located at 16756 Moorpark Street, Encino.

Malibu Lagoon State Beach - Historic Adamson House. Located at 23200 Highway 1.

Pio Pico State Historic Park - Home of the last Mexican Governor of California. Located at 6003 Pioneer Blvd., Whittier.

Watts Towers of Simon Rodia State Historic Park - Folk art sculpture exhibit. Located at 1765 E. 107th Street in the Watts district of Los Angeles.

Will Rogers State Historic Park - Home of famed American humorist. Located at 14253 Sunset in Pacific Palisades.

Los Angeles
Est. 1850

S panish for "the angels," Los Angeles County's natural history reflects the dramatic events of the Ice Age in such famous landmarks as the Mojave Desert and the La Brea Tar Pits. Human events are recorded at sites of Spanish missions, Civil War and W.W. II military activity, and Hollywood filming.

NO. 127 ▲

CASA DE GOVERNOR PÍO PICO

Following the Mexican War, Pío Pico, last Mexican governor, acquired 9,000-acre Rancho Paso de Bartolo and built here an adobe home that was destroyed by the floods of 1883-1884. His second adobe casa, now known as Pío Pico Mansion, represents a compromise between Mexican and American cultures. While living here the ex-Governor was active in the development of American California.

Pio Pico State Historic Park, 6003 Pioneer Blvd, Whittier

NO. 144 ☐

NUESTRA SEÑORA LA REINA DE LOS ANGELES

La Iglesia de Nuestra Senora la Reina de Los Angeles–the Church of Our Lady the Queen of the Angels–was dedicated on December 8, 1822 during California's Mexican era. Originally known as La Iglesia de Nuestra Senora de Los Angeles, the church was the only Catholic church for the pueblo. Today it primarily serves the Hispanic population of Los Angeles.

535 N Main St near Macy St, Los Angeles

NO. 145 ☐

ÁVILA ADOBE

This adobe house was built ca. 1818 by Don Francisco Avila, alcalde (mayor) of Los Angeles in 1810. Used as Commodore Robert Stockton's headquarters in 1847, it was repaired by private subscription in 1929-30 when Olvera Street was opened as a Mexican marketplace. It is the oldest existing house in Los Angeles.

El Pueblo de Los Angeles Historic Monument, Olvera St, Los Angeles

NO. 147 ☐

BANNING PARK

General Phineas Banning, State Senator and pioneer in the development of transportation in Southern California, built this house in the 1850s, soon after founding the town of Wilmington. He and his family lived here until his death in 1885. In 1927 the property was deeded to the city.

401 East M St at Banning Place, Wilmington

NO. 150

BRAND PARK (MEMORY GARDEN)

Brand Park, also called Memory Garden, was given to the city for a park November 4, 1920. It is a part of the original land grant of Mission San Fernando de Rey de España, and the colorful and picturesque atmosphere of the early California missions is preserved in Memory Garden.

15174 San Fernando Mission Blvd, Los Angeles

NO. 151 ☐

CAMPO DE CAHUENGA

"Here was made the Treaty of Cahuenga by General Andrés Pico, commanding forces for Mexico, and Lieutenant-Colonel J. C. Frémont, U.S. Army, for the United States. By this treaty, agreed upon January 13th, 1847, the United States acquired California; finally secured to us by the treaty of Guadalupe Hidalgo, made February 2nd, 1848." This legend was written February 9, 1898 by Mrs. Jessie Benton Frémont.

3919 Lankershim Blvd, North Hollywood

NO. 152 🔔

DOMÍNGUEZ RANCHHOUSE

The central portion of the ranchhouse was built in 1826 by Manuel Domínguez. Rancho San Pedro, ten square leagues granted provisionally by Governor Fages to Juan José Domínguez in 1784, was regranted by Governor Solá to Cristobal Domínguez in 1822. In the battle of Domínguez Ranch, fought here October 8 and 9, 1846, Californians led by José Antonio Carrillo repelled United States forces under Captain William Mervine, U.S. Navy, in an attempt to recapture the Pueblo of Los Angeles.

18127 S Alameda, Compton

NO. 156 ☐

LOS ANGELES PLAZA

A part of the original pueblo lands of El Pueblo de la Reina de Los Angeles de Porciuncula founded in 1781 under the Spanish Laws of the Indies during the reign of King Carlos III, the plaza is located close to the site of the original plaza. It was the center of the settlement founded by Governor Felipe de Neve. When the Plaza Church was completed in 1822, this site was reserved as a public plaza. It was landscaped in 1871 and has served since that date as a public park.

El Pueblo de Los Angeles Historic Monument, 500 block of N Main St, Los Angeles

NO. 157 ☐

MISSION SAN FERNANDO REY DE ESPAÑA

Mission San Fernando Rey de España was founded by Father Lasuén in September 8, 1797. A house belonging to Francisco Reyes, on Encino Rancho, furnished temporary shelter for the missionary in charge. An adobe chapel, built and blessed in December 1806, was damaged by the destructive earthquake of 1812; a new church was completed in 1818.

15151 San Fernando Mission Blvd, Mission Hills

NO. 158 ☐

MISSION SAN GABRIEL ARCÁNGEL

The mission was founded September 8, 1771 by Padres Pedro Benito Cambon and Angel Fernández de la Somera. The present church building was begun during the latter part of the 18th century and completed in the year 1800.

537 W Mission Dr at Junipero St, San Gabriel

NO. 159 ☐

PICO HOUSE (HOTEL)

Pío Pico constructed the Pico House in 1869-70. The first three-story hotel built in Los Angeles, it had about eighty rooms, large windows, a small interior court, and a grand staircase.

El Pueblo de Los Angeles Historic Monument, 400 block of Main St, Los Angeles

NO. 160 ☐

PLUMMER PARK AND OLDEST HOUSE IN HOLLYWOOD

Known as the "Oldest House in Hollywood," this house was built in the 1870s by Eugene Raphael Plummer. Old location:

7377 Santa Monica Blvd, Hollywood (Los Angeles) New location: 23537 Calabasas Rd, Calabasas

NO. 161 ☐

SITE OF MISSION VIEJA

"Mission Vieja," Old Mission, was the name given to the first buildings erected, and later abandoned, by the fathers for Mission San Gabriel Arcángel. The permanent buildings for the mission were located about five miles distant.

SW corner N San Gabriel Blvd and N Lincoln Ave, Montebello

NO. 167 ☐

LA MESA BATTLEFIELD

La Mesa Battlefield served as a campsite for the California forces under General Castro in the summer of 1846, during the United States' occupation of California in the Mexican War. The battle of La Mesa, last military encounter of the war on the California front, was fought here January 9, 1847.

4490 Exchange Ave at Downey Rd, Vernon

NO. 168 🔔/🚫

OAK OF THE GOLDEN DREAM

Francisco López made California's first authenticated gold discovery on March 9, 1842. While gathering wild onions near an oak tree in Placerita Canyon he found gold particles clinging to the roots of the bulbs. The San Fernando placers and nearby San Feliciano Canyon were worked by Sonoran miners using panning, sluicing and dry washing methods. Lopez's find predated James Marshall strike at Sutter's Mill by six years.

Site: Placerita Canyon State and County Park, Placerita Canyon Rd, 4.6 mi NE of Newhall (Los Angeles) Plaque: SE corner I-5 and Lyons Ave, Newhall

NO. 169 🔔
DRUM BARRACKS

Established in 1862, Drum Barracks became the United States military headquarters for Southern California, Arizona, and New Mexico. It was a garrison and base for supplies, and a terminus for camel pack trains operated by the Army until 1863. Abandoned in 1866, the site remains a landmark of the Civil War in California.

1053 Cary St (corner Cary and Opp), Wilmington

NO. 170 ☐
HANCOCK PARK LA BREA

The bones of thousands of prehistoric animals that had been entrapped during the Ice Age in pools of tar that bubbled from beneath the ground were exhumed from this site. First historic reference to the pools, part of the 1840 Rancho La Brea land grant, was recorded by Gaspar de Portolá in 1769; first scientific excavations were made by the University of California in 1906. The site was presented to the County of Los Angeles in 1916 by Captain G. Allan Hancock to be developed as a scientific monument.

Hancock Park, 5801 Wilshire Blvd between Ogden and Curson Sts, Los Angeles

NO. 171
MERCED THEATRE

The Merced Theatre, erected in 1870 on North Main Street next to the Pico House, was the first building built expressly for theatrical purposes in Los Angeles, was built by William Abbot, a cabinetmaker, and named in honor of his wife Merced Garcia.

El Pueblo de Los Angeles Historic Monument, 420 Main St, Los Angeles

NO. 172 ☐
PIONEER OIL REFINERY

In 1875 the Star Oil Company, one of the predecessors of the Standard Oil Company of California, drilled its first Pico Canyon well, which yielded about one hundred barrels per day. The discovery resulted in the erection of the first commercial oil refinery in California the following year.

Site and private plaque at 238 Pine St, Newhall; state plaque at Lang Blvd exit of I-5

NO. 235 ☐
CASA ADOBE DE SAN RAFAEL

In October 1784, José María Verdugo petitioned Pedro Fages, Governor of Alta California, for a grant of land. This grant was the first and one of the largest made. When parts of Rancho San Rafael were sold, Tomás Sánchez, Sheriff of Los Angeles County, purchased a tract of 100 acres and in 1865 built this artistic adobe of the hacienda type, restored in 1932.

1330 Dorothy Dr, Glendale

NO. 289 ☐
FIRST HOME OF POMONA COLLEGE

Pomona College, incorporated October 14, 1887, held its first class in this small frame cottage on September 12, 1888. Those in attendance consisted of a mere handful of eager students, five faculty members, and the president, Professor Edwin C. Norton. Five months later, in January 1889, the college moved to an unfinished boom hotel on a plot of land in the town of Claremont.

SW corner Mission Blvd and S White St, Pomona

NO. 301 Ⓜ
LUGO ADOBE (SITE OF)

The Lugo Adobe, said to have been built in the 1840s by Don Vicente Lugo, was one of the very few two-story houses in the pueblo of Los Angeles. In 1867, Lugo donated this house on the Plaza to St. Vincent's School (forerunner of Loyola University). From the 1880s until it was razed in 1951, the building was occupied by the Chinese.

El Pueblo de Los Angeles Historic Monument, SE corner Los Angeles and Alameda Sts, Los Angeles

NO. 302
OLD MILL

The Old Mill, El Molino Viejo, was designed by Father José María Zalvidea and built of fired bricks and adobe about 1816 to serve Mission San Gabriel. Another grist mill was built in 1823 near the mission and the old mill was gradually abandoned; it passed from mission control in 1846. The property remained in private hands until 1903, when Henry E. Huntington bought the building and used it for a golf clubhouse. Later owners, Mr. and Mrs. James Brehm, had the mill restored in 1928 by Frederick Rupple.

1120 Old Mill Rd, San Marino

NO. 362 ☐
RÓMULO PICO ADOBE (RANCHITO RÓMULO)

The oldest portion of the adobe was built about 1834 by ex-mission Indians. It was enlarged by Eulogio de Celís in 1846, and an upper story added by Rómulo Pico in 1874. The house was restored by Mr. and Mrs. M. R. Harrington in 1930.

10940 N Sepulveda Blvd, Mission Hills

NO. 363 🔔
CENTINELA SPRINGS

Bubbling springs once flowed here from their source in a deep water basin that has existed continuously since the Pleistocene Era. Prehistoric animals, Indians, and early Inglewood settlers were attracted here by the pure artesian water. The springs and valley were named after sentinels guarding cattle in the area.

Centinela Park, 700 Warren Ln, Inglewood

NO. 367 🔔
E. J. BALDWIN'S QUEEN ANNE COTTAGE

Designed by A. A. Bennett for entertaining, the cottage was constructed by Elias Jackson ("Lucky") Baldwin in 1881. Since there was no kitchen, meals were served from the nearby adobe (built by Hugo Reid in 1839) where Baldwin actually lived. The building was restored and dedicated May 18, 1954 as part of Los Angeles State and County Arboretum.

Los Angeles State and County Arboretum, 301 N Baldwin, Arcadia

NO. 368 □

HUGO REID ADOBE

Hugo Reid, a Scotsman, petitioned the government of Mexico to grant him Rancho Santa Anita. His claim strengthened by his marriage to Victoria, a native Indian of the San Gabriel Mission, he received the grant on April 16, 1841. Immediately upon filing his petition, Reid took possession of the land, started to farm and plant vineyards, and built the first house–the Hugo Reid Adobe–in 1839. In 1875, E. J. Baldwin purchased the rancho and in 1879 added a wooden wing to the old adobe.

Los Angeles State and County Arboretum, 301 N Baldwin Ave, Arcadia

NO. 372 🔔

ADOBE DE PALOMARES

Completed about 1854 and restored in 1939, this was the family home of Don Ygnacio Palomares. Governor Juan B. Alvarado granted Rancho San Jose to Don Ygnacio and Don Ricardo Vejar in 1837.

491 E Arrow Hwy, Pomona

NO. 373 □

OLD SALT LAKE

The Indians of this area obtained salt from this lake. Sometime in the 1850s, Johnson and Allanson erected the necessary works to manufacture salt by artificial as well as solar evaporation. The salt yield for 1879 was 450 tons.

SE corner Harbor Dr and Yacht Club Way, Redondo Beach

NO. 380

SITE OF HOME OF DIEGO SEPÚLVEDA

This adobe home, built by Diego Sepúlveda in the 1850s, was the first two-story Monterey-type adobe built in Southern California.

700 block of Channel St, San Pedro

NO. 381

SITE OF OLD WHALING STATION

The whaling industry is said to have been started by Captain Clark in 1864. Captain Frank Anderson, a Portuguese, tried 2,166 barrels of whale oil at this station from 1874 to 1877. The station was abandoned because of a lack of fuel rather than vessels.

Portuguese Bend Club, Palos Verdes Dr. and Maritime Rd, Rancho Palos Verdes

NO. 383

SITE OF ADOBE HOME OF JOSÉ DOLORES SEPÚLVEDA

This adobe was built in 1818. Dolores had trouble getting his land title cleared, so he took a trip to Monterey to get the matter definitely settled and, on his return trip, he was shot with an arrow by a hostile Indian at Mission La Purísima Concepción.

Approx intersection of Madison St and Courtney Way, Torrance

NO. 384 🔔

TIMMS' POINT AND LANDING

In 1852 German immigrant Augustus W. Timms obtained Sepúlveda's Landing on the mudflats near here. He built a wharf, added a warehouse, corral and other facilities to service shipping and the running of stages to Los Angeles. Timms was a pioneer in the development of the harbor and for over fifty years this area was known as Timms Point.

Sampson Way at Southern Pacific Slip, San Pedro

NO. 385🔔
RÍO SAN GABRIEL BATTLEFIELD

Near this site on January 8, 1847, American forces commanded by Captain Robert F. Stockton, U.S. Navy, Commander in Chief, and Brigadier General Stephen W. Kearney, U.S. Army, fought Californians commanded by General José María Flores in the Battle of the Río San Gabriel.

NE corner of Washington Blvd and Bluff Rd, Montebello

NO. 386🔔
LA CASA DE CARRIÓN

This house, built in 1868 by Saturnino Carrión, was restored in 1951 by Paul E. Traweek.

919 Puddingstone Dr, La Verne

NO. 451🔔
THE ORTEGA-VIGARE ADOBE

Erected during mission days, 1792-1805, this is the second oldest adobe in this region. Originally "L"-shaped, it is now only half its original size. In 1859, the adobe became the property of Don Jean Vigare and in the early 1860s, as San Gabriel's first bakery, it was separated from the mission's lime orchard by a high cactus wall.

616 S Ramona St, San Gabriel

NO. 514🔔
POMONA WATER POWER PLANT

The first hydroelectric installation in California for long-distance transmission of alternating current at high voltage was built in 1892 on San Antonio Creek below this spot by the San Antonio Light and Power Company organized by Dr. Cyrus Grandison Baldwin, President of Pomona College. The first high-voltage transformers built by George Westinghouse for this installation provided for transmission of 10,000 volts from the plant to Pomona.

Camp Baldy Rd (P M. 2.0), San Antonio Canyon, 8.1 mi N of State Hwy 166, Claremont

NO. 516☐
WELL NO. "CSO" 4 (PICO NO. 4)

On this site stands CSO-4 (Pico No. 4), California's first commercially productive well. It was spudded in early 1876 under direction of Demetrious G. Scofield who later became the first president of Standard Oil Company of California, and was completed at a depth of 300 feet on September 26, 1876, for an initial flow of 30 barrels of oil a day. Later that year, after the well was deepened to 600 feet with what was perhaps the first steam rig employed in oil well drilling in California, it produced at a rate of 150 barrels a day; it is still producing after 77 years (1953). The success of this well prompted formation of the Pacific Coast Oil Company, a predecessor of Standard Oil Company of California, and led to the construction of the state's first refinery nearby. It was not only the discovery well of the Newhall Field, but was a powerful stimulus to the subsequent development of the California petroleum industry.

On W Pico Canyon Rd, 3.3 mi W of I-5, Newhall

NO. 516-2 🔔

MENTRYVILLE

Named after pioneer oil developer Charles Alexander Mentry, who in 1876 drilled the first successful oil well in California. His restored home and barn and Felton School remain here where the Star Oil Company, one of the predecessors of Standard Oil of California, was born.

27201 W Pico Canyon Rd, 2.8 mi W of I-5, Newhall

NO. 522 ☐

SERRA SPRINGS

The Portolá Expedition of 1769 encamped at this spring, and it is reported that in 1770 Father Serra said Mass here to the Indians of this area. This spring was also the former water supply of the town of Santa Monica. The site is now the campus of the University High School.

University High School Horticulture Area, 11800 Texas Ave, Los Angeles

NO. 531 ☐

LUMMIS HOME

This building was constructed by Charles F. Lummis (1859-1928), author, editor, poet, athlete, librarian, historian, archeologist, etc. He selected this site in 1895 chiefly because of a mammoth, ancient sycamore (El Alisal) which has since died and been replaced by four saplings.

200 E Ave 43 at Pasadena Freeway No. 11, Los Angeles

NO. 536 🔔

ORIGINAL BUILDING OF THE UNIVERSITY OF SOUTHERN CALIFORNIA

Dedicated on September 4, 1880, this original building of the University of Southern California has been continuously in use for educational purposes since October 6, 1880, when its doors were first opened to students by the university's first president, Marion McKinley Bovard. The building was constructed under the guiding hand of Judge Robert M. Widney, the university's leading founder, on land donated by Ozro W. Childs, John G. Downey, and Isaias W. Hellman.

Widney Hall Alumni House, University of Southern CA, Childs Way, between Hoover Blvd and University Ave, Los Angeles

NO. 554 🔔

CECIL B. DeMILLE STUDIO BARN

Cecil B. DeMille rented half of this structure, then used as a barn, as the studio in which was made the first feature-length motion picture in Hollywood–The Squaw Man–in 1913. Associated with Mr. DeMille in making The Squaw Man were Samuel Goldwyn and Jesse Lasky, Sr. Originally located at the corner of Selma and Vine Streets, in 1927 the barn was transferred to Paramount Studios.

2100 N Highland Ave, Hollywood

NO. 556 🔔

RANCHO SAN FRANCISCO

Approximately one-half mile south of the point was the adobe headquarters of Rancho San Francisco, originally built about 1804 as a granary of Mission San

Fernando. The rancho was granted to Antonio de Valle in 1839. Here, in January 1850, William Lewis Manly and John Rogers obtained supplies and animals to rescue their comrades in a California-bound gold-seeking emigrant party that was stranded and starving in Death Valley, some 250 miles to the northeast.

SW corner of "The Old Road" and Henry Mayo Drive, 0.2 mi S of I-5 and State Hwy 126 interchange, Valencia

NO. 567 🔔
ST. VINCENT'S PLACE
This was the site of Saint Vincent's College from 1868 to 1887. The college, now Loyola University, was founded by the Vincentian Fathers in 1865 and was the first institution of higher learning in Southern California.

St. Vincent Court, in alley between Broadway and Hill, and 6th and 7th Sts, Los Angeles

NO. 580 ☐
WELL "ALAMITOS 1"
One of the world's most famous wells. Started on March 23, 1921, it flowed 590 barrels of oil a day when it was completed June 25, 1921, at a depth of 3,114 feet. This discovery well led to the development of one of the most productive oil fields in the world and helped to establish California as a major oil producing state.

NE corner of Temple Ave and Hill St, Signal Hill

NO. 590 🔔
LANG
On September 5, 1876, Charles Crocker, President of the Southern Pacific Company, drove a gold spike here to complete his company's San Joaquin Valley line, the first rail connection of Los Angeles with San Francisco and transcontinental lines.

Soledad Canyon, Lang Station Rd, 0.4 mi S of State Hwy 14 (P.M. 35.6), Shadow Pines Blvd, 4.7 mi E of Canyon Country

NO. 632 🅜
"OLD SHORT CUT"
This is California's first ranger station, built in 1900 by Louie Newcomb and Phillip Begue, early Forest Service men. The cabin took its name from the "Short Cut Canyon Trail," as the cabin was one of the main stopping points on this trail.

Angeles National Forest, Chilao Visitor's Center, Angeles Crest Hwy (State Hwy 2), 27 mi E of La Canada

NO. 637 ☐
CATALINA ADOBE
San Rafael was granted to José María Verdugo on October 20, 1784. Don José died April 12, 1831, leaving his estate to his son Julio and his blind daughter Catalina. This adobe was built for Dona Catalina in the 1830s; she lived here until her death in 1861. Still in excellent condition, the Catalina, or Original Mud Block, Adobe is now in private ownership.

2211 Bonita Dr, Glendale

NO. 646
GRAVE OF GEORGE CARALAMBO, "GREEK GEORGE"

This is the grave of "Greek George," a camel driver from Asia Minor who came to the United States with the second load of camels purchased by the War Department as an experiment to open a wagon road to Fort Tejón from Fort Defiance, New Mexico. Because of the Civil War, the experiment was abandoned. "Greek George" became a naturalized citizen in 1867 under the name of George Allen. He built an adobe home on Santa Monica Boulevard.

Founders' Memorial Park, Broadway at Gregory Ave, Whittier (gravestone in storage, 1993)

NO. 653 🔔
THE CASCADES

This is the terminus of the Los Angeles-Owens River Aqueduct, which brings water 338 miles from the eastern slopes of the Sierra Nevada to the City of Los Angeles. Begun in 1905, the great aqueduct was completed November 5, 1913. The Mono Craters Tunnel project, completed in 1940, extended the system 27 miles to its present northernmost intake near Tioga Pass.

0.1 mi N of intersection of Foothill Blvd and Balboa Blvd, 4 mi NW of San Fernando

NO. 655 🔔
PORTOLÁ TRAIL CAMPSITE (NO. I)

Spanish colonization of California began in 1769 with the expedition of Don Gaspar de Portolá from Mexico. With Captain Don Fernando Rivera v Moncada, Lieutenant Don Pedro Fages, Sgt. José Francisco Ortega, and Fathers Juan Crespí and Francisco Gómez, he and his party camped near this spot on August 2, 1769, en route to Monterey.

Elysian Park entrance, NW corner of N Broadway and Elysian Park Dr, Los Angeles

NO. 656 🔔
BELLA UNION HOTEL SITE

Near this spot stood the Bella Union Hotel, long a social and political center. Here, on October 7, 1858, the first Butterfield Overland Mail stage from the east arrived 21 days after leaving St. Louis. Warren Hall was the driver, and Waterman Ormsby, a reporter, the only through passenger.

Fletcher Bowron Square, 300 block of N Main, between Temple and Aliso Sts, Los Angeles

NO. 658 🔔
WESTERN HOTEL

Erected by the Gilroy family in 1876, this building was purchased in 1902 by George T. Webber, who operated it as the Western Hotel. The Lancaster Chamber of Commerce was organized in its dining room. Between 1905 and 1913, construction crews of the Los Angeles-Owens River Aqueduct were housed here, and it became a center of commercial and social activity in the early life of the community.

557 W Lancaster Blvd, Lancaster

NO. 664 🔔
"HERITAGE HOUSE"

As originally built in 1869 by A. R. Loomis, the house had only two rooms, but other rooms were added by subsequent occupants. It was marked as the "Oldest House in Compton" in 1955; in 1957, it was purchased by the city and moved from 209 South Acacia Street to its present site. It has been restored, refurnished, and renamed by the citizens of Compton as a tribute to early settlers of the community.

NW corner of Willowbrook Ave and Myrrh St, Compton

NO. 665 🔔
PORTOLÁ TRAIL CAMPSITE, NO. 2

The expedition of Don Gaspar de Portolá from Mexico passed this way en route to Monterey to begin the Spanish colonization of California. With Captain Don Fernando Rivera y Moncada, Lieutenant Don Pedro Fages, Sergeant José Francisco Ortega, and Fathers Juan Crespí and Francisco Gómez, Portolá and his party camped near this spot on August 3, 1769.

300 S block of La Cienega Blvd between Olympic and Gregory, Beverly Hills

NO. 669 🔔
GOVERNOR STONEMAN ADOBE, "LOS ROBLES"

This was the site of "Los Robles," the 400-acre estate of Governor George Stoneman. President Rutherford B. Hayes was entertained here in 1880. The first schoolhouse in the San Gabriel Valley, California's first tennis club, and the first municipal Christmas tree of San Marino were located here.

1912 Montrobles Place, San Marino

NO. 681 🔔
PARADOX HYBRID WALNUT TREE

Planted in 1907 by George Weinshank and assistants under the direction of Professor Ralph Smith as part of an experimental planting for the University of California Experiment Station, this tree stands as a monument to the early cooperation of state educational system with local walnut industry.

12300 Whittier Blvd at Mar Vista, Whittier

NO. 688 🔔
LYONS STATION STAGECOACH STOP

This site was the location of a combination store, post office, telegraph office, tavern, and stage depot accommodating travelers during the Kern River gold rush in the early 1850s. A regular stop for Butterfield and other early California stage lines, it was purchased by Sanford and Cyrus Lyons in 1855, and by 1868 at least twenty families lived here. Eternal Valley Memorial Park has called their final resting place "The Garden of the Pioneers."

Eternal Valley Memorial Park, 23287 N Sierra Hwy, near State Hwy 14 and San Fernando Rd, Newhall

NO. 689 ☐
LOS ENCINOS STATE HISTORIC PARK

The Franciscan padres used Encino as their headquarters while exploring the valley before establishing Mission San Fernando in 1797. In 1849 Vincente de la Osa built an adobe with nine rooms. The next owner of El Encino Rancho was Eugene Garnier, who built the existing two-story limestone house in 1872. In December 1891 Domingo Amestoy acquired the property.

Los Encinos State Historic Park, 16756 Moorpark St, Encino

NO. 716 🔔

GRIFFITH RANCH

Originally part of the San Fernando Mission lands, this ranch was purchased by David Wark Griffith, revered pioneer of silent motion pictures, in 1912. It provided the locale for many western thrillers, including *Custer's Last Stand*, and was the inspiration for the immortal production, *Birth of a Nation*. In 1948 it was acquired by Fritz B. Burns, who has perpetuated the Griffith name in memory of the great film pioneer.

12685 Foothill Blvd at Vaughn St, San Fernando

NO. 717 🔔

THE ANGELES NATIONAL FOREST

The first national forest in the State of California and second in the United States, Angeles National Forest was created by proclamation of President Benjamin Harrison on December 20, 1892. The first name given to the forest, "San Gabriel Timberland Reserve," was changed to "San Gabriel National Forest" March 4, 1907 and then to "Angeles National Forest" on July 1, 1908.

San Gabriel Mtns, Clear Creek Vista Point, State Hwy 2 (P.M. 32.8), 8.3 mi N of I-210, La Canada

NO. 718 🔔

SITE OF THE INITIAL UNITED STATES AIR MEET

About a half mile southeast of this spot, on Dominquez Hill in historic Rancho San Pedro, the first air meet in the United States was held during January 10-20, 1910. This area has evolved into one of the world's leading aviation-industrial centers.

18501 S Wilmington Ave, Carson

NO. 730 🔔

OLD PLAZA FIREHOUSE

Dedicated to the firemen of the Los Angeles Fire Department–past, present, and future–who, by their courage and faithful devotion to duty, have protected the lives and property of the citizens of Los Angeles from the ravages of fire since 1871. This was the first building constructed as a fire station in Los Angeles. Built in 1884, it served as a firehouse until 1897. After this it was used for various purposes until restored in 1960 and opened as a museum of fire-fighting equipment of the late 19th century.

El Pueblo de Los Angeles Historic Monument, 501 N Los Angeles St

NO. 744 ☐

THE MIRROR BUILDING (SITE OF BUTTERFIELD STAGE STATION)

The Butterfield Overland Mail Company took an option on this piece of property in August 1858 and acquired it on December 7, 1859. A large brick building containing offices and living quarters, with shops and stables in the rear, was completed in 1860. With the exception of the station at El Paso, Texas, this was the largest and best equipped station on the entire route.

145 S Spring St, Los Angeles

NO. 753

SAN FERNANDO CEMETERY

Earlier known as Morningside Cemetery, this is the oldest nonsectarian cemetery in San Fernando Valley. It was used from the early 1800s until 1939; it was legally abandoned in 1959, when Mrs. Nellis S. Noble donated the site in memory of the pioneers of San Fernando.

SW corner of Bledsoe and Foothill, Sylmar

NO. 789

SITE OF THE LOS ANGELES STAR

Southern California's first newspaper, The Los Angeles Star, was founded in this block on May 17, 1851 and for many years exerted a major influence upon this part of the state. Suspended temporarily from 1864 to 1868, it continued later as an effective voice of the people until its final termination date in 1879.

Fletcher Bowron Square, 300 block of N Main, between Temple and Aliso Sts, Los Angeles

NO. 822

FIRST JEWISH SITE IN LOS ANGELES

The Hebrew Benevolent Society of Los Angeles (1854), first charitable organization in the city, acquired this site from the city council by deed of April 9, 1855. This purchase of a sacred burial ground represented the first organized community effort by the pioneer Jewish settlers.

Chavez Ravine, behind US Naval and Marine Corps Reserve Center, 800 W Lilac Terrace near Lookout Dr, Los Angeles

NO. 840

OLD SANTA MONICA FORESTRY STATION

In 1887, the State Board of Forestry established the nation's first experimental forestry station. Located in Rustic Canyon, the station tested exotic trees for planting in California, established plantations for management studies, and produced planting stock for scientific and conservation purposes. The station was operated by the Board of Forestry until 1893 and by the University of California until 1923.

Rustic Canyon Recreation Center, NW corner of Latimer and Hilltree Rds, Los Angeles

NO. 871

THE GAMBLE HOUSE

Built in 1908, the David B. Gamble House is a tribute to the genius of architects Charles Sumner Greene and Henry Mather Greene. Its design represents a unique California lifestyle and is a masterpiece of American craftsmanship. In 1966 it was made a gift by the Gamble family to the City of Pasadena in a joint agreement with the University of Southern California.

4 Westmoreland Place, Pasadena

NO. 874 🔔
WORKMAN HOME AND FAMILY CEMETERY

William Workman and John Rowland organized the first wagon train of permanent eastern settlers, which arrived in Southern California on November 5, 1841. Together they owned and developed the 48,790-acre La Puente Rancho. Workman began this adobe home in 1842 and remodeled it in 1872 to resemble a manor house in his native England. He also established "El Campo Santo," this region's earliest known private family cemetery, in 1850; the miniature Classic Grecian mausoleum was built in 1919 by grandson Walter P. Temple.

15415 E Don Julian Rd, City of Industry

NO. 881 🔔
SITE OF "PORT LOS ANGELES" LONG WHARF

In 1893 the Southern Pacific Railroad Company completed its 4,720-foot wharf, which served as a deep water port for the Los Angeles area. But after San Pedro became Los Angeles's official harbor in 1897, shipping activity at Port Los Angeles declined and the wharf was finally dismantled. Today, no trace remains of what was once the longest wooden pier in the world.

Will Rogers State Beach lifeguard hdqtrs, 15100 W Pacific Coast Hwy 1 (P.M. 375), Pacific Palisades

NO. 887 🔔
PASADENA PLAYHOUSE

Founded in 1917 by Gilmor Brown, the Pasadena Playhouse was designed by architect Elmer Grey and the cornerstone laid May 31, 1924. In 1928 the College of Theatre Arts was incorporated with the Pasadena Playhouse Association as a non-profit institution. In 1937, the Playhouse received the honorary title "State Theatre of California" from the California Legislature.

39 El Molino Ave, Pasadena

NO. 894
S.S. CATALINA

Commonly referred to as the Great White Steamer, the ship was specially built by William Wrigley to serve his Catalina Island as a passenger ferry. She was christened on May 23, 1924. During World War II, she was requisitioned for use as a troop carrier, but in 1946 she resumed her voyages to Avalon.

Original location: Port of Los Angeles, Catalina Terminal, Berth 96. New location: Ensenada Harbor Ensenada, Mexico

NO. 911
CHATSWORTH CALERA SITE

The Chatsworth Calera is one of the few surviving representative structures of the early 19th century lime industry. This kiln marked the introduction to California of the European industrial process for vitrifying limestone building blocks which were used in the construction of the missions.

From State Hwy 27 and Plummer, go W 2.7 mi to the intersection of Woolsey Canyon Rd and Valley Circle Blvd, site is 500 feet NE of intersection, Chatsworth

NO. 912 🔔

GLENDORA BOUGAINVILLEA

Planted in 1901 by the R. H. Hamlins, early citrus growers, the Glendora bougainvillea is the largest growth of this exotic plant in the United States. The parent stock was brought to California by a whaling ship about 1870. The vines are one of the best remaining illustrations of the image of California as a paradise that was spread by early 20th-century promoters.

400 block of E Bennet Ave at Minnesota Ave, Glendora

NO. 919 🔔

ST. FRANCIS DAM DISASTER SITE

The 185-foot concrete St. Francis Dam, part of the Los Angeles aqueduct system, stood a mile and a half north of this spot. On March 12, 1928, just before midnight, it collapsed and sent over twelve billion gallons of water roaring down the valley of the Santa Clara River. Over 450 lives were lost in this, one of California's greatest disasters.

San Francisquito Power Plant No. 2, 32300 N San Francisquito Canyon Rd, 9.2 mi N of Saugus

NO. 920 🔔

CASA DE SAN PEDRO

The first known commercial structure on the shore of San Pedro Bay was built here in 1823 by the trading firm of McCulloch and Hartnell to store cattle hides from the San Gabriel and San Fernando missions. Richard Henry Dana described this adobe hide house in *Two Years Before the Mast*. Thus began the development of the Port of Los Angeles.

Middle Reservation, Fort MacArthur, 2400 block of Pacific Ave, E side of parade field, 300 feet S of intersection of Meyler and Quartermaster Rds, San Pedro

NO. 933 🔔M

SITE OF LLANO DEL RIO COOPERATIVE COLONY

This was the site of the most important non-religious Utopian experiment in western American history. Its founder, Job Harriman, was Eugene Debs' running mate in the presidential election of 1900. In subsequent years, Harriman became an influential socialist leader and in 1911 was almost elected mayor of Los Angeles. At its height in 1916, the colony contained a thousand members and was a flourishing communitarian experiment dedicated to the principal of cooperation rather than competition.

On State Hwy 138 (P.M. 64.1), Llano

NO. 934

TEMPORARY DETENTION CAMPS FOR JAPANESE AMERICANS– SANTA ANITA ASSEMBLY CENTER AND POMONA ASSEMBLY CENTER

The temporary detention camps (also known as "assembly centers") represent the first phase of the mass incarceration of 97,785 Californians of Japanese ancestry during World War II. Pursuant to Executive Order 9066 signed by President Franklin D. Roosevelt on February 19, 1942, thirteen makeshift detention facilities were constructed at various California racetracks, fairgrounds, and labor camps. These facilities were intended to confine Japanese Americans until more permanent concentration camps, such as those at Manzanar and Tule Lake in California, could be built in isolated areas of the country. Beginning on March 30, 1942, all native-born Americans and long-time legal residents of Japanese ancestry living in California were ordered to surrender themselves for detention.

Arcadia and Pomona

NO. 939 🔔

Twentieth Century Folk Art Environments (Thematic)–OLD TRAPPER'S LODGE

Old Trapper's Lodge is one of California's remarkable Twentieth Century Folk Art Environments. It represents the life work of John Ehn (1897-1981), a self-taught artist who wished to pass on a sense of the Old West, derived from personal experiences, myths, and tall tales. From 1951 to 1981, using his family as models, and incorporating memorabilia, the "Old Trapper" followed his dreams and visions to create the Lodge and its "Boot Hill."

Original location: 10340 Keswick Ave at San Fernando Rd, Sun Valley. New location: Los Angeles Pierce College, Cleveland Park, 6201 Winnelka Ave, Woodland Hills

NO. 947 🔔

"REFORM SCHOOL FOR JUVENILE OFFENDERS" (FRED C. NELLES SCHOOL)

The March 11, 1889 Act of the California Legislature authorized the establishment of a school for juvenile offenders. Dedication and laying of cornerstone was done by Governor R. W. Waterman on February 12, 1890. Officially opened as "Whittier State School" for boys and girls on July 1, 1891. Girls were transferred in 1916 and only boys have been in residence since that time. Renamed "Fred C. Nelles School for Boys" in 1941 ("For Boys" was dropped around 1970). This school has been in continuous operation serving the needs of juvenile offenders since 1891.

Department of the Youth Authority entrance, 11850 E Whittier Blvd, Whittier

NO. 960 🔔

LOS ANGELES MEMORIAL COLISEUM

This stadium was originally completed in 1923. It was partially redesigned and enlarged for the 1932 Olympic Games. Both designs were by architects John and Donald B. Parkinson. The coliseum has witnessed many important sports, political, and historical events. When the games of the XXIIIrd Olympiad began here on July 28, 1984, the coliseum became the first stadium in the world to host the Olympic Games twice.

South end of University of Southern California, 3911 S Figueroa, Los Angeles

NO. 961 🔔

HAROLD LLOYD ESTATE ("GREENACRES")

Greenacres, one of the greatest estates of Hollywood's Golden Era, was built in 1929 for the internationally known silent screen comedian, Harold Lloyd. With its formal gardens, it is one of the finest Mediterranean/Italian Renaissance style residential complexes remaining in the state. The 44-room house was designed by Sumner Spaulding and the gardens planned by A. E. Hansen. The estate is patterned after the Villa Gamberaia near Florence, Italy.

1740 Green Acres Place, Beverly Hills

NO. 963

THE MOJAVE ROAD

Long ago, Mohave Indians used a network of pathways to cross the Mojave Desert. In 1826, American trapper Jedediah Smith used their paths and became the first non-Indian to reach the California coast overland from mid-America. The paths were worked into a military wagon road in 1859. This "Mojave Road" remained a major link between Los Angeles and points east until a railway crossed the desert in 1885.

Site of road runs from Drum Barracks in Wilmington to where State Route 66 crosses Los Angeles County line into San Bernardino County

NO. 965 🔔
POINT DUME

On November 24, 1793, English explorer George Vancouver, commander of an expedition to determine the extent of settlement of the northwest coast of America, named this rocky promontory, Point Dume, after his Franciscan friend, Father Francisco Dumetz, at Mission San Buenaventura. Point Dume is the western terminus of Santa Monica Bay and has been an important landmark for navigators since Vancouver's voyage in 1793.

Point Dume State Beach, corner of Cliffside Dr and Birdview Ave, Malibu

NO. 966 🔔
ADAMSON HOUSE AT MALIBU LAGOON STATE BEACH

Designed by Stiles O. Clements in 1929, this Spanish Colonial Revival home contains the best surviving examples of decorative ceramic tile produced by Malibu Potteries. During its short existence from 1926 to 1932, Malibu Potteries made an outstanding contribution to ceramic art in California through its development and production of a wide range of artistic and colorful decorative tile. The home was built for Merritt Huntley Adamson and Rhoda Rindge Adamson, daughter of

Frederick Hastings Rindge and May Knight Rindge, last owners of the Rancho Malibu Spanish grant.

23200 Pacific Coast Hwy, Malibu

NO. 972 🔔
NAVY AND MARINE CORPS RESERVE CENTER

Designed as the largest enclosed structure without walls in the world by noted California architects Robert Clements and Associates, this Art Deco building, constructed between 1938 and 1941 by the WPA, is the largest and second-oldest Navy Reserve Center in the United Stages. It has served as the induction, separation, and training center for more than 100,000 sailors since World War II well as the filming site for countless motion pictures and television shows.

1700 Stadium Way, Los Angeles

NO. 975 🔔
EL MONTE–FIRST SOUTHERN CALIFORNIA SETTLEMENT BY IMMIGRANTS FROM UNITED STATES

El Monte, on the bank of the San Gabriel River, played a significant part in California's early pioneer history. It was first an encampment on the Old Spanish Trail, an extension of the trail from Missouri to Santa Fe. By the 1850s, some began to call El Monte the "End of the Santa Fe Trail." Early in that decade a permanent settlement was established by immigrants from Texas, the first settlement in Southern California founded by citizens of the United States.

Santa Fe Trail Historical Park, Valley Blvd and Santa Anita Ave, El Monte

NO. 978 🔔

RANCHO LOS CERRITOS HISTORIC SITE

The 27,000-acre Rancho was once part of an 18th-century Spanish land grant to soldier Manuel Nieto. The Monterey-style adobe was constructed in 1844 and served the Temple and Bixby families as headquarters for large-scale cattle and sheep ranching operations in the 19th century. In the 1880s, the land was subdivided for farming and city development.

4600 Virginia Rd, Long Beach

NO. 984 🔔

CASA DE RANCHO SAN ANTONIO (HENRY GAGE MANSION)

Contained within this building are the remaining portions of an adobe house built by Francisco Salvador Lugo and his son Antonio María Lugo. Francisco Lugo was a prominent early landholder and Antonio served as the Alcalde of Los Angeles. They completed the building by 1810. Henry Tifft Gage acquired the property in 1880 and lived here from 1883 until 1924. Gage served as the Governor of California from 1899 to 1903.

7000 E Gage, Bell Gardens

NO. 988

PACIFIC ASIA MUSEUM (GRACE NICHOLSON'S TREASURE HOUSE OF ORIENTAL AND WESTERN ART)

Grace Nicholson, a noted collector and authority on American Indian and Asian Art and artifacts, supervised the design of her combination gallery and museum which was completed in 1929. It has been called an outstanding example of 1920s revival architecture and is unique for its use of Chinese ornamentation.

46 North Los Robles Ave, Pasadena

NO. 990 🔔

CHRISTMAS TREE LANE

The 135 Deodar Cedar trees were planted in 1885 by the Woodbury Family, the founders of Altadena. First organized by F.C. Nash in 1920, the "Mile of Christmas Trees" has been strung with 10,000 lights each holiday season through the efforts of volunteers and the Christmas Tree Lane Association. It is the oldest large-scale Christmas lighting spectacle in Southern California.

Santa Rosa Ave, both sides of street from Woodbuty Ave to Altadena Dr, Altadena

NO. 993

WATTS TOWERS OF SIMON RODIA

The Watts Towers are perhaps the nation's best known work of folk art sculpture. Using simple hand tools, cast off materials (glass, shell, pottery pieces and broken tile) Italian immigrant Simon Rodia spent 30 years building a tribute to his adopted country and a monument to the spirit of individuals who make their dreams tangible. Rodia's Towers inspired many to rally and preserve his work and protect it for the future.

1765 East 107th St, Los Angeles

NO. 997 🔔

TUNA CLUB OF AVALON

The Tuna Club of Avalon marks the birthplace of modern big game sportfishing in 1898. Led by Dr. Charles Frederick Holder, the club's founding members adopted the rules of conduct stressing conservationist ethics and sporting behavior. Today, their work remains the basis for the sport's internationally accepted principles.

100 St. Catherine Way, Avalon

NO. 1006

BEALE'S CUT STAGECOACH PASS

Beale's Cut is the only physical and cultural feature of its kind in the entire Los Angeles Basin. At the time of its construction in 1862, the actual creation and maintenance of the Cut was considered a significant technological and physical feat consisting of breaching the former impassable geographic barrier of the San Gabriel and Santa Susana Mountain ranges. General Edward F. Beale is attributed with the construction of a toll road across the mountains. Beale's Cut was also used as a favorite film-making location by pioneer film maker, David Wark Griffith, and others.

Intersection of Sierra Hwy and Clampitt Rd, Santa Clarita

NO. 1011

FRANK LLOYD WRIGHT TEXTILE BLOCK HOUSE (THEMATIC), FREEMAN HOUSE

The Samuel and Harriet Freeman House, designed by Frank Lloyd Wright and built in 1924, is one of four residences that were designed to be affordable and modular constructed using the cheap building material of concrete. These houses were constructed from a textile block system of handmade concrete tiles held in a matrix of steel bars, anchored and protected by a concrete mixture, and stacked without grout.

1962 Glencoe Way, Los Angeles

NO. 1011

FRANK LLOYD WRIGHT TEXTILE BLOCK HOUSES (THEMATIC), ENNIS HOUSE

This house was designed by Frank Lloyd Wright and built in 1924 for Charles and Mabel Ennis. It is one of four textile block houses registered as Landmark No. 1011.

2655 Glendower Ave, Los Angeles

NO. 1014 🔔

LONG BEACH MARINE STADIUM

Created in 1932 for the rowing events of the Xth Olympiad, the Stadium was the first manmade rowing course in the United States. Its width allowed four teams to race abreast, eliminating additional heats and allowing oarsmen to enter the finals at the peak of their form. Later it served as the venue for the 1968 and 1976 United States men's Olympic rowing trials and the 1984 United States women's Olympic rowing trials. The site remains an important training and competitive center for rowers, including our National and Olympic teams.

Appian Way and Nietro, Long Beach

NO. 1018 🔔

MANHATTAN BEACH STATE PIER

Designed by City Engineer A.L. Harris, this pier was constructed by the City of Manhattan Beach during the years 1917-1920. The roundhouse building was added a year later. Harris' innovative design featured a rounded end to the pier, which helped it withstand the pounding of the Pacific. Although the roundhouse was reconstructed in 1989, the pier itself survives as Southern California's oldest remaining example of early reinforced concrete pier construction.

West of Manhattan Beach Blvd, Manhattan Beach

Madera County

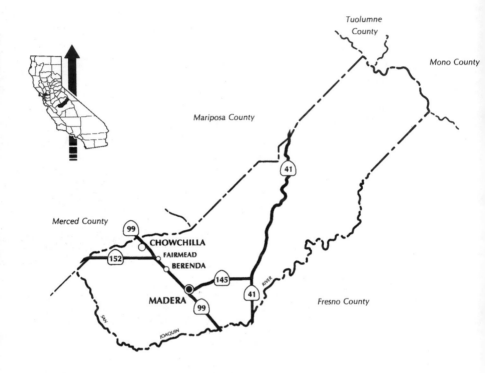

Millerton Lake State Recreation Area - Reconstructed courthouse originally built in 1867. Located 20 miles NE of Fresno.

Wassama Round House State Historic Park - Native American village and archeological site. Located on Highway 49 in Ahwahnee.

Madera
Est. 1893

Natural sloughs and mud flats made the going tough, but Jedediah Smith, Kit Carson, and John C. Frémont, in different expeditions, all passed through Madera's borders in the San Joaquin Valley. Madera County is also the site of the Fresno Indian Reservation, which was established during the 1850s when the Gold Rush provoked resistance from numerous local tribes.

NO. 1001🔔

CALIFORNIA NATIVE AMERICAN CEREMONIAL ROUNDHOUSES (THEMATIC), WASSAMA ROUNDHOUSE

Dating prior to the 1860s, the Wassama Roundhouse was reconstructed in 1985 on the location of the previous four houses. In 1903, the third roundhouse was built using portions of the center pole from the two earlier houses. The roundhouse served as the focal point of spiritual and ceremonial life for many Native Californians. The Wassama Roundhouse continues to serve this purpose.

Wassama Roundhouse State Historic Park, 5.5 mi N of Oakhurst on Hwy 49 to Ahwahnee, then E .4 mi on Round House Rd

Landmark No. 1001

Marin County

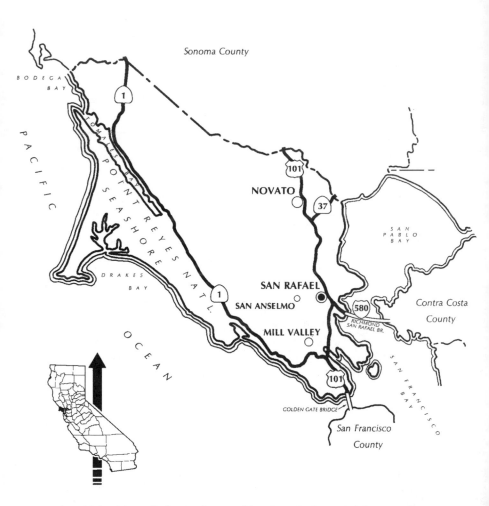

Angel Island State Park - Anchorage of first Spanish ship in San Francisco Bay.

Samuel P. Taylor State Park - Site of first paper mill on the Pacific Coast. Located 15 miles W of San Rafael.

China Camp State Park - Chinese fishing village. Located 2.5 miles E of Highway 101 on San Pedro Road.

Olompali State Historic Park - 1850s adobe preserved amid Victorian structures and gardens. Located 2.5 miles N of Novato on Highway 101.

Marin
Est. 1850

The land to the north of San Francisco Bay, and the bay's largest island – Angel Island – make up Marin County. Rich in the history of early Chinese and Japanese immigration and settlement, the county also reflects early Native American, Spanish, and Mexican cultures.

NO. 207

FIRST SAWMILL IN MARIN COUNTY

This mill was erected by John Reed about 1833-34 on Rancho Corte Madera del Presidio– "the wood cutting place for the Presidio"–present-day Mill Valley. Reed built the first house in Sausalito and the first ferryboat to ply San Francisco Bay.

Old Mill Park, Throckmorton and Cascade Dr, Mill Valley; plaque located at NW corner of Blithedale Ave and Tower Dr

NO. 210

OLDEST HOUSE NORTH OF SAN FRANCISCO BAY

This house was built in 1776 by the father of Camillo Ynitia or Unitia, the last chief of the Olompali Indians. The Indians were taught to make adobe bricks by Lieutenant Bodega and his party while they were surveying and charting the harbor of San Francisco Bay. The old adobe house is inside the house now on the site. (Burned in 1976.)

Olompali State Historic Park, 8901 Redwood Hwy, State Hwy 101 (P.M. 24.8), 3.5 mi N of Novato

NO. 220

MISSION SAN RAFAEL ARCÁNGEL

The San Rafael Arcángel Mission, 20th in the chain of the 21 California missions, was established in 1817 by the Franciscan Order. After the "decree of secularization" in 1834, the buildings gradually fell into ruin. The mission was reconstructed on the original site in 1949.

5th Ave and A St, San Rafael; plaque is at NE corner Merrydale and Southbound 101, San Pedro Rd offramp

NO. 221

SITE OF THE LIGHTER WHARF AT BOLINAS

This wharf was built in the early 1850s to load lumber on lighters to be floated out to the deeper water near the channel, where it was transferred to seagoing vessels for shipment to San Francisco.

At N end of Bolinas Lagoon at jct of State Hwy 1 (P.M. 170) and Olema-Bolinas Rd, 2 mi N of Bolinas

NO. 222

LIME KILNS

Tradition is that the lime kilns were built by Russian stonemasons and worked by Indians during the Russian occupation of Sonoma County, which began in the spring of 1812. The Russians probably used the lime to whitewash their windmills, farm buildings, granaries, storehouses, and cattle yards; to tan hides; and to manufacture brick and tile.

300 ft W of State Hwy 1 (P.M. 22.1), 4.2 mi S of Olema

NO. 529 🔔

ANGEL ISLAND

In 1775, the packet San Carlos, first known Spanish ship to enter San Francisco Bay, anchored in this cove. While here, the commander, Lieut. Juan Manual de Ayala, directed the first survey of the bay. This island, which Ayala named *Isla de los Angeles*, has been a Mexican rancho, a U.S. military post, a bay defense site, and a quarantine and immigration station.

Hospital Cove, Angel Island State Park

NO. 552 🔔

PIONEER PAPER MILL

The first paper mill on the Pacific Coast was built here in November 1856 by Samuel Penfield Taylor. Using water power and later steam, it was replaced in 1884 by a larger steam-powered mill nearby. This mill, closed by the depression of 1893, was destroyed by fire in 1915.

1.3 mi inside Samuel P. Taylor State Park, 18 mi W of Hwy 101 off Sir Francis Drake Blvd, County Hwy A104 (P.M. 171), Lagunitas

NO. 630 🔔

ST. VINCENT'S SCHOOL FOR BOYS

In 1853, Timothy Murphy, Irish-born pioneer of Marin County, gave 317 acres of land to Archbishop Alemany for educational purposes. Here the Sisters of Charity in 1855 founded a school that, as St. Vincent's School for Boys, has been maintained and enlarged by successive archbishops of San Francisco.

0.7 mi E of Hwy 101 on St. Vincent Dr, 4 mi N of San Rafael

NO. 679 🔔

HOME OF LORD CHARLES SNOWDEN FAIRFAX

The home of "Lord" Charles Snowden Fairfax, pioneer and political leader of the 1850s, who served California as an Assemblyman (1853), Speaker of Assembly (1854), and Clerk of the State Supreme Court (1856). A descendant of Scottish barons of the Cameron Fairfax family of Virginia, Fairfax was involved in the last of California's historic political duels as host to the principals and friend of the two antagonists.

Marin Town and Country Club, one block S of intersection of Pastori Ave and Belmont Ave, Fairfax

NO. 917 🔔

GREEN BRAE BRICK KILN

This brick kiln on the San Quentin Peninsula is the only surviving structure of the Remillard Brick Company, once the largest brick manufacturer on the Pacific Coast. During its 103 years of operation, its bricks were used to rebuild Ghirardelli Square, the Palace Hotel, and other San Francisco structures after the 1906 earthquake.

125 E Sir Francis Drake Blvd, Larkspur

NO. 922 🔔

OUTDOOR ART CLUB

The Outdoor Art Club was designed in 1904 by Bernard Maybeck, internationally known American architect. Particularly notable for its unusual roof truss system, the building exemplifies Maybeck's creative use of natural materials. The Club, founded in 1902 by 35 Mill Valley women, is dedicated to preserving the area's natural environment.

1 W Blithedale Ave at Throckmorton, Mill Valley

NO. 924 🔔

CHINA CAMP

One of the earliest, largest, and most productive Chinese fishing villages in California, China Camp was in operation by 1870. The Chinese immigrants and their descendants introduced the use of commercial netting to catch bay shrimp off Point San Pedro. The shrimp were then dried and exported to Chinese throughout the world. China Camp represents the last surviving Chinese shrimp fishing village in California.

At entrance to China Camp Village, China Camp State Park, on N San Pedro Rd, 5.3 mi SE of State Hwy 101, Santa Venetia

NO. 974

GOLDEN GATE BRIDGE

Construction of the bridge started in 1933. Engineer Joseph Strauss and architect Irving Morrow created an extraordinarily beautiful bridge in an extraordinarily beautiful setting. The designs for the Golden Gate Bridge showed the greatest attention to artistic detail, especially on the two streamlined moderne towers. The bridge's 4,200 feet of clear span (from tower to tower) was the longest in the world until 1959. On April 19, 1937, the bridge was completed and the official dedication took place on May 27.

Observation area, N end of bridge

NO. 999 🔔

MARIN COUNTY CIVIC CENTER

The Civic Center Complex was designed by Frank Lloyd Wright (1869-1959) near the end of his long career. The administration Building was completed in 1962 and the Hall of Justice in 1970. They are the only government buildings designed by the distinguished architect that were ever actually constructed. The project fully embodied Wright's ideal of organic architecture—a synthesis of buildings and landscape. In Wright's words, the structures were planned to "melt into the sunburnt hills."

Civic Center, San Rafael (plaque in storage, 3rd floor, County Counsel's Office)

Mariposa County

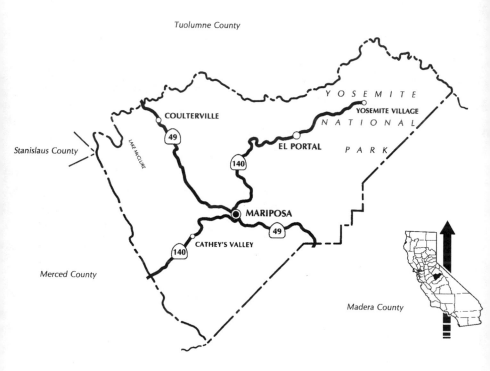

Mariposa
Est. 1850

The wonders of the Yosemite Valley's granite cliffs lie in eastern Mariposa County. The small settlements in the western foothills of the county sprang up during the Gold Rush. The people in these early mining towns made many decisions affecting statewide mining law.

NO. 323
MORMON BAR

Mormon Bar was first mined in 1849 by members of the Mormon Battalion. They, however, stayed only a short time and their places were taken at once by other miners. Later, thousands of Chinese worked the same ground over again.

On small auxiliary rd on right, 500 ft SE of intersection of State Hwy 49 (P.M. 16. 7) and Ben Hur Rd, 1.8 mi S of Mariposa

NO. 331
BEAR VALLEY

First called Johnsonville, Bear Valley had a population of 3,000, including Chinese, Cornish, and Mexicans. During 1850-60 when Col. John C. Frémont's Ride Tree and Josephine Mines were producing, Frémont's elegant hotel, Oso House, was built with lumber brought around the Horn. It no longer stands. After a fire in 1888, structures were rebuilt. Some still standing are Bon Ton Saloon, Trabucco Store, Odd Fellows Hall, school house and remains of jail.

On State Hwy 49 (P.M. 29.2), Bear Valley

NO. 332
COULTERVILLE

George W. Coulter started a tent store here in early 1850 to supply the hundreds of miners working the rich placers of Maxwell, Boneyard, and Black Creeks. He also built the first hotel; water for it was pumped from a well by two Newfoundland dogs. Originally called Banderita from the flag flying over Coulter's store, the settlement became Maxwell Creek when the post office was established in 1853, but the name was changed the following year to honor Coulter. The family of Francisco Bruschi, who erected the first permanent building here, provided the town's leading merchants for over eighty years. Despite their crude methods, and with only wood for fuel, the nearby quartz mines operated for years and produced millions of dollars worth of gold; Andrew Goss built the first stamp mill for crushing their ore.

County Park, NE corner of intersection of County Hwy J20 and State Hwy 132 (P.M. 44.8), Coulterville

NO. 333

HORNITOS

Hornitos, "little ovens," derived its name from the presence of many old Mexican stone graves or tombs built in the shape of little square bake ovens and set on top of the ground. The town seemed to have been settled by an undesirable element driven out of the adjoining town of Quartzburg, but as the placers at Quartzburg gave out, many of its other citizens came to Hornitos. It became the first and the only incorporated town in Mariposa County.

11 mi W of Bear Valley on County Road J16, Hornitos

NO. 518

AGUA FRIA

One-quarter mile north of Carson Creek, a tributary of Agua Fria Creek, was located the town of Agua Fria, in 1850-51 the first county seat of Mariposa County. One of the original 27 counties in California, Mariposa County comprised one-sixth of the state—all of what is now Merced, Madera, Fresno, Tulare, Kings, and Kern Counties—until 1852, while mining was the main industry of region. The town of Mariposa became the seat of government in 1852, and the courthouse there was completed in 1854.

4189 State Hwy 140 (P.M. 172), 3.2 mi W of Mariposa

NO. 527

SAVAGE TRADING POST

Here, in 1849, James D. Savage established a store built of logs. He engaged in trading and mining. In spring of 1850, fearing Indian depredations, he moved to Mariposa Creek; in December his store and others were pillaged and burned. A volunteer battalion was formed and Savage, elected mayor, went in pursuit of the tribe. Their secret hideout in Yosemite Valley was discovered and the war brought to a quick end. Major Savage was killed by a political opponent in August 1852.

On State Hwy 140 (P.M. 43.2), 8 mi W of El Portal

NO. 670

MARIPOSA COUNTY COURTHOUSE

This mortise-and-tenon Greek Revival courthouse, erected in 1854, is California's oldest court of law and has served continuously as the seat of county government since 1854. During the 19th century, landmark mining cases setting legal precedent were tried here, and much United States mining law is based on decisions emanating from this historic courthouse.

10th and Bullion Sts, Mariposa

NO. 790

YOSEMITE VALLEY

On June 30, 1864, in an act signed by President Abraham Lincoln, the United States granted the Yosemite Valley and the Mariposa Big Tree Grove to the State of California to "be held for public use, resort, and recreation . . . inalienable for all time." This, the first federal authorization to preserve scenic and scientific values for public benefit, was the basis for the later concept of state and national park systems. In 1906 the State of California returned the land, considered the first state park in the country, so that it could become part of Yosemite National Park.

Mounted on entrance wall of auditorium bldg, Visitor Center, Yosemite National Park

Landmark No. 790

Mendocino County

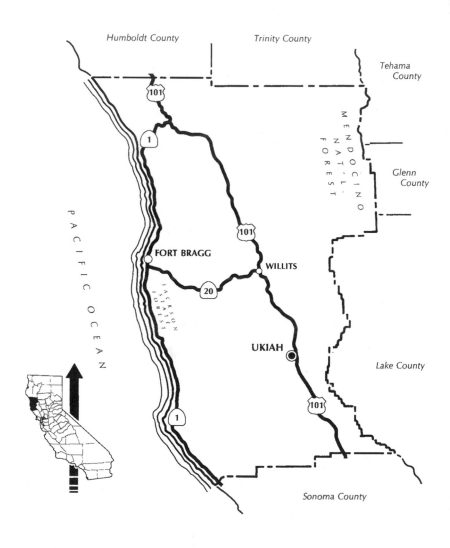

Humboldt County

Trinity County

Tehama County

Mendocino County

Glenn County

PACIFIC OCEAN

MENDOCINO NAT'L. FOREST

FORT BRAGG

WILLITS

JACKSON STATE FOREST

UKIAH

Lake County

Sonoma County

Mendocino
Est. 1850

With its dramatic scenery of rocky coastline, Mendocino County is made up of canyons cut by mountain streams flowing through stands of redwoods and other native trees. Abundant trees drew settlers and lumber companies to exploit the rich resources of the region. Today's attractions include peaceful seaside communities and a cool, humid climate.

NO. 549 🔔

SQUAW ROCK

This early landmark, also called Lover's Leap, is associated with the purported legend of a 19th-century Sanel Indian maiden, Sotuka. Her faithless lover, Chief Cachow, married another; all three were killed when Sotuka, holding a great stone, jumped from the precipice upon the sleeping pair below.

Approx 6 mi S of Hopland on Hwy 101 (P.M. 5.1)

NO. 615 🔔

FORT BRAGG

The fort was established in this vicinity June 11, 1857 by 1st Lieutenant (later Brigadier General) Horatio Gate Gibson, 3rd Artillery, U.S. Army, who named it in honor of his former company commander, Braxton Bragg, later General, CSA. The fort was abandoned in October 1864.

321 Main St, Fort Bragg

NO. 674 🔔

ROUND VALLEY

This valley was discovered by Frank M. Azbill, who arrived from Eden Valley on May 15, 1854. During the same year,

Charles Kelsey from Clear Lake also visited it and George E. White sighted it from Blue Nose.

Inspiration Pt, on State Hwy 162 (P.M. 23.7), 5 mi S of Covelo

NO. 714 🔔

MENDOCINO PRESBYTERIAN CHURCH

This is one of the oldest Protestant churches in continuous use in California. The Presbyterian Church, organized on November 6, 1859, dedicated the redwood building on July 5, 1868.

44831 Main St, Mendocino

NO. 926 🔔

SUN HOUSE

This house, constructed in 1911-12, is a unique Craftsman style redwood building which incorporates northwestern designs into its architecture. The Sun House was designed by George Wilcox and John W. and Grace Carpenter Hudson. Dr. Hudson was a recognized authority on American Indians, and especially California Pomo Indians. Mrs. Hudson, an outstanding artist, became widely known for her paintings of Pomo life.

431 S Main St, Ukiah

NO. 927

TEMPLE OF KUAN TI

One of the oldest of California's Chinese houses of worship in continuous use, the temple may date back as far as 1854, though its documented history reaches only to 1883. The Chinese built many temples in California, but most have been destroyed, and no others remain on the North Coast.

45160 Albion St, Mendocino

Landmark No. 980

NO. 980

UKIAH VICHY SPRINGS RESORT

Frank Marble discovered these springs in 1848, and William Day established a resort here in the 1850s. Ukiah Vichy represents one of the oldest and one of the few continuously operating mineral springs in California. Its waters remain among the most important of the thermal, alkaline-carbonated waters once so highly valued by both European and American believers in hydropathy. It is the only mineral springs in California that resembles the famed Grand Grille Springs of Vichy, France.

2701 Vichy Springs Rd, Ukiah

Landmark No. 926

Landmark No. 927

Landmark No. 615

Merced County

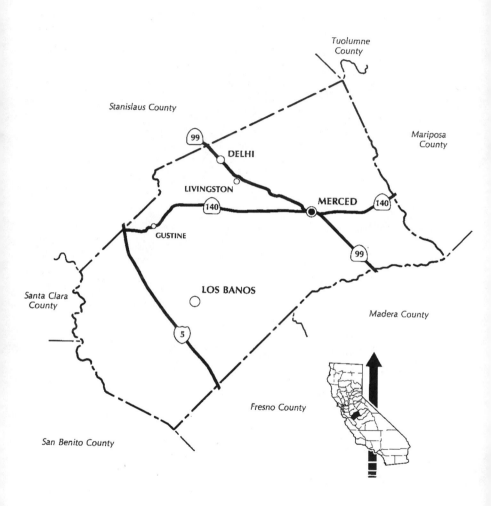

Merced
Est. 1855

Merced County is traversed today by major highways 99 and Interstate 5 and historically the area's travel routes have played an important role. Early Indians established a trail over today's Pacheco Pass and later Spanish explorers also used this crossing. During the Mission Era, Spanish soldiers used the pass as they searched for escaped mission Indians and deserting soldiers. To the east, early trade routes and stage lines ran along the foothills.

NO. 409 ☐
SNELLING COURTHOUSE

This, the first courthouse in Merced County, was erected in 1857. This monument commemorates the 75th anniversary of the organization of Merced County and is dedicated to the memory of our pioneers by Yosemite Parlor No. 24, N.S.G.W., Merced, May 20, 1930.

Main St (Hwy 59) between Second and Third Sts, Snelling

NO. 548 🔔
CANAL FARM INN

This original San Joaquin Valley ranch headquarters of California pioneer and cattle baron Henry Miller (1827-1916) was established in 1873. His farsighted planning and development in the 1870s of a vast gravity irrigation system, and the founding of Los Banos in 1889, provided the basis for this area's present stability and wealth.

1460 E Pacheco Blvd, Los Banos

NO. 550 🔔
LOS BANOS

Los Baños (the baths) del Padre Arroyo, visited as early as 1805 by Spanish explorers, was a favorite place for padres from San Juan Bautista Mission during their travels to the San Joaquin Valley. Its name was changed to Los Banos Creek by later American emigrants. The town of Los Banos was established at its present site in 1889, after the post office of Los Banos was built near the creek in 1874.

Los Banos Park, 803 E Pacheco Blvd, Los Banos

NO. 829 🔔
PACHECO PASS

On June 21, 1805, on his first exploratory journey into the San Joaquin Valley, Lieutenant Gabriel Moraga traversed and recorded this pass. Since then it has been trail, toll road, stagecoach road, and freeway—the principal route between the coastal areas to the west and the great valley and mountains to the east.

Romero Overlook, San Luis Reservoir, 31770 W Hwy 152 (P.M. 8.0), 15 mi W of Los Banos

NO. 934 🔔

TEMPORARY DETENTION CAMPS FOR JAPANESE AMERICANS— MERCED ASSEMBLY CENTER

This was one of 15 temporary detention camps established during World War II to incarcerate persons of Japanese ancestry, a majority of whom were American citizens, without specific charges or trial. From May to September 1942, 4,669 residents of Northern California were detained until permanent relocation camps were built. May the injustices and humiliation suffered here as a result of hysteria, racism, and economic exploitation never recur.

Landmark No. 550

Merced County Fairgrounds, "J" St at 7th St, adjacent to parking lot at entrance to fairgrounds, Merced

Landmark No. 548

Landmark No. 934

Landmark No. 829

Modoc County

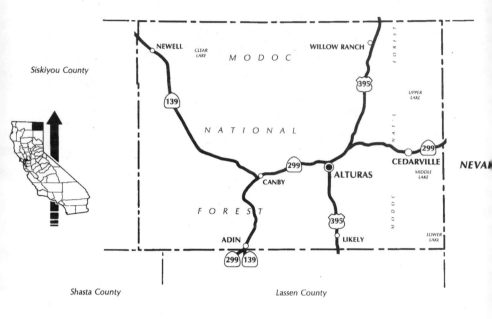

OREGON

Siskiyou County

NEWELL CLEAR LAKE

WILLOW RANCH

MODOC

NATIONAL

FOREST

139

395

UPPER LAKE

NAT'L

299

CEDARVILLE

NEVA

299

ALTURAS

CANBY

MIDDLE LAKE

FOREST

MODOC

395

ADIN

LIKELY

LOWER LAKE

299 139

Shasta County

Lassen County

Modoc
Est. 1874

In the northeastern corner of California, where early emigrants passed into California from Oregon, Modoc County's history reflects bloody conflict with Native Americans. The Modoc Wars are etched in the region's past.

NO. 6
FRÉMONT'S CAMP

John C. Frémont's expedition from Fort Sutter to Upper Klamath Lake, which included Kit Carson and other scouts, camped here May 1-4, 1846. They were the first non-Indians ever to pass this way.

0.7 mi N of old Alturas Hwy (Co Rd 114) and Hwy 139 jct, 12 mi SE of Tule Lake

NO. 8
BLOODY POINT

In 1850 one of the bloodiest massacres of emigrants ever known on the Oregon Trail occurred here when Modoc Indians killed over 90 men, women, and children in a surprise attack. The following year another large party narrowly escaped the same fate, and the Indians succeeded in killing several smaller parties here.

3.0 mi S of Oregon border, then 1.0 mi SW on Co Rd 104, 8.3 mi NW of State Hwy 139, E of Tule Lake

NO. 14 ☐
CRESSLER AND BONNER TRADING POST, 1865

Cressler and Bonner started the first mercantile establishment in Modoc County here, in the first building erected in the town of Cedarville. They carried on a thriving business with emigrants en route to California and Oregon, and later with Surprise Valley settlers.

Cedarville Park, Center St between Bonner and Townsend Sts, Cedarville

NO. 15
BONNER GRADE

The first road from Cedarville to Alturas followed the course of the present highway over Warner Mountains from Surprise Valley. It was named in honor of John H. Bonner, who was instrumental in securing the construction of the road over Bonner Grade in 1869.

Cedar Pass, State Hwy 299 (P.M. 51.3), 6.2 mi W of Cedarville

NO. 16 ☐
INFERNAL CAVERNS BATTLEGROUND, 1867

This is the site of the battle between U.S. troops and Shoshone, Paiute, and Pit Indians on September 26 and 27, 1867. The Indians took refuge in a series of caverns located at the top of a rocky slope. Over a third of the command was killed or wounded in the battle; six soldiers were buried at the foot of the slope.

Ferry Ranch on Co Rd 60, site is 1 mi SW of Ranch, 6.5 mi NW of Likely

NO. 108

BATTLE OF LAND'S RANCH—1872

One of the engagements of the Modoc War took place on December 21, 1872, on what was then known as the Land's Ranch. Army supply wagons, escorted by cavalrymen, had reached camp in safety, but several of the soldiers who had dropped behind were suddenly attacked by Indians hiding among the rocks above the road. Two men were killed and several wounded.

0.1 mi S of intersection of State Hwy 139 (P.M. 40.4) and Co Rd 114, 12.1 mi SE of Tule Lake

NO. 109 ☐

CHIMNEY ROCK

The chimney was cut out of the solid rock by Thomas L. Denson, who came west by the way of the Santa Fe Trail in 1852. In 1870 Denson built his cabin, the second building to be erected in the Pit River Valley, alongside a pyramid-shaped rock, cutting the fireplace and flue out of the solid rock itself.

Beside RR track along State Hwy 395 (P.M. 30.3), 77 mi N of Alturas

NO. 111 ☐

OLD EMIGRANT TRAIL

Near the present Pit River-Happy Camp Road this old pioneer trail, part of one of the earliest roads in northeastern California, is yet easily traced. Trees eight to ten inches in diameter are growing in the old road bed.

5.0 mi NW of Co Rd 84, 9.3 mi NW of Canby

NO. 125 ☐

EVANS AND BAILEY FIGHT—1861

S. D. Evans, Sr. and Joe Bailey, stockmen from Rogue River Valley, Oregon, and 16 of their employees were driving 900 head of beef cattle from Roseburg to the mines at Virginia City, Nevada when they were attacked by Indians and the two owners killed.

On top of hill, 500 ft S of Centerville Rd, 4.9 mi SE of Canby

NO. 430 🔔

FORT BIDWELL

Fort Bidwell, named for John Bidwell, was established in 1865. The fort, which operated until 1893, was one of the last early military posts north of Benicia to be abandoned. From 1898 to 1930, the fort served as a non-reservation boarding school for Indians.

Fort Bidwell Indian Community Center, W end of Bridge St, Fort Bidwell

NO. 546 🔔

APPLEGATE-LASSEN EMIGRANT TRAIL (FANDANGO PASS)

This spot marks the convergence of two pioneer trails used by emigrants during the years 1846-1850. The Applegate Trail, established in 1846, led from the Humboldt River in Nevada to the Willamette Valley in Oregon. The Lassen Cutoff, established by Peter Lassen in 1848, turned south at Goose Lake to the northern mines and settlements of California.

Fandango Pass, 10.8 mi E of State Hwy 395 on Fandango Pass Rd (Co Rd 9), 9.2 mi W of Fort Bidwell

NO. 850-2 🔔

TULE LAKE RELOCATION CENTER

Tule Lake was one of ten American concentration camps established during World War II to incarcerate 110,000 persons of Japanese ancestry, of whom the majority were American citizens, behind barbed wire and guard towers without charge, trial, or establishment of guilt.

These camps are reminders of how racism, economic and political exploitation, and expediency can undermine the constitutional guarantees of United States citizens and aliens alike. May the injustices and humiliation suffered here never recur.

NE corner of State Hwy 139 and Co Rd 176, 75 mi S of Tule Lake

Landmark No. 109

Mono-Inyo Counties

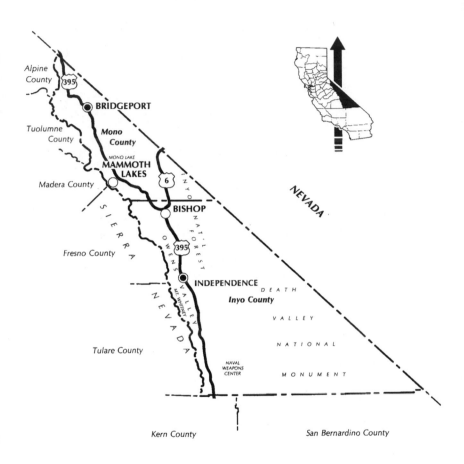

Bodie State Historic Park - Standing, unrestored ghost town. Located E of Highway 395 near Bridgeport.

Mono
Est. 1861

High Sierra mining towns experienced boom and bust in Mono County, leaving remnants of a colorful past. This rugged region of high desert and Sierra peaks makes for scenic traveling along California's eastern border.

NO. 341

BODIE

Gold was discovered here in 1859 by Wm. S. Bodey, after whom the town was named, and the town became the most thriving metropolis of the Mono country. Bodie's mines produced gold valued at more than 100 million dollars. Today a state park, Bodie is one of the best known of the west's "ghost towns."

Bodie State Historic Park, on State Hwy 270, 12.8 mi E of State Hwy 395 (P.M. 69.8), 19.8 mi SE of Bridgeport

NO. 792

DOG TOWN

Site of the first major gold rush to the eastern slope of California's Sierra Nevada, Dog Town derived its name from a popular miners' term for camps with huts or hovels. Ruins lying close to the cliff bordering Dog Town Creek are all that remain of the makeshift dwellings which formed part of the "diggins" here.

On State Hwy 395 (P.M. 69.5), 7 mi S of Bridgeport

NO. 995-1

TRAIL OF THE JOHN C. FRÉMONT 1884 EXPEDITION

In 1844, while exploring and mapping the area of what is presently the western United States, Lt. John C. Frémont's party passed through northern Mono County during the last week of January. After passing through Mono County, Frémont passed over the Sierra and travelled to Sutter's Fort in the Sacramento Valley, where the party rested. To leave California the expedition headed south through the San Joaquin Valley, and then headed easterly to leave California by the Old Spanish Trail to Utah.

Big Bend-Mountain Gate area, Toiyabe National Forest, Bridgeport

Monterey County

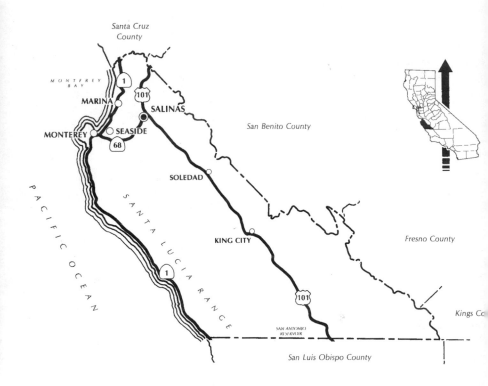

Fremont Peak State Park - Site of fort built by Captain John C. Frémont in 1846. Located 11 miles S of San Juan Bautista.

Monterey State Historic Park - Includes several outstanding examples of early California architecture; capitol of Spanish and Mexican California. Located in Monterey.

Point Sur Lighthouse State Historic Park - 1889 Lighthouse open for tours. Located 19 miles S of Monterey on Highway 1.

Monterey
Est. 1850

Monterey Bay, with its fishhook-shaped peninsula, was first sighted by Spanish explorers in 1542. Established in 1769, the town of Monterey served as both Spanish and Mexican capitol of Alta California. The rich history of early California comes to life in the many adobe buildings that have been preserved and restored.

NO. 1 ☐
CUSTOM HOUSE

Commodore John Drake Sloat raised the American flag over this building on July 7, 1846 to signal the passing of California from Mexican to American rule. Restored through the efforts of the Native Sons of the Golden West with the assistance of the people of California.

Monterey State Historic Park, Custom House Plaza, between Scott and Decatur Sts, Monterey

NO. 105 ☐
ROYAL PRESIDIO CHAPEL OF SAN CARLOS BORROMÉO

Established as a mission by Father Serra, June 3, 1770, this became the royal Presidio Chapel when the mission was moved to Carmel. The chapel was rebuilt with stone in 1791 and became the parish church in 1835, due to secularization. In a dilapidated condition in 1850, it was reconstructed and altered with money donated by Governor Pacheco in 1858.

550 Church St near Figueroa,

NO. 106 ☐
LARKIN HOUSE

The adobe-and-wood Larkin House was built in 1835 by Thomas Oliver Larkin, a Yankee merchant who came to California in April 1832. Since Larkin was the only U.S. consul to California under Mexican rule, his home became the American consulate from 1844 to 1846, and it was also used as military headquarters by Kearny, Mason, and Sherman.

Monterey State Historic Park, SW corner of Jefferson and Calle Principal, Monterey

NO. 126 ☐
COLTON HALL

In this building met the convention that drafted the Constitution under which California was admitted to statehood on September 9, 1850. Robert Semple was chairman and William G. March secretary. The 48 delegates met from September 1 to October 15, 1849 on the upper floor, which ran the length of the main building. The stairway leading to the convention hall was in the rear of the building. Rev. Walter Colton, first American alcalde in Monterey, erected this building as a public hall and schoolhouse; he and Robert Semple established California's first American newspaper in Monterey on August 15, 1846.

Civic Center, Pacific St between Jefferson and Madison, Monterey

NO. 128☐

LANDING PLACE OF SEBASTIAN VIZCAINO AND FRAY JUNÍPERO SERRA

Having entered the harbor the previous evening with his three small vessels, Sebastian Vizcaino landed here on December 17, 1602. Mass was sung by three Carmelite friars and the country taken in the name of the King of Spain. On the same spot, Fray Junípero Serra landed from the San Antonio on June 3, 1770 to join Captain Gaspar de Portolá and Fray Juan Crespí, who had arrived from San Diego overland a week before, in founding the Mission San Carlos de Borroméo de Monterey and the Presidio of Monterey.

Monterey State Historic Park, SW corner of Artillery and Pacific Sts, Monterey

NO. 135

MISSION SAN CARLOS BORROMÉO DE CARMELO

Mission San Carlos was established by Father Serra on June 3, 1770 at the Presidio of Monterey. Finding this location unsuitable, Serra moved the mission to Carmel Valley. In July 1771 he set to work constructing temporary buildings at the new site, and in December 1771 the mission was moved to its permanent location.

SW corner of Lasuen Dr and Rio Rd, Carmel

NO. 136

FIRST THEATER IN CALIFORNIA

This building was built about 1844 as a sailor's lodging house by Jack Swan. In 1848 it was commandeered by a group of mustered-out soldiers of Colonel Stevenson's regiment of New Yorkers looking for a place to put on plays and comedies. The theater afterward served as a whaling station, a lookout station having been added to the roof.

Monterey State Historic Park, SW corner of Scott and Pacific Sts, Monterey

NO. 232 🔔

MISSION SAN ANTONIO DE PADUA

Mission San Antonio de Padua, established on July 14, 1771, was the third in a series of missions founded in Alta California by Father Junípero Serra. Its picturesque setting in the valley of the San Antonio River within the Santa Lucia Range makes it one of today's most outstanding examples of early mission life.

Take Jolon Rd 26.5 mi from Hwy 101, to Hunter-Ligget Military Reservation, 23 mi W of King City

NO. 233 🔔

MISSION NUESTRA SEÑORA DE LA SOLEDAD

This mission, founded October 9, 1791 by Father Fermín Francisco de Lasuén, ministered to the Indians of the Salinas Valley. Governor José Joaquín de Arrillaga died here July 24, 1814 and was buried in the chapel. Prosperous in its early years, Soledad declined after 1825, but Father Vicente Francisco Sarría stayed on in poverty to serve the Indians until his death in 1835, when the mission was secularized. It was regranted to the Bishop of Monterey in 1859. In ruins after 1874, the chapel was reconstructed and dedicated under the auspices of the Native Daughters of the Golden West, October 1955.

Fort Romie Rd (Co Rd G-17), 2.5 mi W of Soledad

NO. 348 🔔

HOUSE OF GOVERNOR ALVARADO

A native of Monterey, Alvarado served as Governor of Mexican California from December 20, 1836 to December 20, 1842. During his administration the increasing influx of Americans and the Russian settlement at Fort Ross began to be regarded as serious problems.

494-498 Alvarado St, Monterey

NO. 351

VÁSQUEZ HOUSE

This adobe house was occupied by a sister of Tiburcio Vásquez, the colorful Monterey bandit of the 1870s.

546 Dutra St, Monterey

NO. 352 □

ROBERT LOUIS STEVENSON HOUSE

In this house in 1879 lived Robert Louis Stevenson, essayist, storyteller, and poet whose contribution to literature delighted the world.

530 Houston St, Monterey

NO. 353

HOUSE OF FOUR WINDS

In the late 1830s, Thomas Oliver Larkin built the House of Four Winds, named for the weather vane in his garden. Tradition says the building was used as an early hall of records.

540 Calle Principal, Monterey

NO. 354

OLD PACIFIC HOUSE

Originally built as a hotel between 1835 and 1847 by James McKinley, the building was known as the Pacific House in 1850, when it housed a public tavern. In later years law offices, a newspaper, small stores, and a ballroom occupied the premises. In 1880 David Jacks bought the property, and in 1954 Miss Margaret Jacks made a gift of the building to the State of California.

Monterey State Historic Park, Custom House Plaza, Monterey

NO. 387

"THE GLASS HOUSE," CASA MATERNA OF THE VALLEJOS

In the 1820s, Don Ignacio Vallejo built the Casa Materna on Bolsa de San Cayetano. Don Ignacio and Dona María Antonio Lugo y Vallejo had 13 children—eight daughters and five sons, one of whom was General Mariano Guadalupe Vallejo.

On edge of bluff 1,000 ft N of intersection of Hillcrest Rd and Salinas Rd, 2.5 mi SE of Watsonville

NO. 494 🔔

RICHARDSON ADOBE

Los Coches Rancho (8,994.2 acres) was granted to María Josefa Soberanes de Richardson by the Mexican government in 1841. Her husband, William Brunner Richardson, a native of Baltimore, Maryland, built the adobe house here in 1843, and planted the nearby locust trees in 1846. This was the site of Captain John C. Frémont's encampment in 1846 and 1847; the adobe was later used as a stage station and post office. It was donated to the State of California in 1958 by Margaret Jacks.

Los Coches Rancho Wayside Campground, NW corner of State Hwy 101 (P.M. 60.5) and Arroyo Seco Rd, 1.5 mi S of Soledad

NO. 532

CASA DE ORO

In the 1850s this building was a general merchandise store operated by Joseph Boston & Co. In later years it was called Casa de Oro because of the unverified story that it had been a gold depository.

Monterey State Historic Park, SW corner of Olivier and Scott, Monterey

NO. 560 ☐

HILL TOWN FERRY

Operated by Hiram Cory, this was one of the first ferries to cross the Salinas River. The Monterey County Board of Supervisors regulated the toll which was, in 1877: buggy and horse, 25 cents; buggy and horses, 37-1/2 cents; four horses and wagon, 85 cents; six horses and wagon, $1; horse and saddle, 25 cents; and man on foot, 12-1/2 cents. The ferry operated until a bridge was built in 1889.

On Old Hwy 68, SW corner of Spreckels Blvd and Old Hwy 68 (P.M. 18.1), 3.0 mi SW of Salinas

NO. 651 🔔

SITE OF THE BATTLE OF NATIVIDAD

Combined American forces under Captains Charles D. Burrass (or Burroughs) and Bluford K. Thompson clashed with Comandante Manuel de Jesús Castro's Californians in this vicinity on November 16, 1846. Casualties on each side consisted of several men killed and wounded. The Americans saved a large herd of horses for Lt. Col. John C. Frémont, who then later proceeded south to participate in the Armistice at Cahuenga in January 1847.

SW corner of San Juan Grade (P.M. 4.9) and Crazy Horse Canyon Rd, 5.0 mi NE of Salinas

NO. 712

SOBERANES ADOBE

Don José Estrada, who built this adobe in 1830, sold the property to Don Feliciano Soberanes. The adobe was the home of the Soberanes family from 1860 until 1922, when Mr. and Mrs. William O'Donnell acquired the property. Mrs. O'Donnell gave the adobe to the State in 1953.

Monterey State Historic Park, 336 Pacific St, Monterey

NO. 713

GUTIÉRREZ ADOBE

In 1841 the municipality of Monterey granted a lot to Joaquín Gutiérrez where he and his wife, Josefa, built an adobe home. The house has been donated to the State by the Monterey Foundation.

Monterey State Historic Park, 590 Calle Principal, Monterey

NO. 839 🔔

CHAUTAUQUA HALL

The first Chautauqua in the West was organized at Pacific Grove in June 1879 for the presentation of "moral attractions" and "the highest grade of concerts and entertainments." Known worldwide as "Chautauqua-by-the-Sea," it made Pacific Grove an unequaled cultural center.

SW corner of 16th St and Central Ave, Pacific Grove

NO. 870 🔔
JOSÉ EUSEBIO BORONDA ADOBE CASA

Built between 1844 and 1848 by José Eusebio Boronda, this is an outstanding example of a Mexican-era rancho adobe. Virtually unaltered since its construction, it shows many features of the "Monterey Colonial" style.

Boronda Adobe Historic Center, 333 Boronda Rd at W Laurel Dr, Salinas

NO. 934 🔔
TEMPORARY DETENTION CAMPS FOR JAPANESE AMERICANS— SALINAS ASSEMBLY CENTER

This monument is dedicated to the 3,586 Monterey Bay area residents of Japanese ancestry, most of whom were American citizens, temporarily confined in the Salinas Rodeo Grounds during World War II, from April to July 1942. They were detained without charges, trial, or establishment of guilt before being incarcerated in permanent camps, mostly at Poston, Arizona. May such injustice and humiliation never recur.

Sherwood Gardens Rodeo Grounds, Sherwood Hall Community Center 940 N Main St, Salinas

NO. 951 🔔
LIGHT STATIONS OF CALIFORNIA (THEMATIC), POINT SUR LIGHT STATION

Spanish explorers and later New England hide and tallow traders found the Big Sur coastline a great hazard. Heavy fogs and extreme winds caused the wreck of many vessels on this coast. The gold rush of 1849 dramatically increased coastal shipping. A lighthouse was clearly needed. President Andrew Johnson signed the Executive Order which reserved the site for lighthouse purposes in 1866. Construction began in 1887 and the lamp was lit on August 1, 1889.

St Hwy 1, 23 mi S of Monterey and 3 mi N of Andrew Molera St Pk

Landmark No. 651

Napa County

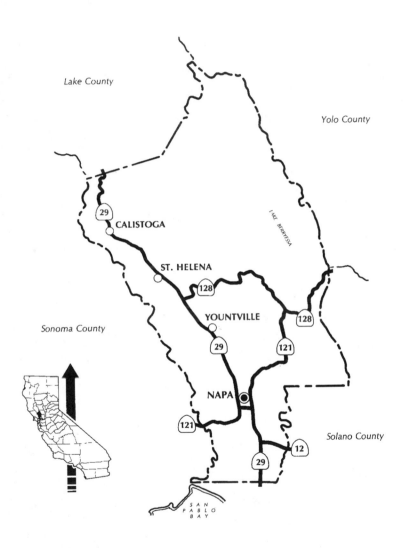

Bale Grist Mill State Historic Park - Water-powered grist mill.
Located 3 miles N of St. Helena.

Napa
Est. 1850

"Napa" is the name for an Indian tribe once known as the bravest of all California natives whose villages occupied the site of the present day town of Napa. The Napa valley is a traveler's delight with its scenic vineyards and tree-covered foothills.

NO. 359 □

OLD BALE MILL

This historic gristmill was erected by Dr. E. T. Bale, grantee of Carne Humana Rancho, in 1846. The mill, with surrounding land, was deeded to the Native Sons of the Golden West by Mrs. W. W. Lyman, and was restored through the efforts of the Native Son Parlors of Napa County.

Bale Grist Mill State Historic Park, Hwy 29 (P.M. 32.1), 3369 N St. Helena Hwy, 3 mi NW of St. Helena

NO. 547 🔔

CHILES MILL

Joseph Ballinger Chiles, who first came to California in 1841, erected the mill on Rancho Catacula 1845-56. The first American flour mill in Northern California, it was still in use in the 1880s. Chiles served as a vice president of the Society of California Pioneers, 1850-53.

SW corner on hillside, Chiles and Pope Rd and Lower Chiles Valley Rd, 3.6 mi N on Hwy 128, Chiles Valley

NO. 561 🔔

SCHRAMSBERG

Founded in 1862 by Jacob Schram, this was the first hillside winery of the Napa Valley. Robert Louis Stevenson, visiting here in 1880, devoted a chapter of his "Silverado Squatters" to Schramsberg and its wines; Ambrose Bierce and Lilly Hitchcock Coit were other cherished friends. The original house and winery have been excellently preserved.

End of Schramsberg Rd, on Hwy 29, 3.1 mi S of Calistoga

NO. 563 🔔

CHARLES KRUG WINERY

Founded in 1861 by Charles Krug (1825-1892), this is the oldest operating winery in Napa Valley. The pioneer winemaker of this world-famous region, Krug made the first commercial wine in Napa County at Napa in 1858.

Krug Ranch, 2800 Main St, St. Helena

NO. 564 🔔

GEORGE YOUNT BLOCKHOUSE

In this vicinity stood the log block-house constructed in 1836 by George Calvert Yount, pioneer settler in Napa County. Nearby was his adobe house, built in 1837, and across the bridge were his grist and saw mills, erected before 1845. Born in North Carolina in 1794, Yount was a trapper, rancher, and miller; he became grantee of the Rancho Caymus and La Jota. He died at Yountville in 1865.

NE corner of Cook Rd and Yount Mill Rd, 1 mi N of Yountville

NO. 682

SITE OF YORK'S CABIN, CALISTOGA

Among the first houses in this area was John York's log cabin, constructed in October 1845. Rebuilt as part of the home of the Kortum family, it was used as a residence until razed in 1930. Nearby was the cabin of David Hudson, also built in October 1845. Calistoga was named by Samuel Brannan.

SW corner Hwy 29 (Foothill Blvd) and Lincoln Ave, Calistoga

NO. 683 🔔

SITE OF HUDSON CABIN, CALISTOGA

David Hudson was one of the early pioneers who helped develop the upper portion of Napa Valley by purchasing land, clearing it, and planting crops and building homes. Hudson built his cabin in October 1845.

NE corner of Hwy 29 (Foothill Blvd) and Lincoln Ave, Calistoga

NO. 684

SAM BRANNAN STORE, CALISTOGA

Sam Brannan arrived in Napa Valley in the late 1850s and purchased a square mile of land at the foot of Mount St. Helena. This is the store he built, in which he made $50,000 in one year.

NW corner of Wapoo Ave and Grant St, 203 Wapoo Ave, Calistoga

NO. 685

SAM BRANNAN COTTAGE, CALISTOGA

Sam Brannan arrived in Napa Valley in the late 1850s with the dream of making it the "Saratoga of California." In 1866 cottages were built and palm trees planted in preparation for the grand opening of the resort. This is the only cottage still standing.

1311 Washington St, Calistoga

NO. 686

SITE OF KELSEY HOUSE, CALISTOGA

Nancy Kelsey arrived in California in 1841 with the Bidwell-Bartleson party and settled with her family south of present-day Calistoga. Now the hearthstone is all that can be seen of the house. The property is owned by the Rockstrohs.

500 ft NW of intersection of State Hwy 29 and Diamond Mtn Rd, 1.1 mi S of Calistoga

NO. 687 ☐

NAPA VALLEY RAILROAD DEPOT, CALISTOGA

The Napa Valley Railroad depot, now the Southern Pacific depot, was built in 1868. Its roundhouse across Lincoln Avenue is gone. On its first trip, this railroad brought people to Calistoga for the elaborate opening of Brannan's summer resort in October 1868.

1458 Lincoln Ave, Calistoga

NO. 693 🔔

GRAVE OF GEORGE C. YOUNT

George Calvert Yount (1794-1865) was the first United States citizen to be ceded a Spanish land grant in Napa Valley (1836). Skilled hunter, frontiersman, craftsman, and farmer, he was the true embodiment of all the finest qualities of an advancing civilization blending with the existing primitive culture. Friend to all, this kindly host of Caymus Rancho encouraged sturdy American pioneers to establish ranches in this area, so it was well populated before the gold rush.

George C. Yount Pioneer Cemetery, Lincoln and Jackson Sts, Yountville

NO. 710☐
ROBERT LOUIS STEVENSON STATE PARK

In the spring of 1880, Robert Louis Stevenson brought his bride to Silverado. He and Fannie Osbourne Stevenson lived here from May 19 until July, while he gathered the notes for *Silverado Squatters*.

Hwy 29 (P.M. 45.5), 75 mi NE of Calistoga

NO. 814 🔔
BERINGER BROTHERS WINERY

Built by Frederick and Jacob Beringer, natives of Mainz, Germany, this winery has the unique distinction of never having ceased operations since its founding in 1876. Here, in the European tradition, were dug underground wine tunnels hundreds of feet in length. These maintain a constant temperature of 58 degrees, a factor considered necessary in the maturing and aging of fine wines.

2000 Main St, St. Helena

NO. 828 🔔
VETERANS HOME OF CALIFORNIA

This home for California's aged and disabled veterans was established in 1884 by Mexican War veterans and members of the Grand Army of the Republic. In January 1897 the Veterans Home Association deeded the home and its 910 acres of land to the State, which has since maintained it.

SW corner of California Dr and Hwy 29, Yountville

NO. 878 🔔
FIRST PRESBYTERIAN CHURCH BUILDING

Designed by pioneer architects R. H. Daley and Theodore Eisen, this church is an outstanding example of late Victorian Gothic architectural styling. It is the best surviving example in this region of the early works associated with Eisen, who later became an important Southern California architect. The church has been in continuous use since its construction in 1874; longest pastorates were those of Richard Wylie and Erwin Bollinger.

1333–3rd St between Randolph and Franklin Sts, Napa

NO. 939 🔔
Twentieth Century Folk Art Environments (Thematic) —LITTO

This is one of California's exceptional Twentieth Century Folk Art Environments. Over a period of 30 years, Emanuele "Litto" Damonte (1896-1985), with the help of his neighbors, collected more than 2,000 hubcaps. All around Hubcap Ranch are constructions and arrangements of hubcaps, bottles, and pulltops which proclaim that "Litto, the Pope Valley Hubcap King," was here.

6654 Pope Valley Rd (P.M. 14.3), 2.1 mi NW of Pope Valley

Nevada County

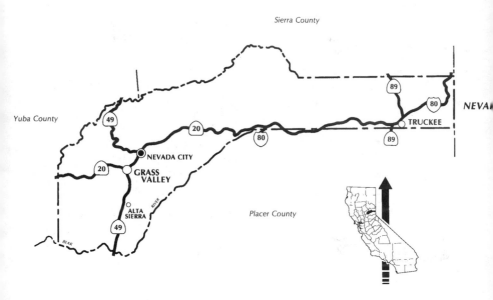

Donner Memorial State Park - Memorializes 1840-50 emigrants. Located 2.6 miles W of Truckee, off I-80.

Empire Mine State Historic Park - Hardrock gold mine, surface buildings and exhibits. Located at 10791 East Empire Street, Grass Valley.

Malakoff Diggins State Historic Park - Hydraulic mining operation. Located 11 miles NE of Nevada City.

Nevada
Est. 1851

Nevada means "snow-covered" in Spanish. During winter months, Nevada County's Eastern border is wholly engulfed in the snows of the Sierra Nevada mountain range. In the 1840s and 1850s many emigrants arrived in California via the overland California Trail which threaded through the infamous Donner Pass.

NO. 134 ☐

DONNER MONUMENT (or) PIONEER MONUMENT

Commemorates the ill-fated Donner party of California-bound emigrants, who wintered here in 1846-1847; many died of exposure and starvation.

Donner Memorial State Park, Old Hwy 40 at I-80 and Truckee exit, Truckee

NO. 247 ☐

THE WORLD'S FIRST LONG-DISTANCE TELEPHONE LINE

The first long-distance telephone in the world, built in 1877 by the Ridge Telephone Company, connected French Corral with French Lake, 58 miles away. It was operated by the Milton Mining Company from a building on this site that had been erected about 1853.

On Pleasant Valley Rd, in center of community of French Corral

NO. 292

HOME OF LOLA MONTEZ

Lola was born in Limerick, Ireland on July 3, 1818, as María Dolores Eliza Rosanna Gilbert. After living in England and on the continent, Lola came to New York in 1851 and settled in Grass Valley in 1852. It was here she built the only home she ever owned and became friends with Lotta Crabtree, who lived up the street. Lola died January 17, 1861 and was bur-

ied in Greenwood Cemetery, New York.

248 Mill St, Grass Valley

NO. 293

HOME OF LOTTA CRABTREE

Lotta Crabtree was born in New York in 1847. In 1852-3 the gold fever brought her family to California. Several months after arriving in San Francisco, Mrs. Crabtree and Lotta went to Grass Valley and with Mr. Crabtree started a boarding house for miners. It was here that Lotta met Lola Montez, who taught her to sing and dance. In Scales, Plumas County, Lotta made her first public appearance, which led to a successful career on stage here and abroad.

238 Mill St, Grass Valley

NO. 294 🔔 🏏

THE LITTLE TOWN OF ROUGH AND READY

Established in 1849 and named in honor of General Zachary Taylor, after the Rough and Ready Company of miners from Wisconsin, this was one of the principal towns of Nevada County. In 1850, articles of secession were drawn up establishing the "Republic of Rough and Ready." As a result of disastrous fires, only a few structures remain today that were built in the 1850s.

NE corner of State Hwy 20 and Mountain Rose Rd, Rough and Ready

NO. 297 ☐ ⚒

SITE OF ONE OF THE FIRST DISCOVERIES OF QUARTZ GOLD IN CALIFORNIA

This tablet commemorates the discovery of gold-bearing quartz and the beginning of quartz mining in California. The discovery was made on Gold Hill by George Knight in October 1850. The occurrence of gold-bearing quartz was undoubtedly noted here and elsewhere about the same time or even earlier, but this discovery created the great excitement that started the development of quartz mining into a great industry. The Gold Hill Mine is credited with a total production of $4,000,000 between 1850 and 1857.

SW corner of Jenkins St and Hocking Ave, Grass Valley

NO. 298 ☐ ⚒

EMPIRE MINE

The Empire Mine was originally located by George D. Roberts in October 1850. In the spring of 1854, the Empire Mining Company was incorporated and in 1865 new works, including a 30-stamp mill, were erected. In 1869 Wm. B. Bourn, Sr. purchased the Empire; when he died, Wm. B. Bourn, Jr. took over its management. The Empire was in constant operation from 1850 to the late 1950s.

Empire Mine State Historic Park, 10791 Empire St, 1.2 mi E of Grass Valley

NO. 390 🔔

BRIDGEPORT (NYES CROSSING) COVERED BRIDGE

Built in 1862 by David Isaac John Wood with lumber from his mill in Sierra County, this bridge was part of the Vir-

ginia Turnpike Company toll road which served the northern mines and the busy Nevada Comstock Lode. Utilizing a combination truss and arch construction, it is one of the oldest housed spans in the west and the longest single-span wood-covered bridge in the United States.

W side of Pleasant Valley Rd at S Fork of the Yuba River 2.7 mi S of French Corral

NO. 628 & 629 🔔 ⚒

ALPHA HYDRAULIC DIGGINGS, OMEGA HYDRAULIC DIGGINGS AND TOWNSITE

One mile north of here were the towns of Alpha and Omega, named by gold miners in the early 1850s. The tremendous hydraulic diggings, visible from near this point, engulfed most of the original townsites. Alpha was the birthplace of famed opera singer Emma Nevada. Mining at Omega continued until 1949, and lumbering operations are carried on there today (1958).

Omega Rest Area, Hwy 20 (P.M. 35. 7), 6 mi E of Washington Rd, Washington

NO. 780-6 🔔

FIRST TRANSCONTINENTAL RAILROAD–TRUCKEE

While construction on Sierra tunnels delayed Central Pacific, advance forces at Truckee began building 40 miles of track east and west of Truckee, moving supplies by wagon and sled, and Summit Tunnel was opened in December 1867. The line reached Truckee April 3, 1868; the Sierra was conquered. Rails reached Reno June 19, and construction advanced eastward toward the meeting with Union Pacific at the rate of one mile daily. On

May 10, 1869, the rails met at Promontory (Utah) to complete the first transcontinental railroad.

SP Depot, 70 Donner Pass Rd, Truckee

NO. 799 🔔
OVERLAND EMIGRANT TRAIL

Over a hundred years ago, this trail resounded to creaking wheels of pioneer wagons and the cries of hardy travelers on their way to the gold fields. It is estimated that over thirty thousand people used this trail in 1849. Here the old trail approaches the present highway.

SE side of Wolf Creek Bridge, State Hwy 49 (P.M. 3.61), 10 mi S of Grass Valley

NO. 832 🔔
SOUTH YUBA CANAL OFFICE

This was the headquarters for the largest network of water flumes and ditches in the state. The South Yuba Canal Water Company was the first incorporated to supply water for hydraulic mining. The original ditch was in use in May 1850, and this company office was in use from 1857 to 1880. The company's holdings later became part of the vast PG&E hydroelectric system.

134 Main St, Nevada City

NO. 843 🔔 🚫
NORTH STAR MINE POWERHOUSE

The North Star Powerhouse, built by A. D. Foote in 1895, was the first complete plant of its kind. Compressed air, generated by Pelton water wheels, furnished power for the entire mine operation. The 30-foot Pelton wheel was the largest in the world, and was in continuous use for over 30 years.

Mining and Pelton Wheel Museum, S Mill at Allison Ranch Rd, Grass Valley

NO. 852 🔔 🚫
NORTH BLOOMFIELD MINING AND GRAVEL COMPANY

This was a major hydraulic gold-mining operation in California. It boasted a vast system of canals and flumes; its 7,800-foot drainage tunnel was termed a feat of engineering skill. It was the principal defendant in an anti-debris lawsuit settled in 1884 by Judge Lorenzo Sawyer's famous decision, which created control that virtually ended hydraulic mining in California.

Malakoff Diggins State Historic Park, 16 mi E of State Hwy 49 on Tyler Foote Crossing Rd; plaque located in park diggins overlook, 28 mi N of Nevada City

NO. 855 🔔
MOUNT SAINT MARY'S CONVENT AND ACADEMY

Built by Reverend Thomas J. Dalton, the Sacred Heart Convent and Holy Angels Orphanage was dedicated May 2, 1865 by Bishop Eugene O'Connell. Under the Sisters of Mercy, it served from 1866 to 1932 as the first orphanage of the Northern Mines. It functioned as an academy from 1868 to 1965 and as a convent from 1866 to 1968.

S Church St between Chapel and Dalton Sts, Grass Valley

NO. 863 🔔

NEVADA THEATRE

California's oldest existing structure erected as a theater, the Nevada, opened September 9, 1865. Celebrities such as Mark Twain, Jack London, and Emma Nevada have appeared on its stage. Closed in 1957, the theatre was later purchased through public donations and reopened May 17, 1968 to again serve the cultural needs of the community.

401 Broad St, Nevada City

NO. 899 🔔

NATIONAL HOTEL

The National Exchange Hotel opened for business on August 20, 1856; the exterior is virtually unchanged since its construction as three brick buildings in 1856. The National is one of the oldest continuously operating hotels west of the Rockies.

211 Broad St, Nevada City

NO. 914 🔔

HOLBROOKE HOTEL

The hotel was built in 1862 around the Golden Gate Saloon, originally constructed in 1852 and the oldest continuously operating saloon in the Mother Lode region. The hotel's one-story field-stone and brick construction is an outstanding example of mid-19th century Mother Lode masonry structures.

212 W Main St, Grass Valley

NO. 1012 🔔

FIRST MANUFACTURING SITE OF THE PELTON WHEEL

The Pelton Water Wheel, first commercially manufactured here at George Allan's Foundry and Machine Works in 1879, was a major advancement in water power utilization and greatly advanced hard-rock mining. Its unique feature was a series of paired buckets, shaped like bowls of spoons and separated by a splitter, that divided the incoming water jets into two parts. By the late 1800s, the Pelton Wheels were providing energy to operate industrial machinery throughout the world. In 1888, Lester Pelton moved his business to San Francisco, but granted continuing manufacturing rights to Allan's Foundry, where the wheels were manufactured into the early 1900s.

325 Spring St, Nevada City

Landmark No. 294

Landmark No. 852

Landmark No. 832

Orange County

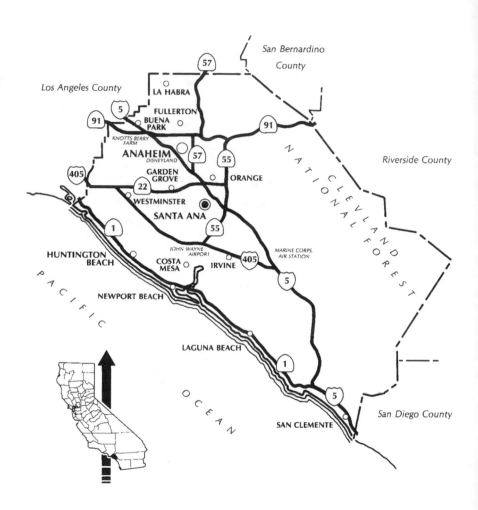

Orange
Est. 1889

The coastal shoreline of today's Orange County served early hide trader's ships at El Embarcadero, located just below Dana Point, which is named for author Richard Henry Dana. Newport Landing, Anaheim Landing, and McFadden Wharf are historic sites that reveal the importance of ocean trade vessels on the early settlements in the once-remote lands in this portion of Southern California.

NO. 112 □

NORTH GATE OF CITY OF ANAHEIM

A wall or fence of willow poles that took root and grew was planted around the Anaheim Colony to keep out the herds of wild cattle that roamed the surrounding country. Gates were erected at the north, east, south, and west ends of the two principal streets of the colony. The north gate, on the highway to Los Angeles, was the main entrance to the city.

775 Anaheim Blvd at North St, Anaheim

NO. 189 🔔

DANA POINT

Named for Richard Henry Dana, author of Two Years Before the Mast, who visited here in 1835. El Embarcadero, the cove below, was used by hide vessels trading with Mission San Juan Capistrano. This trade reached its peak in 1830-1840. In 1818 pirate Hipolito Bouchard, flying an Argentine flag, anchored his fleet here while raiding the mission.

Ken Sampson Overview, S of the Blue Lantern at Santa Clara Ave, Dana Point

NO. 198 🔔

OLD LANDING

On September 10, 1870, Captain Samuel S. Dunnells opened Newport Bay to commerce when they entered it for the first time on the sternwheel steamer Vaquero. The landing was designated "Newport"– a new port–by James Irvine, Benjamin Flint, James McFadden, and Robert McFadden. The McFaddens operated a regular shipping service here during the 1870s and 1880s.

On Dover Dr 500 ft N of State Hwy 1, Newport Beach

NO. 199 □

THE SERRANO ADOBE

Cañada de los Alisos, also called El Toro, was granted to José Serrano in 1842 by Governor Alvarado. Senor Serrano and his relatives erected a number of adobes on the grant, one of which still serves as private living quarters.

Heritage Hill, Serrano Regional Historic Village, NE corner Lake Forest Dr and Serrano Rd, El Toro

NO. 200 🔔
MISSION SAN JUAN CAPISTRANO

Founded in 1776 by Padre Junípero Serra, this is the seventh in the chain of 21 missions established in Alta California to christianize and civilize the Indians. The stone church was destroyed in 1812 earthquake. Expropriated during Mexican rule, the mission was returned to the Catholic church in 1865 by proclamation of President Abraham Lincoln.

NW corner of Ortega Hwy and Camino Capistrano, San Juan Capistrano

NO. 201 🔔
PIONEER HOUSE OF THE MOTHER COLONY

Anaheim's first house, built in 1857 by Founder George Hanson. "The Mother Colony," a German group that left San Francisco to form a grape-growing colony in Southern California, selected the name given to this settlement. The vineyards, which became the largest in California, were destroyed by disease in 1885. The colony then started producing Valencia oranges. Here once resided actress Helena Modjeska and Henryk Sienkiewicz, author of *Quo Vadis.*

414 N West St near Sycamore St, Anaheim

NO. 202 🔔
SILVERADO

Located in Cañada de la Madera (Timber Canyon) was a mining boomtown founded in 1878 when silver was discovered nearby. During the colorful life of its boom, 1878-1881, miners flocking to the area established a thriving community, served daily by stage from Los Angeles and Santa Ana.

Next to Silverado Fire Station #2, end of Silverado Canyon Rd, 3.4 mi E of Silverado post office, Silverado

NO. 203 ☐
RED HILL

In early descriptions it was known as Cerrito de las Ranas, meaning the Hill of the Frogs. In the 1890s this hill became the scene of mining excitement. Its soil composition, very red in color, had caused early American settlers to name it Red Hill.

Church of the Covenant Elementary School, 11911 Red Hill Road, Santa Ana

NO. 204 🔔
OLD SANTA ANA

Portolá camped on the bank of Santa Ana River in 1769, and José Antonio Yorba, a member of the expedition, later returned to Rancho Santiago de Santa Ana. El Camino Real crossed the river in this vicinity. The place was designated Santa Ana by travelers and known by that name until the present town of Santa Ana was founded.

NW corner of Lincoln Ave and Orange Olive Rd, Orange

NO. 205 🔔
MODJESKA'S HOME

Famous as the home of Madame Modjeska, one of the world's greatest actresses, the house was designed by Stanford White in 1888 and built on property called the "Forest of Arden." Sold soon after her retirement, it remains a monument to the woman who contributed immeasurably to the cultural life of Orange County.

Modjeska Canyon, 500 ft E of intersection of Modjeska Canyon Rd and Harding Canyon Rd, 8 mi NE of El Toro

NO. 217

BLACK STAR CANYON INDIAN VILLAGE SITE

The Indians who lived on the village located here had stolen some horses, and the whites followed them back to their camp. After a skirmish, the whites left with the horses that the Indians had not killed. In 1878 the Black Star Coal Mining Company had a mine at the mouth of the canyon.

Black Star Canyon on Black Star Canyon Rd, 6.0 mi N of Silverado Canyon Rd, 9 mi N of Silverado

NO. 218

BARTON MOUND

Juan Flores, who had escaped from San Quentin, was being sought by James Barton with a posse of five men. Near this mound, Flores surprised Barton and three of his men; all four were killed. When Los Angeles learned of the slaughter, posses were formed, and Flores and his men were captured.

SE corner of I-405 and State Hwy 133, 2 mi S of East Irvine

NO. 219 🔔

ANAHEIM LANDING

Soon after the founding of the Mother Colony at Anaheim in 1857, the Anaheim Landing Company established Anaheim Landing as a port for the Santa Ana Valley. Despite treacherous entrance conditions that caused several disasters, regular coastwise trade was carried on here for about 15 years.

NE corner of Seal Beach Blvd and Electric Ave, Seal Beach

NO. 225

FLORES PEAK

In 1857, Juan Flores and a band of outlaws murdered Sheriff James Barton and part of his posse at Barton Mound. Pursued by a posse led by General Andrés Pico, Flores and his men were finally caught on Flores Peak.

Flores Peak, Tucker Wildlife Sanctuary, N side of Modjeska Canyon Rd, Modjeska Canyon

NO. 226 🔔

DON BERNARDO YORBA RANCHHOUSE SITE

Here Don Bernardo Yorba created the greatest rancho of California's Golden Age, combining the Santa Ana Grant awarded to his father by the King of Spain in 1810 and lands granted to him by Governor José Figueroa in 1834. He was the third son of José Antonio Yorba, who came with Don Gaspar de Portolá in 1769 to establish California's first family.

NE corner of Esperanza Rd and Echo Hill Ln, Yorba Linda

NO. 227 🔔

DIEGO SEPÚLVEDA ADOBE

This adobe house was built as a station of Mission San Juan Capistrano. After secularization the property became part of Rancho Santiago de Santa Ana, and the adobe was used as headquarters of Diego Sepúlveda, later owner of the rancho.

Estancia Park, NW corner of Mesa Verde Dr W and Adams Ave, Costa Mesa

NO. 228 □

CARBONDALE

This is the site of the 1878 coal discovery. The mine, called the Santa Clara, was operated by the Southern Pacific. The village of Carbondale was built on the flat. When the mine was closed down, Carbondale's buildings were moved away and today not one remains.

Silverado Community Church entrance, Silverado Canyon Rd, 1.1 mi W of Silverado post office, Silverado

NO. 729

OLD MAIZELAND SCHOOL (RIVERA SCHOOL)

Constructed in 1868, this was the first school in the Rivera District. It was previously located on Shugg Lane, now Slauson Avenue.

Knott's Berry Farm, 8039 Beach Blvd, Buena Park

NO. 775 🔔

SITE OF FIRST WATER-TO-WATER FLIGHT

On May 10, 1912, Glenn L. Martin flew his own plane, built in Santa Ana, from the waters of the Pacific Ocean at Balboa to Catalina Island. This was the first water-to-water flight, and the longest and fastest overwater flight, to that date. On his return to the mainland, Martin carried the day's mail from Catalina–another first.

S end of Main St at Ocean Front (Balboa), Newport Beach

NO. 794 🔔

McFADDEN WHARF

The original wharf on this site was completed in the summer of 1888 by the McFadden brothers. As the seaward terminus of their Santa Ana and Newport Railway it became the funnel through which flowed a major part of the lumber and other goods that built Orange, San Bernardino, and Riverside Counties during the period from 1891 to 1907.

Newport Pier, SE corner of W Ocean Front and McFadden Place, Newport Beach

NO. 837 🔔

ORANGE COUNTY'S ORIGINAL COURTHOUSE

Built in 1900 of Arizona red sandstone, this is the oldest existing county courthouse in Southern California. Significant and far-reaching court decisions were handed down here, including the "Whipstock" case dealing with slant oil drilling, interpretation of farm labor law, and the Overell trial which resulted in law regulating explosives.

211 W Santa Ana Blvd at Broadway, Santa Ana

NO. 918 🔔

OLINDA

From 1897, when oil pioneer Edward L. Doheny brought in the first well, to the 1940s, the boom town of Olinda sprawled over the surrounding hills. To the north was the Chanslor-Candfield Midway Oil Lease and, to the south, the Olinda Crude Oil Lease. Walter Perry Johnson, of Baseball's Hall of Fame, spent his boyhood here.

Carbon Canyon Regional Park, 4442 Carbon Canyon Rd, Brea

NO. 959 🔔

BALBOA PAVILION

This is one of California's last surviving examples of the great waterfront recreational pavilions from the turn of the century. Built in 1905 by the Newport Bay Investment Company, it played a prominent role in the development of Newport Beach as a seaside recreation area. In 1906, it became the southern terminus for the Pacific Electric Railway connecting the beach with downtown Los Angeles. The railway's Red Cars connected the beach with Los Angeles in only one hour.

400 Main St, Balboa

NO. 1004

OLD TOWN IRVINE

Old Town Irvine stands today as a testament to the rich agricultural past of what has become one of California's most heavily urban counties. Founded in 1887 as the distribution and storage center of the 125,000-acre Irvine ranch, Old Town Irvine was to develop over the years a bean and grain storage warehouse (1895) and granary (1947) known as the Irvine Bean and Grain Grower's Building, a blacksmith's shop (1916), a hotel (1913), a general store (1911), and an employees' bungalow (1915). All of these structures have been rehabilitated for commercial uses and their exteriors have been painstakingly maintained.

Sand Canyon Ave and Burt Rd, Irvine

NO. 1015 🔔

RICHARD NIXON BIRTHPLACE

In 1912 Frank and Hannah Nixon built this modest farmhouse on their small citrus ranch. Here Richard Nixon was born, January 9, 1913, and spent his first nine years. He served his country as Congressman, U.S. Senator, Vice President, and 37th President of the United States (1969-1974). He was the first native-born Californian to hold the Presidency. President Nixon achieved significant advances in International Diplomacy by ending U.S. involvement in the Vietnam War, opening lines of communication with China and the Soviet Union, and initiating the Middle East Peace process.

18061 Yorbe Linda Blvd, Yorba Linda

Placer County

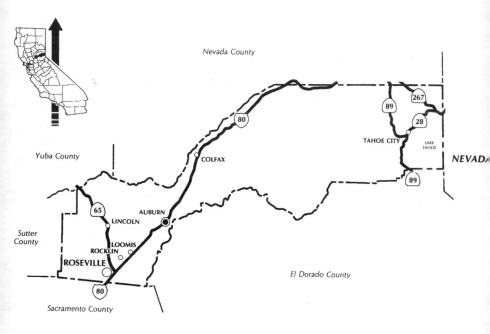

Nevada County

Yuba County

Sutter
County

Sacramento County

El Dorado County

NEVADA

TAHOE CITY

LAKE
TAHOE

COLFAX

AUBURN

LINCOLN

LOOMIS

ROCKLIN

ROSEVILLE

80

65

80

89

89

28

267

Donner Memorial State Park - Memorializes 1840-50 emigrants. Located 2.6 miles W of Truckee, off I-80.

Placer
Est. 1851

Placer is a Spanish word describing surface mining. Gold that had been "placed" in streams or on the ground through natural erosion was processed by panning, rocking, and similar techniques. Such mining efforts made Placer County residents some of the richest in California.

NO. 397 🔔 🪓
TOWN OF DUTCH FLAT

Founded in the spring of 1851 by Joseph and Charles Dornback, from 1854 to 1882 Dutch Flat was noted for its rich hydraulic mines. In 1860 it had the largest voting population in Placer County; Chinese inhabitants numbered about 2,000. Here Theodore Judah and D. W. Strong made the original subscription to build the first transcontinental railroad.

NE corner of Main and Stockton Sts, Dutch Flat

NO. 398 🔔 🪓
YANKEE JIM'S

Gold was discovered here in 1850 by "Yankee Jim," a reputed lawless character, and by 1857 the town was one of the most important in Placer County. The first mining ditch in the county was constructed here by H. Starr and Eugene Phelps. Colonel William McClure introduced hydraulic mining to this area in June of 1853.

SE corner of Colfax Foresthill and Springs Garden Rds, 3.0 mi NE of Forest Hill

NO. 399 🔔 🪓
TOWN OF FOREST HILL

Gold was discovered here in 1850, the same year the first "forest house" was built. In 1852 the Jenny Lind Mine, which produced over a million dollars in gold, was discovered. Mines in this immediate vicinity produced over ten million dollars up to 1868. The town was an important trading post and was famed for its beautiful forest.

24540 Main St, Forest Hill

NO. 400 🔔 🪓
VIRGINIATOWN

Founded June 1851, the town was commonly called "Virginia." Over 2,000 miners worked rich deposits here. In 1852 Captain John Brislow built California's first railroad to carry pay dirt one mile, to Auburn Ravine. It was the site of Philip Armour's and George Aldrich's butcher shop, said to have led to founding of the famous Chicago Armour meatpacking company.

4725 Virginiatown Rd, 0.2 mi SE of Fowler and Virginiatown Rds, 7 mi NW of Newcastle

NO. 401 🔔 🏚

IOWA HILL

Gold was discovered here in 1853, and by 1856 weekly production was estimated at one hundred thousand dollars. The total value of gold produced up to 1880 is placed at twenty million dollars. The town was destroyed by fire in 1857 and again in 1862; each time it was rebuilt with more substantial buildings, but the last big fire, in 1922, destroyed most of the town.

0.1 mi SW of post office on Iowa Hill Rd, Iowa Hill

NO. 402 🔔 🏚

TOWN OF MICHIGAN BLUFF

Founded in 1850 and first known as Michigan City, the town was located on the slope one-half mile from here. Leland Stanford, who gained wealth and fame in California, operated a store in Michigan City from 1853 to 1855. In 1858 the town became undermined and unsafe so it was moved to this location and renamed Michigan Bluff.

Intersection of Gorman Ranch and Auburn-Foresthill Rds, Michigan Bluff

NO. 403 🔔

EMIGRANT GAP

The spring of 1845 saw the first covered wagons surmount the Sierra Nevada. They left the valley, ascended to the ridge, and turned westward to old Emigrant Gap, where they were lowered by ropes to the floor of Bear Valley. Hundreds followed before, during, and after the gold rush. This was a hazardous portion of the overland emigrant trail.

Emigrant Gap Vista Pt, Interstate 80 (P.M. 55.5), Emigrant Gap

NO. 404 🔔 🏚

CITY OF AUBURN

Gold was discovered near here by Claude Chana on May 16, 1848. First known as "North Fork" or "Woods Dry Diggins," the settlement was given the name Auburn in the fall of 1849. It soon became an important mining town, trading post, and stage terminal, and also became the county seat of Sutter County in 1850 and of Placer County in 1851. It was destroyed by fires in 1855, 1859, and 1863.

SW corner of Maple St and Lincoln Way, Auburn

NO. 405 🔔 🏚

TOWN OF GOLD RUN

Originally called Mountain Springs, Gold Run was founded in 1854 by O. W. Hollenbeck. It was famed for its hydraulic mines, which from 1865 to 1878 shipped $6,125,000 in gold. Five water ditches passed through the town to serve the mining companies, but they had to cease operations in 1882 when a court decision made hydraulic mining unprofitable.

NW corner of I-80 and Magra Rd; plaque across the street from post office, Gold Run

NO. 463 🔔 🏚

OPHIR

Founded in 1849 as "The Spanish Corral," Ophir received its Biblical name in 1850 because of its rich placers. The most populous town in Placer County in 1852, polling 500 votes, Ophir was almost totally destroyed by fire in July 1853 but later became the center of quartz mining in the county.

SW corner of Lozanos and Bald Hill Rds, 3 mi W of Auburn

NO. 585

PIONEER EXPRESS TRAIL

Between 1849 and 1854, Pioneer Express riders rode this gold rush trail to the many populous mining camps on the American River bars now covered by Folsom Lake–Beals, Condemned, Dotons, Long, Horseshoe, Rattlesnake, and Oregon–on the route to Auburn and beyond.

Folsom Lake State Recreation Area, Beals Point unit, 0.3 mi N on levee; plaque on riding trail, Folsom

NO. 724

PIONEER SKI AREA OF AMERICA, SQUAW VALLEY

The VIII Olympic Winter Games of 1960 commemorated a century of sport skiing in California. By 1860 the Sierra Nevada–particularly at the mining towns of Whiskey Diggings, Poker Flat, Port Wine, Onion Valley, La Porte, and Johnsville, some 60 miles north of Squaw Valley–saw the first organized ski clubs and competition in the western hemisphere.

Squaw Valley Sports Center, Squaw Valley Rd, Squaw Valley

NO. 780-1

FIRST TRANSCONTINENTAL RAILROAD–ROSEVILLE

Central Pacific graders arrived at Junction on November 23, 1863, and when track reached there on April 25, 1864, trains began making the 18-mile run to and from Sacramento daily. The new line crossed a line reaching northward from Folsom that the California Central had begun in 1858 and abandoned in 1868.

Junction, now called Roseville, became a major railroad distribution center.

Old Town Roseville, intersection of Lincoln and Pacific Sts, Roseville

NO. 780-2

FIRST TRANSCONTINENTAL RAILROAD–ROCKLIN

Central Pacific reached Rocklin, 22 miles from its Sacramento terminus, in May 1864, when the railroad established a major locomotive terminal here. Trains moving over the Sierra were generally cut in two sections at this point in order to ascend the grade. The first CP freight movement was three carloads of Rocklin granite pulled by the engine Governor Stanford. The terminal was moved to Roseville April 18, 1908.

SE corner of Rocklin Rd and First St, Rocklin

NO. 780-3

FIRST TRANSCONTINENTAL RAILROAD–NEWCASTLE

Regular freight and passenger trains began operating over the first 31 miles of Central Pacific's line to Newcastle on June 10, 1864, when political opposition and lack of money stopped further construction during that mild winter. Construction was resumed in April 1865. At this point, stagecoaches transferred passengers from the Dutch Flat Wagon Road.

SW corner of Main and Page Sts, Newcastle

NO. 780-4 🔔

FIRST TRANSCONTINENTAL RAILROAD–AUBURN

After an 11-month delay due to political opposition and lack of money, Central Pacific tracks reached Auburn May 13, 1865, and regular service began. Government loans became available when the railroad completed its first 40 miles, four miles east of here. With the new funds, Central Pacific augmented its forces with the first Chinese laborers, and work began again in earnest.

639 Lincoln Way, Auburn

NO. 780-5 🔔

FIRST TRANSCONTINENTAL RAILROAD–COLFAX

Central Pacific rails reached Illinois-town on September 1, 1865, and train service began four days later. Renamed by Governor Stanford in honor of Schuyler Colfax, Speaker of the House of Representatives and later Ulysses S. Grant's Vice President, the town was for ten months a vital construction supply depot and junction point for stage lines. The real assault on the Sierra began here.

Red Caboose Museum, NE corner of Main and Grass Valley Sts, Colfax

NO. 797 🔔

LAKE TAHOE OUTLET GATES

Conflicting control of these gates, first built in 1870, resulted in the two-decade "Tahoe Water War" between lakeshore owners and downstream Truckee River water users. The dispute was settled in 1910-11 when techniques for determining water content in snow, developed by Dr. James E. Church, Jr., made possible the accurate prediction and control of the seasonal rise in lake and river levels.

73 N Lake Blvd (Hwy 89), at SW corner of Truckee River Bridge, Tahoe City

NO. 799-2 🔔

OVERLAND EMIGRANT TRAIL

Over a hundred years ago, this trail resounded to creaking wheels of pioneer wagons and the cries of hardy travelers on their way to the gold fields. It is estimated that over thirty thousand people used this trail in 1849. Rocks near this site still bear the marks of wagon wheels. For those early travelers, the next ordeal was a tortuous descent into Bear Valley.

Big Bend Ranger Station, 2008 Hampshire Rocks Rd (old Hwy 40), 8 mi W of Soda Springs

NO. 885 🔔

GRIFFITH QUARRY

Established in the fall of 1864 by Mr. Griffith Griffith, a native of Wales, the quarry located near this site supplied high-quality granite for a number of the important buildings in San Francisco and Sacramento, including portions of the state capitol. This was also the site of the state's first successful commercial granite polishing mill, erected in 1874.

SE corner of Taylor and Rock Springs Rds, Penryn

Landmark No. 780-2

Landmark No. 797

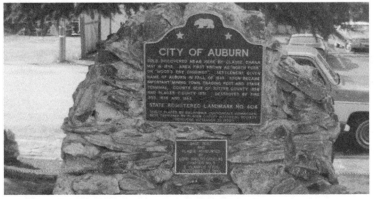

Landmark No. 404

Plumas County

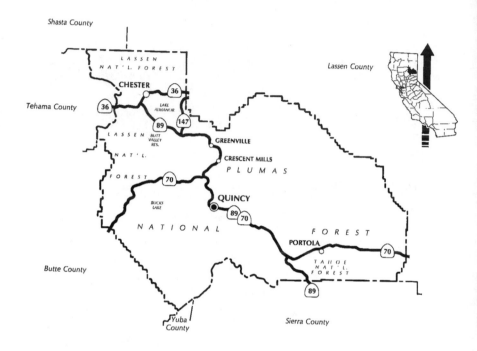

Plumas-Eureka State Park - Early mine and stamp mill. Located 5 miles W of Blairsden.

Plumas
Est. 1854

El Río de las Plumas, "the river of feathers," lends its name to Plumas County. Captain Luís Argüello named the river, having been impressed by the many floating feathers on the water. Plumas County also contains Beckwourth Pass, the lowest summit of the High Sierra, which quickly became a favorite route of wagon trains.

NO. 184 ☐
PETER LASSEN MARKER (SITE OF LASSEN TRADING POST)

In the summer of 1850, Lassen and a companion, Isidore Meyerwitz, went to Indian Valley and selected a suitable location for a ranch, where they erected a log cabin in 1851 to house their trading post. In 1855 Lassen moved to Honey Lake Valley, Lassen County, where he resided as a miner and farmer until he was killed from ambush while prospecting in 1859.

On North Valley Rd, 4.5 mi E of Greenville

NO. 196 🔔
JAMISON CITY, EUREKA MILLS, JOHNSTOWN, AND THE FAMOUS EUREKA MINE

Along the Pioneer Trail lies Jamison City and mine, large producer and famous for its 52-pound nugget. Eureka Mill and mine yielded $17 million to Cornish miners and others. Johnstown, now Johnsville, is a well-preserved '49er town.

Plumas-Eureka State Park, from Hwy 70, go S on State Hwy 89, then W on County Road A14, 5 mi SW of Blairsden

NO. 197 ☐
BUCK'S LAKE

This was the site of a ranch established by Horace Bucklin and Francis Walker in 1850. Later came a large hotel, post office, and express office. The site is now inundated by Buck's Dam and Reservoir.

Buck's Lake Lodge Marina, Buck's Lake Rd, 15.7 mi W of Quincy via Buck's Lake Rd W

NO. 212 ☐
PIONEER GRAVE (GRIZZLY CREEK)

The legend, as told by the pioneers: "The lad was returning to Marysville from a trip to the mines; he, having packed a trainload of provisions to the mines, was returning with gold dust. He was murdered and robbed. Later a comrade carved his name, age, etc., on a tree. P. Linthiouh, died September, 1852, age 19."

On Buck's Lake Rd, 3.5 mi W of Buck's Lake, 19.2 mi W of Quincy

NO. 213 ☐
RABBIT CREEK HOTEL MONUMENT

La Porte, first known as Rabbit Creek, was one of the most important settlements in the southern part of Plumas County. In the fall of 1852, Eli S. Lester built the Rabbit Creek Hotel, the first house in town.

SW corner of Main and Church Sts, La Porte

NO. 231 □

ELIZABETHTOWN

Tate's Ravine was named in the spring of 1852, when Alex and Frank Tate discovered gold there. Lewis Stark and his family came across the plains to settle here in September 1852. A very rich mine was opened up and the place grew in population. Soon the miners wanted a new name for the settlement, so they called it Elizabethtown in honor of Stark's daughter, the village's only unmarried woman.

On dirt rd, 0.4 mi NW of State Hwy 70 (P.M. 41.6), 1.8 mi N of Quincy

NO. 336 □

BECKWOURTH PASS

Beckwourth Pass, at an elevation of 5,221 feet, the lowest pass in the Sierra Nevada, was discovered in 1851 by James P. Beckwourth. The monument is dedicated to the discoverer and to the pioneers who passed along this trail.

Roadside rest area, Beckwourth 's Pass, State Hwy 70 (P.M. 95.8), 1.5 mi E of Chilcoot

NO. 337 🔔

RICH BAR

Gold was first found here in July 1850 by miners coming over the mountains from the Yuba Diggins, and there was much production during early 1850s along this east branch of the Feather River's north fork. Here "Dame Shirley" (Louise Amelia Knapp Smith Clappe) wrote her Letters From the California Mines, one of the classics of the gold rush.

Rich Bar, on State Hwy 70 (P.M. 18.8), 4 mi SE of Belden, 23.6 mi NW of Quincy

NO. 479

SITE OF AMERICAN RANCH AND HOTEL

James H. Bradley in 1854 built the American Hotel, the first sawed-lumber house in Quincy. On March 18, 1854, three commissioners met there to form a new county from a portion of Butte County, and the hotel became the county seat of Plumas County until a more suitable location could be found. Plumas Lodge No. 60, F. & A.M., instituted May 1, 1854, met in an upstairs room in the hotel until their new Quincy temple was completed in 1855.

355 Main St, Quincy

NO. 480

SITE OF PLUMAS HOUSE

The first and second Plumas Houses were built on this site. The second was built in 1866 by James and Jane Edwards. This hotel, the center of Quincy's social and business life for more than thirty years, burned to the ground on June 23, 1923.

SW corner of Main and Court Sts, Quincy

NO. 481 □

SPANISH RANCH AND MEADOW VALLEY

Miners going to the East Branch, Middle Fork, or North Fork of the Feather River separated at Spanish Rancho, established in July 1850 by two Spaniards, and at Meadow Valley, 2.5 miles from Spanish Ranch.

On Spanish Ranch side rd, Buck's Lake Rd, 5.8 mi W of Quincy

NO. 625 □

PIONEER SCHOOLHOUSE

In 1857 the residents of the eastern end of American Valley built a school, the first schoolhouse in Plumas County. On July 2, 1857, Mr. S. A. Ballou was engaged as teacher for 19 children. The building is now used for kindergarten purposes (1957).

Plumas Co Fairgrounds, 2 mi E of Quincy via E Main St and Fairgrounds Rd

NO. 723 🔔

PIONEER SKI AREA OF AMERICA, JOHNSVILLE

The first sport ski area in the western hemisphere was in the Sierra Nevada, and by 1860 races were being held in the Plumas-Sierra region. The mining towns of Whiskey Diggings, Poker Flat, Port Wine, Onion Valley, La Porte, Jamison City, and Johnsville organized the earliest ski clubs and annual competitions.

Plumas-Eureka State Park, from Hwy 70 go S on State Hwy 89, then W on County Road A14, 5 mi SW of Blairsden

Landmark No. 337

Landmark No. 196

Riverside County

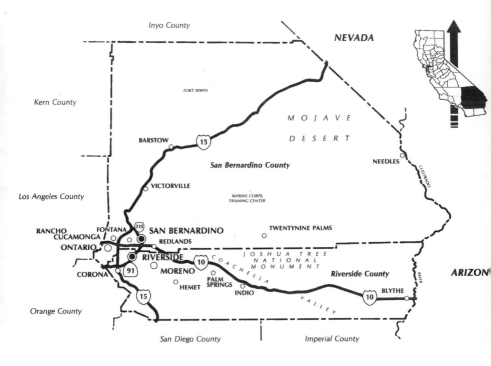

California Citrus State Historic Park - Commemorates citrus industry. Located at 9400 Dufferin Avenue in Riverside.

Riverside
Est. 1893

U nsolved mysteries of ancient Indian history pervade this county which encompasses much of the Mojave Desert to the border of Nevada. Modern tribes have no lore explaining the rich drawings, carvings and writings of the area. Some say the Aztecs ventured into present day Riverside County to hunt, leaving their marks near springs and watering places. Many old trails through Riverside County made it the gateway to the California coast.

NO. 20 ☐

PARENT WASHINGTON NAVEL ORANGE TREE

The tree was introduced into the United States from Bahia, Brazil, by the U.S. Department of Agriculture in 1870. Twelve young trees were received and buds from them were propagated on sweet orange seedlings. In 1873 two of these greenhouse-grown trees, which were distributed throughout the United States, were sent to Mrs. Eliza Tibbets in Riverside.

City Park, SW corner of Magnolia and Arlington Sts, Riverside

NO. 101 ▲

GIANT DESERT FIGURES

Times of origin and meaning of these giant figures, the largest of which is 167 feet long and the smallest 95 feet, remain a mystery. There are three figures, two of animals and one of a coiled serpent, and some interesting lines. (Sandstone pebbles glazed on one side with "desert varnish," strewn over the surface of the mesa, have been moved away, leaving the earth forming the figures; the pebbles were placed in windrows about the edge as an outline.)

On Hwy 95 (P.M. 15.3), 16 mi N of Blythe

NO. 102

SITE OF LOUIS RUBIDOUX HOUSE

In 1844 Louis Rubidoux arrived in California with his family and, shortly thereafter, purchased the Jurupa Rancho. He became one of the most prosperous stock raisers in Southern California, and also planted orchards and vineyards, raised grain, built the first grist mill in the area, and operated a winery.

5575 block, Mission Blvd, Rubidoux

NO. 103 ☐

SITE OF DE ANZA CAMP, MARCH 1774

On March 16, 1774, Juan Bautista de Anza, explorer and colonizer, led the first non-Indian explorers to cross the mountains into California through this pass (named by him San Carlos) on their way from Tubac, Arizona to Monterey. On December 27, 1775, on a second expedition into California, Anza led through this pass the party of Spaniards from Sonora who became the founders of San Francisco.

On Cary Ranch 60901 Coyote Canyon Rd, 7 mi SW of Anza

NO. 104 🔔

SITE OF INDIAN VILLAGE OF POCHEA

Pochea was one of a cluster of Indian villages forming the very large settlement of Pahsitnah, which extended along the ridge east and west of Ramona Bowl. Pahsitnah was thriving when the Spanish first passed by in 1774. A tragic story tells of the natives contracting smallpox from Europeans, a terrible epidemic spreading, and some survivors fleeing to the area of the present Soboba Reservation.

Ramona Bowl, 27400 S Girard St, Hemet, plaque located near restrooms

NO. 185 Ⓜ

SERRANO BOULDER

As early as 1818, Don Leandro Serrano had cattle, sheep, cultivated land, and orchards in Temescal Valley. The boulder placed by residents of Temescal Valley marks the site of the first house in Riverside County, erected by Leandro Serrano about May 1824.

From I-15, take Old Temescal Canyon Rd S 0.4 mi to Lawson Rd, then go W 0.2 mi to dirt rd, then S 0.1 mi to site, 9 mi S of Corona

NO. 186 🔔

SERRANO TANNING VATS

Nearby, two vats were built in 1819 by the Luiseño Indians under the direction of Leandro Serrano, first non-Indian settler in what is now Riverside County. The vats were used in making leather from cow hides. In 1981 the vats were restored and placed here by the Billy Holcomb Chapter of E Clampus Vitus.

NW corner of I-15 and Old Temescal Rd, 8 mi SE of Corona

NO. 187

CARVED ROCK

The petroglyphs were carved by the Luiseño Indians; their meaning is said to be: "A chief died here. These are his plumes, his portrait, his sign, and the animals sacred to him." The Luiseño Indians who lived in Temescal Valley belonged to the Shoshoean linguistic group. The rock has been damaged by vandals.

In canyon, 0.4 mi N of I-15 (P.M. 32.5), 8 mi S of Corona

NO. 188 ☐

BUTTERFIELD STAGE STATION

Site of Butterfield Stage Station where mail was delivered and horses changed. The first stage carrying overland mail left Tipton, Missouri on September 15, 1858 and, passing through Temescal, arrived in Los Angeles October 7, 1858.

20730 Temescal Canyon Rd, 7 mi S of Corona

NO. 190 ☐

PAINTED ROCK

In tribute to the earliest record of any people in this region, the Santa Fe Railway has preserved this rock with its ancient pictograph, and the Committee of the Corona Women's Improvement Club has placed this tablet.

From Temescal Canyon Rd, go 0.1 mi NE on Dawson Canyon Rd, then go 0.1 mi E on Gravel Pit Rd, then 0.2 mi S along railroad track berm; site is 50 ft W of berm, 7 mi S of Corona

NO. 224 ☐

RUINS OF THIRD SERRANO ADOBE

Don Leandro Serrano set out orchards and vineyards and cultivated some of the fertile lands of the Temescal Valley. In the 1840s he built his third adobe, which the Serrano family occupied until 1898, on the well-traveled road between San Diego and Los Angeles.

NE corner of I-15 and Old Temescal Road, 8 mi SE of Corona

NO. 303 Ⓜ

SITE OF OLD RUBIDOUX GRIST MILL

One of the first grist mills in this part of Southern California was built by Louis Rubidoux on the Rancho Jurupa in 1846-47. Then the only mill there of its kind, it supplied a great need. Louis Rubidoux, a pioneer builder, was one of the first permanent American citizens in the valley.

5540 Molina Way, Rubidoux

NO. 557 🔔

HEMET MAZE STONE

This pictograph, representing a maze, is an outstanding example of the work of prehistoric peoples. It, with 5.75 acres of land, was donated to Riverside County as a county park on April 16, 1956 by Mr. and Mrs. Rodger E. Miller.

From State Hwy 74, go N 3.2 mi on California Ave to Maze Stone Park, Hemet

NO. 638 🔔

OLD TEMESCAL ROAD

This route was used by Luiseño and Gabrieleno Indians, whose villages were nearby. Leandro Serrano established a home here in 1820. Jackson and Warner traveled the road in 1831, and Frémont in 1848. It was the southern emigrant road for gold seekers from 1849 to 1851, the Overland Mail route from 1858 to 1861, and a military road between Los Angeles and San Diego from 1861 to 1865.

On Old Hwy 71, 0.9 mi S of I-15 and Temescal Canyon Rd interchange, 11 mi S of Corona

NO. 738 ☐

CORONA FOUNDERS MONUMENT

R. B. Taylor, George L. Joy, Samuel Merrill, A. S. Garretson, and Adolph Rimpau, after purchasing lands of La Sierra Rancho and El Temescal grant, founded the citrus colony and town of Corona on May 4, 1886.

Corona City Park, 100 block of 6th St (Hwy 71), Corona

NO. 749 🔔

SAAHATPA

Chief Juan Antonio and his band of Cahuilla Indians helped white settlers in the San Bernardino area defend their property and livestock against outlaws during the 1840s and 1850s. In late 1851, Juan Antonio, his warriors and their families, settled at nearby Saahatpa. During the winter of 1862-63, a smallpox epidemic swept through Southern California killing many Native Americans, including Juan Antonio. Cahuilla tradition asserts that the U.S. Government sent Army blankets that were contaminated with smallpox. After this disaster, Saahatpa was abandoned.

Brookside Rest Area, W-bound I-10, 3 mi W of junction of I-10 and Hwy 60

NO. 761 🔔

MISSION INN

Frank A. Miller (1857-1935) made the adobe bricks for a small 12-room guest house that he opened in 1876. Over the years he added to the building to create this remarkable Mission Revival style building.

7th between Main and Orange, Riverside

NO. 787 ☐

DE ANZA CROSSING OF THE SANTA ANA RIVER, 1775 AND 1776

On January 1, 1776, the first party of colonists to come overland to the Pacific Coast crossed the Santa Ana River south of this marker and camped between here and the river. Recruited in the presidios of Sonora, Mexico and led by Lieutenant Colonel Juan Bautista de Anza, who had established the trail a year earlier, this humble and heroic band of 242 men, women, and children continued north to found San Francisco, thus setting a boundary to Russian expansion from the north. Prior to the opening of de Anza's trail, three precarious missions were maintained by uncertain ocean voyages; the flourishing missions and ranchos of Spanish California sprang from the droves of cattle, sheep, and horses brought over the trail.

Site is near Union Pacific Bridge, Jurupa Heights; plaque is located between clubhouse and No. 1 tee, Jurupa Hills Country Club Golf Course, 6161 Moraga Ave, Riverside

NO. 943 🔔

CORNELIUS AND MERCEDES JENSON RANCH

Danish sea captain Cornelius Jensen sailed to San Francisco during the Gold Rush to sell his cargo. In 1854 he settled in Agua Mansa, established a store, and married Mercedes Alvarado, a descendant of a pioneer Californio family. The Jensens purchased this ranch in 1865 and began planting vineyards and orchards. They used local materials to build their house which is of Danish vernacular design. The Jensens made this ranch an important civic, social, business, and agricultural center.

4350 Riverview Dr, Rubidoux

NO. 948 🔔

SITE OF BLYTHE INTAKE

On July 17, 1877, Thomas Blythe, a San Francisco financier, filed the first legal claim for Colorado River water rights. Oliver Callaway planned a diversion dam and canal which opened in 1877 to irrigate the Palo Verde Valley. This made possible the settlement and development of the valley.

Intake Service, on US. Hwy 95, 4.5 mi N of Blythe at entrance to Palo Verde Diversion Dam

NO. 985 🔔

DESERT TRAINING CENTER, CALIFORNIA-ARIZONA MANEUVER AREA (ESTABLISHED BY MAJOR GENERAL GEORGE S. PATTON, JR.) – CAMP YOUNG

The D.T.C. was established by Major General George S. Patton, Jr., in response to a need to train American combat troops for battle in North Africa during World War II. The camp, which began operation in 1942, covered 18,000 square miles. It was the largest military training ground ever to exist. Over one million men were trained at the eleven sub-camps (seven in California).

General Patton Memorial Museum, Chiriaco Summit, from Interstate 10 exit N at Chiriaco Summit, 28 mi E of Indio

NO. 985 ☐

DESERT TRAINING CENTER, CALIFORNIA-ARIZONA MANEUVER AREA (ESTABLISHED BY MAJOR GENERAL GEORGE S. PATTON, JR.) – CAMP COXCOMB

Camp Coxcomb was established at this site in the Spring of 1942. It was one of twelve such camps built in the southwestern desert to harden and train United States troops for service on the battlefields of World War II. The Desert Training Center was a simulated theater of operations that included portions of California, Arizona and Nevada. The other camps were Young, Granite, Iron Mountain, Ibis, Clipper, Pilot Knob, Laguna, Horn, Hyder, Bouse and Rice. A total of 13 infantry divisions and 7 armored divisions plus numerous smaller units were trained in this harsh environment. The Training Center was in operation for almost 2 years and was closed early in 1944 when the last units were shipped overseas. During the brief period of operation over one million American soldiers were trained for combat.

45 mi E of Indio on I-10, exit at Desert Center and go 18 mi N on SR 177

NO. 985 ☐

DESERT TRAINING CENTER, CALIFORNIA-ARIZONA MANEUVER AREA (ESTABLISHED BY MAJOR GENERAL GEORGE S. PATTON, JR.) – CAMP GRANITE

Camp Granite was established at this site in the Spring of 1942. See previous entry for full description.

45 mi E of Indio on I-10, N on Hwy 177 approx 25 mi, rt on Hwy 62 for 5.4 mi

NO. 989 🔔
SOVIET TRANSPOLAR LANDING SITE

Three miles west of this site, on July 14, 1937, three Soviet aviators completed a transpolar flight from Moscow in 62 hours, 17 minutes, establishing a new world's nonstop distance record of 6,305 miles. The huge single-engine aircraft, an Ant-25 Military Reconnaissance Monoplane, was shipped back to the Soviet Union and placed in a museum. Aircraft commander Mikhail Gromov, co-pilot Andrei Yumashev and navigator Sergei Danilin became generals in World War II.

Near intersection of Cottonwood and Sanderson Sts, W of San Jacinto

NO. 992 🔔
SITE OF CONTRACTOR'S GENERAL HOSPITAL

In 1933, Dr. Sidney R. Garfield opened Contractor's General Hospital six miles west of here. His modest facility successfully delivered health care to Colorado River Aqueduct workers through a prepaid insurance plan. Later, in association with industrialist Henry J. Kaiser, Dr. Garfield applied the lessons he first learned at the hospital to create his enduring legacy: Kaiser Permanente, the nation's largest nonprofit prepaid health care program.

Next to post office, Ragsdale Rd, Desert Center

NO. 1005
SANTA ROSA RANCHO

Located on the Santa Rosa Plateau Preserve, the historical site of the Santa Rosa Rancho is a prime example of various historical phases of cattle ranching in Southern California. Archeological evidence gathered from the site indicates that various bands of Luiseño Indians established village and religious sites on the land. No other historic rancho site in Southern California retains so much of its original setting undisturbed.

22115 Tenaja Rd, intersection Clinton Keith Rd and Tenaja Rd, Murieta

NO. 1009 🔔
RAMONA BOWL, SITE OF THE RAMONA PAGEANT

Within this valley was laid part of the scene, and here resided a number of the characters portrayed in Helen Hunt Jackson's historical novel, "Ramona," which depicted life and presented the status of the Indians on many great ranchos in early California beginning around the 1850s. The story, dramatized by the late Garnet Holme, was first presented on this site April 13, 1923, becoming an annual event.

27400 Ramona Bowl Rd, Hemet

Landmark No. 101

Landmark No. 943

Sacramento County

California State Capitol Museum - Restored main wing of capitol, 1906 vintage rooms. Located in Capitol Park, Sacramento.

California State Railroad Museum - Historic railroad equipment, exhibits, and programs. Located at 125 "I" Street, Old Sacramento.

Folsom Powerhouse State Historic Park - Supplied 11,000 volts to Sacramento in 1895. Located in Folsom.

Governor's Mansion State Historic Park - Home of 13 governors of California. Located at 16th and H Streets, Sacramento.

Leland Stanford Mansion State Historic Park - Governor Stanford's Sacramento residence. Located at 800 "N" Street, Sacramento.

Old Sacramento State Historic Park - Gateway to the mines, and starting point of the Central Pacific Railroad. Located in Sacramento.

State Indian Museum - Outstanding collection of Indian artifacts. Located at 2618 K Street, Sacramento.

Sutter's Fort State Historic Park - Founded by Captain John H. Sutter in 1839. Located at 27th and L Streets, Sacramento.

Sacramento
Est. 1850

The region where the Sacramento and American Rivers converge has seen humanity converge in the pageant of history. From the establishment of Sutter's Fort, which welcomed tired and hungry overland emigrants, to the Gold Rush of Forty-niners outfitting themselves with pick, pan, and shovel, to the building of the western terminus of the Transcontinental Railroad, Sacramento County has fostered events of worldwide magnitude.

NO. 366 ☐
PIONEER TELEGRAPH STATION

Erroneously called the Pony Express Terminal, this was the location of the office occupied by the State Telegraph Company, 1863-1868, and the Western Union Telegraph Company, 1868-1915.

1015–2nd St, Old Sacramento, Sacramento

NO. 439 Ⓜ
SITE OF GRIST MILL BUILT BY JARED DIXON SHELDON, 1846-47

Jared Dixon (Joaquin) Sheldon built his grist mill on Omochumnes Rancho, granted to him by the Mexican government in 1823. Born in Vermont on January 8, 1813, Sheldon came to California in 1832. He was shot July 11,1851 in a quarrel over a dam he had built that flooded miners' claims.

On the W side of Meiss Rd, 0.9 mi SW of Sloughhouse

NO. 464 🔔 🚫
PRAIRIE CITY

Site of Prairie City, mining town and center of trade in California's gold rush days. In July 1853, at the height of its prosperity, Prairie City included 15 stores and 10 boarding houses and hotels; two stage lines operated daily. A quartz mill that cost $50,000 to build operated here in the 1850s.

NE corner of Prairie City Rd, 500 ft N of State Hwy 50.

NO. 468 Ⓜ 🚫
MICHIGAN BAR

Now practically obliterated by hydraulic and dredging operations, the booming town of Michigan Bar once contained 1,500 population. Gold was discovered here in 1849 by citizens of Michigan, after whom the settlement was named. Pottery works, once largest in the state, were located here, and town contained a post office and Wells Fargo agency.

State Hwy 16, (P.M. 22.4) 0.1 mi E of Michigan Bar Rd

NO. 525 🔔
SUTTER'S FORT

John Augustus Sutter, born of Swiss parents in Germany, arrived in New York in July 1834 and in California in July 1839. He founded the fort in 1839 to protect "New Helvetia," his 76-square-mile Mexican land grant. Of the original fort, the two-story central building, made of adobe and oak, remains; the fort's outer walls and rooms, which had disappeared by the 1860s, were reconstructed after the State acquired the property in 1890.

Sutter's Fort State Historic Park, 27th and L Sts, Sacramento

NO. 526 🔔
CALIFORNIA'S FIRST PASSENGER RAILROAD

The Sacramento Valley Railroad, running from Sacramento to Folsom, was begun at this site on February 12, 1855. The passenger terminal was located here; the turntable and freight depot were at Third and Front Streets. Completion of the railroad was celebrated at Folsom on February 22, 1856.

SW corner of 3rd and R Sts, Sacramento

NO. 558 🔔
TERMINAL OF CALIFORNIA'S FIRST PASSENGER RAILROAD

Completion of the 22-mile Sacramento Valley Railroad line from Sacramento to Folsom was celebrated here February 22, 1856 by enthusiastic residents of both cities. The new line, commenced February 12,1855, was built by noted pioneer engineer Theodore Dehone Judah.

Leidesdorff Plaza, NE corner of intersection of Reading and Sutter, Folsom

NO. 566 🔔
SACRAMENTO CITY CEMETERY

Resting place of California pioneers, this cemetery was established in 1850. Many of the victims of the cholera epidemic of that year are buried here. Included among the graves of illustrious Californians are those of John Bigler, Newton Booth, and William Irwin, Governors of California; General George Wright, hero of the Mexican War; Mark Hopkins, cobuilder of the Central Pacific Railroad; General Albert M. Winn, founder of the Native Sons of the Golden West; Hardin Bigelow, first mayor of Sacramento; William S. Hamilton, son of Alexander Hamilton; E. B. Crocker, founder of the Crocker Art Gallery; and Reverend O. C. Wheeler, organizer in 1850 of the first Baptist Church.

SW corner of Broadway and 10th Sts, Sacramento

NO. 575 🔔
SLOUGHHOUSE

Sloughhouse, prominent hotel and stage station on the road to the Amador mines, was a favorite stopping place for travelers such as Leland Stanford. Constructed in 1850 by Jared Dixon Sheldon, it was destroyed by fire in 1890 and rebuilt the same year. Many descendants of pioneers of the community of Sloughhouse, which developed near Sheldon's establishment, still live in this fertile valley of the Cosumnes.

Meiss St, across from post office, Sloughhouse

NO. 591 🔔
SUTTER'S LANDING

Captain John A. Sutter, after coming up the Sacramento River from Yerba Buena in August 1839, landed approximately two hundred feet north of here, at what was then the south bank of the American River. A short time thereafter he established a permanent camp, and later built his fort. Sutter and his men were the first non-Indian settlers within the present city limits of Sacramento.

NE corner of 28th and C Sts, in Stanford Park, Sacramento

NO. 592 ☐
NEW HELVETIA CEMETERY

This was the site of Sacramento's first cemetery, established by Captain John A. Sutter in 1849.

NE corner of Alhambra Blvd and J St, Sacramento

NO. 593 ☐
SUTTERVILLE

Sutter laid out a townsite here in 1844, about two miles below the embarcadero. In 1847, George Zins built one of the first brick structures erected in California here.

Sutterville Rd, vicinity of Land Park Dr, Sacramento

NO. 594
SITE OF CHINA SLOUGH

The site of the slough, which formerly extended from 3rd to 5th Streets and north of I Street in Sacramento, is now occupied by the Southern Pacific depot.

SP Depot, NE corner of 4th and I Sts, Sacramento

NO. 595
EAGLE THEATER

This is the site of the first building in California constructed as a theater in 1849. The theater was reconstructed in 1974.

Old Sacramento State Historic Park, 925 Front St, Sacramento

NO. 596
SITE OF HOME OF NEWTON BOOTH

This is the site of the store and home of Newton Booth, Governor of California 1871-1873 and U.S. Senator 1873-1879.

1015-17 Front St, Sacramento

NO. 597
WHAT CHEER HOUSE

The celebrated hotel was constructed on this site in 1853. State offices were located here in 1855.

SE corner of Front and K Sts, Sacramento

NO. 598
SITE OF STAGE AND RAILROAD (FIRST)

This is the site of the terminal of stages of the 1850s and of the Sacramento Valley Railroad in 1855.

Old Sacramento State Historic Park, NW corner of Front and K Sts, Sacramento

NO. 599
E. B. CROCKER ART GALLERY

This building was erected in 1870 to house the private art collection of Judge and Mrs. E. B. Crocker. The building and its contents were donated to the City of Sacramento in 1884 by Mrs. Crocker.

216 O St, Sacramento

NO. 600

HEADQUARTERS OF THE "BIG FOUR"

(This landmark number has been retired and this landmark site is now included as part of the registration of Old Sacramento, Landmark No. 812.)

Old Sacramento State Historic Park, Sacramento

NO. 601

WESTERN HOTEL

Constructed by William Land in 1875, this hotel was one of the largest in the West. It was built on sites of earlier hotels of 1853-1854.

Parking lot, 200 ft NE of intersection of 2nd and K Sts, Sacramento

NO. 602

EBNER'S HOTEL

This hotel was built by Charles Ebner in 1856. It is said that Captain Sutter was a frequent visitor here.

116 K St, Old Sacramento

NO. 603 ☐

LADY ADAMS BUILDING

This store and office building was erected in 1852 from materials brought around the Horn in the ship Lady Adams.

117-19 K St, Old Sacramento

NO. 604

SITE OF SAM BRANNAN HOUSE

This building, erected by Henry E. Robinson in 1853 on land owned by Sam Brannan, was used as the first meeting place of the Pioneer Association and other organizations of early days.

112 J St, Old Sacramento

NO. 605

SITE OF SACRAMENTO UNION

Erected in 1851, this structure was occupied by the *Sacramento Union* in 1852. The newspaper began its career March 19, 1851 at 21 J Street, Sacramento.

121 J St, Old Sacramento

NO. 606 🔔

B. F. HASTINGS BUILDING

This structure, erected in 1852-53, was occupied during the 1850s by the B. F. Hastings Bank, Wells Fargo & Co., various state officials, the Sacramento Valley Railroad, and the Alta Telegraph Co. During April 1860–May 1861, the Alta Telegraph Co. and its successor, the California State Telegraph Co., were the agents here for the Central Overland Pony Express, owned and operated by the firm of Russell, Majors, and Waddell. The first overland journey eastward of the Pony Express was begun from this historic site on April 4, 1860.

1000 2nd St, plaque located on wall at 2nd St, between J and I Sts, Old Sacramento

NO. 607

ADAMS AND COMPANY BUILDING

Erected in the fall of 1853, this building was occupied during 1853-1855 by Adams and Co.'s express and banking house. The Alta Telegraph Co., California State Telegraph Co., Pacific Express Co., California Stage Co., Sacramento City Bank, and

Wells Fargo & Co. also had offices here in the 1850s. During May-October 1861, Wells Fargo & Co. were agents here of the western portion of the Central Overland Pony Express until it was discontinued on October 26, 1861 on completion of the transcontinental telegraph.

1014–2nd St, Old Sacramento

NO. 608
SITE OF ORLEANS HOTEL
This hotel, erected in 1852, served as a depot for stage companies and others.

1018–2nd St, Old Sacramento

NO. 609
D. O. MILLS BANK BUILDING
Erected in 1852, this building housed one of the oldest and largest banks of early-day California.

100 ft from SE corner of intersection of 2nd and J Sts, Old Sacramento

NO. 610
OVERTON BUILDING
This building was constructed in 1852 and was occupied in the 1850s by various state offices and commercial companies.

Parking lot, 300 ft NE of intersection of 2nd and J Sts, Old Sacramento

NO. 611
ORIGINAL SACRAMENTO BEE BUILDING
The Sacramento Bee was founded in 1857; its first issue was dated February 3, 1857. Its early home was in this two-story brick building on the west side of Third Street.

Under N-bound offramp of I-5, W side of 3rd St between J and K Sts, Sacramento

NO. 612 □
PIONEER MUTUAL VOLUNTEER FIREHOUSE
Erected in 1854, this structure was occupied by Engine Co. No. 1, the oldest fire company of California.

200 ft NE of intersection of 3rd and J Sts, Sacramento

NO. 613
SITE OF CONGREGATIONAL CHURCH
In 1849, the Rev. Joseph A. Benton organized the first church in Sacramento.

915–6th St, Sacramento

NO. 614 🔔
STANFORD-LATHROP HOME
The house was originally designed in 1857 by Seth Babson and was purchased by Leland Stanford in 1861. It served as the state executive office from 1861 to 1867, before the completion of the State Capitol. It was later extensively remodeled and enlarged. In 1900 Jane Lathrop Stanford gave the house to the Roman Catholic Diocese of Sacramento to create the Stanford-Lathrop Memorial Home for Friendless Children.

Leland Stanford Mansion State Historic Park, 800 N St, Sacramento

NO. 633 🔔

OLD FOLSOM POWERHOUSE

In the 1850s, Horatio Gates Livermore and later his sons, Horatio P. and Charles E., pioneered the development of ditches and dams on the American River for industry and agriculture. One historic result was Folsom Powerhouse, which began operations in July 1895. Power was delivered to Sacramento at 11,000 volts, a new achievement in long-distance high-voltage transmission which the capital celebrated by a grand electric carnival September 9, 1895. The original generating plant, still in place, remained in continuous operation until 1952. The plant was donated by Pacific Gas and Electric Co. to the State of California to preserve its historical values.

Folsom Powerhouse State Park, Greenback Lane, Folsom

NO. 633-2 🔔

OLD FOLSOM POWERHOUSE– SACRAMENTO STATION A

The first distribution point of electricity for a major city, Station A was constructed in 1894 by the Sacramento Electric Power and Light Company to receive power generated from Folsom Powerhouse. The first transmission of electricity was on July 13, 1895. This power distribution network resulted in the first overhead wire streetcar system in the Central Valley.

NE corner of 6th and H Sts, Sacramento

NO. 654 🔔

SITE OF THE FIRST JEWISH SYNAGOGUE OWNED BY A CONGREGATION ON THE PACIFIC COAST

The building that stood on this site was prefabricated in Baltimore and shipped around Cape Horn in 1849. It originally housed the Methodist Episcopal Church, whose trustees sold the edifice on June 4, 1852 to Alexander Myer, Joseph Levison, and Charles Friedman, Officers of the Association of the Children of Israel (B'nai Israel), to serve as the first synagogue on the Pacific Coast, dedicated on September 3, 1852. The congregation followed the orthodox tradition until 1880, when it became an adherent of reform Judaism.

In sidewalk, 7th St between Capitol and L, Sacramento

NO. 654-1

CHEVRA KADDISHA (HOME OF PEACE CEMETERY)

This site was the first Jewish cemetery in California. On November 12, 1850, R. J. Watson gave a Deed of Trust to Louis Schaul: "Lot number four in the square between thirty-second and thirty-third and J and K Streets . . . for the Sacramento City Hebrew Association for a burial ground."

3230 J St, Sacramento

NO. 657
GRAVE OF ALEXANDER HAMILTON WILLARD

Willard, a native of New Hampshire who died March 6, 1865, was perhaps the last survivor of the exploring party sent out by President Jefferson under Captain Meriwether Lewis to discover the course and sources of the Missouri River.

Franklin Cemetery, Franklin

NO. 666 🔔
CAMP UNION, SUTTERVILLE

Organized here on October 8, 1861, the 5th Infantry Regiment, California Volunteers was trained by Brevet Brigadier General George W. Bowie for duty against Confederate forces in Arizona, New Mexico, and Texas. The troops aided the stricken capital in this year of the great flood. Company F (Sacramento Rangers), 2nd Cavalry Regiment, California Volunteers, organized in Sacramento August 29, 1861, later served here. This company furnished a large number of officers for other units of the California Volunteers.

NE corner of Sutterville and Land Park Dr, Sacramento

NO. 680 🔔
MURPHY'S RANCH

This is the site of the beginning of the United States' conquest of California. On June 10, 1846, American settlers led by Ezekial Merritt overpowered Mexican soldiers under Lieutenant Francisco Arce and took their horses from the corral of the Murphy Ranch on the north bank of the Cosumnes River. The "Bear Flag" action in Sonoma followed on June 14, 1846.

Near SW corner of Grant Line Rd and Hwy 99, Elk Grove

NO. 697 🔔
FIVE MILE HOUSE–OVERLAND PONY EXPRESS ROUTE IN CALIFORNIA

Departing at 2:45 a.m. from the Alta Telegraph Co. in Sacramento, rider Sam (Bill) Hamilton carried the first mail of the Central Overland Pony Express eastward on April 4, 1860. Quickly changing ponies at the Five Mile House, he sped on to the next stop at Fifteen Mile Station.

On campus of California State University, on Jed Smith Dr at N side of Guy West Bridge, Sacramento

NO. 698 🔔
FIFTEEN MILE HOUSE–OVERLAND PONY EXPRESS ROUTE IN CALIFORNIA

Owned and operated from 1957 as a stage station by Henry F. W. Deterding, this was the site of the second remount station of the Central Overland Pony Express during March-July 1860. Sam (Bill) Hamilton, carrying the first eastward mail of the Pony Express, changed ponies here on April 4, 1860.

On White Rock Rd, 0.2 mi E of intersection of Sunrise Blvd and White Rock Rd, Rancho Cordova

NO. 702 🔔

FOLSOM—OVERLAND PONY EXPRESS ROUTE IN CALIFORNIA

Gold rush and railroad town, Folsom became the western terminus of the Central Overland Pony Express on July 1, 1860. During its first few months, the express mail had been run by pony to and from Sacramento, but beginning July 1, 1860, the Sacramento Valley Railroad carried it between Sacramento and Folsom until Placerville was made the terminus.

819 Sutter St near Decatur, Folsom

NO. 719 🔔

GRAVE OF ELITHA CUMI DONNER WILDER

This survivor of the ill-fated Donner party was the daughter of George and Mary Blue Donner. Born near Springfield, Illinois in 1832, she arrived in California in December 1846 with her sister, Leanna Charity Donner, and was rescued by the first relief party to reach the tragic scene. Married to Benjamin W. Wilder in 1853, she died on July 4, 1923, survived by her sister and two children.

Elk Grove Masonic Cemetery, Row C; Lot 2, Elk Grove Blvd, Elk Grove

NO. 745 🔔

THE COLOMA ROAD–SUTTER'S FORT

Sutter's Fort, established by Capt. John A. Sutter in August 1839, marked the western end of the Coloma Road. Opened in 1847, this road ran from the fort to Sutter's sawmill at Coloma. Used by James W. Marshall in January 1848 to bring the

news of the gold discovery to Sutter, it was traversed later by thousands of miners going to and from the diggings. In 1849 the Coloma Road became the route of California's first stageline, established by James E. Birch.

NE corner of 28th and L Sts, Sacramento

NO. 746 🔔

THE COLOMA ROAD–NIMBUS DAM

Alder Springs, south of this point, marks the old Coloma Road, running between Sutter's Fort and Cul-luh-mah (Coloma). Established in 1847, this road was used by James W. Marshall in January 1848 to bring the first gold from Sutter's Mill to the fort. Later, traveled by thousands to and from the diggings, it became the route of California's first stageline, established in 1849 by James E. Birch.

From Hwy 50, go N on Hazel Ave, take first rd to right, plaque located in day use area, Nimbus Flat, Lake Natoma, Folsom Lake State Recreation Area

NO. 780 🔔

FIRST TRANSCONTINENTAL RAILROAD

Here, on January 8, 1863, Governor Leland Stanford turned the first spade of earth to begin construction of the Central Pacific Railroad. After more than six years of labor, crews of the Central Pacific Railroad from the west and the Union Pacific Railroad from the east met at Promontory, Utah where, on May 10, 1869, Stanford drove the gold spike signifying completion of the First Transcontinental Railroad. The Central Pacific Railroad, forerunner of the Southern Pacific Company, was planned by Theodore D. Judah and constructed largely through the efforts of the "Big Four"–Sacramento businessmen Leland Stanford, Collis P. Huntington, Charles Crocker, and Mark Hopkins.

Old Sacramento State Historic Park, Sacramento; California State Railroad Museum, rear lounge area

NO. 780-8 🔔

FIRST TRANSCONTINENTAL RAILROAD–WESTERN BASE OF THE SIERRA NEVADA

On January 12, 1864, President Abraham Lincoln decreed that the western base of the Sierra Nevada began where the Central Pacific Railroad crossed Arcade Creek. The hardships of railroad construction through mountains resulted in increased government subsidies that gave the company impetus to finish the transcontinental railroad.

Haggin Oaks Municipal Golf Course, N side of clubhouse, 3645 Fulton Ave, Sacramento

NO. 812 🔔

OLD SACRAMENTO

Founded in December 1848 by John A. Sutter, Jr., Sacramento was an outgrowth of Sutter's Fort established by his father, Captain John A. Sutter, in 1839. State capital since 1854, during the gold rush it was a major distribution point, a commercial and agricultural center, and terminus for wagon train, stagecoach, riverboat, telegraph, pony express, and the first transcontinental railroad.

Old Sacramento State Historic Park; plaque located on wall at 2nd St between J and I Sts, Sacramento

NO. 817 🔔

SITE OF FIRST COUNTY FREE LIBRARY BRANCH IN CALIFORNIA

Through the efforts of Miss Harriet G. Eddy, then principal of Elk Grove Union High School, in 1908 Elk Grove acquired the first county free library branch in California. Subsequently, California's county free library branch system has become one of the most outstanding in America.

9125 Elk Grove Blvd, Elk Grove

NO. 823 🔔

GOVERNOR'S MANSION

This mansard-styled Victorian house was built for Albert Gallatin in 1877. Acquired by the State, it served as the first official Governor's residence; Governor George C. Pardee and his family moved in during November 1903. It was home for 13 Governors over a span of 64 years.

SW corner of 16th and H Sts, Sacramento

NO. 869

SITE OF FIRST AND SECOND STATE CAPITOLS AT SACRAMENTO

Sacramento's first County Courthouse, formerly located on this site, served as California's State Capitol from January 16, 1852 to May 4, 1852 and from March 1, 1854 to May 15, 1854, when it housed the third and fifth sessions of the State Legislature.

NW corner of 7th and I Sts, Sacramento

NO. 872 🔔

CALIFORNIA'S CAPITOL COMPLEX

The historic Capitol was designed by architects M. F. Butler and Ruben Clark. Its style is an adaptation of Roman Corinthian architecture. Work began in 1860 and by late 1869 the Capitol was partly occupied. In 1874, construction ended at a cost of $2.45 million. The west wing which once housed all branches of government is now a legislative facility. Its design and construction are tributes to California's pioneer architects, craftsmen, and builders.

E of intersection of 10th St and Capitol Mall, Sacramento

NO. 900

NISIPOWINAN VILLAGE SITE

This was the location of the most significant Indian village and cemetery of this region. The Nisipowinan, part of the Maidu tribe, had a strong economic and cultural interaction with Capt. John A. Sutter's settlement in the 1840s.

Discovery Park, archery range, E end of park, NE side of I-5 and Richards Blvd, Sacramento

NO. 934

TEMPORARY DETENTION CAMPS FOR JAPANESE AMERICANS– SACRAMENTO ASSEMBLY CENTER

The temporary detention camps (also known as "assembly centers") represent the first phase of the mass incarceration of 97,785 Californians of Japanese ancestry during World War II. Pursuant to Executive Order 9066 signed by President Franklin D. Roosevelt on February 19, 1942, thirteen makeshift detention facilities were constructed at various California racetracks, fairgrounds, and labor camps. These facilities were intended to confine Japanese Americans until more permanent concentration camps, such as those at Manzanar and Tule Lake in California, could be built in isolated areas of the country. Beginning on March 30, 1942, all native-born Americans and long-time legal residents of Japanese ancestry living in California were ordered to surrender themselves for detention.

Walerga Park, NW corner of Palm Ave and College Oak Drive, Sacramento

NO. 967 🔔

CALIFORNIA ALMOND GROWERS EXCHANGE PROCESSING FACILITY

The California Almond Growers Exchange, founded in 1910, was the first successful grower-owned cooperative for marketing California almonds. It pioneered in many fields, including almond production, mechanization, and marketing. The first structure on this property was built in 1915 and was designed to mechanize almond processing. This shelling plant was one of the earliest structures of its type, and contained the world's first mechanical cracker.

1809 C St, Sacramento

NO. 991

STATE INDIAN MUSEUM

The State Indian Museum was built fifty years ago as California's first state-run museum devoted to Indian cultures. It continues to serve the same purpose today, displaying an updated (1984) major exhibit on California's Indian peoples.

2618 "K" St, Sacramento

NO. 1013 🔔

SITE OF THE FIRST AFRICAN AMERICAN EPISCOPAL CHURCH ESTABLISHED ON THE PACIFIC COAST

This is the site of the first church building associated with an African American religious congregation on the Pacific Coast. The church was the Methodist Church of Colored People of Sacramento City, formally organized in 1850. In 1851 the congregation was admitted into the African Methodist Episcopal Church, becoming the first African Methodist Episcopal Church on the Pacific Coast. First known as Bethel, the name was later changed to St. Andrews. The original 1850 wooden church building was the site of the first statewide convention of the California Colored Citizens which met November 20-22, 1855.

715 Seventh St, Sacramento

San Benito County

San Juan Bautista State Historic Park - Mission trade center, bandit headquarters. Located in San Juan Bautista.

San Benito
Est. 1874

Father Juan Crespí named San Benito Creek for "Saint Benedict" in 1772. Natural features include the Gabilan mountain range with its famous Pinnacles, the New Idria Quicksilver Mines and the San Andreas Fault, with California's largest mission church at its edge — the Mission San Juan Bautista.

NO. 179 ☐

CASTRO HOUSE

In the 1840s the Castro House was built to house General José Castro's administrative office and his secretary. In 1848 Castro sold the house to Patrick Breen, survivor of the ill-fated Donner party of 1846, and the Breen family lived here for many years.

San Juan Bautista State Historic Park, 2nd and Washington Sts, San Juan Bautista

NO. 180

PLAZA HOTEL

In 1858 Angelo Zanetta added a second story to a one-story adobe barracks built in 1813-14 for soldiers who represented the Spanish government and operated it as a hotel for many years. Because San Juan Bautista was one of the main stage stops between San Francisco and Los Angeles, the Plaza Hotel became famous throughout California.

San Juan Bautista State Historic Park, 2nd and Mariposa Sts, San Juan Bautista

NO. 181 🔔

FREMONT PEAK

On March 6, 1846, Captain John C. Frémont built a fort here on Gabilan (Gavilan) Peak (Fremont Peak). He unfurled his colors and for four days awaited the attack of a force of Californians. The battle did not materialize by the night of March 9, and Frémont broke camp and departed for Oregon.

Fremont Peak State Park, 11 mi S of Hwy 156 via San Juan Canyon Rd (Co Rd G1); plaque located in Abbey Park, SE corner of Fourth and Muckelem Sts, San Juan Bautista

NO. 195 ☐

MISSION SAN JUAN BAUTISTA AND PLAZA

Founded June 24, 1790, Mission San Juan Bautista, partly destroyed by the earthquakes of 1800 and 1906, was repeatedly restored. The two bells it now uses were salvaged from its original chime. The plaza on its south, surrounded by old adobes, has witnessed many historic scenes, including General Frémont's activities in 1846.

2nd and Mariposa Sts, San Juan Bautista

NO. 324 🔔

NEW IDRIA MINE

Named for Idria Mine in Austria, the New Idria ranks among the most famous quicksilver mines of the world. Mission fathers, before American occupation, made assays and determined the ore to be cinnabar; mining began in the 1850s, and in 1881 between two and three hundred men were employed.

Plaque located NW corner of State Hwy 25 and Panoche Rd (J1); site located on San Carlos Peak, from Paicines, 30 mi E on Panoche Rd (J1) to New Idria Rd, then 21 mi S to mine

San Bernardino County

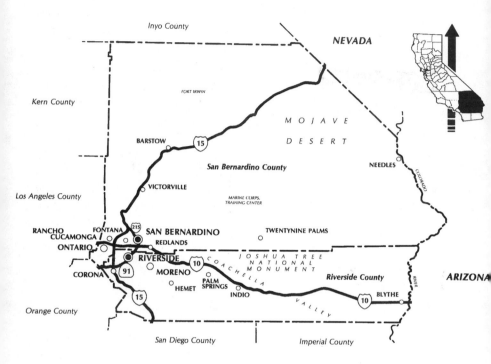

Providence Mountains State Recreation Area - Features early tourist attraction Mitchell Caverns. Located 40 miles W of Needles.

San Bernardino
Est. 1853

San Bernardino County is the largest county in the nation and indeed larger even than nine individual states. The Mojave Desert region, with its fragile, drought-adapted plants and animals occupies 90% of San Bernardino County.

NO. 42 🔔
SAN BERNARDINO ASISTENCIA

This branch of San Gabriel Mission was constructed about 1830 on the San Bernardino Rancho. During the 1840s its buildings were used by José del Carmen Lugo as part of his rancho grant. After its sale to the Mormons, it was occupied by Bishop Tenney in the 1850s and by Dr. Benjamin Barton in the 1860s. Its restoration was completed in 1937 by the Works Progress Administration, assisted by the San Bernardino County Historical Society.

26930 Barton Rd, E of Nevada St, Redlands

NO. 43 🔔
THE ZANJA

Spanish missionaries introduced the principle of irrigation in San Bernardino Valley, thus opening the way to settlement. Franciscan fathers engineered, and Indians dug, this first ditch, or "zanja," in 1819-20. It supported the San Bernardino Asistencia, the Rancho San Bernardino, then pioneer ranches and orchards and finally Redlands' domestic water supply.

Sylvan Park, University St, Redlands

NO. 44 ☐
SITE OF MORMON STOCKADE

On this site in 1839 was built the first house in San Bernardino, the home of José del Carmen Lugo, one of the grantees of the San Bernardino Rancho. In 1851 a stockade of logs was built here as a protection against the Indians; in it more than a hundred families lived for over a year.

San Bernardino County Courthouse, Arrowhead Ave and Court St, San Bernardino

NO. 95 ☐
GUACHAMA RANCHERIA

Guachama Rancheria, renamed San Bernardino on May 20, 1810 by Francisco Dumetz, became the San Bernardino Rancho of the Mission San Gabriel in 1819. The adobe administration building stood 70 yards north of this spot; an enramada served as the chapel, and a zanja was constructed to bring water from the mountains for irrigation. Control by mission fathers ended in 1834.

25894 Mission Rd, SW of high powerline towers on N side of st, Redlands

NO. 96 M

MORMON ROAD

When the Mormons came to the San Bernardino valley in 1851 they needed suitable lumber to construct their homes and stockade. To bring in lumber from the mountains they built an 11-mile wagon road that required about a thousand days' labor to complete.

Waterman Canyon, State Hwy 18 (P.M. 17.15), 0.5 mi W of Crestline

NO. 121 □

AGUA MANSA

Don Juan Bandini, owner of the Jurupa Rancho, donated parts of his rancho to a group of New Mexican colonists in 1845 on the understanding that they would aid in repelling Indian raids on his stock. The community was named Agua Mansa–Gentle Water–and was prosperous until 1862, when a great flood suddenly swept down the Santa Ana, carrying away the village of adobe buildings and covering the fields with sand and gravel. The village was rebuilt on higher ground, but never regained its former prosperity.

Agua Mansa Cemetery, 270 E Agua Mansa Rd, Colton

NO. 191 🔔

YORBA-SLAUGHTER ADOBE

This example of early California architecture was built in 1850-53 by Raimundo Yorba. Purchased in 1868 by Fenton Mercer Slaughter, it was preserved as a memorial to him by his daughter, Julia Slaughter Fuqua.

17127 Pomona-Rincon Rd, 5.5 mi S of Chino

NO. 360 🔔

TAPIA ADOBE (SITE OF)

In 1839 Governor Juan Alvarado granted the 13,000-acre tract called Cucamonga to Tiburcio Tapia, an ex-soldier who was a prominent merchant and alcalde in Los Angeles. A half-mile west of this marker Tapia, employing Indian laborers, immediately built an adobe house on a vantage point on Red Hill. The large adobe was abandoned in 1858 when Tapia's heirs sold the rancho. The adobe soon disintegrated into its native earth. This marker is located on land which once was a part of Tapia's rancho.

8916 Foothill Blvd, Cucamonga

NO. 490 □

CUCAMONGA RANCHO WINERY

Established by Tiburcio Tapia, to whom the Cucamonga Rancho was granted March 3, 1839, by Governor Juan Bautista Alvarado of Mexico.

8916 Foothill Blvd, Cucamonga

NO. 528 🔔

YUCAIPA ADOBE

Constructed in 1842 by Diego Sepúlveda, nephew of Antonio María Lugo, this is believed to be the oldest house in San Bernardino County. The land, formerly controlled by San Gabriel Mission, was part of the Rancho San Bernardino granted to the Lugos in 1842. The adobe's later owners included John Brown, Sr., James W. Waters, and the Dunlap family; it was acquired by San Bernardino County in 1955.

32183 Kentucky St, Yucaipa

NO. 573 □

SYCAMORE GROVE

Sycamore Valley ranch, formerly called Sycamore Grove, was first camp of the Mormon pioneers. Captain Jefferson Hunt, Amasa Lyman, Charles C. Rich, David Seely, and Andrew Lytle stopped here in June 1851.

Glen Helen Regional Park, 2555 Devore Rd, 0.7 mi W of Devore

NO. 576 □

SANTA FE AND SALT LAKE TRAIL MONUMENT

Erected in 1917 in honor of the brave pioneers of California who traveled the Santa Fe and Salt Lake Trail in 1849 by Sheldon Stoddard, Sydney P. Waite, John Brown, Jr., George Miller, George M. Cooley, Silas C. Cox, Richard Weir, and Jasper N. Corbett.

S end Wagon Train Rd, SE corner I-15 (P.M. 21.4) and State Hwy 138, 17 mi N of San Bernardino

NO. 577 □

MORMON TRAIL MONUMENT

In June 1851, 500 Mormon pioneers came through this pass to enter the San Bernardino Valley, where they established a prosperous community.

W Cajon Canyon, State Hwy 138 (P.M. 10. 7), 3.6 mi W of I-15, 20 mi N of San Bernardino

NO. 578 □

STODDARD-WAITE MONUMENT

This monument marks the western extension of the Santa Fe Trail traveled by Sheldon Stoddard and Sydney P. Waite in 1849.

Elsie Arey May Nature Center NW corner of I-15 (P.M. 20.0) and Cleghorn Rd, 16 mi N of San Bernardino

NO. 579 □

DALEY TOLL ROAD MONUMENT

The Daley Road, built by Edward Daley and Co. in 1870, was one of the first roads into the San Bernardino Mountains that could accommodate wagons. It was a toll road until 1890, when it became a county road. Now a Forest Service fire road, it is not open to the public.

On State Hwy 18 (P.M. 23.3), at Daley Canyon Rd, 0.6 mi E of Rim Forest

NO. 617 □

FORT BENSON

This is the site of an adobe fortification erected about 1856-57 by the "Independent" faction in a dispute with the Mormons over a land title. The fort was maintained for about a year. This also is the site of the Indian village of Jumuba, and Jedediah Smith camped here in January 1827.

10600 Hunts Lane, Colton

NO. 618 □

GARCÉS-SMITH MONUMENT

This monument marks an old Indian trail, the Mojave Trail, used by Father Garcés in March 1776 on his trip from Needles to San Gabriel. The same trail was used by Jedediah Smith in 1826 on his first trip through San Bernardino Valley.

Call San Bernardino National Forest, Cajon Ranger District, 714/887-2576 for permission to view plaque and directions

NO. 619

HOLCOMB VALLEY

Southern California's largest gold rush followed the discovery of rich placer deposits by William F. Holcomb and Ben Choteau on May 4, 1860. Miners rushed to the valley and established boom towns. Belleville, the largest, rivaled San Bernardino in population and almost became the county seat. Violence and hangings were common in this remote valley. Over time, major placer and quartz mining declined although some activity continues today. Belleville Holcomb Valley, on Rd No. 3N16, 4.3 mi NW of Big Bear City.

Plaque at Big Bear Valley Historical Society Museum in Big Bear City Park on Green Way Dr

NO. 620

YUCAIPA RANCHERIA

Yucaipa Valley supported a large population of Serrano Indians. The fertile valley was watered by springs and creeks. The Indians called this area 'Yucaipat" which meant "wet lands." These Native Americans lived at this village site most of the year, with occasional excursions to the mountains to gather acorns and other food items during the harvesting season.

32183 Kentucky St, Yucaipa

NO. 622

HARRY WADE EXIT ROUTE

After getting to Death Valley with the ill-fated 1849 caravan, Harry Wade found this exit route for his ox-drawn wagon and thereby saved his life and the lives of his wife and children. At this point the Wade party came upon the known Spanish Trail to Cajón Pass.

4 mi S of Death Valley National Monument on State Hwy 127 (P.M. 29.8), 30 mi N of Baker

NO. 717

THE ANGELES NATIONAL FOREST

The first national forest in the State of California and second in the United States, Angeles National Forest was created by proclamation of President Benjamin Harrison on December 20, 1892. The first name given to the forest, "San Gabriel Timberland Reserve," was changed to "San Gabriel National Forest" March 4, 1907 and then to "Angeles National Forest" on July 1, 1908.

San Gabriel Mtns, Clear Creek vista point, State Hwy 2 (P.M. 32.8), 8.3 mi N of I-210, La Canada

NO. 725

OLD BEAR VALLEY DAM

In 1884 Frank Brown built an unusual dam here to supply irrigation water for the Redlands area. The single-arch granite dam formed Big Bear Lake, then the world's largest man-made lake. Engineers claimed the dam would not hold, and declared it "The Eighth Wonder of the World" when it did. The old dam is usually underwater because of the 20-foot higher dam built 200 feet west in 1912.

W edge of Big Bear Lake, intersection of State Hwys 18 and 38, 4.8 mi W of Big Bear Lake Village

NO. 737 🔔
CHIMNEY ROCK

Conflicts between Indians and white settlers over the rich lands of the San Bernardino Mountains culminated in the battle at Chimney Rock on February 16, 1867. Although the Indians defended themselves fiercely, they were forced to retreat into the desert. In the years following, the Indians' traditional mountain food gathering areas were lost to white encroachment.

On State Hwy 18 (P.M. 76.9) at Rabbit Springs Rd, 3.2 mi W of Lucerne Valley

NO. 774 🔔
SEARLES LAKE BORAX DISCOVERY

John Searles discovered borax on the nearby surface of Searles Lake in 1862. With his brother Dennis, he formed the San Bernardino Borax Mining Company in 1873 and operated it until 1897. The chemicals in Searles Lake–borax, potash, soda ash, salt cake, and lithium–were deposited here by the runoff waters from melting ice-age glaciers; John Searles' discovery has proved to be the world's richest chemical storehouse, containing half the natural elements known to man.

Roadside rest area, Trona Rd at Center St, Trona

NO. 781 🔔
NATIONAL OLD TRAILS MONUMENT

An old Indian trail, still visible in some places, ran roughly parallel to the Colorado River on the California side. This is the route followed by Garcés and his Mojave guides in 1776 and by Jedediah Smith in 1826.

On shoulder of NW corner of Colorado River Bridge, North K St, Needles

NO. 782 🔔
TOWN OF CALICO

The Calico Mining District, which had a peak population of 3,000, produced between $13 and $20 million in silver and $9 million in borate minerals between 1881 and 1907. On April 6, 1881, several claims were located that formed the Silver King, largest mine in the district. Profitable mining of silver in the area ceased in 1896.

4 mi NW of I-15 on Ghost Town Rd, Yermo

NO. 859 🔔
VON SCHMIDT STATE BOUNDARY MONUMENT

This boundary monument, a cast iron column erected in 1873, marks the southern terminus of the California-Nevada State boundary established by A. W. Von Schmidt's 1872-73 survey. Von Schmidt's line, the first officially recognized oblique state line between California and Nevada, erred slightly; the boundary was later corrected to the present line, 3/4 mile to the north.

On E side of Pew Rd (River Rd), 2.6 mi S of state line, 14 mi N of Needles

NO. 892 🔔

HARVEY HOUSE

In 1893 Fred Harvey, founder and operator of the Santa Fe Harvey Houses, took over the operation of all hotel and restaurants on the Santa Fe line, including the one at Barstow (then Waterman Junction) constructed in 1885. In 1908 this Harvey House burned, and in 1910-13 the present Spanish-Moorish structure designed by architect Mary E. J. Coulter was constructed. It is the best surviving example of California's depot-hotels of the turn of the century.

Santa Fe Depot, SW corner of First Ave and Riverside Dr, plaque located at Mojave River Museum, 270 E Virginia Way, Barstow

NO. 939

Twentieth Century Folk Art Environments (Thematic)–POSSUM TROT

Calvin and Ruby Black began building Possum Trot in 1954 as an attraction for their rock shop as well as an artistic expression. Calvin carved the dolls, each representing someone important in his life, and Ruby made clothes for them. The animated displays were designed to entertain visitors.

Ghost Town Rd, 1.5 mi N of I-15, 4 mi NW of Yermo

NO. 939

Twentieth Century Folk Art Environments (Thematic)–HULA VILLE

Miles Mahan began building Hula Ville in 1955 after retiring as a "carny," or carnival worker. Over the years, he put his statues and poems together in the desert,

on Interstate 15 near Hesperia.

On Amargosa Rd, 2.0 mi W of I-15 and Phelan Rd, 6 mi NW of Hesperia

NO. 942 🔔

SITE OF THE RANCHO CHINO ADOBE OF ISAAC WILLIAMS

Near this site, Isaac Williams in 1841 built a large adobe home, located on the 22,000-acre Rancho Chino which he acquired from his father-in-law Antonio Lugo. The "Battle of Chino" occurred at the adobe on September 26-27, 1846, during which 24 Americans were captured by a group of about 50 Californios. Located on the Southern Immigrant Trail to California, the adobe later became an inn and stage stop famous for its hospitality.

Chino Fire Station No. 2, 4440 Eucalyptus Ave, one block W of State Hwy 71 and Pipeline Ave, 3 mi SW of Chino

NO. 950 🔔

UNITED STATES RABBIT EXPERIMENTAL STATION

In March 1928, the Federal Government established the first and only experimental station in the United States devoted solely to research on the breeding and raising of rabbits on a five-acre property donated by A. B. Miller of Fontana. The station successfully pioneered new techniques of rabbit care and breeding until 1965 when the City of Fontana acquired the property for use as a senior citizens facility.

Josephine Knoph Senior Citizen Center of Fontana, 8384 Cypress Ave at Seville Ave, Fontana

NO. 963 🔔

THE MOJAVE ROAD

Long ago, Mohave Indians used a network of pathways to cross the Mojave Desert. In 1826, American trapper Jedediah Smith used their paths and became the first non-Indian to reach the California coast overland from mid-America. The paths were worked into a military wagon road in 1859. This "Mojave Road" remained a major link between Los Angeles and points east until a railway crossed the desert in 1885.

Midway Rest Area, N-bound I-15, 30 mi NE of Barstow

NO. 963-1 🔔

CAMP CADY (ON THE MOJAVE ROAD)

Camp Cady was located on the Mojave Road which connected Los Angeles to Albuquerque. Non-Indian travel on this and the nearby Salt Lake Road was beset by Paiutes, Mohaves, and Chemehuevis defending their homeland. To protect both roads, Camp Cady was established by U.S. Dragoons in 1860. The main building was a stout mud redoubt. Improved camp structures were built 1/2 mile west in 1868. After peace was achieved, the military withdrew in 1871. This protection provided by Camp Cady enabled travelers, merchandise, and mail using both roads to boost California's economy and growth.

24 mi N of Barstow take Harvard Rd offramp from I-15, turn rt, go .8 mi to Cherokee Rd, turn left and go 2.5 mi and turn rt at second fence line. At end of dirt rd.

NO. 977 ☐

THE ARROWHEAD

Located in the foothills of the San Bernardino Mountains directly above the City of San Bernardino, the arrowhead landmark can be seen for miles around. This important landmark has for centuries been a symbol of the San Bernardino Valley to the Native Indians and then to the pioneers and settlers that followed. It is believed to be a natural landmark. The face of the arrowhead consists of light quartz, supporting a growth of short white sage. This lighter vegetation shows in sharp contrast to the surrounding chaparral and greasewood. Indians who inhabited the San Bernardino Valley believed that the arrowhead pointed the way to the hot mineral springs below, with healing qualities, and thus considered it holy ground. Through the years, numerous forest fires have caused some erosion. But the arrowhead landmark continues to preserve its uniqueness and remains a symbol of the "pioneer spirit" of the San Bernardino Valley.

N of softball field in Wildwood Park, at intersection of Waterman and 40th St, Hwy 18, San Bernardino

NO. 985 ☐

DESERT TRAINING CENTER, CALIFORNIA-ARIZONA MANEUVER AREA (ESTABLISHED BY MAJOR GENERAL GEORGE S. PATTON, JR.) — CAMP IRON MOUNTAIN

Iron Mountain Divisional Camp was established at this site in the Spring of 1942. One of eleven such camps built in the California-Arizona Desert to harden and train United States troops for service on the battlefields of World War II. The first major unit trained here was the 3rd Armored Division followed by elements of the 4th, 5th, 6th, and 7th Armored Divisions. In all, one million men trained in the desert before the Training Center was officially closed in May of 1944. The most unique feature built at this camp is the huge relief map built into the desert floor. It can still be seen (1985).

45 mi E of Indio on I-10, take Hwy 177 N to right on Hwy 62, plaque is 5.4 mi

NO. 985 ☐

DESERT TRAINING CENTER, CALIFORNIA-ARIZONA MANEUVER AREA (ESTABLISHED BY MAJOR GENERAL GEORGE S. PATTON, JR.) — CAMP CLIPPER

Camp Clipper was established at a site that reached from Essex Road to this location in the Spring of 1942. It was one of twelve such camps built in the southwestern deserts to harden and train United States troops for service on the battlefields of World War II. The Desert Training Center was a simulated theater of operations that included portions of California, Arizona, and Nevada. The other camps were Young, Coxcomb, Iron Mountain, Ibis, Granite, Pilot Knob, Laguna, Horn, Ryder, Bouse and Rice. A total of 13

infantry divisions and 7 armored divisions plus numerous smaller units were trained in this harsh environment. The Training Center was in operation for almost two years and was closed early in 1944 when the last units were shipped overseas. During the brief period of operation over one million American soldiers were trained for combat. The 33rd and 93rd Infantry Divisions were trained here.

37 mi W of Needles on I-40 and 115 mi E of Barstow at Fenner Rest Area eastbound

NO. 985 ☐

DESERT TRAINING CENTER, CALIFORNIA-ARIZONA MANEUVER AREA (ESTABLISHED BY MAJOR GENERAL GEORGE S. PATTON, JR.) — CAMP IBIS

Camp Ibis was established at this site in the Spring of 1942–one of eleven such camps built in the California-Arizona Desert to harden and train United States Troops for service on the battlefields of World War II. The 440th AAA AW Battalion was activated per General Order No. 1 at Camp Haan, CA on July 1, 1942. It trained at Camp M.A.A.R. (Irwin), Camps Young, Iron Mountain, Ibis, and then Camps Pickett, VA and Steward, GA. The battalion shipped out to England in December 1943 and landed in Normandy on D-3. The unit earned 5 Battle Stars and 2 Foreign Awards while serving with the 1st, 3rd, 7th, and 9th U.S. Armies; the 1st French Army and the 2nd British Army; 7 different corps and 5 different divisions. The 440th AAA AW BN was deactivated in December 1944.

8 mi E of Needles on Hwy 40 go N on Hwy 95 1.9 mi

NO. 994 🔔

A.K. SMILEY PUBLIC LIBRARY

Albert K. Smiley, a leader of the city's library movement, donated this building and park to the citizens of Redlands in 1898. Through his generosity, Redlands was given one of California's few privately funded libraries of that era. In 1906, he also contributed a wing, built to blend with the original design for this outstanding Mission Revival library.

125 West Vine St, Redlands

NO. 1019

KIMBERLY CREST

Kimberly Crest, constructed in 1897, is an excellent example of Chateauesque architecture. Near the residence is a Chateauesque-style carriage house. Terraced Italian gardens designed in 1908 stretch almost a thousand yards from the entrance of the residence down to the entrance of the grounds.

1325 Prospect Dr, Redlands

Landmark No. 977

San Diego County

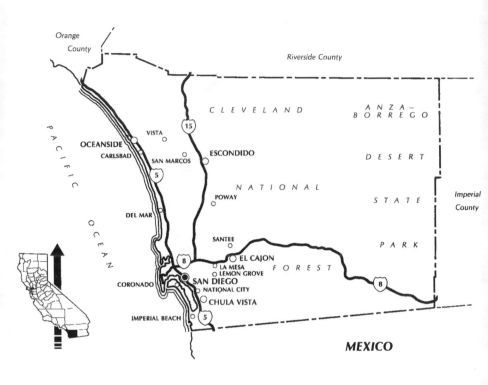

Anza-Borrego Desert State Park - Pioneer trail and early stage route. Located 65 miles NE of San Diego.

Cuyamaca Rancho State Park - Early gold mining area. Located 9 miles N of I-8 on Highway 79.

Old Town San Diego State Historic Park - Birthplace of San Diego. Located in San Diego's Old Town.

San Pasqual Battlefield State Historic Park - Site of U.S. and Mexican battle, 1846. Located 8 miles SE of Escondido on Highway 78.

San Diego
Est. 1850

On November 12, 1602 Sebastian Vizcaino named San Diego Bay in celebration of the Feast of San Diego, after Franciscan saint and Spanish native St. Didacus. Geographically split into thirds, San Diego County is bordered on the west by the Pacific Coast. The Cleveland National Forest occupies the center portion, the Anza-Borrego Desert lies to the east.

NO. 49 🔔

ADOBE CHAPEL OF THE IMMACULATE CONCEPTION

Originally built as the home of San Diego's John Brown in 1850. The house was converted to a church by Don José Aguirre in 1858. Father Antonio D. Ubach, formerly a missionary among the Indians, was parish priest here from 1866 to 1907. It is said that he was the model for "Father Gaspara" in Helen Hunt Jackson's Ramona. In 1937 the WPA rebuilt the adobe chapel close to its original site.

3950 Conde St, between Congress St and San Diego Ave, Old Town, San Diego

NO. 50 🔔

BALLAST POINT WHALING STATION SITE

Late in 1857, the three Johnson brothers and the twin Packard brothers came to this site to survey possibilities for a station to "try out" or extract whale oil. Their operations began the next year. In 1869 the U.S. Government acquired the property for Fort Rosecrans and in 1873 whaling operations at Ballast Point ended.

Base of Ballast Point, S end of Rosecrans St, where historic markers are on a half circle, U.S. Naval Submarine Base, San Diego

NO. 51 🔔

OLD POINT LOMA LIGHTHOUSE

This lighthouse, built in 1854, was one of the first eight lighthouses on the Pacific Coast. It continued in use until 1891, when the new Pelican Point Lighthouse began operating. The Point Loma Lighthouse became the site of the Cabrillo National Monument in 1913. During World War II, the Navy used it as a signal tower. Today the lighthouse remains the central feature of the Point Loma Preserve.

Cabrillo National Monument, Point Loma, San Diego

NO. 52 🔔

MISSION DAM AND FLUME

After many attempts dated back to 1774 to provide a reliable source of water for crops and livestock for Mission San Diego de Alcala, a dam and flume system was finished between 1813 and 1816 by Indian laborers and Franciscan Missionaries to divert waters of the San Diego River for a distance of 6 miles. The aqueduct system continued in existence until 1831 when constant flooding caused the dam and flume to fall into disrepair. They were not repaired due to secularization of the missions.

In parking lot on N side of Fr. Junipero Serra Trail in Mission Trails Regional Park near NE entrance, San Diego

NO. 53 □

CASA DE ESTUDILLO

Three generations of Don José María Estudillo's family made their home in Casa de Estudillo. Rich in historical background, the casa is often pointed out, erroneously, as Ramona's marriage place.

SE corner of San Diego Ave and Mason St, Old Town San Diego State Historic Park

NO. 54 🔔

FORT STOCKTON

Fortified briefly by Carlos Carrillo in 1828, this site became Fort Dupont (July-November 1846) after American forces took Old Town during the Mexican War. Retaken and held briefly by the Californios, it fell once more to the Americans, who renamed it Fort Stockton and used it as campaign headquarters for ending the Californio revolt in early 1847. The Mormon Battalion stayed here later that year. The post was abandoned on September 25, 1848.

Top of hill W of Presidio Dr in Presidio Park, Old Town, San Diego

NO. 55 🔔

FORT ROSECRANS NATIONAL CEMETERY

A burial ground before 1847, this graveyard became an Army post cemetery in the 1860s. It is the final resting place for most who fell at San Pasqual in 1846, and for the USS Bennington victims of 1905. It became Fort Rosecrans National Cemetery in 1934 and was placed under the Veterans Administration National Cemetery System in 1973. Over 50,000 who served the U.S. honorably in war and peace lie here.

Cabrillo Memorial Dr Point Loma, San Diego

NO. 56 🔔

CABRILLO LANDING SITE

Seeking the mythical Strait of Anián (the Northwest Passage) for Spain, on September 28, 1542, Iberian navigator Juan Rodríguez Cabrillo brought his three ships to Ballast Point, the first European landing on the coast of Alta California.

Base of Ballast Point, S end of Rosecrans St, where historic markers are on a half circle, U.S. Naval Submarine Base, San Diego

NO. 57 🔔

LA PUNTA DE LOS MUERTOS

Sailors and marines were buried here in 1782, when San Diego Bay was surveyed and charted by Don Juan Pantoja y Arriaga, pilot, and Don José Továr, mate, of the royal frigates *La Princesa* and *La Favorita* under command of Don Augustín de Echeverria.

SE corner of Market St and Pacific Hwy (State Hwy 163), San Diego

NO. 59 🔔

SAN DIEGO PRESIDIO SITE

Soldiers, sailors, Indians, and Franciscan missionaries from New Spain occupied the land at Presidio Hill on May 17, 1769 as a military outpost. Two months later, Fr. Junípero Serra established the first San Diego Mission on Presidio Hill. Officially proclaimed a Spanish Presidio on January 1, 1774, the fortress was later occupied by a succession of Mexican forces. The Presidio was abandoned in 1837 after San Diego became a pueblo.

Next to parking lot across Presidio Dr from Serra Museum, Presidio Park, Old Town, San Diego

NO. 60

CASA DE LÓPEZ

Built about 1835 by Juan Francisco López, one of San Diego's early Spanish settlers, the Casa Larga, or Long House, was among the first substantial houses built in the Pueblo of San Diego. In 1846 it was the home of José Matias Moreno, secretary to Pío Pico, California's last Mexican governor.

3890 Twiggs St, Old Town, San Diego

NO. 61

OLD LA PLAYA

From 1770 to 1870, this was San Diego's port. Over the Brookline hide house, Americans unofficially raised a U.S. flag in 1829. At that time La Playa was a thriving trading and shipping village. Richard Henry Dana's account of the hide business in *Two Years Before the Mast* is based on his hide-droghing experience here in 1835-36. The U.S. Navy later acquired the site and operated a coaling station and a quarantine station here. It is now a Navy research center.

On left side of Rosecrans St, at entrance to Military Reserve, Point Loma, San Diego

NO. 62

FORT ROSECRANS

President Millard Fillmore's executive order of 1852 created a U.S. Preserve on Point Loma. From 1870 to 1873 the coast artillery corpsmen evicted whalers from the site in order to begin the military installation. In 1899 it was named for William S. Rosecrans, Civil War general and Califor-

nia congressman. Major fortifications were constructed in 1891-1903 and 1941-1943. Transferred to the U.S. Navy in 1957, it became a submarine support facility.

Base of Ballast Point, S end of Rosecrans St, where historic markers are on a half circle, U.S. Naval Submarine Base, San Diego

NO. 63

PLAZA, SAN DIEGO VIEJO (WASHINGTON SQUARE)

This plaza was established as the center of the Mexican Pueblo of San Diego which elected its first ajuntamiento in 1834. On July 29, 1846, at 4 p.m., Lieutenant Stephen C. Rowan, U.S.N., from the U.S. Sloop-of-War Cyane, raised the American flag over the plaza.

Old Town Plaza (Washington Square), Old Town San Diego State Historic Park

NO. 64

"OLD LANDING," SITE OF EL DESEMBARCADERO

El Desembarcadero was one of the first landmarks designated during the first year of the landmark program. The site was recognized as the landing place for small boats carrying freight and passengers to Old San Diego. It was also believed to be the place visited in 1769 by the crews of the *San Antonio* and *San Carlos* in their search for fresh water.

Inside NTC, NE side of Farragut St near Truxton St, U.S. Naval Submarine Base, San Diego

NO. 65 🔔

THE WHALEY HOUSE

This house, in which the San Diego County Court met for about 20 years, was the first brick building to be erected in San Diego County. The bricks were made at Thomas Whaley's own kiln in Old Town in 1856, and the walls were finished with plaster made from ground seashells. Five generations of the Whaley family have occupied the old home.

2482 San Diego Ave, Old Town, San Diego

NO. 66

CONGRESS HALL SITE

This building was originally a two-story public house built by George Dewitt Clinton Washington Robinson about 1867. From this building one of the last survivors of the pony express rode north.

Vacant lot, S side of 2734 Calhoun St, Old Town San Diego State Historic Park

NO. 67 🔔

"SERRA PALM" (SITE)

Site of the palm planted in 1769 by Padre Junípero Serra when he arrived at San Diego. Here the four divisions of the Portolá Expedition met on July 1, 1769. The famous "El Camino Real," most celebrated trail in California, begins here.

Presidio Park, SE corner of Taylor St and Presidio Dr, San Diego

NO. 68 🔔

El CAMPO SANTO

El Campo Santo once included the adobe chapel on Conde Street, in which was buried José Antonio Aguirre, and where funeral services were held for María Victoria Domínguez Estudillo and Cave Johnson Couts, and many distinguished early San Diegans. Between 1849 and 1897, 477 persons were buried in these grounds. Antonio Garra was the most eminent of many Native Americans interred here. A number of graves were relocated after 1874. A street railway bisected the cemetery in 1894. The wall around this portion was built in 1933. Restoration has continued to the present (1994).

On San Diego Ave between Arista and Conde Sts, San Diego; plaque currently in storage

NO. 69 🔔

SITE OF FORT GUIJARROS

An outpost of Spain's far-flung empire at its greatest extent, this fort was completed before 1800 from plans drawn by Alberto de Córdoba in 1795. Its major action came under Corporal José Velásquez on March 22, 1803, in the "Battle of San Diego Bay" with the American Brig *Lelia Byrd*, which was smuggling sea otter pelts.

Base of Ballast Point, S end of Rosecrans St, where historic markers are on a half circle, U.S. Naval Submarine Base, San Diego

NO. 70 ☐

CASA DE PEDRORENA

This was the home of Miguel de Pedrorena, who arrived in San Diego Viejo in 1838. Don Miguel was a member of the Constitutional Convention at Monterey in 1849.

2616 San Diego Ave, Old Town San Diego State Historic Park

NO. 71

CASA DE MACHADO

This adobe house, constructed about 1832 by José Manuel Machado, pioneer leatherjacket soldier of the Spanish Army who arrived at San Diego Presidio about 1782, is now used as a community church.

Park visitor center Old Town San Diego State Historic Park

NO. 72 □

CASA DE BANDINI

This adobe house was constructed about 1827 by José and Juan Bandini. As headquarters of Commodore Robert F. Stockton in 1846, it was the place where Kit Carson and Edward Beale delivered their urgent message of December 9, 1846, calling for reinforcements to be rushed to the aid of General Kearny.

On NE corner of Mason and Calhoun Sts, Old Town San Diego State Historic Park

NO. 73

CASA DE STEWART

Adobe house constructed by José Manuel Machado in 1830s for his daughter Rosa, wife of John C. Stewart. Stewart was a shipmate of Richard Henry Dana, Jr. who describes his 1859 visit to this house in *Two Years Before the Mast*.

NW corner of Congress and Mason Sts, Old Town San Diego State Historic Park

NO. 74 🔔

CASA DE CARRILLO

Presidio Comandante Francisco María Ruiz built this house next to his 1808 pear garden late in 1821 for his close relative and fellow soldier, Joaquín Carrillo, and his large family. From this adobe dwelling, in April 1829, daughter Josefa Carrillo eloped to Chile with Henry Delano Fitch. When Ruiz died in 1839 and Joaquín soon afterwards, son Ramon Carrillo sold this property to Lorenzo Soto. It was transferred several times before 1932, deteriorating gradually, until George Marston and associates restored the house and grounds and deeded them to the City of San Diego as a golf course.

About 100 ft NE of Juan St on Wallace St, Presidio Golf Course, San Diego

NO. 75

SITE OF CASA DE COTA

This adobe is said to have been built about 1835 by Juan or Ramon Cota.

NW corner of Twiggs and Congress Sts, Old Town, San Diego

NO. 239 🔔

MISSION SAN LUÍS REY DE FRANCIA

Founded June 12, 1798 by Father Lasuén, then president of the California missions, and administered by Father Peyrí, Mission San Luís Rey is notable for its impressive architecture–a composite of Spanish, Moorish, and Mexican.

On State Hwy 76 (4050 Mission Ave) at Rancho Del Oro Dr, Oceanside

NO. 242 🔔

MISSION SAN DIEGO DE ALCALA

On Sunday, July 16, 1769, Fathers Junípero Serra, Juan Vizcaino, and Fernando Parrón raised and blessed a cross to establish Alta California's first mission. Relocated from Presidio Hill to this site in August 1774, the mission was the Mother of those founded in California by the Franciscan Order. The present buildings, first completed in 1813, were rebuilt in stages from 1915 to 1931 after many years of deterioration. They have been in use as a parish church since February 1941.

Mission San Diego de Alcala, 10818 San Diego Mission Rd, San Diego

NO. 243 🔔

ASISTENCIA DE SAN ANTONIO

Notable for its bell tower, or campanile, the chapel was built by Father Peyrí in 1816. Almost destroyed by earthquake and storm, it was later restored.

Mission on Pala Mission Rd; plaque on State Hwy 76 (P.M. 23.6), Pala

NO. 244 🔔

DERBY DIKE

Until 1853 the erratic San Diego River dumped tons of debris into the harbor or poured into False Bay, now Mission Bay. At times it threatened to destroy Old Town San Diego. Lieutenant George Horatio Derby, U.S. Topographical Corps, built a dike that diverted the waters into False Bay. This was the first effort to tame the river, and one of the first U.S. Government projects in California. The river was not fully harnessed until the 1950s.

Presidio Park, SE corner of Taylor St and Presidio Dr, San Diego

NO. 304 🔔

VALLECITO STAGE DEPOT (STATION)

A reconstruction (1934) of Vallecito Stage Station built in 1852 at the edge of the Great Colorado Desert. It was an important stop on the first official transcontinental route, serving the San Diego-San Antonio ("Jackass") mail line (1857-1859), the Butterfield Overland Stage Line, and the southern emigrant caravans.

Vallecito Stage Station County Park, on County Rd S2 (P.M. 34.7), 3.7 mi NW of Agua Caliente Springs

NO. 311 🔔

WARNER'S RANCH

In 1844, Governor Manuel Micheltorena granted 44,322 acres to Juan José Warner, who built this house. General Kearny passed here in 1846, and the Mormon Battalion in 1847. The first Butterfield Stage stopped at this ranch on October 6, 1858, on its 2,600-mile, 24-day trip from Tipton, Missouri to San Francisco, the southern overland route into California.

On County Hwy S2 (P.M. 0.7), 0.7 mi E of junc of State Hwy 79, 4 mi SE of Warner Springs

NO. 369 🔔

CHAPEL OF SANTA YSABEL (SITE OF)

The first mass at a site nearby was celebrated September 20, 1818 by Father Fernando Martin. By 1822, Santa Ysabel was an asistencia, or mission outpost, that had a chapel, a granary, several houses, a cemetery, and about 450 neophytes. After secularization in the 1830s, priestly visits became rare. When the roof caved in, after 1850, ramadas were erected against one wall and services were held there. Tradition asserts this site has been used for religious services since 1818. The present chapel was constructed in 1924.

On State Hwy 79 (P.M. 21.8), 1.4 mi N of Santa Ysabel

NO. 411 🔔
CAMPO STONE STORE

The pioneer Gaskill brothers of 1868 built a frame store which was raided on December 4, 1875 by border bandits. This fort-like replacement of summer 1885 was bought in 1896 by E. T. Aiken, resold to Klauber Wangenheim, 1889, and operated by Henry Marcus Johnson as the Mountain Commercial Company until 1925. In disrepair, it was bought after 1938 by E. M. Statler, given to San Diego County, and restored, 1943-48, as a museum.

State Hwy 94 (P.M. 50.6), at Campo Cr, Campo

NO. 412 🔔 ☐
JULIAN

Following the discovery of gold nearby during the winter of 1869-70, this valley became the commercial and social center of a thriving mining district. Ex-Confederate soldier Drury D. Bailey laid out the town on his farmland and named it for his cousin and fellow native of Georgia, Michael S. Julian. By 1906 most mines were unprofitable. Since then the area has become more famous for the variety and quality of its apple crop.

Private plaque: Julian Memorial Park, Washington and Fourth Sts, Julian State plaque: In front of Town Hall, Julian

NO. 425 ☐
LA CAÑADA DE LOS COCHES RANCHO

Commemorating Cañada de Los Coches Rancho, smallest Mexican grant in California, granted in 1843 to Apolinaria Lorenzana by Governor Manuel Micheltorena. This is the site of the old grist mill.

13468 Old Hwy 80, Lakeside

NO. 452 🔔
MULE HILL

On December 7, 1846, the day following the Battle of San Pasqual fought five miles east of here, General Stephen Kearny's command, on its way to San Diego, was again attacked by Californians. The Americans counterattacked and occupied this hill until December 11. Short of food, they ate mule meat and named the place "Mule Hill."

On Pomerado Rd, 0.1 mi E of I-15, 5 mi SE of Escondido

NO. 472 🔔
BOX CANYON

The old road, known as the Sonora, Colorado River, or Southern Emigrant Trail and later as the Butterfield Overland Mail Route, traversed Box Canyon just east of here. On January 19, 1847, the Mormon Battalion under the command of Lieutenant Colonel Philip St. G. Cooke, using hand tools, hewed a passage through the rocky walls of the narrow gorge for their wagons and opened the first road into Southern California.

On County Rd S2 (P.M. 25.7), 8.6 mi S of State Hwy 78, Anza-Borrego Desert State Park

NO. 482 🔔

CAMP WRIGHT

Camp Wright, named for Brigadier General George Wright, United States Army, who commanded the Pacific Department and California District from 1861 to 1865, was first established October 18, 1861 on Warner's Ranch to guard the line of communication between California and Arizona. The camp was moved to this site by Major Edwin A. Rigg, First California Volunteers, about November 23, 1861 and was abandoned December 1866.

State Hwy 79 (P.M. 49.3), Oak Grove

NO. 491

THE EXCHANGE HOTEL

This tablet marks the site of the Exchange Hotel. Here, on June 29,1851, Masons met for the first time in San Diego and organized the lodge which became San Diego Lodge No. 35, F. & A.M., the oldest lodge of Masons in Southern California.

2729 San Diego Ave, Old Town San Diego State Historic Park

NO. 502 🔔

OAK GROVE STAGE STATION

Oak Grove is one of the few remaining stations on the Butterfield Overland Mail route, which operated between San Francisco and two eastern terminals–St. Louis, Missouri and Memphis, Tennessee–from September 15, 1858 to March 2, 1861. During the Civil War the station was used as a hospital for nearby Camp Wright.

State Hwy 79 (P.M. 49.4), Oak Grove

NO. 523 🔔

SAN DIEGO BARRACKS

New San Diego was established as a quartermaster depot by Captain Nathaniel Lyon, 2nd U.S. Infantry, in 1850-51 to supply military establishments in Southern California. The name of the post was changed from New San Diego to San Diego Barracks by General Orders No. 2, Military Division of the Pacific, San Francisco, April 5, 1879. San Diego Barracks continued to operate as a subpost of Fort Rosecrans until abandoned December 15, 1921.

700 block of Harbor-Market Sts, San Francisco

NO. 533 🔔

SAN PASQUAL BATTLEFIELD STATE HISTORIC PARK

While marching to the conquest and occupation of California during the Mexican War, a detachment of 1st U.S. Dragoons under the command of Brigadier General Stephen W. Kearny was met on this site by native California lancers under the command of General Andrés Pico. In this battle, fought on December 6, 1846, severe losses were incurred by the American forces. The native Californians withdrew after Kearny had rallied his men on the field. Gallant action on the part of both forces characterized the Battle of San Pasqual, one of the significant actions during the Mexican War of 1846-1848.

San Pasqual Battlefield State Historic Park, State Hwy 78 (P.M. 25.1) at Old Pasqual Rd, 7 mi SE of Escondido

NO. 538 🔔

FIRST PUBLICLY OWNED SCHOOL BUILDING

The first public schoolhouse in this county, the Mason Street School—District No. 1, was erected at this site in 1865, when San Diego County covered an area larger than three New England states. It was restored by popular subscription in 1955.

3966 Mason St, Old Town San Diego State Historic Park

NO. 562 🔔

LA CHRISTIANITA

Near this spring, the first Christian baptism in Alta California was performed by Padre Francisco Gómez, a member of the Portolá Expedition, in 1769.

Site and plaque in Camp Pendleton, Los Cristianitos Canyon, on Cristianitos Rd, 0.4 mi N. of intersection of San Mateo Rd, 3 mi E of I-5 at San Clemente; plaque in San Clemente Civic Center 100 Avenida Presidio, San Clemente

NO. 616 🔔

LAS FLORES ASISTENCIA

From 1823 to the 1840s, the tile-roofed adobe chapel and hostel at Las Flores, built by Father Antonio Peyrí, served as the asistencia to Mission San Luís Rey and provided comfort to travelers on El Camino Real. The adobe structure and adjacent corral were the site of the April 1838 battle between Juan Bautista Alvarado and Carlos Antonio Carrillo contesting the provincial governorship of Alta California.

Camp Pendleton Marine Base; plaque located on hill 1,000 ft W of Orange Co Boy Scouts Adobe, 0.6 mi SE of Las Pulgas gate, 0.9 mi SW of I-15 (P.M. 62.0) at Las Pulgas Rd, 10 mi S of San Clemente

NO. 626 🔔

BANCROFT RANCH HOUSE

Adobe built about 1850 by A. S. Ensworth. Home of Capt. Rufus K. Porter and family. Curved timbers brought from the *Alarissa Andrews*, famed coaling hulk formerly of the Pacific Mail Steamship Co. Historian Hubert Howe Bancroft later owned this estate and here wrote a part of his monumental History of California.

One block E of Memory and Bancroft Dr, Spring Valley

NO. 634 🔔

EL VADO

This route was opened by Captain Juan Bautista de Anza and Father Francisco Garces in 1774. Anza's expedition of 1775, a group of 240 soldiers and settlers coming from Sonora to found San Francisco, encamped near El Vado (The Ford) for three days and two nights, December 20-22, 1775.

6 mi NW of Borrego Springs on Borrego Springs Rd (dirt), Anza -Borrego Desert State Park, ask at Visitor Center

NO. 635 🔔

LOS PUERTECITOS

Juan Bautista de Anza's expedition marched through this little pass December 19, 1775 on its way to strengthen Spanish colonization in California. Many of the 240 members of the party were recruited from Mexico to be the first residents of San Francisco. They had camped the preceding night somewhere in the wide flats just east of this monument.

On State Hwy 78 (P.M. 93.8), 1.6 mi E of Ocotillo Wells

NO. 639 🔔

PALM SPRINGS

Here Mexican pioneers coming to California between 1862 and 1866 rested among the palms; here, too, came mountain men, the Army of the West, the Mormon Battalion, a boundary commission, '49ers, a railway survey team, the Butterfield Overland Mail stages, and the California Legion. This was the site of the Butterfield stage station built in 1858 by Warren F. Hall.

On Vallecito Creek Rd, 1.6 mi E of County Rd S2 (P.M. 43.1), 6.3 mi SE of Agua Caliente Springs, Anza-Borrego Desert State Park

NO. 647 🔔

BUTTERFIELD OVERLAND MAIL ROUTE

This pass, Puerta, between the desert and the cooler valleys to the north, was used by the Mormon Battalion, Kearny's Army of the West, the Butterfield Overland Mail stages, and emigrants who eventually settled the West. The eroded scar on the left was the route of the Butterfield stages, 1858-1861. The road on the right served as a county road until recent years.

Blair Valley, 0.5 mi E of County Rd S2 (P.M. 23.0), 5.8 mi S of State Hwy 78, Anza-Borrego Desert State Park

NO. 673 🔔

SAN GREGORIO

Somewhere in this narrow valley, perhaps on this very spot, the Anza Expeditions of 1774 and 1775 made their camps. Water for the 240 people and over 800 head of stock on the 1775 march was obtained from a series of wells, deeper than the height of a man, dug into the sandy bottom of the wash.

Borrego Sink, 3 mi SE of Palm Canyon and Peg Leg Rds, Anza -Borrego Desert State Park, ask at Visitor Center

NO. 711 ☐

MONTGOMERY MEMORIAL

At Otay Mesa, in 1883, John Joseph Montgomery made the first flight in a heavier-than-air craft 20 years before the Wrights. Montgomery made many more glider flights before accepting a professorship at Santa Clara College, where he continued his interest in aviation.

Montgomery-Walker Park, NE corner of Coronado Ave and Beyer Blvd, South San Diego

NO. 750 🔔

PEG LEG SMITH MONUMENT

Thomas L. Smith, better known as "Peg Leg," 1801-1866, was a mountain man, prospector, and spinner of tall tales. Legends regarding his lost gold mine have grown through the years, and countless people have searched the desert for its fabulous wealth. The mine could be within a few miles of this monument.

Henderson Canyon Rd, 1,000 ft N of Pegleg Rd, Anza-Borrego Desert State Park

NO. 764 🔔

SITE OF THE KATE O. SESSIONS NURSERY

This plaque commemorates the life and influence of a woman who envisioned a beautiful San Diego. On this site she operated a nursery and gained world renown as a horticulturist; she was the first woman to receive the International Meyer Medal in genetics.

NW corner of Garnet Ave and Pico St, San Diego

NO. 784 🔔

EL CAMINO REAL (AS FATHER SERRA KNEW IT AND HELPED BLAZE IT)

This plaque was placed on the 250th anniversary of the birth of California's apostle, Padre Junípero Serra, OFM, to mark El Camino Real as he knew it and helped blaze it.

Mission San Diego de Alcala, 10818 San Diego Mission Rd, San Diego to Mission San Francisco de Asis, San Francisco.

NO. 785 🔔

SANTA CATARINA

This spring was named by Captain Juan Bautista de Anza when his overland exploration party camped here on March 14, 1774, on the journey that opened the Anza Trail from Sonora into Alta California. Anza's colonizing expedition of 1775, consisting of 240 persons and over 800 head of livestock, camped here the night of December 23.

Santa Catarina Springs, 10 mi NW of Borrego Springs (4-wheel drive dirt rd), Anza-Borrego Desert State Park, ask at Visitor Center

NO. 793 🔔

SAN FELIPE VALLEY AND STAGE STATION

Here the southern trail of explorers, trappers, soldiers, and emigrants crossed ancient trade routes of Kamia, Cahuilla, Diegueno, and Luiseño Indians. On the flat southwest across the creek, Warren F. Hall built and operated the San Felipe home station of the Butterfield Mail, which operated from 1858 to 1861. Later the station was used by Banning Stages and by the military during the Civil War.

On County Hwy S2 (P.M. 15.9), 0.9 mi NW of intersection of State Hwy 78, near Anza-Borrego Desert State Park

NO. 798 🔔

SAN DIEGO STATE COLLEGE, SITE OF FIRST DOCTORATE DEGREE GRANTED BY THE CALIFORNIA STATE COLLEGE SYSTEM

Under the Master Plan for Higher Education adopted in 1960, the colleges in the newly established California College System were given degrees with the University of California, and independent degrees to individuals who have made unusual contributions toward learning and civilization. San Diego State College was the first of the California State Colleges to do so when, on June 7, 1963 it conferred an honorary doctorate upon the late President of the United States, John Fitzgerald Kennedy.

San Diego State University, N end of Aztec Bowl, across from parking lot "W," at intersection of Scripps Terrace and Canyon Crest Dr, San Diego

NO. 818 🔔

FIRST MILITARY FLYING SCHOOL IN AMERICA

The flat lands beyond have been a part of aviation history since Glenn Curtiss founded the first military flying school in America here on January 17, 1911. The Army operated Rockwell Field until January 31, 1939; the Navy commissioned the present air station on November 8, 1917.

Sunset Park, 200 block of Ocean Blvd, at entrance to Gate 5, Naval Air Station, North Island, Coronado

NO. 830 🔔

OLD TOWN SAN DIEGO STATE HISTORIC PARK

Settled by pensioned soldiers from the presidio and their families, Old Town grew into a cluster of adobe houses and garden plots in the early 1800s. By 1835, "it was composed of about 40 dark brown looking huts." The Stars and Stripes was first raised over the plaza in 1846 by Marines from the U.S.S. Cyane.

Old Town San Diego State Historic Park, plaque located W side of plaza at 4016 Wallace St, San Diego

NO. 844 🔔

HOTEL DEL CORONADO

This Victorian hotel, built in 1887, is one of America's largest wooden buildings. Few seaside resort hotels of this significant architectural style remain in America. The hotel has hosted several Presidents and other national figures.

Hotel Garden Patio, 1500 Orange Ave, Coronado

NO. 858 🔔

PEDRO FAGES TRAIL

On October 29, 1772, headed east from San Diego in search of army deserters, Colonel Pedro Fages made the first entry by a European into Oriflamme Canyon. From there, Fages and his men traveled on through Cajón Pass and around the Mojave and the Central Valley to eventually reach Mission San Luís Obispo, discovering the Colorado desert and the San Joaquin Valley.

1.7 mi SE on Sunrise Hwy (County Rd S1, P.M. 36) from intersection with Hwy 79 (P.M. 14.5), 8 mi SE of Julian

NO. 891 🔔

SPANISH LANDING

Near this point, sea and land parties of the Portolá-Serra expedition met in 1769. Two ships, the *San Antonio* and *San Carlos*, anchored on May 4-5 and the scurvy-weakened survivors of the voyage established a camp, where on May 14 and July 1 they greeted the parties coming overland from Baja California. Together, they began the Spanish occupation of Alta California.

Spanish Landing Park, Harbor Dr San Diego

NO. 940 🔔

RANCHO GUAJOME

Formerly attached to Mission San Luís Rey, this 2,219-acre ranch was briefly owned by two mission Indians and then came into the hands of Don Abel Stearns; Ysidora Bandini acquired it on her marriage to Col. Cave Johnson Couts. The adobe ranch house, built in 1852-53, is one of the finest extant examples of the traditional Spanish-Mexican one-story hacienda with an inner-outer courtyard plan. San Diego County acquired it in 1973 for the Guajome Regional Park.

Rancho Guajome Regional Park, 2210 N Santa Fe Ave, 4 mi E of Mission San Luis Rey, 3.3 mi N of Vista

NO. 982 🔔

HISTORIC PLANNED COMMUNITY OF RANCHO SANTA FE

Rancho Santa Fe began as Rancho San Dieguito, a land grant of nearly 9,000 acres made to Juan María Osuna in 1845. The Santa Fe Railway Company later used the land to plant thousands of eucalyptus trees for use as railroad ties. In the 1920s Rancho Santa Fe became one of the state's first planned communities unified by a single architectural theme, the Spanish Colonial Revival. Lilian Rice, one of California's first successful women architects, supervised the development and designed many of the buildings.

Village Green in front of The Inn, Rancho Santa Fe

NO. 1020 🔔

LEO CARRILLO RANCH (RANCHO DE LOS KIOTES)

Between 1937 and 1940, these adobe and wood buildings were built by actor Leo Carrillo as a retreat, working ranch, and tribute to old California culture and architecture. The Leo Carrillo Ranch, with its Flying "LC" brand, originally covered 2,538 acres and was frequented by Carrillo and his friends until 1960. Leo Carrillo was a strong, positive, and well-loved role model who sought to celebrate California's early Spanish heritage, through a life of good deeds and charitable causes.

4758 Palomar Airport Rd, Carlsbad

Landmark No. 51

Landmark No. 982

San Francisco County

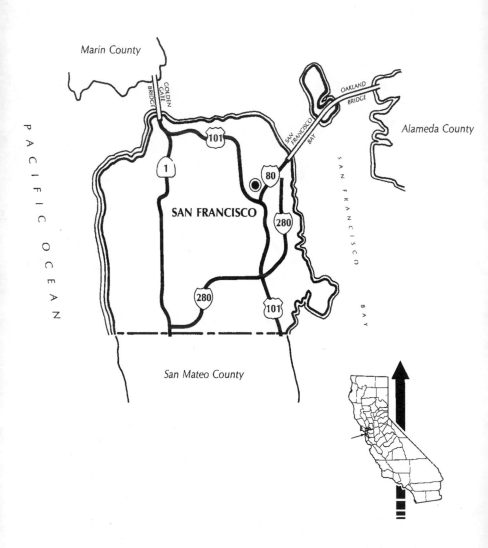

Marin County

PACIFIC OCEAN

GOLDEN GATE BRIDGE

OAKLAND BRIDGE

Alameda County

SAN FRANCISCO BAY

101

1

80

280

SAN FRANCISCO

SAN FRANCISCO BAY

280

101

San Mateo County

San Francisco
Est. 1850

San Francisco County derives its name from the Mission San Francisco de Asís, named for St. Francis of Assisi, founder of the Franciscan order. The county encompasses the urban center at the tip of the San Francisco Peninsula, Treasure Island and the seven Farallon Islands. Many Forty-niners disembarked from ships at this spectacular port to begin the trek to the foothills and their promise of fortune.

NO. 79 🔔
PRESIDIO OF SAN FRANCISCO

Formally established on September 17, 1776, the San Francisco Presidio has been used as a military headquarters by Spain, Mexico, and the United States. It was a major command post during the Mexican War, Civil War, Spanish-American War, World Wars I and II, and the Korean War, and remains a symbol of United States authority in the Pacific.

SW corner of Funston Ave and Lincoln Blvd, San Francisco

NO. 80 🔔
MONTGOMERY BLOCK

This is the site of San Francisco's first fire-proof building, erected in 1853 by Henry Wager Halleck. It was the headquarters for many outstanding lawyers, financiers, writers, actors, and artists. James King of William, editor of the *Bulletin*, died here on May 14, 1856 after being shot by James Casey. This building escaped destruction in the fire of 1906.

600 Montgomery St, San Francisco

NO. 81 ☐
LANDING PLACE OF CAPTAIN J. B. MONTGOMERY

In the early morning of July 9, 1846, "when the water came up to Montgomery Street," Commander John B. Montgomery landed near this spot from the U.S. Sloop-of-War Portsmouth to raise the Stars and Stripes on the Plaza, now Portsmouth Square.

552 Montgomery St, SE corner of Montgomery and Clay, San Francisco

NO. 82 ☐
CASTILLO DE SAN JOAQUÍN

The first ship to enter San Francisco Bay, the San Carlos (Captain Ayala), dropped anchor off this point August 5, 1775. Lieutenant-Colonel Don Juan Bautista de Anza planted the cross on Cantil Blanco (White Cliff) March 28, 1776. The first fortification, Castillo de San Joaquín, was completed December 8, 1794 by José Joaquín de Arrillaga, sixth Governor of California. In 1853 United States Army engineers cut down the cliff and built Fort Point, renamed Fort Winfield Scott in 1882. This fort, a partial replica of Fort Sumter, is the only brick fort west of the Mississippi; its seawall has stood undamaged for over a hundred years.

SE corner of Fort Wall, Fort Point, San Francisco (below Golden Gate Bridge)

NO. 83 ☐

SHORELINE MARKERS

"This tablet marks the shoreline of San Francisco Bay at the time of the discovery of gold in California, January 24, 1848. Map reproduced above delineates old shoreline."

Plaque in sidewalk, NE corner of Bush and Market Sts, San Francisco

NO. 84 🔔

RINCON HILL

A fashionable neighborhood in the 1860s, Rincon Hill was the home of William Tecumseh Sherman, William C. Ralston, William Gwin, H. H. Bancroft, and others. By the 1880s the hill, already partially leveled, became a working class district. Today it is nearly invisible beneath the Bay Bridge. This plaque is mounted on the retaining wall of St. Mary's Hospital, built 1861 but destroyed in the fire of 1906.

NE corner of Rincon and Bryant Sts, San Francisco

NO. 85

OFFICE OF THE STAR NEWSPAPER

On this site January 9, 1847, the first newspaper in San Francisco–the *California Star* later known as *The Alta Californian*–was published by Samuel Brannan with Elbert P. Jones as editor.

SW corner of Washington St and Brenham Place, San Francisco

NO. 86 ☐

CALIFORNIA THEATRE

On this site on January 18, 1869, the California Theatre, built by William C. Ralston, opened with the following stock company: John McCullough, Lawrence

Barrett, Harry Edwards, Willie Edouin, E. B. Holmes, William Mastayer, John T. Raymond, W. F. Burroughs, W. H. Sadley Smith, John Wilson, Edward J. Buckley, Mrs. Judah Emelie Melville, Elizabeth Saunders, Annette Ince, Marie E. Gordon, Sophie Edwin, Minnie Walton, and Julia Buckley. Among artists who played here were Charles W. Couldock, Edwin Adams, John Broughan, Edwin Booth, Barton Hill, Walter Montgomery, Mrs. D. P. Bowers, Adelaide Neilson, and Lotta Crabtree. This theater remained a brilliant center of drama until August 11, 1888.

430 Bush St between Kearny and Grant, San Francisco

NO. 87 🔔

SITE OF FIRST U.S. BRANCH MINT IN CALIFORNIA

The first United States branch mint in San Francisco was authorized by Congress July 3, 1852 and opened for operation April 3, 1854. Dr. L. A. Birdsall was the first superintendent; J. Huston, first minter; and A. Haraszthy, first assayer.

608-610 Commercial St near Montgomery, San Francisco

NO. 88 🏛

NIANTIC HOTEL (BUILDING)

The emigrant ship *Niantic* stood on this spot in the early days "when the water came up to Montgomery Street." Converted to other uses, it was covered with a shingle roof with offices and stores on the deck, at the level of which was constructed a wide balcony surmounted by a veranda. The hull was divided into warehouses entered by doorways on the sides. The fire of May 3, 1851 destroyed all but the submerged hulk, which later was utilized as the foundation for the Niantic Hotel, a famous hostelry that stood until 1872.

In lower level of Two Transamerica Center 505 Sansome at Clay, San Francisco

NO. 89
SITE OF PARROTT GRANITE BLOCK

The Parrott Block was erected in 1852 by John Parrott, an importer and banker. The three-story building, built by Chinese labor, was of granite blocks brought from China. The 1906 earthquake and fire did little damage to the building, which soon thereafter reopened for business. In 1926 it was demolished to make way for the Financial Center Building.

NW corner of California and Montgomery, San Francisco

NO. 90 ☐
FORT GUNNYBAGS

This is the site of the headquarters of the Vigilance Committee of 1856. On June 21, 1856, Judge David S. Terry was arrested and confined in a cell. The committee, fearing that his friends might attempt to rescue him, decided to fortify the building with gunnysacks filled with sand.

S side of Sacramento between Davis and Front, San Francisco

NO. 91 ☐
TELEGRAPH HILL

A signal station was erected on Telegraph Hill in 1849 from which to observe the incoming vessels; a tall pole with movable arms was used to signal to the people in the town below whether sailing vessels or the sidewheel vessels of the Pacific

mail were passing through the Golden Gate. In September 1853, the first telegraph in California, which extended eight miles to Point Lobos, was stationed here, giving the hill its name.

Lobby of Coit Tower, Telegraph Hill, San Francisco

NO. 119 ☐
PORTSMOUTH PLAZA

Named for U.S.S. Portsmouth, commanded by Captain John B. Montgomery, after whom Montgomery Street was named. It was here on the plaza that Captain Montgomery first raised the American flag near the Mexican adobe custom house on July 9, 1846. Center of many early-day activities, this plaza was the site of: the first public school building, erected in 1847 on the southwest corner of plaza, where religious services and many public meetings were held; the dramatic announcement of gold discovery made on May 11, 1848, when Sam Brannan displayed glittering samples to crowds; mass meeting to urge election of delegates to Monterey Constitutional Convention on June 12, 1849; refuge for citizens following conflagrations of 1849, 1850, 1851, and 1906; citizens' assembly on July 16, 1849 to organize against depredations of a lawless body called "The Hounds;" memorial services held August 29, 1850, following death of President Zachary Taylor; first Admission Day celebration held October 29, 1850, when the steamship Oregon brought the news that California had become 31st state on September 9; an indignation meeting, organized June 1, 1852, to protest against the city council's purchase of the Jenny Lind Theatre to be used as a city hall; commemorative services held for Henry Daly, August 10, 1852; and an oration delivered by Colonel E. D. Baker on September 18, 1859, over the body of U. S. Senator David C. Broderick, killed in duel with Chief Justice David S. Terry. Robert Louis Stevenson spent many hours here during his visit to the city in 1879-1880.

Portsmouth Square Park, on Kearny between Clay and Washington, San Francisco

NO. 192 🔔
"EL DORADO," "PARKER HOUSE," AND "DENNISON'S EXCHANGE"

The "El Dorado," the "Parker House," and "Dennison's Exchange" were among the most famous hotel and gambling resorts around San Francisco in the early 1850s. The Jenny Lind Theatre replaced the Parker House in 1850. The third Jenny Lind Theatre, opened by Tom Maguire on October 4, 1851 on the same site as the two preceding it, which were destroyed in the fires of 1851, was purchased by the City of San Francisco in 1852 for use as the city hall.

750 Kearny St at Merchant, San Francisco

NO. 236 🔔
ENTRANCE OF THE SAN CARLOS INTO SAN FRANCISCO BAY

On August 5, 1775, the Spanish packet San Carlos, under the command of Lieutenant Juan Manuel de Ayala, became the first ship to enter San Francisco Bay. His crew spent a month and a half surveying the bay from its southernmost reaches to the northern end of present-day Suisun Bay. The San Carlos departed September 18, 1775.

Aquatic Park, NW corner of Beach and Larkin Sts, San Francisco

NO. 327 □
MISSION SAN FRANCISCO DE ASIS (MISSION DOLORES)

The sixth mission to be founded was San Francisco de Asis. This mission was dedicated by Father Junípero Serra on October 9, 1776; construction of mission buildings was completed 1784. Mission Dolores has none of the usual arches, arcades, and towers which adorn the more elaborate sister missions, but nonetheless its massive simplicity makes it impressive.

Dolores St between 16th and 17th Sts, San Francisco

NO. 327-1 🔔
SITE OF ORIGINAL MISSION DOLORES CHAPEL AND DOLORES LAGOON

On June 29, 1776, Father Francisco Palou, a member of the Anza Expedition, had a brushwood shelter built here on the edge of a now vanished lake, Lago de los Dolores (Lake of the Sorrows), and offered the first mass. The first mission was a log and thatch structure dedicated on October 9, 1776 when the necessary church documents arrived. The present Mission Dolores was dedicated in 1791.

Site: Camp and Albion Sts, San Francisco (plaque in storage)

NO. 328
LONG WHARF

In the spring of 1848, the old Central or Long Wharf was built "from the bank in the middle of the block between Sacramento and Clay Streets, where

Leidesdorff Street now is, 800 feet into the Bay." After 1850 it was extended 2,000 feet and the Pacific mail steamers and other large vessels anchored there. Central or Long Wharf is now Commercial Street.

Intersection of Leidesdorff and Commercial Sts, San Francisco

NO. 408 □

SITE OF THE FIRST MEETING OF FREEMASONS HELD IN CALIFORNIA

On November 9, 1849, a charter was granted by the Grand Lodge of the District of Columbia for the organization of California Lodge No. 13, now California Lodge No. 1 of the Free and Accepted Masons. On November 23, 1848, Levi Stowell was appointed master of the new lodge, and on November 15, 1849, the lodge was formally organized under the charter.

728 Montgomery St, San Francisco

NO. 453 🔔

LUCAS, TURNER & CO. BANK (SHERMAN'S BANK)

William Tecumseh Sherman established the branch bank of Lucas, Turner & Co. in San Francisco in 1853, and settled the firm in its own building on the northeast corner of Jackson and Montgomery Streets in the spring of 1854. He successfully carried the bank through the financial crisis of 1855, and remained until it discontinued business in 1857.

NE corner of Montgomery and Jackson, San Francisco

NO. 454 🔔

WOODWARD'S GARDENS

R. B. Woodward opened his gardens to the public in 1866 as an amusement park catering to all tastes, and it remained San Francisco's most popular resort until it closed in 1892. The Gardens once occupied the block bounded by Mission, Duboce, Valencia, and 14th Streets; the main entrance was on Mission.

SW corner of Mission and Duboce Sts, San Francisco

NO. 459 🔔

SITE OF BRICK BUILDING OF THE FIRM OF MELLUS AND HOWARD

In the Mellus and Howard Warehouse, erected on this site in 1848, the Society of California Pioneers, oldest historical society in the state, was organized August 31, 1850 to collect and preserve the history of California. W. D. M. Howard was its first president.

555 Montgomery at Clay, San Francisco

NO. 462 🔔

SITE OF FIRST JEWISH RELIGIOUS SERVICES IN SAN FRANCISCO

In a second-floor room in a store that once stood here, forty pioneers of the Jewish faith gathered on September 26, 1849, Yom Kippur (5610), and participated in the first Jewish religious services in San Francisco.

735 Montgomery between Washington and Jackson, San Francisco

NO. 500 🔔

EASTERN TERMINUS OF CLAY STREET HILL RAILROAD

The Clay Street Hill Railroad Company, the first cable railroad system in the world, was invented and installed by Andrew S. Hallidie. It started operation on August 1, 1873 and ceased on February 15, 1942.

Portsmouth Plaza, Clay and Kearny, San Francisco

NO. 587 🏛

FIRST PUBLIC SCHOOL

This is the site of the first public school in California. It was opened on April 3, 1848 on the southwest corner of Portsmouth Square.

Portsmouth Plaza, Clay and Brenham Sts, San Francisco

NO. 623 🔔

UNION SQUARE

This was the center of San Francisco in pioneer days, deeded for public use January 3, 1850 during the administration of John White Geary, first mayor and postmaster, and later Governor of Kansas and Pennsylvania. The name originated in 1860 when public meetings were held here in support of the Union.

NE corner of Geary and Powell, San Francisco

NO. 650 🔔

SITE OF THE WHAT CHEER HOUSE

This is the site of the famous What Cheer House, a unique hotel opened in 1852 by R. B. Woodward and destroyed by the fire of 1906. The What Cheer House catered to men only, permitted no liquor on the premises, and housed San Francisco's first free library and first museum.

SW corner of Sacramento and Leidesdorff Sts, San Francisco

NO. 691 🔔

SARCOPHAGUS OF THOMAS STARR KING

Apostle of liberty, humanitarian, Unitarian minister, who in the Civil War bound California to the Union and led her to excel all other states in support of the United States Sanitary Commission that preceded the American Red Cross. His statue, together with that of Father Junípero Serra, represents California in the National Capitol, and his name is borne by a Yosemite peak—"A man to match our mountains."

First Unitarian Church, Franklin between Starr King and Geary, San Francisco

NO. 696 🔔

WESTERN BUSINESS HEADQUARTERS OF RUSSELL, MAJORS, AND WADDELL—FOUNDERS, OWNERS, AND OPERATORS OF THE PONY EXPRESS

This was the site of the western business headquarters of Russell, Majors, and Waddell-founders, owners, and operators of the Pony Express, 1860-1861. The firm's main office was in Leavenworth, Kansas; W. W. Finney was the western representative in San Francisco.

601 Montgomery St at Clay, San Francisco

NO. 754 🔔

SITE OF THE MARK HOPKINS INSTITUTE OF ART

In February 1893, Mr. Edward F. Searles donated the Hopkins Mansion to the University of California in trust for the San Francisco Art Institute for "instruction in and illustration of the fine arts, music, and literature," and as San Francisco's first cultural center.

SE corner of California at Mason, San Francisco

NO. 760 🔔

SITE OF LAUREL HILL CEMETERY

The builders of the West, civic and military leaders, jurists, inventors, artists, and eleven United States Senators are buried here, on the most revered of San Francisco's hills.

3333 California St at Walnut, San Francisco

NO. 772 🔔

ORIGINAL SITE OF ST. MARY'S COLLEGE

In August 1863, Archbishop Joseph Sadoc Alemany, OP, opened St. Mary's College here with a faculty of two diocesan priests, four laymen, and two student teachers. In August 1868, at the invitation of the archbishop, Brother Justin McMahon and seven Christian Brothers took charge of St. Mary's.

Intersection of Mission and College Sts, San Francisco

NO. 784 🔔

EL CAMINO REAL (AS FATHER SERRA KNEW IT AND HELPED BLAZE IT)

This plaque was placed on the 250th anniversary of the birth of California's apostle, Padre Junípero Serra, OFM, to mark El Camino Real as he knew it and helped blaze it.

Mission San Diego de Alcala, San Diego to Mission San Francisco de Asis, Dolores St, between 16th and 17th Sts, San Francisco

NO. 791 🔔

ORIGINAL SITE OF THE BANCROFT LIBRARY

In 1860 Hubert Howe Bancroft began to collect the wealth of material which was to result in the writing of his monumental history of western North America. His library was located here in 1881; in 1905 it was purchased by the University of California and moved the following year to Berkeley.

1538 Valencia St, San Francisco

NO. 810 🔔

SITE OF OLD ST. MARY'S CHURCH

The first building erected as a cathedral in California, Old St. Mary's served the Archdiocese of San Francisco from 1854 to 1891. Once the city's most prominent building, it is built of brick brought "around the Horn" in sailing ships, and much of its stonework was quarried and cut in China.

NE corner of California and Grant Ave; plaque on Grant Ave entrance, San Francisco

NO. 819 🔔
HUDSON'S BAY COMPANY HEADQUARTERS

On this block, then on Yerba Buena's waterfront, stood the California headquarters of the Hudson's Bay Company. Their chief trader, William G. Tae, purchased the property and started operations in 1841. This venture caused wide speculation about British intentions. Inadequate profits, a declining fur catch, and pressure of U.S. expansion caused Hudson's Bay Company to end its California operations.

505 Montgomery between Sacramento and Commercial Sts, San Francisco

NO. 841 🔔
THE CONSERVATORY

California's first municipal greenhouse was completed in 1879. Patterned after The Conservatory, Kew Gardens, England, it was a distinguished example of late Victorian style using early techniques of mass production and assembly of simple glass units. It was given to the City of San Francisco by public-spirited citizens.

Golden Gate Park, 0.5 mi W of John McLearn Lodge on J F Kennedy Dr, San Francisco

NO. 861 🔔
SITE OF FIRST CALIFORNIA STATE FAIR

California's first state fair was held on this site on October 4, 1854. Sponsored by the California State Agricultural Society, the exhibition of "horses, cattle, mules, and other stock, and agricultural, mechanical, and domestic manufacture and produc-

tions" promoted the new state's growing agricultural industry. A different city held the fair each year, until Sacramento became the permanent location in 1861.

269 Bush at Montgomery St, San Francisco

NO. 875 🔔
OLD UNITED STATES MINT

This is San Francisco's second mint (1869), California's only such Federal Greek Revival structure. Due to unsurpassed productivity, it became a sub-treasury in 1874. Intact after the 1906 disaster, it served as clearinghouse-bank, thus aiding in the city's reconstruction. Closed in 1937, it was restored in 1972-76 by Mint Director Mary Brooks.

In lobby of Old Mint, 88–5th St at Mission St, San Francisco

NO. 876
CITY OF PARIS BUILDING

It was 1850 when the Verdier brothers, immigrants from France, opened a store aboard the ship *La Ville de Paris* to serve the Argonauts passing through San Francisco's harbor. In 1896 the business, which stayed in the family for over a century and a quarter, moved into a new building designed by architect Clinton Day; damaged by the 1906 earthquake, its interior was reconstructed by architects John Bakewell and Arthur J. Brown. The old City of Paris building was one of the finest examples of the beaux-arts style of commercial building in California.

SE corner of Geary and Stockton Sts, San Francisco

NO. 937 🔔

SITE OF INVENTION OF THE THREE-REEL BELL SLOT MACHINE

Charles August Fey invented the first coin-operated, three-reel slot machine in San Francisco in 1895. Fey continued to manufacture the popular "Liberty Bell" gaming devices in a workshop located at 406 Market Street from 1897 to 1906, until the workshop was destroyed by the 1906 earthquake and fire. The international popularity of the bell slot machines attested to Fey's ingenuity as an enterprising inventor whose basic design continues to be used in mechanical gaming devices today.

Traffic island on N side of Market St between Bush and Battery Sts, San Francisco

NO. 941 🔺

FARNSWORTH'S GREEN STREET LAB

In a simple laboratory on this site, 202 Green Street, Philo Taylor Farnsworth, U.S. pioneer in electronics, invented and patented the first operational all-electronic "television system." On September 7, 1927 the 21-year-old inventor and several dedicated assistants successfully transmitted the first all-electronic television image, the major breakthrough that brought the practical form of this invention to mankind. Further patents formulated here covered the basic concepts essential to modern television. The genius of Green Street, as he was known, died in 1971.

NW corner of Sansome and Green Sts, San Francisco

NO. 964

BIRTHPLACE OF THE UNITED NATIONS, WAR MEMORIAL COMPLEX

President Franklin D. Roosevelt designated the War Memorial Complex in San Francisco to be the place that the United Nations Conference for International Organization would convene on April 25, 1945. Fifty nations participated in the drafting of the United Nations Charter which was unanimously adopted June 25 and signed by representatives of the 50 nations in the War Memorial Veterans Building on June 26. The site of the signing of the Charter is one of the most significant historical landmark sites in the world for 20th century events.

Civic Center San Francisco

NO. 974

GOLDEN GATE BRIDGE

Construction of the bridge started in 1933. Engineer Joseph Strauss and architect Irving Morrow created an extraordinarily beautiful bridge in an extraordinarily beautiful setting. The designs for the Golden Gate Bridge showed the greatest attention to artistic detail, especially on the two streamline moderne towers. The bridge's 4,200 feet of clear span (from tower to tower) was the longest in world until 1959. On April 19, 1937, the bridge was completed and the official dedication took place on May 27th.

Toll Gate area, S end of bridge

NO. 987 🔔

TREASURE ISLAND–GOLDEN GATE INTERNATIONAL EXPOSITION, 1939-40

This artificial island was constructed of bay sand in 1936-7. It was the site of the Golden Gate International Exposition, February 18, 1939-September 29, 1940. Tall towers, gigantic goddesses and dazzling lighting effects turned the Island into a "Magic City." The exposition celebrated the ascendancy of California and San Francisco as economic, political and cultural forces in the increasingly important Pacific Region. From 1939 to 1944 the Island was the landing site for flights of the China Clipper. Treasure Island has been a U.S. Naval Station since 1941.

Naval Station, Treasure Island, San Francisco

NO. 1002

SITE OF THE FIRST DYNAMITE FACTORY IN UNITED STATES

The first commercial manufacturing of dynamite in the U.S. occurred in what is now Glen Canyon Park. On March 19, 1868, the Giant Powder Company began production at its first manufacturing plant, under exclusive license from Alfred Nobel to produce his new explosive in America. The factory did not last long. On November 26, 1869, an explosion completely destroyed the entire facility, turning every one of the buildings on the place, and the surrounding fencing, into "hundreds of pieces," according to a newpaper account. The company moved its operations elsewhere, an action that was to be repeated again in the future under similar circumstances, until it moved to its permanent and final home at Point Pinole on San Pablo Bay.

Glen Canyon Park, San Francisco

NO. 1010 🔔

ORIGINAL SITE OF THE THIRD BAPTIST CHURCH (FORMERLY THE FIRST COLORED BAPTIST CHURCH)

In August 1852, Abraham Brown, Thomas Bundy, Thomas Davenport, Willie Denton, Harry Fields, George Lewis, Fielding Spotts, and Eliza and William Davis organized the church in the Davis home. The congregation purchased the old First Baptist Church and moved it to this location in 1854. The church is now located at 1399 McAllister Street.

Corner Grant Ave and Greenwich, San Francisco

Landmark No. 691

Landmark No. 937

Landmark No. 784

San Joaquin County

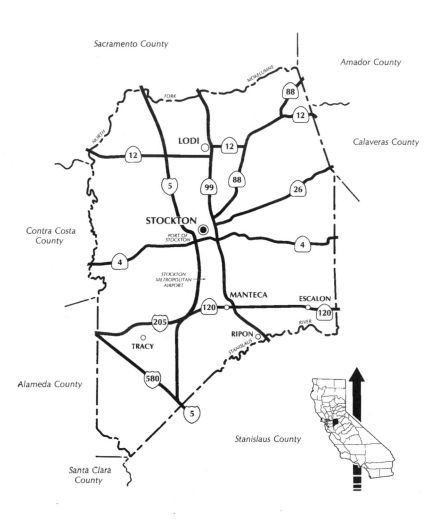

Sacramento County

Amador County

MOKELUMNE

FORK

88

12

NORTH

Calaveras County

LODI

12

12

5

99

88

26

STOCKTON

Contra Costa
County

PORT OF
STOCKTON

4

4

STOCKTON
METROPOLITAN
AIRPORT

MANTECA

ESCALON

120

120

205

RIVER

580

RIPON

STANISLAUS

TRACY

Alameda County

5

Stanislaus County

Santa Clara
County

San Joaquin
Est. 1850

The many waterways of the San Joaquin, Cosumnes, Mokelumne, and Calaveras Rivers and abundant sloughs create a rich marshland for waterfowl and other wildlife. Stockton, the county seat, is centrally located amidst a maze of highways connecting the county to the river delta, the bay area and the Sierra Nevada foothills.

NO. 149 [M]

BENSON'S FERRY

This river ferry, established in 1849, was purchased by John A. Benson in 1850. In 1852, Benson laid out the then-principal wagon road between Sacramento and Stockton. Following Benson's murder in 1859, the ferry was operated by his son-in-law, Ed Gayetty.

S bank of N Fork Mokelumne River 100 ft W of County Rd J8, 3 mi N of Thornton

NO. 155 □

LONE STAR MILL

A sawmill built in 1852 on the Mokelumne River was removed to Hodge and (David S.) Terry's ranch in 1854 and a flour mill attached the following year. The mill burned in 1856 and was rebuilt on its present site as the Lone Star Mill.

Entrance to Stillman L. Magee Park, Mackville Rd, 1 mi N of Clements

NO. 162 [M]

SITE OF MOKELUMNE CITY

Established in 1850, its prospects were bright. The second largest town in the county, it had deep water communication with San Francisco all year round, an advantage not possessed by any other town in the county except Stockton. The floods of 1862 destroyed the town.

200 ft N of intersection of Cameron Rd and Thornton Rd, 3 mi N of Thornton

NO. 163

SITE OF WOOD'S FERRY AND WOOD'S BRIDGE

In 1852, immediately after his arrival and completion of his cabin, Wood proceeded to build a ferryboat and establish the crossing known as Wood's Ferry. In 1858, he built a toll bridge at the old ferry crossing, charging $1 for a pair of animals and wagon, and .50 extra for every additional pair of animals with the wagon.

Present bridge is approx location of original ferry and bridge, County Hwy J10, Woodbridge

NO. 165 🔔

WEBER POINT

Site of a two-story adobe-and-redwood house built in 1850 by Charles M. Weber, founder and pioneer developer of Stockton. One of the first elaborate residences and landscaped gardens in the San Joaquin Valley, it remained Captain Weber's home until his death in 1881.

On Center St between Channel and Miner Sts, Stockton

NO. 178 🔔

SITE OF FIRST BUILDING IN PRESENT CITY OF STOCKTON

In August 1844, the first settlers arrived at Rancho del Campo de los Franceses. One of the company, Thomas Lindsay, built the first dwelling, a tule hut, on this site. He was later murdered by Indians and buried here by travelers. The Point was formed by the junction of McLeod's Lake and Miner's Channel.

City Hall, on Civic St between Miner and El Dorado Sts, Stockton

NO. 214

SITE OF BATTLE BETWEEN FORCES UNDER GENERAL VALLEJO AND SAN JOAQUIN VALLEY INDIANS

In 1829, the Governor-General of California directed Vallejo to punish the Cosumnes Indians for their raids on local ranches. The battle is one of the few fought in California in which cannons were actually used.

10 mi S of Manteca on Two Rivers Rd, take S Manteca Rd to Trahern, turn right 1/4 mi, left on Two Rivers Rd to Indian Valley Resort, 200 yards SE of confluence of San Joaquin and Stanislaus Rivers on N bank of Stanislaus

NO. 358

TOWN OF WOODBRIDGE

In 1852 Jeremiah H. Woods and Alexander McQueen established a ferry across the Mokelumne River at this point. As a result, a new road from Stockton to Sacramento by way of Wood's Ferry was established. In 1858 Woods built a bridge at the site of the ferry from which the town, laid out in April 1859, took its name.

On County Hwy J10, Woodbridge

NO. 365 ☐

LOCKEFORD (LOCKE'S FORD)

It was on this hill that Dr. Dean Jewett Locke and his brother Elmer H. Locke built the first cabin on this section in 1851. Disturbed by grizzly bears, they spent their first nights in the oak trees. Dr. Locke, physician for the Boston and Newton Joint Stock Company, left Boston on April 16, 1849 to cross the plains and arrive at Sacramento on September 16, 1849. Because he built and maintained a ford across the Mokelumne River, his wife, Delia Hammond Locke, in 1859 named the town he laid out on his ranch Lockeford.

0.6 mi N on Elliotte Rd, Lockeford

NO. 436 🔔

NEW HOPE

Approximately six miles west of this spot, 20 Mormon pioneers from the ship Brooklyn founded the first known agricultural colony in San Joaquin Valley, planting the first wheat and crops that they irrigated by the pole and bucket method. They erected three log houses and operated a sawmill and a ferry across Stanislaus. Their settlement later became known as Stanislaus City.

Ripon City Park, Fourth and Locust Sts, Ripon

NO. 437 🔔
FIRST LANDING PLACE OF SAILING LAUNCH COMET

First known sail launch to ascend San Joaquin River from San Francisco landed here autumn, 1846. It carried 20 Mormon pioneers who founded New Hope Agricultural Project on Stanislaus. A yoke of oxen and span of mules were driven from Marsh's Landing (Antioch) by two men who followed a crude map drawn by Merritt the trapper. Two years later Doak and Bonsell operated here the first ferry on San Joaquin River.

From I-5 take Manthey Rd interchange, take W side frontage rd, go N 1 mi to N bank of San Joaquin River; plaque located at entrance to Mossdale Crossing Park and Ramp, 2.0 mi N of intersection of I-5 and I-205, Tracy

NO. 513 🔔
BURIAL PLACE OF JOHN BROWN ("JUAN FLACO")

In 1846, during American conquest of California, John Brown –nicknamed Juan Flaco – rode from Los Angeles to San Francisco in four days to warn Commodore Stockton of the siege of Los Angeles, and troops were sent to secure the city. This "Paul Revere of California," who lived in Stockton from 1851 to 1859, is buried in the former Citizen's Cemetery near this site.

1100 E Weber St at N Union St, Stockton

NO. 520 🔔
SAN JOAQUIN VALLEY COLLEGE

Built through subscription by the residents of Woodbridge and dedicated as Woodbridge Seminary in 1879 by the United Brethren Church, this was the site of San Joaquin Valley College from 1882 to 1897. It was then used as Woods Grammar School until 1922, when the building was dismantled.

18500 N Lilac St, Woodbridge

NO. 668 🔔
FRENCH CAMP

Here was the terminus of the Oregon-California Trail used from about 1832 to 1845 by the French-Canadian trappers employed by the Hudson's Bay Company. Every year Michel La Framboise, among others, met fur hunters camped with their families here. In 1844 Charles M. Weber and William Gulnac promoted the first white settlers' colony on Rancho del Campo de los Franceses, which included French Camp and the site of Stockton.

On Elm St at French Camp School, French Camp

NO. 740 🔔
CARNEGIE

A city of 3,500 population from 1895-1912, the town had a post office, company store, hotels, saloons, bandstand, and hundreds of homes. The Carnegie Brick and Pottery Company had 45 kilns and 13 tall smokestacks; clay came from the famous Tesla Coal Mine, four miles to the west. Town and plant were served by the Alameda and San Joaquin Railroad.

Carnegie State Vehicular Recreation Area, 5.9 mi W of I-580 on Corral Hollow Rd, 9 mi SW of Tracy

NO. 755 📛

CORRAL HOLLOW

The Edward B. Carrell home was built here at the site of an Indian village on El Camino Viejo, an old Spanish trail. Through here passed the '49ers and the first mail to the Tuolumne mines; men and animals received food and drink at Wright's Zink House five hundred yards north of here.

1.5 mi W of I-580 on Corral Hollow Rd, 6.5 mi SW of Tracy

NO. 765 🔔

TEMPLE ISRAEL CEMETERY

Donated by Captain Charles M. Weber in 1851 for use as a cemetery by the Jewish community of Stockton, this is the oldest Jewish cemetery in continuous use in California and west of the Rocky Mountains.

On E Acacia St between N Pilgrim and N Union Sts, Stockton

NO. 777 🔔

SITE OF SAN JOAQUIN CITY

This river town was established in 1849. Pioneers and freight wagons following post roads to the southern mines crossed the river nearby at Durham's Ferry, and as a terminal for riverboats, the town played an important part in development of west side grain farming and cattle raising.

1.4 mi N of county line on County Hwy J3, SE of Tracy

NO. 780-7 🔔

FIRST TRANSCONTINENTAL RAILROAD–SITE OF COMPLETION OF PACIFIC RAILROAD

The construction of the San Joaquin River bridge completed the last link of the transcontinental railroad. Building has proceeded simultaneously from the bay area and Sacramento to meet at the San Joaquin River. The first train crossed the bridge on September 8, 1869.

From I-5 take Manthey Rd interchange, take W side frontage rd and go N 1.9 mi to N bank of San Joaquin River; plaque located at entrance to Mossdale Crossing Park and Ramp, 2.0 mi N of intersection of I–5 and I-205, Tracy

NO. 801 ☐

REUEL COLT GRIDLEY MONUMENT

Erected in honor of the soldier's friend, Reuel Colt Gridley, by Rawlins Post, Grand Army of the Republic, and the citizens of Stockton in gratitude for services rendered Union soldiers during the War of the Rebellion, when he collected $275,000 for the Sanitary Commission by selling and reselling a sack of flour.

Stockton Rural Cemetery near Memory Chapel, Cemetery Ln and E Pine St, Stockton

NO. 931 🔔

LODI ARCH

Designed by architect E. B. Brown and built in 1907 for the Lodi Tokay Carnival, the arch served as an entrance into Lodi and a symbol of agricultural and commercial growth. Essentially unaltered since construction, the structure is one of few remaining Mission Revival ceremonial arches left within California.

SE corner of E Pine and S Sacramento Sts, Lodi

NO. 934 🔔

TEMPORARY DETENTION CAMPS FOR JAPANESE AMERICANS— STOCKTON ASSEMBLY CENTER

Here, within the confines of San Joaquin County Fairgrounds, enclosed by barbed wire and housed in temporary barracks, 4,217 San Joaquin County residents of Japanese ancestry, predominately American citizens, were interned from May 10 to October 17, 1942 under Executive Order 9066. May such usurpation of civil, social, and economic rights, without specific charges or trial, never again occur.

Administration Bldg, San Joaquin County Fairgrounds, Airport Way, Stockton

NO. 935 🔔

CALIFORNIA CHICORY WORKS

The partnership of C. A. Bachmann and Charles H. W. Brandt, formed in 1885, was the largest chicory supplier in America while operating at this site during the 1890s. Chicory roots are roasted, ground, and used as a mixture with or substitute for coffee. Using its own ship, *The Dora*, and the finest German equipment to process the chicory, the company shipped its product to market until about 1911.

1672 W Bowman Rd, 2.2 mi W of I-5, French Camp

NO. 995

TRAIL OF THE JOHN C. FRÉMONT 1844 EXPEDITION

Frémont's historic second overland expedition of 1843-44 was the first in which he reached California. He and his companions entered California in the dead of winter, camped across the snowbound Sierra, spent a month at Sutter's Fort in the Sacramento Valley, and then continued south through the San Joaquin Valley. Frémont's report added to the growing American interest in the Far West and California, making this 1844 expedition one of the most influential events in American westward expansion. Frémont camped at this site on March 26, 1844.

NW corner of junction of Hwy 88 and Calaveras River

NO. 1016

STOCKTON DEVELOPMENTAL CENTER

The Stockton Developmental Center began in 1853 as the Insane Asylum of California at Stockton. It was founded on 100 acres with ready access to the goldfields on land donated by Captain Charles Weber, founder of Stockton. California's Legislature was convinced that the turbulence of the Gold Rush had caused many to suffer from mental problems, and that the existing hospitals were inadequate to cope with large numbers of people with mental and emotional conditions. Consequently it authorized the establishment of the Stockton Hospital, the first public hospital in California to serve the mentally ill. California's mental hospital is one of the oldest in the west, and early on was recognized for its progressive forms of treatment.

510 E Magnolia St, Stockton

San Luis Obispo County

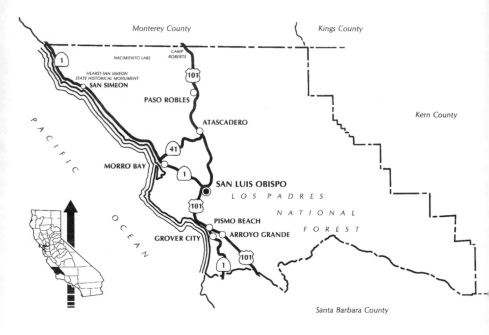

Hearst San Simeon State Historical Monument - Home of distinguished Californian, William Randolph Hearst. Located 9 miles N of Cambria, Highway 1.

San Luis Obispo
Est. 1850

San Luis Obispo County boasts a generous length of Pacific Coast shoreline and its jewel, California's only castle, Hearst San Simeon State Historical Monument. During the Spanish Era of Alta California, two missions sprang up around the large Indian population here. Along the coast, Morro Rock stands as a maritime navigational landmark.

NO. 325 🔔

MISSION SAN LUÍS OBISPO DE TOLOSA

Founded by Fray Junípero Serra, OFM, first president of the California missions, Mission San Luís Obispo was the fifth in a chain of 21 missions stretching from San Diego to Sonoma. Built by the Chumash Indians living in the area, its combination of belfry and vestibule is unique among California missions. In 1846 John C. Frémont and his California Battalion quartered here while engaged in the war with Mexico.

Monterey between Chorro and Broad Sts, San Luis Obispo

NO. 326 🔔

MISSION SAN MIGUEL ARCÁNGEL

This site was selected because of the great number of Salinan Indians that lived in the vicinity. Fray Fermín Francisco de Lasuén, OFM, second president of the California missions, founded San Miguel Arcángel on July 25, 1797. The 16th in a chain of 21 Franciscan missions, it influenced not only the native population, but the history of California as a whole.

SW corner of Mission St and San Luis Obispo Rd, San Miguel

NO. 364

SANTA MARGARITA ASISTENCIA (SITE OF)

This asistencia served as an outpost or chapel and storehouse for Mission San Luís Obispo. Here the mission padres and the Indians carried on extensive grain cultivation.

Rancho Santa Margarita Hay Barn (private property, no trespassing), 1/4 mi N of intersection of Yerba Buena Ave and F St, Santa Margarita

NO. 542 🔔

ESTRELLA ADOBE CHURCH

This was the first Protestant church to be erected in the northern part of San Luis Obispo County. Construction was completed in 1878; restoration was completed in 1952.

On Airport Rd, 2.5 mi N of State Hwy 46, Paso Robles

NO. 640 🔔
HEARST SAN SIMEON STATE HISTORICAL MONUMENT

Here on the historic Piedra Blanca Rancho, between 1919 and 1947, William Randolph Hearst created La Cuesta Encantada (The Enchanted Hill), including La Casa Grande and adjacent buildings with their rare art treasures and beautiful gardens. The Hearst Corporation presented it to the State of California in 1958 as a memorial to William Randolph Hearst, donated in the name of his mother, Phoebe Apperson Hearst.

Hearst San Simeon State Historical Monument, plaque located in entrance rest area, State Hwy 1, San Simeon

NO. 720 🔔
DALLIDET ADOBE

This was the home of Pierre Hyppolite Dallidet, a native of France, who settled in San Luis Obispo in 1853 and became a vineyardist. His son, Paul Dallidet, gave it to the San Luis Obispo County Historical Society in 1953, in memory of the Dallidet family that had occupied it for a century.

1309 Toro at Pacific, San Luis Obispo

NO. 726 🔔
THE SEBASTIAN STORE

This is the oldest store building along the north coast of San Luis Obispo County. Built in the 1860s at Whaling Point, one-half mile to the west, it was moved to its present location in 1878. It has been operated by the Sebastian family for over half a century.

San Simeon Road, San Simeon

NO. 802 🔔
AH LOUIS STORE

Ah Louis' Store, established in 1874, was the first Chinese store in the county. It sold general merchandise and herbs and served as a bank, counting house, and post office for the numerous Chinese coolies who dug the eight tunnels through the Mountains of Cuesta for the Southern Pacific Railroad, 1884 to 1894.

800 Palm St at Chorro St, San Luis Obispo

NO. 821 🔔
MORRO ROCK

An important mariner's navigational landfall for over three hundred years, Morro Reef was chronicled in the diaries of Portolá, Fr. Crespí, and Costanso in 1769, when they camped near this area on their trek to find Monterey. Sometimes called the "Gibraltar of the Pacific," it is the last in the famous chain of nine peaks that starts in the City of San Luis Obispo.

Located in city park, foot of Morro Rock, on Embarcadero Rd, 0.4 mi NW of Morro Bay

NO. 936 🔔
RÍOS-CALEDONIA ADOBE

This imposing building is an excellent example of California's Mexican-era architecture. With Indian labor, Petronilo Ríos built the two-story adobe about 1846 as his residence and the headquarters for his sheep and cattle operations. Named "Caledonia" in the 1860s, it served as a hotel and stop on the stage route between Los Angeles and San Francisco until 1886. Restoration was begun in 1968 by the Friends of the Adobes.

700 Mission St, San Miguel

NO. 939 🔔

Twentieth Century Folk Art Environments (Thematic) —NITT WITT RIDGE

Nitt Witt Ridge, one of California's remarkable Twentieth Century Folk Art Environments, is the creation of Arthur Harold Beal (der Tinkerpaw or Capt. Nitt Witt), a Cambria Pines pioneer, who sculpted the land using hand tools and indigenous materials, remarkable inventiveness, and self-taught skills. A blend of native materials and contemporary elements, impressive in its sheer mass and meticulous placement, it is a revealing memorial to Art's unique cosmic humor and zest for life.

Nitt Witt Ridge, 881 Hillcrest Dr, Cambria Pines

NO. 958 🔔

ADMINISTRATION AND VETERAN'S MEMORIAL BUILDING

This building, dedicated in 1914 and completed in 1918, was the headquarters for the Atascadero Colony, a model community envisioned by Edward G. Lewis. Designed by Walter D. Bliss of San Francisco and built of reinforced concrete and locally produced brick, it had also served as a private school for boys, a veteran's memorial building, and county offices. It is currently the seat of municipal government.

6500 Palma Ave, Atascadero

Landmark No. 936

San Mateo County

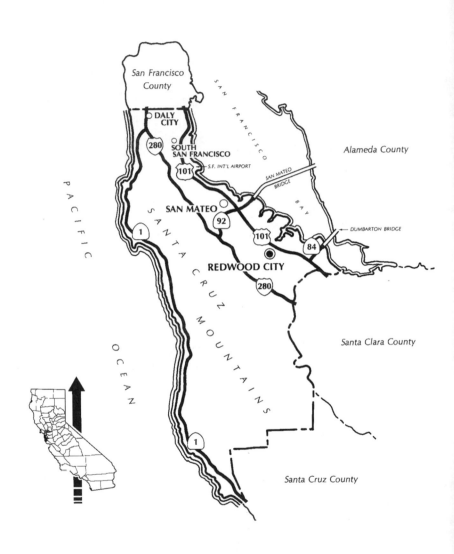

San Francisco
County

DALY
CITY

280

SOUTH
SAN FRANCISCO

101   S.F. INT'L AIRPORT

Alameda County

SAN MATEO BRIDGE

PACIFIC

SAN MATEO

92

101

DUMBARTON BRIDGE

84

1

REDWOOD CITY

SANTA CRUZ MOUNTAINS

280

BAY

Santa Clara County

OCEAN

1

Santa Cruz County

San Mateo
Est. 1856

The rugged Santa Cruz Mountains separate the coastline of San Mateo County from its web of urban development along the eastern edge of San Francisco Bay. Highway 1 winds along the rocky Pacific shoreline, roughly tracing the route of Portolá's expedition of 1769.

NO. 2 🔔
PORTOLÁ JOURNEY'S END

In 1769 the Portolá expedition of 63 men and 200 horses and mules camped near El Palo Alto, the tall tree. They had traveled from San Diego in search of Monterey but discovered instead the Bay of San Francisco. Finding the bay too large to go around, and deciding that Monterey had been bypassed, they ended the search and returned to San Diego.

Intersection of E Creek Dr and Alma St, Menlo Park

NO. 19 🔔
BRODERICK-TERRY DUELING PLACE

In the early morning of September 13, 1859, U.S. Senator David C. Broderick and Chief Justice David S. Terry of the California Supreme Court fought the famous duel that ended dueling in California in a ravine east of here, near the shore of Lake Merced. Senator Broderick was mortally wounded. The site is marked with a monument and granite shafts where the two men stood.

1100 Lake Merced Blvd, Daly City

NO. 21
PORTOLÁ EXPEDITION CAMP

The Portolá Expedition of 1769 camped close to the mouth of Pilarcitos Creek on October 28 and 29. Portolá himself was very ill.

Mouth of Pilarcitos Creek, 1/2 mi W of State Hwy 1 (P.M.. 29.0), Half Moon Bay

NO. 22
PORTOLÁ EXPEDITION CAMP

The Portolá Expedition of 1769 camped on the south bank of Purísima Creek on October 27. The Indian village on the north bank of the creek was named "Las Pulgas" by the army engineer with the party because the soldiers who occupied some abandoned Indian huts became covered with fleas.

Mouth of Purisima Creek, 1/2 mi W of State Hwy 1 (P.M. 24.6), 4.1 mi S of Half Moon Bay

NO. 23
PORTOLÁ EXPEDITION CAMP

The Portolá Expedition of 1769 camped October 23 near the mouth of Gazos Creek.

State Hwy 1 (P.M. 5.75) at Gazos Creek Rd, 79 mi S of Pescadero Rd

NO. 24 🔔

PORTOLÁ EXPEDITION CAMP

The Portolá Expedition of 1769 camped near the San Pedro Creek, where there was an Indian village, from October 31 to November 3. To that camp scouting parties brought news of a body of water to the east.

SE corner of Crespi Dr and State Hwy 1, Pacifica

NO. 25

PORTOLÁ EXPEDITION CAMP

The Portolá Expedition of 1769 camped October 30 on a stream at the foot of Montara Mountain, which now blocked their way. Needing food badly, here the explorers found a plentiful supply of mussels. They named the camp "El Rincón de las Almejas."

On Martini Creek at foot of Montara Mtn, 1/2 mi E of State Hwy 1 (P.M. 37.2), 0.9 mi N of Montara

NO. 26 🔔

PORTOLÁ EXPEDITION CAMP

On October 24, the Portolá Expedition camped at an Indian rancheria on San Gregorio Creek, about one-half league from its mouth. Tired and sick, they rested here over the 25th and 26th.

San Gregorio State Beach, State Hwy 1 (P.M. 18.1), 0.1 mi S of State Hwy 84 intersection, 10.8 mi S of Half Moon Bay

NO. 27 ☐

PORTOLÁ EXPEDITION CAMP

The Portolá Expedition of 1769 camped near a lagoon now covered by San Andreas Lake on November 4. They camped here a second time on November 12, on their return trip.

Take Millbrae Ave interchange I-280, go N to intersection of Skyline Blvd and Hillcrest Blvd; plaque 500 ft W on Hillcrest Blvd, Millbrae

NO. 47 🔔

ANZA EXPEDITION CAMP

Here on the banks of San Mateo Creek Captain J. B. de Anza camped March 29, 1776, after exploring the peninsula and selecting the sites for the Mission and Presidio of San Francisco. The party of families, soldiers, and priests, on their way to establish San Francisco, also camped here for three days, June 24-27, 1776.

From El Camino Real (State Hwy 82), go W one block on W 3rd Ave, turn N on Arroyo Court, go 1/2 block and turn left; plaque is 300 ft W, San Mateo

NO. 48

ANZA EXPEDITION CAMP

The Anza Expedition of 1776, on its way up the peninsula to locate sites for the Presidio and Mission of San Francisco, camped here on March 26 at a dry watercourse a short league beyond Arroyo de San Mateo.

El Camino Real and Ralston, Burlingame

NO. 92

PORTOLÁ EXPEDITION CAMP

On November 11, the Portolá Expedition of 1769 traveled two leagues, about 5.26 miles, to a point in the lower Cañada de Reymundo, and made their first camp on their return trip.

Pulgas Water Temple, on Canada Rd (P.M. 3.1), 6 mi N of Woodside

NO. 93 🔔

WOODSIDE STORE

Built in 1854 among sawmills and red-wood groves by Dr. R. O. Tripp and M. A. Parkhurst, the store was operated by Dr. Tripp (who also served as dentist, librarian, postmaster, and community leader) until his death in 1909. It was purchased by the County of San Mateo in 1940 and opened as a public museum on September 7, 1947.

SW corner of Tripp Rd and Kings Mint Rd, Woodside

NO. 94

PORTOLÁ EXPEDITION CAMP

The Portolá Expedition of 1769 camped on November 5 at a "laguna grande" which today is covered by the Upper Crystal Springs Lake.

Crystal Springs Dam, on Skyline Blvd (P.M. 13.7), 0.1 mi S of Crystal Springs Rd, 4 mi W of San Mateo

NO. 343

OLD STORE AT LA HONDA

In the winter of 1861-62, John L. Sears settled in the mountains 17 miles from Redwood City. He named the place La Honda and built a store that was some-times called the "Bandit-Built Store" be-cause two men that he employed-Jim and Bob Younger, newcomers to the area-were later proved to be members of the James Boys gang.

State Hwy 84 (P.M. 8.91), NW corner of La Honda and Sears Ranch Rds, La Honda

NO. 375

TUNITAS BEACH, INDIAN VILLAGE SITE ON PORTOLÁ ROUTE

The Portolá Expedition of 1769 discovered this Indian village on Tunitas Creek, in the southwest corner of Rancho Cañada de Verde y Arroyo de la Purísima; the rancho was granted to José María Alviso in 1838.

Mouth of Tunitas Creek at Tunitas Beach, 1,000 ft W of State Hwy 1 (P.M. 20.9), 6.8 mi S of Half Moon Bay

NO. 391 🔔

SÁNCHEZ ADOBE

This is the home of Francisco Sánchez (1805-1862), alcalde of San Francisco and commandante of militia under the Mexican Republic, grantee of the 8,926-acre Rancho San Pedro, and later a respected American citizen. His house, built 1842-46, afterwards was owned and remodeled by General Edward Kirkpatrick; it was purchased by the County of San Mateo in 1947 to be preserved as a public museum.

Sanchez Adobe County Park, SW corner of Linda Mar Blvd and Seville Dr, Pacifica

NO. 393 □
"THE HOSPICE" (OUTPOST OF MISSION DOLORES)

Here stood the Hospice built around 1800 by the Spanish Padres on El Camino Real to break the journey from Santa Clara and serve the Indians of Mission Dolores.

SW corner of Baywood and El Camino Real, San Mateo

NO. 394 🔔
SITE OF THE DISCOVERY OF SAN FRANCISCO BAY

On October 31,1769, Captain Gaspar de Portolá was camped by the creek at the south of this valley when scouting parties brought news of a body of water to the east. On November 4, the expedition advanced. Turning inland, the party climbed to the summit of Sweeney Ridge and beheld the Bay of San Francisco for the first time.

Sweeney Ridge, from Hwy 1 take Fassler Ave, then trail to site in Pacifica; plaque located SE corner of Crespi Dr and State Hwy 1, Pacifica

NO. 474 🔔
SITE OF THE FORMER VILLAGE OF SEARSVILLE

Here stood the lumbermen's village of Searsville whose first settler, John Sears, arrived in 1854. Across the road, west of this monument, stood a hotel. The school, store, blacksmith shop, and dwellings were to the southeast, some on the site of the present lake and others overlooking it. These buildings were removed in 1891, as water rose behind the new dam.

NW corner intersection of Sandhill and Portola Rds, Woodside

NO. 478 🔔
SITE OF SAN MATEO COUNTY'S FIRST SAWMILL

About 300 feet south of this monument, on the banks of the Alambique Creek, stood San Mateo County's first sawmill, built by Charles Brown in 1847. About the same time, Dennis Martin was building a second mill, also run by waterpower, on San Francisquito Creek. These mills were similar to the famous Sutter's Mill at Coloma, site of James Marshall's 1848 gold discovery.

On Portola Rd, 0.2 mi S of intersection of Woodside Rd (State Hwy 84) and Portola Rd, Woodside

NO. 816
UNION CEMETERY

The name of this cemetery, established before the first shots were fired at Fort Sumter, reflects the controversy that brought on the Civil War. On March 16, 1859, the purchase of six acres was consummated but the cemetery association, not being a corporate body, did not take title to the property. Instead it was deeded "to John B. Weller, Governor of California and his successors in office . . . in trust for the use and benefit of the Union Cemetery Association of San Mateo County."

200 block of Woodside Rd (State Hwy 84), NW corner of El Camino Real and Woodside Rd, Redwood City

NO. 825 🔔
CASA DE TABLETA

This structure, built by Felix Buelna in the 1850s, served as a gambling retreat and meeting place for Mexican-

Californios. It was strategically located on the earliest trail used both by rancheros and American settlers crossing the peninsula to the coast. Acquired by an American in 1868, it has continued to serve under various names as a roadhouse and saloon.

3915 Alpine Rd at Arastradero Rd, town of Portola Valley

NO. 846 🔔

BURLINGAME RAILROAD STATION

This first permanent building in the Mission Revival style of architecture opened for service on October 10, 1894. Designed by George H. Howard and J. B. Mathison, it was financed by local residents and the Southern Pacific Railroad. The roof used 18th-century tiles from the Mission San Antonio de Padua at Jolon and the Mission Dolores Asistencia at San Mateo.

290 California Dr at Burlingame Ave, Burlingame

NO. 856 🔔

RALSTON HALL

This redwood structure was completed in 1868 by William Chapman Ralston, San Francisco financier. Incorporating Count Cipriani's earlier villa, this enlarged mansion with its mirrored ballroom became the symbol of the extravagance of California's Silver Age. It anticipated features later incorporated into Ralston's Palace Hotel in San Francisco.

Campus of College of Notre Dame, 1500 Ralston Ave, Belmont

NO. 886 🔔

CAROLANDS

Harriet Pullman Carolan, heiress to the Pullman railroad car company fortune, constructed this lavish mini-palace in 1915-16, the focal point of a fully landscaped 500-acre estate. Willis Polk supervised construction of the American Renaissance-design residence, which is an adaptation of Vaux le Vicomte, also prototype for the Palace of Versailles. In the early 1950s, Countess Lillian Remillard Dandini acquired the chateau and the six remaining acres of land.

565 Remillard Rd, Hillsborough

NO. 906 🔔

STEELE BROTHERS DAIRY RANCHES

Beginning in the 1850s, the Steele brothers pioneered one of the first large-scale commercial cheese and dairy businesses in California. They extended their operations from Point Reyes to Rancho Punta de Año Nuevo in 1862. This 7,000-acre ranch consisted of five dairies extending from Gazos Creek to Point Año Nuevo. For a century the Steele brothers' dairy ranches were of importance in California's agricultural development.

Año Nuevo State Reserve, NW corner of State Hwy 1 (P.M. 0.9) and New Year's Creek Rd, 14 mi S of Pescadero

NO. 907 🔔

FILOLI

Filoli, built as the home of mining entrepreneur William B. Bourn II, was the last great residential commission of one of California's most important architects, Willis Polk. Built in Georgian Revival style with its formal gardens, Filoli is an outstanding example of the grand estates of the late 1800s.

Filoli Center, Canada Rd (P.M. 2. 7), 5 mi N of Woodside

NO. 909 🔔

OUR LADY OF THE WAYSIDE

This country church, built in 1912, was the first design of architect Timothy L. Pflueger to be executed. Pflueger, who had just begun work for James Miller, shows his awareness of the Spanish California missions in the style, which contrasts with the large commercial buildings and art deco theaters for which he later became recognized. Construction of this church was initiated by a non-denominational club, The Family.

930 Portola Rd, town of Portola Valley

NO. 930 🔔

PIGEON POINT LIGHTHOUSE

This brick lighthouse was built to incorporate a French first order Fresnel lens. Although no longer used, the lens is still operable in the lantern room. Previously the lens had been installed at Cape Hatteras, North Carolina. It first flashed over the Pacific in November 1872, and the lighthouse has served continuously without structural modifications since that time.

Pigeon Point Light Station, 0.2 mi W of intersection of State Hwy 1 (P.M. 8.0) and Pigeon Point Rd, 17 mi N of Davenport

NO. 934

TEMPORARY DETENTION CAMPS FOR JAPANESE AMERICANS— TANFORAN ASSEMBLY CENTER

The temporary detention camps (also known as "assembly centers") represent the first phase of the mass incarceration of 97,785 Californians of Japanese ancestry during World War II. Pursuant to Executive Order 9066 signed by President Franklin D. Roosevelt on February 19, 1942, thirteen makeshift detention facilities were constructed at various California racetracks, fairgrounds, and labor camps. These facilities were intended to confine Japanese Americans until more permanent concentration camps, such as those at Manzanar and Tule Lake in California, could be built in isolated areas of the country. Beginning on March 30, 1942, all native-born Americans and long-time legal residents of Japanese ancestry living in California were ordered to surrender themselves for detention.

Tanforan Park Shopping Center, El Camino Real, San Bruno

NO. 939

Twentieth Century Folk Art Environments (Thematic) —CAPIDRO

The late John Guidici, a retired gardener, began landscaping his Menlo Park house in 1932, using mostly cement, local sand, and the shells that were available free at local beaches.

262 Princeton Rd, Menlo Park

NO. 949 🔔

FIRST CONGREGATIONAL CHURCH OF PESCADERO

Built in May 1867, this is the oldest church building on its original site within the San Mateo-Santa Clara County region. Its Classical Revival style reflects the cultural background of pioneer Yankee settlers of the south San Francisco peninsula coast. The steeple was appended to the bell tower in 1890. During repairs caused by a minor fire in 1940, the social hall was added.

San Gregorio St, Pescadero

NO. 955 🔔

MENLO PARK RAILROAD STATION

This building, constructed in 1867 by the San Francisco and San Jose Railroad Company, is the oldest railroad passenger station in California. The Victorian ornamentation was added in the 1890s when the station was remodeled to serve the newly-opened Stanford University. The extension on the northwest was added to accommodate increased traffic generated by the establishment of Camp Fremont nearby during World War I.

1100 Merrill Ave, Menlo Park

Landmark No. 825

Landmark No. 93

Santa Barbara County

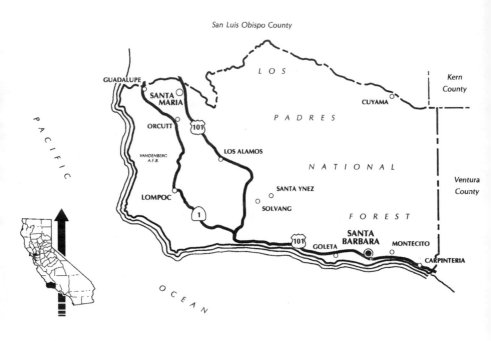

Chumash Painted Cave State Historic Park - Native American Rock Art. Located on San Marcos Pass.

El Presidio de Santa Barbara State Historic Park - Spanish presidio established 1782. Located at 135 E. Canon Perdido, Santa Barbara.

La Purísima Mission State Historic Park - The 11th Franciscan Mission, 1813. Located 4 miles NE of Lompoc on Highway 1.

Santa Barbara
Est. 1850

With its rich history of native American culture, mission settlement, and early Mexican land grants, this oceanside county of Southern California still preserves the flavor of its early beginnings. Spanish explorer Vizcaíno named the channel between the coastline and the Channel Islands in 1602, for Saint Barbara, the name later used for the county.

NO. 248 ☐

GAVIOTA PASS

Here, on Christmas Day, 1846, natives and soldiers from the Presidio of Santa Barbara lay in ambush for Lieutenant Colonel John C. Frémont, U.S.A., and his battalion. Frémont learned of the plot and, guided by Benjamin Foxen and his son William, came instead over the San Marcos Pass, to capture Santa Barbara without bloodshed.

N-bound State Hwy 101 rest stop (P.M. 46.9), 1.5 mi NW of Gaviota

NO. 305

MISSION SANTA INÉS

This mission was founded in 1804 by Father Estévan Tapís to reach the Indians living east of the Coast Range. Construction was completed in 1817. It was through the efforts of Father Alexander Buckler, starting in 1904, that Mission Santa Inés was restored to as much as possible of its old charm and grace.

1760 Mission Dr, Solvang

NO. 306 🔔

BURTON MOUND

Thought to have once been the Indian village of Syujtun, this site has yielded some of the most important archeological evidence found in California. In 1542 the village was recorded by Cabrillo while on his voyage of discovery, and again in 1769 by Fr. Crespí and the redoubtable Portolá. Don Luís Burton, after whom the mound was named, acquired the property in 1860.

129 W Mason St at Burton Circle, Santa Barbara

NO. 307 🔔

CASA DE LA GUERRA

A common council was duly elected near this site on August 26, 1850, two weeks before California statehood. The City of Santa Barbara held its first official meeting here in 1875; the first city hall was erected here, and the area is still center of city's governmental activities. The plaza was the scene of early Santa Barbara fiestas, and the hospitality at the de la Guerra house set standards for Santa Barbara.

El Paseo Plaza, SE corner of De La Guerra St and De La Guerra Plaza, Santa Barbara

NO. 308 🔔

COVARRUBIAS ADOBE

The adobe was built by Indian labor in 1817 for Don Domingo Carrillo. In 1838, his daughter married Don José María Covarrubias, who in 1852 became the first federal elector from California. Descendants of these families, many of them leaders in public affairs, occupied this house for over a century. John R. Southworth moved and rebuilt the "Historic Adobe" here in 1924 as part of a civic program of historic preservation. Los Adobes de los Rancheros acquired the property in 1938 as headquarters for Los Rancheros Visitadores and for the use and enjoyment of the people.

715 N Santa Barbara St, Santa Barbara

NO. 309 🔔

MISSION SANTA BARBARA

Santa Barbara Mission was founded December 4, 1786. Portions of five units of its extensive waterworks, built by Indian labor and preserved in this part, are a filter house, Spanish gristmill, sections of aqueducts, and two reservoirs, the larger of which, built in 1806, is used today as part of the city water system. The fountain and lavadero are nearby, in front of the mission, and a dam built in 1807 is located in the Santa Barbara Botanic Garden, one and one-half miles up Mission Canyon. Only ruins remain of the mission's pottery kiln, guard house, and tanning vats.

2201 Laguna St; plaque located in Mission Historical Park, 1,000 ft W at old 1806 Reservoir, Santa Barbara

NO. 340 🔔

MISSION LA PURÍSIMA

Established December 8, 1787, by Father Lasuén, the mission was badly damaged by an earthquake in 1812. Removed from control of Franciscans during secularization of the missions, it was abandoned in 1834. State and National Park Services and the Civilian Conservation Corps restored major and many small structures and the water system so that today La Purisima is the only example in California of a complete mission.

La Purísima Mission State Historic Park, N side of intersection of Mission Gate Rd and Purisima Rd, on State Hwy 246, 3 mi E of Lompoc.

NO. 361 🔔

OLD LOBERO THEATRE

José Lobero opened the region's first legitimate theatre on this site on February 22, 1873. For many years the old theatre was the center of social life in Santa Barbara. A new Lobero Theatre, opened in 1924 on the same site, continues to serve the cultural interests of the area.

33 E Canon Perdido St, Santa Barbara

NO. 535 🔔

CARPINTERIA AND INDIAN VILLAGE OF MISHOPSHNOW

The Chumash Indian village of Mishopshnow, discovered by Juan Rodríguez Cabrillo on August 14, 1542, was located one-fourth mile southwest of the monument. Fray Juan Crespí of the Gaspar de Portolá Expedition named it San Roque on August 17, 1769. Portolá's soldiers, observing the Indians building wooden canoes, called the village La Carpinteria–the Carpenter's Shop.

Carpinteria Valley Museum of History, 950 Maple Ave; second plaque located at 1,000 S Carpinteria Ave, Carpinteria

NO. 559 🔔

HASTINGS ADOBE

Built in 1854 by Captain Horatio Gates Trussell of Orland, Maine, the adobe is partly constructed of material from the wreck of the S.S. *Winfield* Scott on Anacapa Island. The Winchesters acquired the adobe in 1882 and Katherine Bagg Hastings, niece of Miss Sarah Winchester, bequeathed it to the Santa Barbara Historical Society in 1935.

412 W Montecito St, Santa Barbara

NO. 582 ☐

WELL "HILL 4"

This well, spudded September 26, 1905, and completed April 30, 1906, is the first oil well in which a water shutoff was attained by pumping cement through the tubing and back of the casing—forerunner of the modern cementing technique. It was drilled to a depth of 2,507 feet by Union Oil Company of California; 1,872 feet of 10-inch casing and 2,237 feet of 8-inch casing were so securely cemented off that the well produced for over forty-five years.

Mission Hills District; plaque is located 1.6 mi N of Union Oil Co. Production Office; office is located off of Rucker Rd, 5 mi NE of Lompoc

NO. 636 🔔

ROYAL SPANISH PRESIDIO

This presidio was established April 19-21, 1782 by Governor Felipe de Neve, Padre Junípero Serra, and Lieutenant José Francisco Ortega, under orders of King Carlos III to provide the benefits of government for the inhabitants of the Santa Barbara Channel region of California.

El Presidio de Santa Barbara State Historic Park, NW corner of Santa Barbara and Canyon Perdido Sts, Santa Barbara

NO. 721 🔔

CARRILLO ADOBE

Daniel Hill of Massachusetts built this adobe about 1825 for his bride, Rafaela L. Ortega y Olivera. She was the granddaughter of José Francisco Ortega, founder and first commandante of the Royal Presidio of Santa Barbara.

11 E Carrillo St, Santa Barbara

NO. 877 🔔

CHAPEL OF SAN RAMON

This redwood frame chapel, erected in 1875 by Frederick and Ramona Foxen Wickenden, illustrates the transition between the architecture of the old missions and the frame churches of the American settlers. It is a unique example of the use of wood to create strong, simple forms that had formerly been executed in adobe.

SW corner of Tepusquet and Foxen Canyon Rds, 15 mi SE of Santa Maria

NO. 928 🔔

SITE OF ORIGINAL MISSION AND REMAINING RUINS OF BUILDINGS OF MISSION DE LA PURÍSIMA CONCEPCIÓN DE MARÍA SANTISIMA

The ruins at this site are part of the original Mission La Purísima, founded by Padre Fermín de Lasuén on December 8, 1787, as the 11th in the chain of Spanish Missions in California. The mission was destroyed by earthquake on December 12, 1812; the present Mision (mission) La Purisima was then established several miles away.

5085 'T" St at E Locust Ave, Lompoc

Santa Clara County

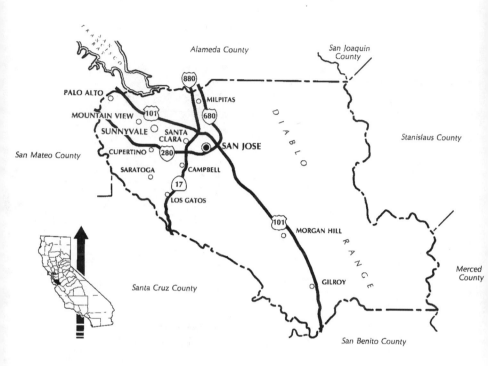

Palo Alto
Mountain View
Sunnyvale
Santa Clara
Cupertino
Saratoga
Campbell
Los Gatos
San Jose
Milpitas
Morgan Hill
Gilroy

Alameda County
San Joaquin County
Stanislaus County
Merced County
San Benito County
Santa Cruz County
San Mateo County

DIABLO RANGE

Santa Clara
Est. 1850

Southof the San Francisco Bay, Santa Clara County is prolific in unique developments: from agricultural "firsts" to architectural treasures; from Spanish missions to modern-era churches; from mines to motion pictures — Santa Clara County has it all.

NO. 249 🔔

OLD ADOBE WOMAN'S CLUB

This adobe, among the oldest in Santa Clara Valley, was one of several continuous rows of homes built in 1792-1800 as dwellings for the Indian families of Mission Santa Clara. It links the Franciscan padres' labors with California of today.

3260 The Alameda between Benton and Franklin Sts, Santa Clara

NO. 250 ⓜ

OLD SITES OF MISSION SANTA CLARA DE ASIS AND OLD SPANISH BRIDGE

The first mission in this valley, Mission Santa Clara de Thamien, was established at this site by Franciscan Padres Tomás de la Peña and Joseph Antonio Marguia January 17, 1777. Here, at the Indian village of So-co-is-u-ka, they erected a cross and shelter for worship to bring Christianity to the Costanoan Indians.

SE corner of Central Expressway and De la Cruz Blvd, Santa Clara

NO. 259 🔔

VASQUEZ TREE AND SITE OF 21-MILE HOUSE

This famous tavern and stage stop was located 21 miles from San Jose on the road to Monterey. The 21-Mile-House was built in 1852 by William Host beneath a spreading oak that later was called the Vasquez Tree. The house was sold to William Tennant in November 1852. Now destroyed, this stopping station was a place where horses could be changed, fed, and stabled, and where tired and hungry passengers could refresh themselves.

NW corner of Tennant Ave and Monterey Hwy (Old 101), Morgan Hill

NO. 260 🔔

SANTA CLARA CAMPAIGN TREATY SITE

After an armed confrontation on January 2 and a meeting the following day, Marine Captain Ward Marston, commander of the United States expeditionary force, and Francisco Sánchez, leader of the Mexican-Californian ranchers, agreed to a treaty here on January 7, 1847. U.S. forces were to recognize the rights of the Californians and end seizures of their property.

Civic Center Park, NE corner of El Camino Real and Lincoln St, Santa Clara

NO. 338 🔔

MISSION SANTA CLARA

Founded nearby on the edge of the Guadalupe River on January 12, 1777, this is the first California mission to honor a woman–Clare of Assisi. The mission, which once had the largest Indian population of any in California, was moved after floods and earthquake; its fifth church was dedicated on this site in 1825. In 1851 Santa Clara College was established in the old mission buildings.

In front of Mission Church, Univ of Santa Clara, The Alameda and Lexington St, Santa Clara

NO. 339 🔔

NEW ALMADEN MINE

The Indians used pigment from this cinnabar hill for paint. Mercury was mined as early as 1845. The gold discovery made mercury indispensable, and the mine, the most productive in America, became world famous. It sold for $1,700,700 in 1864.

On N-bound old Hwy 101 (P.M. 27.5) (Monterey Rd), 1/2 mi S of Ford Rd, San Jose

NO. 339-1 🔔

NEW ALMADEN MINE

Here, along Arroyo de los Alamitos Creek, Luís Cabolla and Antonio Suñol did the first mining in California as they worked New Almaden ore in their arrastra. In constant production since 1845, the mine has produced more than a million flasks of quicksilver valued at over $50 million.

Bulmore Park, Almaden Rd and Almaden Way, New Almaden

NO. 416

EDWIN MARKHAM HOME

Markham was born at Oregon City April 23, 1852 and later moved to a cattle ranch near Suisun. Later he and his mother moved to San Jose, and Markham entered the State Normal School, from which he graduated in 1872. Markham lived and taught school in many places but made this home his main residence, and it was here that he wrote *The Man with the Hoe.*

432 S 8th St, San Jose

NO. 417 🔔

FIRST NORMAL SCHOOL IN CALIFORNIA (SAN JOSE STATE COLLEGE)

Originally founded as a private institution, "Minns' Evening Normal School," in 1857, the school became a public institution by act of the State Legislature on May 2, 1862. In 1868 the board of trustees took up the matter of permanent location, and Washington Square in San Jose was chosen. Destroyed by fire February 11, 1880 and heavily damaged by the 1906 earthquake, the school was rebuilt after each disaster.

San Jose State University, located on Tower Hall in Washington Square, NE corner of San Carlos and 4th Sts, San Jose

NO. 433 🔔

FIRST SITE OF EL PUEBLO DE SAN JOSÉ DE GUADALUPE

Within a year after the opening of the first overland route from Mexico to Alta California, Governor Felipe de Neve authorized establishment of California's first civil settlement. Lieutenant José Joaquín Moraga arrived in the Santa Clara Valley with 14 settlers and their families on November 29, 1777 to found El Pueblo de San José de Guadalupe near the present civic center.

Front parking lot planter, City Hall, 151 W Mission St, San Jose

NO. 434 🔔
SITE OF "CITY GARDENS"– NURSERY OF LOUIS PELLIER

Pellier, native of Saint-Hippolyte, France and founder of California's prune industry, came to California in 1849. In October 1850 he established a nursery called City Gardens. Here, aided by his brothers Pierre and Jean, who came over from France at a later date, he introduced the French prune—la petite prune d'Agen–into California during the winter of 1856-57.

100 block of W St James St, San Jose

NO. 435 🔔
SARATOGA

The Anza exploring party passed through the Saratoga area March 25, 1776. Lumbering in the mountains, which began in 1847 and continued many years, brought the area's first settlers in 1850. Among other industries established were a lime quarry (1850s), grist mill (1854), tannery (1863), paper mill (1868), and pasteboard mill (1870). Pacific Congress Springs was a popular resort from 1866 to 1942. Farmers here pioneered in fruit industry and held Blossom Festivals beginning in 1900, after the end of a drought.

Located in park, SE corner of junction of Hwys 9 and 85, Saratoga

NO. 447 🔔
GUBSERVILLE

Named after Frank Gubser, a German immigrant and barber, Gubserville was an important stage, mail, and teamster stop on the road between San Jose and Saratoga. Gubser served as the village's first and only postmaster, beginning July 5, 1882. Gubserville ceased to exist officially when the post office was discontinued on April 15, 1897.

1481 Saratoga Ave, San Jose

NO. 448 🔔
PATCHEN

"Mountain Charley" McKiernan, one of the earliest residents of the Santa Cruz Mountains, settled near here in 1850, and John Martin Schultheis and his wife homesteaded land about a mile from here in 1852. Their home was still standing in 1950. The Patchen Post Office, named for a famous racehorse, was located in this vicinity from 1872 to the 1920s.

Intersection of Old Santa Cruz Hwy (P.M. 3.57) and Mtn Charlie Rd, 1.2 mi SE of Holy City

NO. 458 🔔
FORBES FLOUR MILL

This is all that remains of the four-story stone flour mill built in 1854 by James Alexander Forbes. The town that grew around this building was first called Forbes Mill, then Forbestown, and finally Los Gatos.

Forbes Mill Museum, 75 Church St, Los Gatos

NO. 461 🔔
SITE OF CALIFORNIA'S FIRST STATE CAPITOL

Directly opposite this tablet was located the first State Capitol Building, in which California's first Legislature assembled in December 1849. San Jose was the seat of government from 1849 to 1851.

City Park Plaza, 100 block, S Market St, San Jose

NO. 489 🔔
MORELAND SCHOOL

Established in 1851 as a subscription school meeting in private homes, this is the oldest rural school district in California. Its first teacher, Charles LaFollette, 1851, taught for three months; the second teacher, Abraham H. Featherman, stayed six months. Through efforts of Samuel Curtis Rogers, its third teacher, who taught from 1852 to 1854, the first public school building, formerly the home of Zechariah Moreland, was obtained in 1852. In 1853 Rogers secured organization of the school as Santa Clara Township School District No. 2; the school was renamed in Moreland's honor in 1862.

4335 Payne Ave at Saratoga, San Jose

NO. 505 🔔
ALMADEN VINEYARDS

On this site, in 1852, Charles LeFranc made the first commercial planting of fine European wine grapes in Santa Clara County to found Almaden Vineyards. LeFranc imported cuttings from vines in the celebrated wine districts of his native France, shipping them by sailing ship around the Horn.

1530 Blossom Hill Rd, San Jose

NO. 524
SITE OF JUANA BRIONES DE MIRANDA HOME ON RANCHO LA PURÍSIMA CONCEPCIÓN

In 1843 Apolinario Miranda, husband of Juana Briones de Miranda, was sent before the subprefect for not living harmoniously with his wife and, shortly thereafter, Juana and her seven children arrived at Rancho la Purísima Concepción. In 1856 this property was duly confirmed to her, and she lived in this adobe until, crippled by rheumatism, she was forced to move.

4157 Old Adobe Rd, Palo Alto

NO. 644 🔔
MARTIN MURPHY HOME AND ESTATE (SITE)

Martin Murphy, Jr. arrived in California with his family in 1844 in the first wagon train to cross the Sierra Nevada. The founder of Sunnyvale, he constructed here his prefabricated lumber house, brought around the Horn in 1849. Members of the Murphy family lived here continuously until 1953, when the property was acquired by the City of Sunnyvale. The house was destroyed by fire in 1961.

Martin Murphy, Jr. Historical Park, corner of N Sunnyvale and California Aves, Sunnyvale

NO. 733 🔔
PAUL MASSON MOUNTAIN WINERY

Premium wines and champagne have flowed continuously since 1852 from the winery that bears the name of Paul Masson, even during Prohibition under a special government license. Twice partially destroyed by earthquake and fire, the original sandstone walls still stand. The 12th-century Spanish Romanesque portal came around the Horn.

Turn N off State Hwy 9 (P.M. 5.6), go 0.3 mi on Pierce Rd and turn left on Paul Masson Mtn Winery Rd, continue for 1.2 mi to winery, Saratoga

NO. 800 🔔

ARROYO DE SAN JOSEPH CUPERTINO

This arroyo honoring San Joseph, patron saint of flight and students, was first discovered and traversed by Spanish explorers in 1769. On March 25-26, 1776, Colonel Juan Bautista de Anza made it his encampment No. 93, as mapped by his cartographer, Padre Pedro Font, on his journey to the San Francisco Bay area where he initiated a colony, a mission, and a presidio.

Monta Vista High School W parking lot, 21840 McClellan Rd, Cupertino

NO. 813 🔔

MONTGOMERY HILL

Three-quarters of a mile northeast is Montgomery Hill, site of the 55 successful flights of John Joseph Montgomery's "aeroplane" that demonstrated aerodynamic developments still indispensable to modern aircraft. Montgomery combined his engineering skill with the basic principles of aerodynamics that he discovered to produce a heavier-than-air flying machine which had complete control: cambered wing, rear stabilizer, flexible wingtips, and wing-warping aileron.

Entrance to Evergreen College, 0.5 mi E of intersection of San Felipe and Yerba Buena Rds, San Jose

NO. 834 🔔

EADWEARD MUYBRIDGE AND THE DEVELOPMENT OF MOTION PICTURES

In commemoration of the motion picture research conducted in 1878 and 1879 by Eadweard Muybridge at the Palo Alto Stock Farm, now the site of Stanford University. This extensive photographic experiment portraying the attitudes of animals in motion was conceived by and executed under the direction and patronage of Leland Stanford. Consecutive instantaneous exposures were provided for a battery of 24 cameras fitted with electroshutters.

Stanford University, Campus Dr W across from Stanford Driving Range, Palo Alto

NO. 836 🔔

PIONEER ELECTRONICS RESEARCH LABORATORY

This is the original site of the laboratory and factory of Federal Telegraph Company, founded in 1909 by Cyril F. Elwell. Here, Dr. Lee de Forest, inventor of the three-element radio vacuum tube, devised the first vacuum tube amplifier and oscillator in 1911-13. Worldwide developments based on this research led to modern radio communication, television, and the electronics age.

In sidewalk, SE corner of Channing Ave and Emerson St, Palo Alto

NO. 854 🔔

OLD POST OFFICE

Constructed by the United States government in 1892, this was the first federal building in San Jose. It served as U.S. Post Office from 1892 to 1933. Designed by Willoughby Edbrooke and constructed of locally quarried sandstone, this Romanesque-style structure is the last of its kind on the West Coast.

110 S Market St, San Jose

NO. 857 🔔

JOHN ADAMS SQUIRE HOUSE

Designed by T. Paterson Ross and constructed in 1904 by builder George W. Mosher, this house is a notable example of California's interpretation of the Greco-Roman Classic Revival movement in America.

900 University Ave, Palo Alto

NO. 866 🔔

LUÍS MARÍA PERALTA ADOBE

The last vestige of El Pueblo de San José de Guadalupe. This simple adobe was rehabilitated in the mid-19th century. It is believed to have been built before 1800 by Manuel Gonzalez, an Apache, who was one of the Pueblo Pobladores founders. It was later owned and occupied by Sgt. Peralta, pueblo comisionado from 1807 to 1822, who also came to California with the Anza expedition in 1775-76.

184 W St John St, San Jose

NO. 868 🔔

WINCHESTER HOUSE

Built by Sarah Winchester, widow of rifle manufacturer William Winchester, this unique structure includes many outstanding elements of Victorian architecture and fine craftsmanship. Construction began in 1884 and continued without interruption until Mrs. Winchester's death in 1922. The continual building and remodeling created a 160-room house covering an area of six acres.

525 S Winchester Blvd, San Jose

NO. 888 🔔

HAYES MANSION

Jay Orley and Everis A. Hayes built this Mission Revival style mansion, designed by George W. Page in 1904. The Hayes brothers were early San Jose *Mercury* publishers, prominent valley politicians, and were actively involved in establishing the Santa Clara Valley fruit industry. The mansion consists of 62 rooms, 11 fireplaces, and was paneled in over a dozen different woods.

200 Edenvale Ave, San Jose

NO. 895 🔔

HOSTESS HOUSE

Designed by Julia Morgan for the YWCA, this building originally served Camp Fremont as a meeting place for servicemen and visitors, and was dedicated in 1919 to those who died in World War I. Moved from its original site to Palo Alto to become the first municipally sponsored community center in the nation, it is the only remaining structure from California's World War I Army training camps.

27 Mitchell Ln, near NE corner of University Ave and El Camino Real, Palo Alto

NO. 898 🔔

ROBERTO-SUÑOL ADOBE

This historic adobe was built in 1836 by a native Californian, Roberto Balermino, on Rancho de los Coches, which was officially granted to him by Governor Micheltorena in 1844. The one-story dwelling was enlarged in 1847 by the new owner, Antonio Suñol; the second story and balcony were added in 1853 by Captain Stefano Splivalo.

770 Lincoln Ave, San Jose

NO. 902 🔔

FIRST UNITARIAN CHURCH OF SAN JOSE

This church's architectural character is generally described as Richardsonian Romanesque; it is one of the few churches in America patterned after the traditional Unitarian churches of Transylvania. Designed by architect G. W. Page and erected in 1891-92, the building has served its congregation continuously since construction.

160 N 3rd St, San Jose

NO. 903 🔔

KOTANI-EN

Kotani-En is a classical Japanese residence in the formal style of a 13th-century estate with tile roofed walls surrounding a tea house, shrine, gardens, and ponds. Constructed for Max M. Cohen in 1918-1924 of mahogany, cedar, bamboo, and ceramic tile by master artisan Takashima and eleven craftsmen from Japan, Kotani-En represents a harmonious union of art and nature in a two-acre rustic environment. Kotani-En is a prominent example of Japanese landscape architecture in America.

15891 Ravine Rd, Los Gatos

NO. 904 🔔

CHARLES COPELAND MORSE RESIDENCE

C. C. Morse of Ferry-Morse Seed Company fame built this mansion, claimed to be the largest remaining late Queen Anne-style Victorian residence in the City of Santa Clara in 1892. Morse was a pioneer in the seed industry whose work had a substantial impact upon the economic growth of California.

981 Fremont St, Santa Clara

NO. 910 🔔

ST. JOSEPH'S CATHOLIC CHURCH

Established in 1803, St. Joseph's was the first non-mission church in a Spanish California settlement. The present edifice, designed in Italian baroque style by noted architect Bryan C. Clinch, is the fourth to be built at the original site. Its cornerstone was laid March 19, 1876, and it was dedicated April 22,1877.

90 S Market St at San Fernando St, San Jose

NO. 913 🔔

LOU HENRY HOOVER HOUSE

This 1919 residence, a unique blend of pueblo and international style elements, embodies Mrs. Herbert Hoover's innovative architectural concepts. It was executed by architects A. B. Clark, Charles Davis, and Birge Clark, and was maintained as the Hoover family home from 1920 to 1944; it was here that Hoover received news of his election as President of the United States in 1928. Upon Mrs. Hoover's death, the house was given to Stanford University.

623 Mirada Rd; plaque located 100 ft S of intersection of Cabrillo and Santa Ynez Aves, Stanford University, Palo Alto

NO. 945

FIRST SUCCESSFUL INTRODUCTION OF THE HONEYBEE TO CALIFORNIA

Here, on the 1,939-acre Rancho Potrero de Santa Clara, Christopher A. Shelton in early March 1853 introduced the honeybee to California. In Aspinwall, Panama, Shelton purchased 12 beehives from a New Yorker and transported them by rail, "bongo," pack mule, and steamship to San Francisco. Only enough bees survived to fill one hive, but these quickly propagated, laying the foundation for California's modern bee-keeping industry.

San Jose Municipal Airport, 1661 Airport Blvd, San Jose

NO. 952 🔔

SITE OF WORLD'S FIRST BROADCASTING STATION

On this corner stood the Garden City Bank Building, where Charles D. Herrold established Station FN, the first radio broadcasting station in the world. As a pioneer in wireless telephony (radio), Herrold established the first station in 1909 to transmit radio programs of music and news to a listening audience on a regular basis.

SW corner of First and San Fernando Sts, San Jose

NO. 969 🔔

HOME SITE OF SARAH WALLIS

Sarah Armstrong Wallis (1825-1905) was a pioneer in the campaign for women's voting rights. In 1870 she was elected president of California's first statewide suffrage organization which in 1873 in-

corporated as the California State Woman Suffrage Education Association. The home she built on this site, Mayfield Farm, was a center of suffrage activities attracting state and national leaders such as Susan B. Anthony, Elizabeth Cady Stanton, and Ulysses S. Grant.

S side of La Selva Dr between Military Way and Magnolia Dr, Palo Alto

NO. 976 🔔

BIRTHPLACE OF "SILICON VALLEY"

This garage is the birthplace of the world's first high-technology region, "Silicon Valley." The idea for such a region originated with Dr. Frederick Terman, a Stanford University professor who encouraged his students to start up their own electronics companies in the area instead of joining established firms in the East. The first two students to follow his advice were William R. Hewlett and David Packard, who in 1938 began developing their first product, an audio oscillator, in this garage.

367 Addison Ave, Palo Alto

NO. 1000 🔔

SITE OF INVENTION OF THE FIRST COMMERCIALLY PRACTICABLE INTEGRATED CIRCUIT

At this site in 1959, Dr. Robert Noyce of Fairchild Semiconductor Corporation invented the first integrated circuit that could be produced commercially. Based on "planar" technology, an earlier Fairchild breakthrough, Noyce's invention consisted of a complete electronic circuit inside a small silicon chip. His innovation helped revolutionize "Silicon

Valley's" semicondutor electronics industry, and brought profound change to the lives of people everywhere.

844 E Charleston Rd, Palo Alto

NO. 1017

GILROY YAMATO HOT SPRINGS RESORT

Under the guidance of the George Room and William McDonald families during the years of 1865 of Francisco Cantua's discovery to the 1930s, Gilroy Hot Springs was a popular health and family resort oriented around a single hot mineral spring located near Coyote Creek. In 1938 the resort was purchased by H.K. Sakata, a successful Japanese American farmer from Watsonville. Renamed the Gilroy Yamato Hot Springs, it was the only Japanese American owned commercial hot springs in California. The resort served as a recreational and spiritual center for Japanese Americans before World War II and briefly as a hostel after the war for those returning from internment camps.

9.5 mi NE of junction of New Ave and Roop Rd on Hot Springs Rd, Gilroy

Landmark No. 904

Santa Cruz County

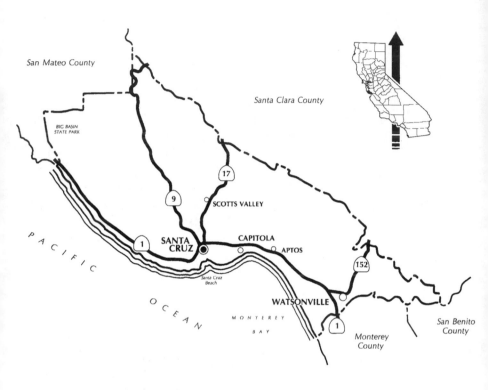

Big Basin Redwoods State Park - Beginning of the California State Park System. Located 20 miles N of Santa Cruz.

Santa Cruz Mission State Historic Park - Only original structure of Santa Cruz Mission. Located on Mission and School Streets, Santa Cruz.

Santa Cruz
Est. 1850

Santa Cruz County surrounds the northern portion of Monterey Bay. Its beaches are famous for swimming, camping, and the only oceanside amusement park operating on the West Coast. The redwood forests of the Santa Cruz mountains inspired the formation of the Sempervirens Club, which established Big Basin as the first California State Park in 1902.

NO. 342 🔔

SITE OF MISSION SANTA CRUZ

Mision la Exaltación de la Santa Cruz, the 12th Franciscan Mission, was consecrated by Father Fermín Lasuén in August 1791. In 1793 the adobe church was built where the Holy Cross Catholic Church is now located. The mission was damaged by several earthquakes and finally collapsed in 1857. Plaza Park is located at the center of the mission complex which contained 32 buildings at the time of its secularization in 1834; the last building remains on School Street.

Plaza Park, NE corner of Mission and Emmet Sts, Santa Cruz

NO. 449 🔔

GLENWOOD

This historic town was founded by Charles C. Martin, who came around the Horn in 1847, and his wife, Hannah Carver Martin, who crossed the Isthmus. Martin first homesteaded the area in 1851 and operated a tollgate and station for stagecoaches crossing the mountains. Later he developed a lumber mill, winery, store, and the Glenwood Resort Hotel.

4171 Glenwood Dr, 0.4 mi N of Glenwood cutoff rd (Martin Rd), NE of Scotts Valley

NO. 469 🔔

SITE OF CENTER OF VILLA DE BRANCIFORTE

These school grounds were the center of Villa de Branciforte, founded in 1797 by Governor Diego de Borica of California on orders from Spain through Viceroy Branciforte in Mexico. The settlement existed as a separate township until 1905, when it was annexed to the city of Santa Cruz.

SW corner of Water and Branciforte, Santa Cruz

NO. 583 🔔

FELTON COVERED BRIDGE

Built in 1892-93 and believed to be the tallest covered bridge in the country, it stood as the only entry to Felton for 45 years. In 1937 it was retired from active service to become a pedestrian bridge and figured prominently in many films of that period. After suffering damage in the winter storms of 1982, it was restored to its original elegance in 1987 using native materials and local talent.

Covered Bridge Rd and Graham Hill Rd, Felton

NO. 827 🔔

BIG BASIN REDWOODS STATE PARK

A group of conservationists led by Andrew P. Hill camped at the base of Slippery Rock on May 15, 1900 and formed the Sempervirens Club to preserve the redwoods of Big Basin. Their efforts resulted in deeding 3,500 acres of primeval forest to the State on September 20, 1902 to mark the beginning of the California State Park System.

Slippery Rock Memorial, Big Basin Redwoods State Park, State Hwy 236 (P.M. 8.7), Big Basin

NO. 860 🔔

SUPERINTENDENT'S OFFICE

This building is Capitola's oldest commercial structure. It served as head quarters for F. A. Hihn's operations from approximately 1883 to 1919, when he owned and developed what was then known as "Camp Capitola" into the first seaside resort in the state.

201 Monterey Ave, Capitola

NO. 983 🔔

SANTA CRUZ BEACH BOARDWALK

A local landmark since 1907, this boardwalk was one of the first amusement parks in California. It is now the only oceanside amusement park operating on the West Coast. The boardwalk is the site of two rare attractions, the 1911 carousel and the 1924 Giant Dipper roller coaster. Both were manufactured by members of the Looff family, some of the nation's earliest and most prominent makers of amusement rides.

400 Beach St, Santa Cruz

NO. 998

RANCHO SAN ANDRÉS CASTRO ADOBE

The Castro Adobe is an outstanding example of Monterey Colonial architectural styling. The adobe functioned as a regional social center due to the importance of its location as the governing seat of the Castro family rural empire, which reached across seven land grants to include over a quarter of a million acres.

184 Old Adobe Rd, Watsonville

Landmark No. 860

Landmark No. 983

Shasta County

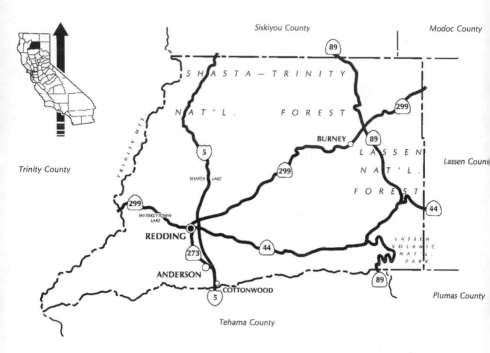

Shasta State Historic Park - Old Shasta courthouse, other buildings.
Located 5 miles W of Redding on Highway 299.

Shasta
Est. 1850

Shasta County is bordered by the Trinity Mountains to the west and the Cascade Range to the east, featuring the Lassen Volcanic National Park. Although Shasta's jewels include Lassen Peak and Lake Shasta, Siskiyou County to the north claims the spectacular landmark Mount Shasta.

NO. 10 🔔
READING ADOBE

This was the home of Pierson Barton Reading (1816-1868), a California pioneer of 1843. He was a major in Frémont's California Battalion which fought in the Mexican War. He was a signer of the Capitulation of Cahuenga and discovered gold in 1040. Major Reading is buried nearby.

Near entrance to Reading Island Park, 213 Adobe Rd, 5.8 mi E of Cottonwood

NO. 11 ☐
NOBLE PASS ROUTE

William H. Noble, accompanied by a party of citizens, showed the route for a wagon road across the Sierra Nevada in May 1852. It was from this point that emigrants got their first glimpse of the Sacramento Valley.

Lassen Volcanic National Park, on park Hwy, 0.2 mi E of park marker no. 60, 3.7 mi from NW entrance on State Hwy 44

NO. 32 ☐ 🚫
READING'S BAR

Major Pierson B. Reading and his Indians washed out the first gold in Shasta County on a bar at the mouth of the canyon of Clear Creek in March 1848.

Clear Creek Bridge, on Clear Creek Rd, 6.9 mi W of old Hwy 99 W Redding

NO. 33 ☐
SOUTHERN'S STAGE STATION

This is the site of the famous Southern Hotel and Stage Station built by Simeon Fisher Southern. The original building, a log cabin, was built in 1859. During a half-century many noted people who made early California history were entertained in this hotel.

On old Hwy 99, 0.7 mi SW of Sims exit, 6.9 mi S of Castella

NO. 58 ☐
OLD CALIFORNIA-OREGON ROAD

This marks the location of the main artery of travel used by pioneers between the Trinity River and the northern mines of California and Oregon.

NW corner of Hwy 99 (P.M. 7.12) and Spring Gulch Rd, 1.7 mi N of Anderson

NO. 77 🔔 🚫

OLD TOWN OF SHASTA

Founded in 1849 as Reading's Springs, the town was named Shasta June 8, 1850. It was the second county seat for Shasta County, 1851-1888, and the metropolis of northern California during the 1850s. Here, until 1861, the road ended and the Oregon pack trail began. It is the home of the Western Star Lodge No. 2, F. & A.M., whose charter was brought across the plains in the Peter Lassen party of 1848. In 1851, Dr. Benjamin Shurtleff, pioneer physician and Shasta's first and only alcalde, built his home. The Shasta Courier was founded in 1851. The entire business section of Shasta was destroyed by fire in 1853.

Shasta State Historic Park, State Hwy 299, NW corner of Main Stand Trinity Alley, Shasta

NO. 78 ☐ 🚫

CLEAR CREEK

Five miles up the creek, at Reading's Bar, is the site of the discovery of gold by Major Pierson B. Reading and his Indian laborers in 1848.

Old Hwy 99 and Canyon Rd, S Redding

NO. 116 🔔

BATTLE ROCK

Battle of the Crags was fought below Battle Rock in June 1855. This conflict between the Modoc Indians and the settlers resulted from miners destroying the native fishing waters in the Lower Soda Springs area. Settlers led by Squire Reuben Gibson and Mountain Joe Doblondy, with local Indians led by their Chief Weilputus, engaged Modocs, killed their Chief Dorcas Della, and dispersed them. Poet Joaquin Miller and other settlers were wounded.

On lawn at entrance station, Castle Crags State Park, 1 mi W of I-5 (P.M. 63.6), Castella

NO. 120 ☐

DERSCH HOMESTEAD

Here in 1850 "Doc" Baker established a stopping place for emigrants on the Lassen and Nobles Trails. George and Anna Maria Dersch took up a homestead on the land in 1861. A history of troubled relations between Indians and settlers led to an Indian raid on the ranch in 1866 in which Mrs. Dersch was killed. A posse was formed and killed most of the Indians at their Dye Creek Camp.

Rte 1, Box 273, Dersch Rd at Bear Creek, 10 mi E of Anderson

NO. 131 🚫

WHISKEYTOWN

Settled by gold miners in 1849, the town was first called Whiskey Creek for the stream on which it was located, but later the name was changed to Whiskeytown. A barrel of whiskey lost off a pack mule christened the stream with the popular drink of that day. The town is inundated by Whiskeytown Reservoir.

Intersection of Whiskey Creek Rd and State Hwy 299, 11.3 mi W of Redding on Hwy 299

NO. 148 ☐

BASS HILL

On the summit of Bass Hill a remnant of the California-Oregon stage road crosses the Pacific Highway and descends to the Pit River. Because this was a favorite "holdup" spot in stage-coach days, a marker has been placed there in memory of W. L. Smith, division stage agent of the California and Oregon Stage Company, and of the pioneer stage drivers along this road.

Bridge Bay Resort parking lot, Bridge Bay turnoff and I-5, 6 mi N of Central Valley

NO. 166

FRENCH GULCH

Founded nearby by French miners in 1849, the town of Morrowville, relocated here, was the center of one of the state's richest gold producing areas. Total production was over $20,000,000. One of California's first stamp mills operated at the nearby Franklin Mine. From 1856 to 1858 French Gulch was the trailhead on the western branch of the California-Oregon Trail. St. Rose Catholic Church was founded in 1856. As a supply and stopping place, the town rivaled Shasta.

3 mi E of Hwy 299 (P.M. 8.6) on Trinity Hill Rd, French Gulch

NO. 355 ☐

FORT CROOK (SITE OF)

Established July I, 1857 by Lieutenant George Crook for protection of the immigrants and settlers, Fort Crook was later commanded by Captain John W. Gardner

and Captain McGregor. The boundaries of the fort were set at one mile in every direction from the flagpole. Abandoned June 1, 1869.

SE corner of McArthur Rd (County A -19) and Soldier Mtn Dr 2 mi NW of Glenburn

NO. 377 🔔

PIONEER BABY'S GRAVE

Charles, infant son of George and Helena Cohn Brownstein of Red Bluff, died December 14, 1864. He was buried near land established by the Shasta Hebrew Congregation as a Jewish cemetery in 1857, one of the earliest such cemeteries in the region. Since there was no Jewish burial ground in Red Bluff, Charles' parents made the arduous journey to Shasta to lay their baby to rest. Concern for the fate of the grave led to the rerouting of Highway 299 in 1923.

0.75 mi W of Shasta on State Hwy 299

NO. 379 ☐

FORT READING

Fort Reading, established on May 26, 1852 by Second Lieutenant E. N. Davis, Co. E, 2nd Infantry on the orders of Lieutenant Colonel George M. Wright, was the first and largest fort in Northern California. It was named in honor of Pierson Barton Reading and stood in a clearing of 10 acres. The fort was abandoned in June 1867.

0.6 mi E of intersection of Deschutes and Dersch Rds, 6 mi NE of Anderson

NO. 483 □

FATHER RINALDI'S FOUNDATION OF 1856

In the summer of 1853 Archbishop Alemany of San Francisco sent Father Florian Schwenninger to take over the mission of Shasta County. In the later part of 1853 a small wooden church was built. In 1855 Father Schwenninger moved over to Weaverville and Shasta's new priest, Father Raphael Rinaldi, decided to build a structure of cut stone to replace the small wooden church that had served since 1853. In 1857 the cornerstone of the church was laid, but for some reason its walls never rose; the foundation can still be seen (1963).

NW corner of intersection of Red Bluff Rd and Crocker Alley, Shasta

NO. 519 🔔

BELL'S BRIDGE

Erected in 1851 by J. J. Bell, this was an important toll bridge on the road from Shasta City to Tehama. Bell's Mansion, erected in 1859 on Clear Creek, was a favorite stopping place for miners on their way to the Shasta, Trinity, and Siskiyou gold fields.

SW corner of old Hwy 99 and Clear Creek Rd, Redding

NO. 555 🔔

LOCKHART FERRY

Established by Samuel Lockhart in 1856 as a link in the first wagon road from Yreka to Red Bluff, the Lockhart Ferry crossed below the confluence of the Fall and Pit Rivers near this spot. After a massacre in December 1856, the ferry was reestablished in 1857 below Fall River Falls.

On State Hwy 299 (P.M. 91.3), NW of Long St, 0.3 mi W of Fall River Mills

NO. 759 🔔

SITE OF FIRST SCHOOL IN FALL RIVER VALLEY

In 1868, the first school in Fall River Valley was built near this spot. The windowless building was of log construction and measured 20 feet by 30 feet. About 1870 the first sawmill in the valley was built at Dana, and lumber was obtained to put a floor in the schoolhouse and build school desks.

On State Hwy 299 (P.M. 99.0), 0.4 mi W of Lassen Co line, 3.6 mi E of McArthur

Landmark No. 77

Landmark No. 77

Sierra County

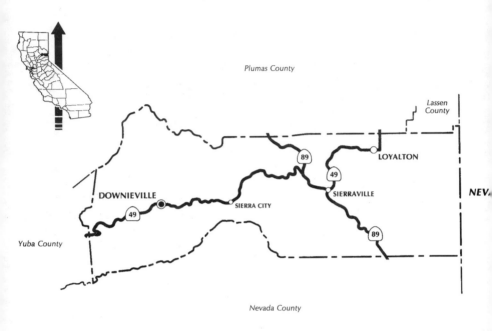

Sierra
Est. 1852

Sierra County is named for the Sierra Nevadas, "snow-covered, saw-toothed mountains." The county is not as mountainous as its name suggests and includes remote sections of scenic highways that wind through small towns established during the Gold Rush.

NO. 421 □
HENNESS PASS ROAD

The main emigrant trail between Virginia City, Nevada and Marysville, California, the Henness Pass Road was in use as early as 1849. At that time, this was the only road through the Henness Pass.

SW corner intersection of Ridge and Henness Pass Rds, 3.3 mi W of Alleghany

NO. 695 🔔
PLUM VALLEY HOUSE

In 1854, John Bope built the Plum Valley House of hewn logs and whipsawn lumber. Named for the wild plums which grow in the area, it was a toll station on the Henness Pass Road between Marysville and Virginia City.

On Ridge Rd, 8.6 mi E of State Hwy 49 and 9.0 mi W of Alleghany

NO. 971 🔔
SIERRA COUNTY SHERIFF'S GALLOWS

On November 27, 1885, 20-year-old James O'Neill was hanged from this gallows for the August 7, 1884 murder of Webber Lake dairyman John Woodward. That execution, conducted by Sheriff Samuel C. Stewart approximately 100 feet west of this site, was the last legal execution in Sierra County and the only time this gallows was used. Changes in State law in 1891 ended local executions in California, and further changes in 1941 ended hanging as a means of legal execution within the state.

Sierra County Jail Yard, Downieville

Siskiyou County

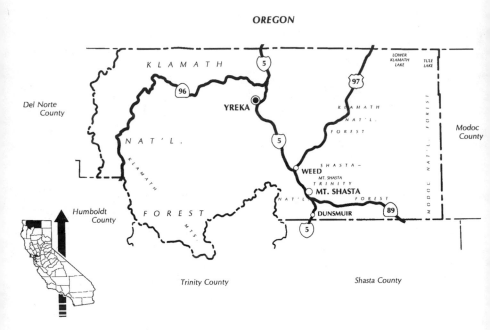

Siskiyou
Est. 1852

M ount Shasta is a dormant volcano, shrouded in glacial ice, that dominates the landscape of Siskiyou and neighboring counties. Siskiyou Pass, the county's namesake, lies a few miles north on Highway 5. This majestic northern county contains portions of the Klamath, Modoc and Shasta-Trinity National Forests.

NO. 9 🔔
CAPTAIN JACK'S STRONGHOLD

From this fortress, Captain Jack and his Indian forces successfully resisted capture by U.S. Army troops from December 1, 1872 to April 18, 1873.

3.8 mi W of NE entrance to Lava Beds National Monument (Sec 15, T46N, R4E, 2.5 mi W of Modoc Co line), 8.3 mi S of Tule Lake

NO. 13 ☐
GUILLEM'S GRAVEYARD

Almost 100 soldiers killed in action during the Modoc Indian War of 1872-73 were buried here. The bodies were moved to the National Cemetery in Washington, D.C. in the early 1890s.

In Lava Beds National Monument, 7.5 mi W of NE entrance, 4 mi S of Tule Lake

NO. 110 🔔
CANBY'S CROSS-1873

General E. R. S. Canby was murdered here in April 1873 while holding a peace parley with Captain Jack and Indian chiefs under a flag of truce. Eleazer Thomas, peace commissioner, was likewise slain.

In Lava Beds National Monument, about 0.5 mi E of park's N entrance, 8.3 mi S of Tule Lake

NO. 317 ☐
SITE OF FORT JONES

Companies A and B of the First United States Dragoons established a military post here on October 16, 1852. Named in honor of Colonel Roger Jones, brevet major general and the Adjutant General of the Army 1825-52, this fort was garrisoned by Company 3, 4th U.S. Infantry from April 23, 1853 until it was abandoned on June 23, 1858. This monument is dedicated this 14th day of July, 1946, to the officers and men who served here, among them Sergeants James Bryan and John Griffin and Private Gundor Salverson who upon their discharge became pioneer settlers of this valley.

On E Side Rd, 0.5 mi SE of intersection of E Side Rd and State Hwy 3, Fort Jones

NO. 396 □

STRAWBERRY VALLEY STAGE STATION

Across the road from this marker stood the Strawberry Valley Stage Station which served the patrons of the line from its completion in 1857 until 1886, when railroad construction reached the valley. The small building across the road was the Berryvale Post Office, which operated from 1870 to 1887; its first postmaster was Justin Hinckley Sisson. Behind the marker stood the famous Sisson Hotel; well known to mountain climbers, fishermen, hunters, and vacationers throughout California, it was built about 1865 by J. H. Sisson and in 1916 was destroyed by fire. The Mount Shasta trout hatchery was founded in 1888, but J. H. Sisson had started rearing trout to stock the streams in the vicinity in 1877. When the business center was moved to its present location on the railroad in 1886, its name was changed from Strawberry Valley to Sisson, and in 1923 the town was renamed Mount Shasta City.

SW corner of W Jessie St and Old Stage Rd, 1 mi W of Mt Shasta

NO. 517 🔔

EMIGRANT TRAIL CROSSING OF PRESENT HIGHWAY

As early as 1852 wagon trains of overland emigrants crossed six hundred feet to the north of this monument, into Shasta Valley and Yreka; the monument also marks the point where the 1857 military pass from Fort Crook emerged to join the westward emigrant road.

State Hwy 97 (P.M. 14.5), at Military Pass Rd, 14.5 mi NE of Weed

NO. 901 🔔

WEST MINER STREET—THIRD STREET HISTORIC DISTRICT, YREKA

Founded in March 1851 with the discovery of gold in the nearby "flats," Yreka quickly became the commercial and transportation hub for the surrounding communities and mining camps. Yreka's tents and shanties gave way to more substantial commercial and residential buildings seen on West Miner and Third Streets which remain as tangible evidence of the town 19th-century regional prominence.

SW corner of Miner St and Broadway, Yreka

Landmark No. 110

Landmark No. 110

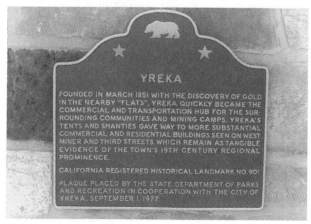

Landmark No. 901

Solano County

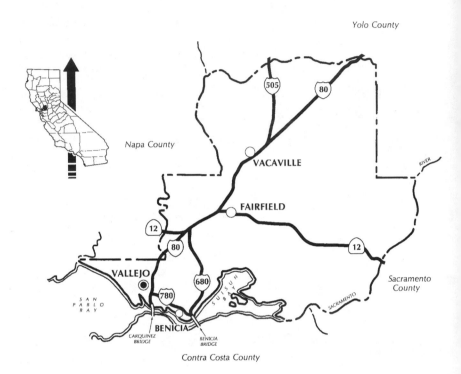

Benicia Capitol State Historic Park - Oldest California State Capitol building. Located in the town of Benicia.

Solano
Est. 1850

Two cities in Solano County were early State Capitals — Vallejo and Benicia. Today's visitor might think the naval shipyards at Mare Island reflect only modern military use of the Suisun Bay. But the first naval yard in this area was established in 1854. The county also has an historic arsenal, shipyard, and barracks.

NO. 153 🔔
BENICIA CAPITOL

Erected in 1852, ostensibly as Benicia's City Hall, this historic building was one of the four locations of the "Capitol on Wheels," from February 4, 1853 to February 25, 1854. It was deeded to the State in 1951.

NW corner of 1st and G Sts, Benicia

NO. 174 ☐
FIRST BUILDING ERECTED IN CALIFORNIA BY MASONIC LODGE FOR USE AS A HALL

The first Masonic hall built in California was begun in the summer of 1850, occupied by the lodge October 14, 1850, and formally dedicated December 27, 1850. This building served as the Masonic Temple for Benicia Lodge No. 5 until 1888, when the new temple was occupied. Used by a boys' club prior to World War I and by the American Legion shortly after the war, it was reacquired by Benicia Lodge No. 5 in 1950.

110 W J St, Benicia

NO. 175 ☐
SITE OF FIRST PROTESTANT CHURCH

On April 15, 1849, the Reverend Sylvester Woodbridge, Jr., organized the first Presbyterian Church of Benicia, the first Protestant church established in California with an ordained resident pastor. The church was disbanded in 1875.

Benicia City Park, K St between 1st and 2nd Sts, Benicia

NO. 176 ☐
BENICIA ARSENAL

Captain Charles P. Stone, with 21 enlisted men, established Benicia Arsenal as an ordnance depot in August 1851. The first building, a small wooden powder magazine, was erected in September 1851. Between 1853 and 1863, Congress authorized $550,000 to be spent on the establishment, and some 15 stone and frame buildings were constructed. The arsenal was first called "California Ordnance Depot," then "Benicia Arsenal Depot," and finally, in the spring of 1852, "Benicia Arsenal." It played an important role in crises such as the Indian wars. Some of its original buildings are in use today. Descendants of the men who established Benicia Arsenal are still living in Benicia and other parts of California.

Main gate of port area, intersection of Adams and Jefferson Sts, Benicia

NO. 177🔔
SITE OF FORMER BENICIA BARRACKS

Benicia Barracks, established on April 30, 1849 and organized by Brevet Lt. Col. Silas Casey, 2nd U.S. Infantry, was the U.S. Army headquarters for the Department of the Pacific from 1851-1857. Also known as the "Post near Benicia," it remained a garrison installation until 1898. The post hospital, built in 1856, is the only remaining structure associated with the original Barracks. The Barracks became part of the Benicia Arsenal, which closed in 1964.

Francesca Terrace Park, across from the Benicia National Guard Armory, 711 Hillcrest Ave, Benicia

NO. 534 🔔
VACA-PEÑA ADOBE

This is the site of the 10-square-league Rancho Los Putos that Governor Pío Pico granted to Juan Felipe Peña and Manuel Cabeza Vaca in 1845. The Peña Adobe, erected here in 1843, is still owned by the descendants of their families (1955). The nearby town of Vacaville was established in 1851 on land that Vaca sold to William McDaniel.

Take Pena Adobe Rd interchange on I-80, go NE 0.5 mi on Pena Adobe Rd to Pena Adobe Park, Vacaville

NO. 574☐
SITE OF STATE CAPITOL AT VALLEJO

Vallejo was the official seat of State government from February 4, 1851 to February 4, 1853.

Located in NW corner of city parking lot, 200 block of York St, between Sacramento and Santa Clara Sts,

NO. 751🔔
FIRST U.S. NAVAL STATION IN THE PACIFIC

Mare Island Navy Yard was established September 16, 1854 by Commander David G. Farragut, U.S.N., on a site selected in 1852 by a commission headed by Commodore John D. Sloat, U.S.N. Mare Island had the Navy's first shipyard, ammunition depot, hospital, Marine barracks, cemetery, chapel, and radio station in the Pacific.

Entrance to Mare Island Naval Shipyard, main gate, SW corner of Tennessee St and Mare Island Way, Vallejo

NO. 779 🔔
ROCKVILLE STONE CHAPEL

The cornerstone of this chapel, erected by pioneers of Methodist Episcopal Church South with volunteer labor and donated funds, was laid October 3, 1856 on a site supplied by Landy and Sarah Alford, and the chapel was dedicated February 1857. By 1929, the chapel had deteriorated and the church deeded it to Rockville Public Cemetery District as a pioneer monument. It was restored in 1940.

Rockville Cemetery, Suisun Valley Rd, 0.2 mi N of Rockville

NO. 795

BENICIA SEMINARY

Founded in 1852 as the Young Ladies' Seminary of Benicia, Mills College was acquired from Mary Atkins by Cyrus and Susan Mills in 1865 and moved to its present site in Oakland in 1871. It was chartered as a college by the State of California in 1885.

City park, Military W St between 1st and 2nd Sts, Benicia

NO. 804

UNIVERSITY OF CALIFORNIA EXPERIMENTAL FARM, WOLFSKILL GRANT

In 1842, John R. Wolfskill arrived here, laden with fruit seeds and cuttings. A true horticulturist, he became the father of the fruit industry in this region. In 1937 his daughter, Mrs. Frances Wolfskill Taylor Wilson, bequeathed 107.28 acres to the University of California for an experimental farm. The university's research at this portion of Rancho Río de los Putos has enriched the state's horticultural industry.

University of California Experimental Farm, Putah Creek Rd, 1.5 mi SW of Winters

NO. 862

SAINT PAUL'S EPISCOPAL CHURCH

Designed in 1859 by Lt. Julian McAllister and built by shipwrights of the Pacific Mail and Steamship Company, St. Paul's is an outstanding example of early California Gothic ecclesiastical architecture. Notable for its fine craftsmanship, this building has continuously served the Episcopal Church since its consecration by the Rt. Rev. William Ingraham Kip in 1860.

120 E J St at 1st St, Benicia

NO. 880

FISCHER-HANLON HOUSE

In 1849, Joseph Fisher, a Swiss immigrant, came to Benicia. After joining a butcher partnership, Fischer purchased this lot on July 1, 1858 and moved the house, reputed to be an old hotel, onto it. The building, an outstanding example of East Coast Federalist styling, illustrates architectural diffusion during the Gold Rush.

135 W G St, Benicia

NO. 973

TURNER/ROBERTSON SHIPYARD, 1883-1918

In 1882, Matthew Turner of San Francisco relocated his shipyard to Benicia. Turner, the most prodigious shipbuilder in North America, constructed 228 vessels, 169 of which were launched here. In 1913, the shipyard was purchased by James Robertson, who operated it until 1918. The yard sways, and the Whaler Stamboul, used as a shipyard work platform, are visible at low tide.

Matthew Turner Shipyard Park, foot of W 12th St off of W K St, Benicia

Sonoma County

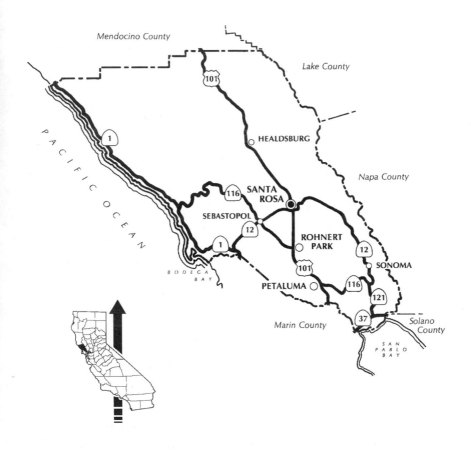

Fort Ross State Historic Park - Outpost of Russian-American Fur Company. Located 13 miles N of Jenner on Highway 1.

Jack London State Historic Park - The author's ranch and home, Wolfhouse Ruins. Located 1 mile W of Glen Ellen.

Petaluma Adobe State Historic Park - Vallejo's adobe ranch house, 1834. Located 4 miles E of Petaluma on Highway 101.

Sonoma State Historic Park - Mission, barracks, and Vallejo Home. Located in and adjacent to Sonoma.

Sonoma
Est. 1850

Sonoma County is a treasure of diverse history, from the Mexican-era mission and barracks in the town of Sonoma, to the Russian outpost of Fort Ross on the rocky coast. Sonoma County's historic vineyards and wineries, the home of Mariano G. Vallejo, and the Petaluma Adobe are just a few of the gems in this county of historical riches.

NO. 3 🔔
MISSION SAN FRANCISCO SOLANO

On July 4, 1823, Padre José Altamira founded this northernmost of California's Franciscan missions, the only one established in California under independent Mexico. In 1834, secularization orders were carried out by Military Commandant M. G. Vallejo, and Mission San Francisco Solano became a parish church serving the Pueblo and Sonoma Valley until it was sold in 1881.

Sonoma State Historic Park, NW corner of Spain at 1st St E, Sonoma

NO. 4 ☐
GENERAL M. G. VALLEJO HOME

The home of General Mariano Guadalupe Vallejo, known as "Lachryma Montis" (Tears of the Mountain), was built in 1850. Its name was derived from the springs that now are the source of Sonoma's water supply. General Vallejo, born at Monterey July 7, 1808, was commander of the northern Mexican frontier, founder of the Pueblo of Sonoma, and a member of the first Constitutional Convention of California.

Vallejo Home, Sonoma State Historic Park, Spain at 3rd St W Sonoma

NO. 5 🔔
FORT ROSS

Founded in 1812 by Russians from Alaska. When Russians withdrew to Alaska in 1841, Captain Sutter bought the improvements and supplies. The State acquired the fort in 1906 and the remaining buildings–Greek Orthodox Chapel, Commandant's Quarters, and Stockade–were restored. The chapel, destroyed by fire in 1970, was reconstructed in 1974.

19005 Coast Hwy, State Hwy 1 (P.M. 33.0), 12 mi N of Jenner

NO. 7 ☐
BEAR FLAG MONUMENT

On June 14, 1846, the Bear Flag Party raised the Bear Flag on this spot and declared California free from Mexican rule. Following the raising of the American flag at Monterey July 7, 1846 by Commodore John Drake Sloat, on July 9 the Bear Flag was hauled down and the American flag raised in its place by Lieutenant Joseph W. Revere, U.S.A., who had been sent to Sonoma from San Francisco by Commander John B. Montgomery of the U.S. Sloop-of-War Portsmouth.

Sonoma Plaza, E Spain and 1st St E, Sonoma Plaza

NO. 17 □

BLUE WING INN

Erected by General M. G. Vallejo about 1840 to accommodate emigrants and other travelers, the Inn was purchased in gold rush days by Cooper and Spriggs, two retired sea-faring men, and operated as hotel and store. It was among first hostelries in Northern California. Notable guests, according to local tradition, included John C. Frémont, U. S. Grant, Governor Pío Pico, Kit Carson, Fighting Joe Hooker, William T. Sherman, Phil Sheridan, and members of the Bear Flag Party.

Sonoma State Historic Park, 133 E Spain St, Sonoma

NO. 18 🔔

PETALUMA ADOBE

It took about ten years to complete this building, begun in 1834 as a result of General M. G. Vallejo's order to settle the area. On Vallejo's 66,000-acre rancho such necessities as candles, soap, blankets, shoes, and saddles were manufactured by native artisans in shops which included a tannery, smithy, and grist mill.

Adobe at 3325 Adobe Rd, plaque located 6 mi W of site, 300 ft NW of intersection of Old Redwood Hwy and Adobe Rd, Petaluma

NO. 234 □

LUTHER BURBANK HOME AND GARDEN

In this garden Luther Burbank wrought with living plants to bring to the world greater fertility, wealth, and beauty, developing new varieties that produced better fruits and more beautiful flowers.

200 block of Santa Rosa Ave, Santa Rosa

NO. 237 🔔

TEMELEC HALL

This structure was erected in 1858 by Captain Granville P. Swift, a member of the Bear Flag Party, using stone quarried here by native Indian labor. General Percifor F. Smith, U.S. military commander in California, lived in the little house nearby in 1849.

Temelec Adult Community, 220 Temelec Circle, 3 mi SE of Sonoma

NO. 316 □

PRESIDIO OF SONOMA (SONOMA BARRACKS)

Sonoma Barracks was erected in 1836 by General M. G. Vallejo. It became the headquarters of the Bear Flag Party, which in June 1846 proclaimed a "California Republic" and raised the Bear Flag on Sonoma's Plaza. Twenty-three days later, on July 7, 1846, Commodore John Drake Sloat took possession of California for the United States government. Stevenson's Regiment, Company C, U.S.A., occupied the barracks in April 1847.

Sonoma State Historic Park, NW corner of E Spain and 1st St E, Sonoma

NO. 392 🔔

BUENA VISTA WINERY AND VINEYARDS

Founded in 1857, this is the birthplace of California wine. Its founder, Colonel Agoston Haraszthy, called the father of the state's wine industry, toured Europe in 1861 to gather grape vine cuttings; he also oversaw planting the vineyards and digging wine storage tunnels into the limestone rock of the hillsides.

18000 Old Winery Rd, 2 mi NE of Sonoma

NO. 392-1

SITE OF HARASZTHY VILLA

Here Count Agoston Haraszthy, "Father of California Viticulture," built an imposing villa in 1857-58, as his home. California's first formal Vintage Celebration, a masked ball, was held at this site on October 23, 1864. General and Mrs. Mariano Guadalupe Vallejo were guests of honor. While living here, Haraszthy oversaw operations of the Winery and Buena Vista Vinicultural Society.

Castle Rd near Buena Vista Winery, Sonoma

NO. 496 🔔

SWISS HOTEL

The Swiss Hotel was constructed about 1850 by Don Salvador Vallejo. This adobe adjoined his first Sonoma dwelling, built in 1836. Occupied by various pioneers, in 1861 it was the house of Dr. Victor J. Faure, vintner of prize-winning wines made from the grapes of the Vallejo family vineyards. Later, it was used as a hotel and restaurant.

18 W Spain St, Sonoma

NO. 501 🔔

SALVADOR VALLEJO ADOBE

This was the home of Captain Salvador Vallejo, brother of General Mariano G. Vallejo, who founded Sonoma. The adobe was built by Indian labor between 1836 and 1846, and was occupied by Captain Vallejo and his family until the Bear Flag Party seized Sonoma on June 4, 1846. Cumberland College, a Presbyterian coeducational boarding school, was located here from 1858 to 1864.

421-1st St W Sonoma

NO. 621 🔔

ITALIAN SWISS COLONY

Here in 1881 Italian immigrants established an agricultural colony. Choice wines produced from grape plantings from the Old World soon brought wide acclaim. By 1905, 10 gold medals had been awarded these wines at international competition.

SE corner of Asti Rd and Asti Post Office Rd, Asti

NO. 627 🔔

UNION HOTEL AND UNION HALL

The original hotel was a one-story adobe; the adjoining hall was a one-story frame structure. After the fire of 1866, a two-story stone hotel and a two story frame hall with rooms upstairs for hotel guests were built. The Union Hotel was conducted as a hotel until 1955, when the Bank of America acquired the property.

35 Napa and 1st St W Sonoma

NO. 667 🔔

NASH ADOBE

This house was built by H. A. Green in 1847. Here John H. Nash was taken prisoner by Lieutenant William T. Sherman in July 1847 for refusing to relinquish his post as alcalde to Lilburn W. Boggs. The adobe was restored in 1931 by Zolita Bates, great-granddaughter of Nancy Patton Adler, who lived here after her 1848 marriage to Lewis Adler, pioneer merchant of San Francisco and Sonoma.

579–1st St E, Sonoma

NO. 692 🔔

HOOD HOUSE

This was the site of Rancho los Guilucos (18,833 acres), which Governor Juan Bautista Alvarado granted to John Wilson and his wife, Ramona Carrillo, sister-in-law of General Mariano Guadalupe Vallejo, in 1839. The house, constructed in 1858 by William Hood for his bride, Elsia Shaw of Sonoma, incorporates the original bricks fired on the property. The property was purchased in 1943 by the California Department of the Youth Authority for Los Guilucos School for Girls.

Hood Mansion, Santa Rosa Jr College, 7501 Sonoma Hwy (Hwy 12), Santa Rosa

NO. 739 🔔

VINEYARD AND WINERY (SAN FRANCISCO SOLANO MISSION VINEYARD)

Here the Franciscan Fathers of San Francisco Solano de Sonoma Mission produced sacramental wine from the first vineyard in Sonoma Valley, planted in 1825. After secularization of the mission in 1835, General Mariano G. Vallejo, Commandant of Alta California's northern frontier, produced prize-winning wines from these grapes. A young immigrant from Italy, Samuele Sebastiani, with his wife Elvira, purchased this property in the early 1900s. Since that time, he and his family have continued with distinction the traditions handed down to them. Much of the original mission vineyard is still planted to choice wine grapes.

394–4th St E at Spain St, Sonoma

NO. 743 🔔

JACK LONDON STATE HISTORIC PARK

This is the "House of Happy Walls," built in 1919 by Charmian K. London in memory of her husband, renowned author Jack London. Here are housed many of his works and the collection gathered in their travels throughout the world. In 1960 Charmian's house, the ruins of Jack's "Wolf House," and his grave were presented to the State by his nephew, Irving Shepard.

Glen Ellen

NO. 820 🔔

ST. TERESA'S CHURCH

Constructed of redwood in 1859 by New England ship's carpenters on land donated by Jasper O'Farrell, the church has served this coastal community continuously for over a century. Father Louis Rossi was appointed pastor on March 8, 1860, and Archbishop Alemany dedicated the church on June 2, 1861.

Bodega Hwy near Bodega Ln, Bodega

NO. 833 🔔

BODEGA BAY AND HARBOR

Discovered in 1602-03 by Vizcaino's expedition, the bay was named by Bodega in his survey of 1775. The harbor was used in 1790 by Colnett and in 1809 and 1811 by the Kusov expeditions. The Russian-American company and their Aleut hunters used the bay as an outpost until 1841; Stephen Smith took control in 1843. Pioneer ships of many nations used Bodega Bay as an anchorage.

Doran Park, 1.6 mi W of State Hwy 1 (P.M. 9.4), on Doran Beach Rd, 0.5 mi S of Bodega Bay

NO. 835

COOPER'S SAWMILL

In 1834, Mariano G. Vallejo's brother-in-law, John B. R. Cooper, constructed California's first known power-operated commercial sawmill. In addition to sawing redwood lumber, the mill and surrounding settlement served as a barrier to Russian encroachment from the west. Located on Mark West Creek, the waterpowered mill was destroyed by flood in the winter of 1840-41.

SW corner, intersection of Mirabel and River Rds (P.M. 174) near Mirabel Park, 8 mi W of Santa Rosa

NO. 879

COTATI DOWNTOWN PLAZA

Cotati's hexagonal town plan, one of only two such in the United States, was designed during the 1890s by Newton Smyth as an alternative to the traditional grid. Each of the streets surrounding the six-sided town plaza, where early settler Dr. Thomas Page's barn once stood, is named after one of Page's sons; "Cotati" derives from the name of a local Indian chief.

Downtown plaza, SE corner of Old Redwood Hwy and E Cotati Ave, Cotati

NO. 893

WALTERS RANCH HOP KILN

This is the most significant surviving example of a stone hop kiln in the North Coast region. Built by Angelo "Skinny" Sodini in 1905, it served the Russian River Valley and North Coast regions, once the major hop-growing areas in the West. In the latter part of the 19th century, Sol Walters purchased 380 acres, part of the Sotoyome Rancho patented in 1853, from Josefa Fitch.

6050 Westside Rd, Healdsburg

NO. 915

PETRIFIED FOREST

The petrified forest, historically and scientifically significant as the state's only petrified forest dating from the Eocene period, is unique in its size, scope, and variety of petrification. Discovered in 1870, the forest is about a mile long by half a mile wide.

4100 Petrified Forest Rd, 5 mi NW of Calistoga

NO. 939

Twentieth Century Folk Art Environments (Thematic)–JOHN MEDICA GARDENS

"Trying to make it look better," John Medica spent 20 years transforming a barren hillside into a magical garden of plants and creative stone works. Castles were his greatest triumph. A native of Yugoslavia, self-taught, Medica created an oasis for people and animals to enjoy. This imaginative assemblage is one of California's remarkable Twentieth Century Folk Art Environments.

5000 Medica Rd, Santa Rosa

NO. 981 🔔

ICARIA-SPERANZA COMMUNE

Icaria-Speranza was a Utopian community based on the writings of French philosopher Etienne Cabet. In 1881, at Cloverdale, French immigrant families led by the Dehay and Leroux families began their social experiment in cooperative living based on solidarity and depending on an agrarian economy. It lasted until 1886. Icaria-Speranza was the only Icarian Colony in California and the last of seven established throughout the United States. On this site stood the Icarian schoolhouse, deeded to the county in 1886.

W side of Asti Rd, 1.68 mi N of Asti Post Office Rd, S of Cloverdale

Landmark No. 5

Landmark No. 893

Landmark No. 692

Landmark No. 3

Landmark No. 820

Stanislaus County

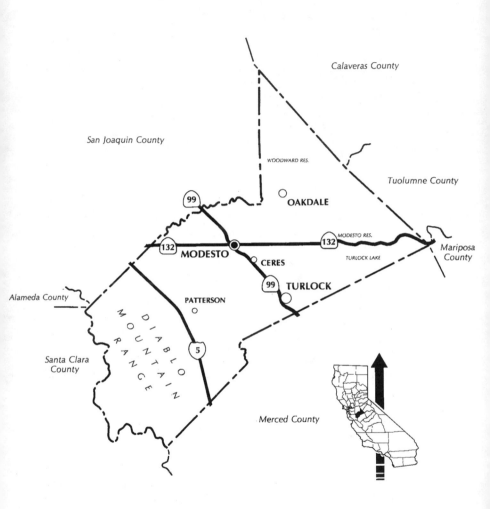

Stanislaus
Est. 1854

T he history of Stanislaus County was partially shaped by the Stanislaus and Tuolumne rivers that wind through the area. Early miners and settlers needed a means for crossing the rivers, so several ferries were established. This territory was a part of "El Camino Viejo," a route used in the Spanish and Mexican periods of California history.

NO. 347
KNIGHTS FERRY

Once called Dentville, this picturesque mining center and trading post was founded in 1849. An early ferry carried Argonauts on their way to the southern mines. The rare wooden covered bridge, reportedly designed by U. S. Grant, brother-in-law of the Dent brothers, and the old flour mill were built there in 1854. The town served as the county seat from 1862 to 1872.

On Sonora Rd, 1.4 mi W of State Hwy 120 (P.M. 16.4), Knights Ferry

NO. 414
LA GRANGE

French settlers originally established the community of French Bar along the Tuolumne River in 1850. After the destructive floods of 1851-52, citizens of French Bar relocated one mile upstream above the floodplain. Renamed La Grange, the new town prospered as a mining and agricultural community, and served as the county seat of Stanislaus County from 1856 to 1862.

30173 Yosemite Blvd., La Grange

NO. 415
THE WILLMS RANCH

Arriving in California October 12, 1849, John R. Willms and John H. Kappelmann engaged in the hotel and butcher businesses in Buena Vista, in what is now Stanislaus County. They bought up mining claims and settler's claims until, by 1852, they had a tract of 3,600 acres. The "KW" brand was the first in Tuolumne County in 1852. After the death of Kappelmann, Willms carried on alone, and the ranch has been owned by the Willms family ever since.

On Willms Rd, 1.3 mi S of State Hwy 120 (P.M. 170), 1.9 mi S of Knights Ferry

NO. 418
EMPIRE CITY

This memorial is dedicated to the memory of the pioneer men and women of Empire City and vicinity. Located one-half mile west of here on the banks of the Tuolumne River, Empire City was the head of navigation and the site of the second courthouse of Stanislaus County. Records remained here from October 1854 to December 1855.

0.1 mi S on County Hwy J-7 Empire

NO. 934

TEMPORARY DETENTION CAMPS FOR JAPANESE AMERICANS— TURLOCK ASSEMBLY CENTER

The temporary detention camps (also known as "assembly centers") represent the first phase of the mass incarceration of 97,785 Californians of Japanese ancestry during World War II. Pursuant to Executive Order 9066 signed by President Franklin D. Roosevelt on February 19, 1942, thirteen makeshift detention facilities were constructed at various California racetracks, fairgrounds, and labor camps. These facilities were intended to confine Japanese Americans until more permanent concentration camps, such as those at Manzanar and Tule Lake in California, could be built in isolated areas of the country. Beginning on March 30, 1942, all native-born Americans and long-time legal residents of Japanese ancestry living in California were ordered to surrender themselves for detention.

Site: Arboga Community, 6 mi S of Marysville on Arboga Rd

Landmark No. 347

Landmark No. 872

Sutter-Yuba Counties

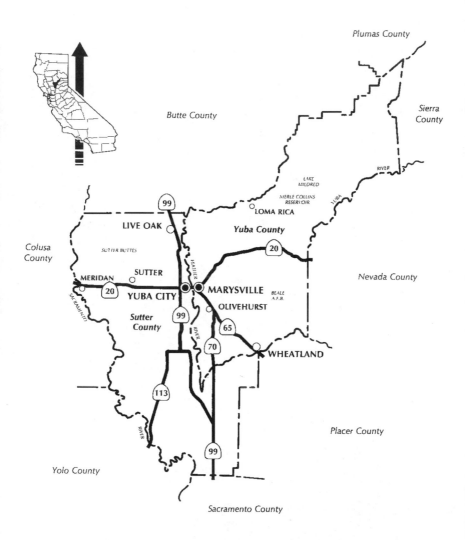

Sutter

Est. 1850

Early explorers and trappers noted the buttes, or small mountains, rising in the midst of the valley. The buttes and the county are named for John Sutter, whose Hock Farm was established nearby as an agricultural enterprise in the 1841. The Sacramento river flows through this county, and served the development of early navigation of the upper river.

NO. 346 🔔

HOCK FARM (SITE OF)

This memorial is constructed of the original iron from the fort of Hock Farm, the first non-Indian settlement in Sutter County. Established in 1841 by John Augustus Sutter, the fort and farm buildings were located on the banks of the Feather River opposite this point.

Plaque located on State Hwy 99 at Messick Rd; site at 5320 Garden Hwy at intersection of Messick Rd, 6.7 mi S of Yuba City

NO. 929 🔔

SITE OF PROPAGATION OF THE THOMPSON SEEDLESS GRAPE

William Thompson, an Englishman, and his family settled here in 1863. In 1872 he sent to New York for three cuttings called Lady de Coverly of which only one survived. The grape, first publicly displayed in Marysville in 1875, became known as Thompson's seedless grape. Today, thousands of acres have been planted in California for the production of raisins, bulk wine, and table grapes.

9001 Colusa Hwy, State Hwy 20 (P.M. 7.7), 8 mi W of Yuba City

Landmark No. 346

Tehama County

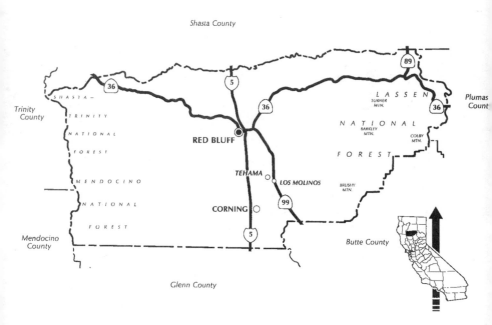

William B. Ide Adobe State Historic Park - Commemorates Bear Flag Republic President. Located 1.5 miles N of Red Bluff.

Tehama
Est. 1856

In 1844, John Bidwell led a party to explore the area we know today as Tehama County. Many members of the party later successfully petitioned the Mexican government for land grants. These "ranchos" proved to be the beginning of a thriving agricultural industry.

NO. 12 🔔

RESIDENCE OF GENERAL WILLIAM B. IDE

General Ide came to California with his family in 1845. Ide helped organize the revolt against the Mexican mandate requiring Americans to leave California, and was the first and only President of the California Republic, under Bear Flag Party proclamation.

William B. Ide Adobe State Historic Park, 3040 Adobe Rd, 1.5 mi N of Red Bluff

NO. 117

HOME OF MRS. JOHN BROWN

In 1864 the widow of John Brown, the famous abolitionist of Harpers Ferry, came to Red Bluff with her children. So great was the admiration for John Brown in that area that a considerable sum of money was raised to provide his widow and children with a home. Mrs. Brown lived there until the summer of 1870, when she and her children moved to Humboldt County.

135 Main St, Red Bluff

NO. 183 🔔

FIRST TEHAMA COUNTY COURTHOUSE

Tehama County's Board of Supervisors and other county officials first met in rented rooms in the Union Hotel, later called Heider House. The county seat remained here from May 1856 to March 1857, when it was moved to Red Bluff. The Heider House was destroyed by fire in 1908. This property is part of original land grant to Robert Hasty Thomes, 1844.

75 ft E of intersection of 2nd and D Sts, Tehama

NO. 357 ☐

INDIAN MILITARY POST, NOMI LACKEE INDIAN RESERVATION

An Indian military post from 1854 to 1866, the Nomi Lackee Indian Reservation controlled 300 to 2,500 militant Indians. U.S. Survey of 1858 showed the reservation to cover 25,139.71 acres. The Indians moved to Round Valley in 1866.

On Osborn Rd, 3.9 mi N of Flournoy

Trinity County

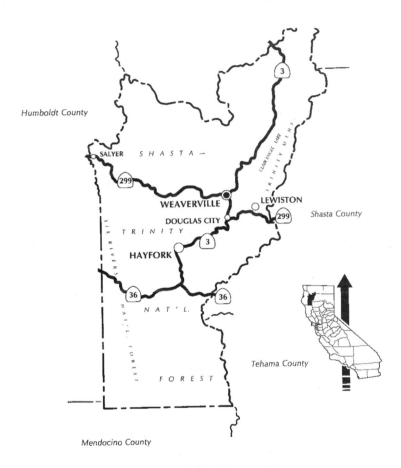

Weaverville Joss House State Historic Park - Chinese temple of late gold rush period. Located on Highway 299 in Weaverville.

Trinity
Est. 1850

This rugged, mountainous county reflects the boom and bust of the gold rush period. Small mining towns and camps once lined the rivers and streams. Weaverville is a well preserved remnant of the early mining days. Its Chinese temple displays early artifacts from China.

NO. 709 🔔

WEAVERVILLE JOSS HOUSE

Hundreds of Chinese miners came to the Weaverville area in the 1850s and prospered despite hardships, discrimination, and tax on foreign miners. The first house of worship burned in 1873; the Chinese continued their religious traditions in the present temple, dedicated April 18, 1874. Moon Lim Lee, trustee and grandson of one of its contributors, gift-deeded the "Temple Amongst the Forest Beneath the Clouds" to the State.

SW corner of State Hwy 299 and Oregon St, Weaverville

NO. 778 🔔

LA GRANGE MINE (HYDRAULIC)

This mine, originally known as the Oregon Mountain Group of Claims, first operated about 1862. In 1892 the mine was purchased by the La Grange Hydraulic Gold Mining Company, which brought water from Stuart's Fork through 29 miles of ditch, tunnels, and flume to deliver it to the mine pit under a 650-foot head. Over 100,000,000 yards of gravel were processed to produce $3,500,000 in gold. Large-scale operations ceased in 1918.

State Hwy 299 (P.M. 478), 4 mi W of Weaverville

Landmark No. 778

Tulare County

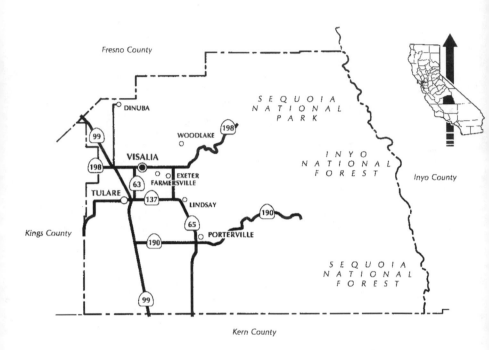

Colonel Allensworth State Historic Park - Only
California town founded and governed by African-
Americans. Located 17 miles N of Wasco.

Tulare
Est. 1852

T ulare is a Spanish word meaning "a place of many tules, or rushes." This fertile land provided Native Americans with abundance since ancient times, as evidenced in their many village sites. The county's rich ethnic history includes the establishment of the first Tule Indian Reservation, a Japanese Detention Camp and Allensworth, the only California town founded and governed by African Americans.

NO. 388 🔔
FIRST TULE RIVER INDIAN RESERVATION

A reservation was originally established in 1857, and Indians from a widespread area were brought here. The natives of the vicinity, the Koyeti tribe towards the west and the Yandanchi tribe toward the east, were branches of the Yokuts Indians that occupied the San Joaquin Valley. The Tule River Indian Reservation was moved to its present location, 10 miles to the southeast in 1873.

Alta Vista School, 2293 E Crabtree Ave, Porterville

NO. 389 🔔
KAWEAH POST OFFICE, KAWEAH COLONY

The Kaweah cooperative colony was a utopian project started in 1886. For several years it attracted international attention; many settlers came here and actually did much to further their ideals. Unable to secure title to the land, and experiencing internal difficulties, the organization ceased to exist after 1892, leaving the Kaweah Post Office as one of its tangible reminders.

43795 N Fork Dr, Kaweah

NO. 410 🔔
CHARTER OAK OR ELECTION TREE

Under this tree on July 10, 1852, a party commanded by Major James D. Savage conducted the election by which Tulare County was organized. Woodville, site of Wood's cabin, and the first county seat, was located about one-half mile south of this marker. This general area, the delta of the Kaweah River, was also known as the "Four Creeks County."

On Charter Oak Dr 0.3 mi W of Rd 180, 7 mi E of Visalia

NO. 413 🔔
TAILHOLT

Tailholt began as a gold mining camp about 1856 during the Kern River gold rush, when gold was obtained from placer and shaft operations. Mining has been carried on intermittently since the time of discovery, with a considerable settlement here during active periods. The town's name was changed to White River about 1870.

SW corner of County Hwy M109 (old Springville stage rte) and County Hwy M12, 8.0 mi S of Fountain Springs

NO. 471

BUTTERFIELD STAGE ROUTE

This route, following an earlier emigrant trail, was laid out in the 1850s as part of the Stockton-Los Angeles Road. It was used from 1858 to 1861 by the Butterfield Overland Mail stages to carry the first overland mail service on a regular schedule between St. Louis and San Francisco.

SW corner of Hermosa St (Ave 228) and State Hwy 65, 1 mi W of Lindsay

NO. 473 ♠

TULE RIVER STAGE STATION

Here Peter Goodhue operated an emigrant trail stopping place on the bank of the Tule River from 1854 until the river changed its course in 1862. This became a Butterfield Overland and mail stage station, 1858-61. It was kept in 1860 by R. Porter Putnam, who in 1864 founded Porterville.

Porterville Public Park, SW corner of N Main St and W Henderson Ave

NO. 648 ♠

FOUNTAIN SPRINGS

The settlement of Fountain Springs was established before 1855, 1-1/2 miles northwest of this point, at the junction of the Stockton-Los Angeles Road and the road to the Kern River gold mines. From 1858 to 1861, Fountain Springs was a station on the Butterfield Overland Mail route.

SW corner of County Rds J22 and M 109 (old Springville stage rte), Fountain Springs

NO. 934

TEMPORARY DETENTION CAMPS FOR JAPANESE AMERICANS— TULARE ASSEMBLY CENTER

The temporary detention camps (also known as "assembly centers") represent the first phase of the mass incarceration of 97,785 Californians of Japanese ancestry during World War II. Pursuant to Executive Order 9066 signed by President Franklin D. Roosevelt on February 19, 1942, thirteen makeshift detention facilities were constructed at various California racetracks, fairgrounds, and labor camps. These facilities were intended to confine Japanese Americans until more permanent concentration camps, such as those at Manzanar and Tule Lake in California, could be built in isolated areas of the country. Beginning on March 30, 1942, all native-born Americans and long-time legal residents of Japanese ancestry living in California were ordered to surrender themselves for detention.

Tulare County Fairgrounds, Tulare

Landmark No. 648

Landmark No. 389

Tuolumne County

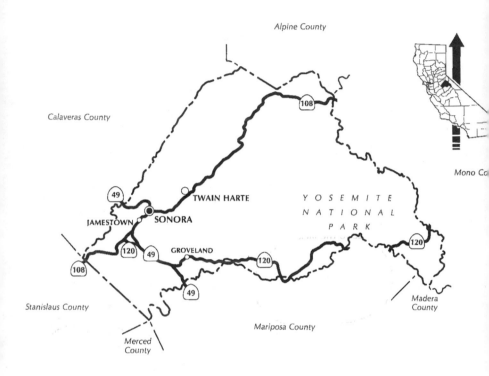

Columbia State Historic Park - Restored California gold rush town. Located 4 miles N of Sonora.

Railtown 1897 State Historic Park - Historic railroading exhibit. Located on 5th Avenue, Jamestown.

Tuolumne
Est. 1850

A treasure of natural wonders and lively gold rush history, Tuolumne County offers visitors vivid scenery. A portion of Yosemite National Park lies within the county, along with giant redwood groves and impressive geological features. Both Bret Harte and Mark Twain wrote stories set in this area during the Gold Rush.

NO. 122 □
MONTEZUMA

First record of Montezuma was June 1850 when partners Solomon Miller and Peter K. Aurand, proprietors of the "Montezuma Tent," were attacked and Aurand killed by a group of Mexicans during the foreign miners tax excitement of that period. Due to the lack of water, little mining occurred here until 1852 when a ditch and flume were completed bringing water for placer mining. Two types of mining were carried on, placer operations on the flats and tunnels extending under Table Mountain. The gravel produced 3-1/2 C. per pan in the mid 50s. The yield was from $5 to $10 per day. One placer nugget found in 1853 weighed 18 lbs. 8 oz. By late 1852 the population was about 800. At its zenith Montezuma City had four saloons, two hotels, Adams Express Co., post office, church, some homes, and many tents and cabins. The town was nearly destroyed by an incendiary fire which started in Clarks Hotel on June 29, 1866.

On State Hwy 49 (P.M. 11.3), 2.5 mi N of Chinese Camp

NO. 123 🔔
COLUMBIA

Columbia, the "Gem of the Southern Mines," became a town of 4,000 to 5,000 in the 1850s, following the discovery of gold here by the Hildreth party March 27, 1850. Gold shipments, estimated at $87,000,000, declined rapidly after 1858, but Columbia never became a ghost town. Columbia State Historic Park was created in 1945 to preserve its historic buildings and sites.

Columbia State Historic Park, NW corner of Washington and Broadway Sts, Columbia

NO. 124 🔔
TUTTLETOWN

This early-day stopping place for men and mounts was named for Judge Anson A. H. Tuttle, who built the first log cabin here in 1848. Stones used in the base for the plaque are from the old Swerer store built in 1854, remains of which still exist (1949). Mark Twain traded here. Tuttletown Hotel, built in 1852 and still standing in 1949, was last operated by John Edwards.

On State Hwy 49 (P.M. 24.8) at Wilcox Ranch Rd, Tuttletown

NO. 138

MARK TWAIN CABIN

This is a replica of Mark Twain's cabin, with original chimney and fireplace. Here on Jackass Hill, young Mark Twain, while guest of the Gillis Brothers in 1864-65, gathered material for *The Jumping Frog of Calaveras County*, which first brought him fame, and for *Roughing It*.

1 mi NW of Tuttletown off State Hwy 49

NO. 139

ST. JAMES EPISCOPAL CHURCH

The seventh parish of the Protestant Episcopal Church in California, St. James is the oldest Episcopal Church building in the state. The first services were held in the church on October 4, 1859, and it was consecrated by Rt. Rev. Wm. Ingraham Kip in 1870.

Intersection of N Washington (State Hwy 49) and Elkin Sts, Sonora

NO. 140

WELLS FARGO EXPRESS COMPANY BUILDING

This building, erected in 1849 by the Walkerly brothers, was subsequently owned by the Morris brothers. It housed a general merchandise store in connection with the office of Adams Express Company, predecessor of Wells Fargo & Company. The original express agents were Sol Miller, C. W. H. Solinsky, and the Morris brothers.

SW corner of Main St and Solinsky Alley, Chinese Camp

NO. 395

SHAW'S FLAT

In 1850 this community was alive with gold miners. James D. Fair, after whom the Fairmont Hotel in San Francisco is named, was one of the most notable. The Mississippi House, built in 1850, contains many relics including the original bar and post office with its grill and mailboxes. On a nearby hill stands the old bell, given by miners, which summoned men to work and announced the convening of various courts. According to tradition, a local bartender added to his income by panning the gold dust dropped on his muddy boots as he served customers.

SE corner of Shaw's Flat Rd and Mt Brow Rd, 2.6 mi SW of Columbia

NO. 406

BIG OAK FLAT

First called Savage Diggins after the man who discovered gold here in 1848, the town was renamed Big Oak Flat about 1850 after the giant oak tree that stood in the center of town, near this spot. The oak, which was about 13 feet in diameter, was undermined in 1869 and burned in 1890; only pieces remained in 1949. Rich placer and lode mines are reported to have yielded $28,000,000 during the town's heyday. Stone buildings erected in 1852 were still standing in 1949.

On State Hwy 120 (P.M. 30.2), Big Oak Flat

NO. 407 □ 🗶

SUMMERSVILLE (TUOLUMNE)

The area's first non-Indian settlers, the Franklin Summers family, arrived in 1854 and built a log cabin a half mile west of this spot, the geographical center of East Belt Placer Gold Rush from 1856 to 1857. In 1858, James Blakely discovered the first quartz lode half a mile east of here and named it "Eureka." The mine became the nucleus of the town of Summersville, which was later called Carters and finally became Tuolumne. Other mining towns lively in gold rush days were Long Gulch, two miles south, and Cherokee, two miles north.

In island, center of Carter St at intersection with Tuolumne Rd, Tuolumne

NO. 419 🔔 🗶

JACKSONVILLE

Near this site stood the historic town of Jacksonville, now inundated by the waters of Don Pedro Reservoir. The town was settled by Julian Smart, who planted the first garden and orchard in the spring of 1849, and named for Colonel A. M. Jackson. In 1850 it was the principal river town in the area and the center for thousands of miners working the rich bed of the Tuolumne River.

Vista point at N approach to Don Pedro Bridge, State Hwy 120 (P.M. 19.4), 3.5 mi SE of Chinese Camp

NO. 420 □ 🗶

SOULSBYVILLE

Site of the famous Soulsby Mine (discovered by Benjamin Soulsby), Soulsbyville is the first community in Tuolumne County to be founded (1855) entirely upon the operation of a lode mine. First to work the mine were hard rock miners from Cornwall, England; the first group of 499 Cornishmen arrived in 1858.

NW corner of Soulsbyville Rd and Community Dr, Soulsbyville

NO. 422 □

SONORA-MONO ROAD

Jedediah Smith is reputed to have been the first white man to cross over or near Sonora Pass in 1827. A portion of the road was built by Tuolumne County Water Company in 1852 and a toll gate, fine hotel, and stables were located near this spot in the 1850s. Surveyed to Bridgeport, Mono County in 1860, the road was completed in 1864, when a six-horse team took three weeks for the round trip between Sonora and Bridgeport.

On State Hwy 108 (P.M. 14.5) at Sugar Pine cutoff, Sugar Pine

NO. 423 🗶 🗶

CHINESE CAMP

Reportedly founded about 1849 by a group of Englishmen who employed Chinese as miners, Chinese Camp was headquarters for stagelines in early 1850s and for several California Chinese mining companies. Much surface gold was found on hills and flats. The first Chinese tong war in the state was fought near here between the Sam Yap and Yan Woo Tongs. Stone and brick post office, built in 1854, is still in use. The St. Francis Xavier Catholic Church, built in 1855, was restored in 1949; its first pastor was Father Henry Aleric.

NW corner of State Hwy 120 (P.M. 15.9) and Main St, Chinese Camp

NO. 424 ☐

SAWMILL FLAT

Its name derived from two sawmills erected here to supply mining timbers in the early 1850s, Sawmill Flat was rich in pocket gold in its heyday; population at one time was 1,000. The mining camp of a Mexican woman, Dona Elisa Martínez, at north end of the flat, is reported to have been a hideout of the famous bandit Joaquin Murieta. The legendary "Battle of Sawmill Flat" would have taken place here.

22041 Sawmill Flat Rd, 2 mi SE of Columbia

NO. 431 ☐ 🪓

JAMESTOWN

James Woods first discovered gold in Tuolumne County west of this point, on Woods Creek, shortly before the town was founded by Colonel George James on August 8, 1848. Large quantities of gold were recovered from the stream. The town became known as gateway to the Mother Lode and the southern mines.

NE corner of Main and Donovan Sts, Jamestown

NO. 432 ☐ 🪓

SPRINGFIELD

Springfield received its name from the abundant springs gushing from limestone boulders. The town with its stores, shops, and hotel built around a plaza once boasted 2,000 inhabitants. It is believed to have been founded by Dona Josefa Valmesada, a Mexican woman of means with the reputation of aiding Americans in the war with Mexico. During the town's heyday, 150 miners' carts could be seen on the road, hauling gold-bearing dirt to Springfield springs for washing.

At intersection of Springfield and Horseshoe Bend Rds, 1.1 mi SW of Columbia

NO. 438 ☐

PARROTT'S FERRY

This is the site of the ferry crossing established in 1860 by Thomas H. Parrott that connected the mining towns of Tuttletown and Vallecito. The ferry was in operation until 1903, when the first bridge was built. The ferryboat, of flatbottom wooden construction, was propelled on heavy cables anchored in a large boulder. Still visible (1949) at low water on the Calaveras side of the river is the sandbag dam built to form a small lake that stored enough water to float the ferries in dry periods.

Vista area on Calaveras side of Columbia-Vallecito Highway Bridge, Stanislaus River Parrott's Ferry Rd, 5 mi NW of Columbia

NO. 445 ☐ 🪓

CHEROKEE

Gold was discovered here in 1853 by the Scott brothers, descendants of Cherokee Indians. Scars of placer "diggins" in every little arroyo in Cherokee Valley, healed over by Mother Nature, were later replaced by a quartz mine. Present-day productive farms in this area were once rich placer grounds.

On Confidence-Tuolumne City Rd (P.M. 8.5), 2 mi N of Tuolumne City

NO. 446 ☐ 🖾

GROVELAND

Formerly called "First Garrote" because of the hanging of a Mexican for stealing a horse, Groveland was built in 1849 as shown by dated adobe brick taken from a partition; adobe buildings were still standing in 1949. Gold was discovered here in 1849, and thousands of dollars in placer gold were taken from mines on Garrote Creek, Big Creek, and other diggings.

On NE corner of Main (State Hwy 120) and Back Sts, Groveland

NO. 460 ☐ 🖾

SECOND GARROTE

A sizable settlement was established at this rich placer location in 1849 by miners spreading east from Big Oak Flat and Groveland. The famous hangman's tree, part of which still stands (1950), is reported to have been instrumental in the death of a number of lawbreakers during the heyday of this locality.

On State Hwy 120 (P.M. 34. 7), 2.4 mi SE of Groveland

Landmark No. 864

Ventura County

Ventura
Est. 1873

Spanish explorer Cabrillo is believed to have stopped on these shores in 1542 and encountered Chumash Indians, with their skillfully crafted canoes. The Portolá expedition of 1769 also camped for a few nights in this coastal region. In 1782, Father Junipero Serra established his ninth and final mission here, called San Buenaventura, from which the city and county of Ventura get their names.

NO. 113 ☐

SITE OF JUNÍPERO SERRA'S CROSS

The first cross on the hill known as "La Loma de la Cruz," or the Hill of the Cross, was erected by Junípero Serra at the founding of the Mission San Buenaventura on March 31, 1782. This was the ninth and last mission founded by Father Serra in California.

Grant Park, at end of Ferro Dr, Ventura

NO. 114

OLD MISSION RESERVOIR

Part of the mission water system for Mission San Buenaventura, this was the settling tank or receiving reservoir from which water was distributed to the church and to the few Spanish families who lived near the mission.

Eastwood Park, N of Valdez Alley, 115 E Main St, Ventura

NO. 114-1

SAN BUENAVENTURA MISSION AQUEDUCT

The aqueduct at Canada Larga Road is two surviving sections of viaduct about 100 feet long and made of cobble stone and mortar. Originally, the watercourse ran from a point on the Ventura River about 1/2 mile north of the remaining ruins and carried the water to holding tanks behind the San Buenaventura Mission, a total of about 7 miles. The aqueduct was built by Chumash Indians 1805-15 to meet the needs of the mission population and consisted of both ditches and elevated stone masonry. The entire water system was destroyed by floods and abandoned in 1862.

234 Canada Larga Rd, Ventura

NO. 115 🔔

OLIVAS ADOBE

Continuous use has preserved this adobe, the only early two-story adobe in the Santa Clara Valley. A small one-story adobe built in 1837 was enlarged in 1849 by Don Raimundo Olivas, a prosperous cattle rancher.

4200 Olivas Park, Ventura

NO. 310

MISSION SAN BUENAVENTURA

This mission, established in 1782, was the ninth and the last to be dedicated by Father Junípero Serra. The first chapel and church were destroyed; the present mission church was begun in 1793 and completed in 1809.

210 E Main St at Figueroa, Ventura

NO. 553 ☐
RANCHO CAMULOS

On January 22, 1839, Governor Juan Alvarado granted the 48,815-acre Rancho San Francisco to Antonio del Valle. Jacoba Feliz filed a claim against this grant that was dismissed on June 8, 1857. The Del Valle family chose to live on the Rancho at Camulos, later known as the Home of Ramona.

On State Hwy 126 (P.M. 30.6), 2.2 mi E of Piru

NO. 624 ☐
WARRING PARK

On August 11, 1769, the explorers and priests accompanying Portolá found a populous village of Piru Indians near this point. Carrying their bowstrings loose, the Indians offered necklaces of stones, in exchange for which Portolá presented them with beads.

Warring Park, 700 block of Orchard St, Piru

NO. 659 🔔
STAGECOACH INN

Originally located some 200 yards to the north, the Stagecoach Inn was built in 1876. Its redwood lumber came by sea and was freighted up the steep Conejo Grade by multiteam wagons. From 1887 to 1901, the hotel served as a regular depot for the Coast Stage Line, which carried both passengers and mail. In 1965 it was moved to its present location.

51 S Ventu Park Rd, Newbury Park

NO. 727 ☐
PORTOLÁ EXPEDITION

On August 11, 1769, the Portolá Expedition arrived at the junction of the Arroyo Mupu and Santa Paula Creek, at a place they named the Holy Martyrs Ipolito and Cassiano. The priests of the Mission San Buenaventura here established the Asistencia Santa Paula, where they held services for the Mupu Indians.

Santa Paula Boys Club Recreation Center, 1400 block of Harvard Blvd, Santa Paula

NO. 756 🔔
SYCAMORE TREE

In 1846 General John C. Frémont passed this sycamore tree on his way to sign a treaty with General Andrés Pico to secure California for annexation to the United States. The tree has served as a resting place, a polling place, a temporary post office, and an outdoor chapel.

On State Hwy 126 (P.M. 16.7) at Hall Rd, 4 mi E of Santa Paula

NO. 847 🔔
VENTURA COUNTY COURTHOUSE

The courthouse was designed in 1910 by one of the early pioneers of architecture in Southern California—Albert C. Martin, Sr. Dedicated in July 1913, the structure is an outstanding example of neoclassic architecture, a style prevalent in the United States at the turn of the century. The courthouse is an extremely well-proportioned building, and is rich in detail and materials not likely to be found elsewhere in the Southern California area.

501 Poli St. at N California St, Ventura

NO. 939 🔔

Twentieth Century Folk Art Environments (Thematic)–GRANDMA PRISBREY'S BOTTLE VILLAGE

This fantastic assemblage is one of California's remarkable Twentieth Century Folk Art Environments. In 1956, Tressa Prisbrey, then nearly 60 years old, started building a fanciful "village" of shrines, walkways, sculptures, and buildings from recycled items and discards from the local dump. She worked for 25 years creating one structure after another to house her collections. Today, Bottle Village is composed of 13 buildings and 20 sculptures.

4595 Cochran St, Simi Valley

NO. 979 🔔

RANCHO SIMI

This is the site of the headquarters of the Spanish Rancho San José de Nuestra Senora de Altagarcia y Simi. The name derives from "Shimiji," the name of the Chumash village here before the Spanish. At 113,000 acres, Rancho Simi was one of the state's largest land grants. Two prominent Spanish and Mexican family names are connected with the Rancho: Santiago Pico who first received the grant, and José de la Guerra who purchased the Rancho in 1842. Two rooms of original adobe remain, part of the Strathearn home built in 1892-93.

Robert P Strathearn Historical Park, 137 Strathearn Place, Simi Valley

NO. 996

UNION OIL COMPANY BUILDING

The Santa Paula Hardware Company Building, more commonly referred to as the Union Oil Company Building, is significant for its historical importance as the birthplace of the Union Oil Company on October 17, 1890. The building continued to serve as a field division office after the main headquarters moved to Los Angeles in 1900. In 1950 the Union Oil Museum was established and in 1990, for its Centennial Celebration, the building was restored to its original appearance and reopened as a new state-of-the-art oil museum.

1003 E Main St, Santa Paula

Yolo County

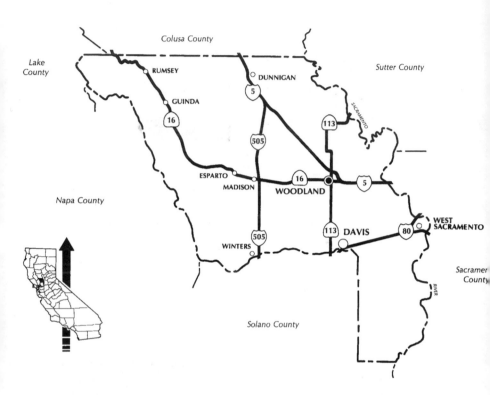

Woodland Opera House State Historic Park - Restored
Victorian Opera House of the 1890s. Located on the corner
of Main and Second Streets in Woodland.

Yolo
Est. 1850

Yolo County has 147 archeological sites and was named for a tribe of Patwin Indians. The rich valley soil and its rivers provided fertile hunting for Native Americans, and, later, fur trappers. The same fertile soil made this prime agricultural land for early settlers.

NO. 851 🔔
WOODLAND OPERA HOUSE

The first opera house to serve the Sacramento Valley was built on this site in 1885. The present structure, built in 1895-96, continues to represent an important center for theatrical arts of that period. Erected by David M. Hershey and incorporating the classic American playhouse interior, it served vast agricultural regions of the Sacramento Valley. Motion picture competition hastened its closing in 1913.

W side of 2nd St between Main St and Dead Cat Alley, Woodland

NO. 864 🏠
GABLE MANSION

The Gable Mansion, an outstanding example of 19th-century Victorian Italianate architecture, is one of the last of its style, size, and proportion in California. This structure was built in 1885 for Amos and Harvey Gable, pioneer Yolo County ranchers.

659–1st St, Woodland

Landmark No. 864

Yuba - Sutter Counties

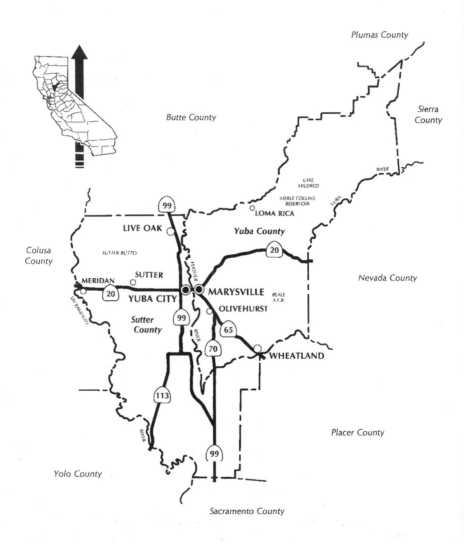

Yuba
Est. 1850

Much of Yuba County once belonged to Captain John Sutter, who sublet his agricultural lands. One such property, Johnson's Ranch, near present-day Wheatland, served as the western terminus of the California Emigrant Trail through Donner Pass. Indeed, seven members of the Donner Party arrived here in the winter of 1846-47, the first part of the party to end their mountain crossing ordeal.

NO. 320 🔔
TIMBUCTOO

In 1855, Timbuctoo was the largest town in eastern Yuba County. At the height of its prosperity it contained a church, theater, stores, hotels, and saloons, a Wells Fargo office, and the Stewart Bros. store which was restored in 1928 and dedicated to the town's pioneer men and women.

Plaque located on State Hwy 20 (P.M. 14.9); site on Timbuctoo Rd, 1.0 mi W of Smartville

NO. 321
SMARTSVILLE

The first building at Smartsville (the post office is called Smartville) was built in the spring of 1856 by a Mr. Smart. The Church of the Immaculate Conception (organized in 1852 in Rose's Bar) was built in 1861, and in 1863 the Union Church was erected. One of the prominent features of the landscape of the town today is its churches.

On State Hwy 20, Smartville

NO. 493 🔔
JOHNSON'S RANCH

The first settlement reached in California by emigrant trains using the Emigrant ("Donner") Trail, this was an original part of the 1844 Don Pablo Gutiérrez land grant. It was sold at auction to William Johnson in 1845, and in 1849 part of the ranch was set aside as a government reserve—Camp Far West. In 1866, the town of Wheatland was laid out on a portion of the grant.

Tomita Park, Front St, between Fourth and Main Sts, Wheatland

NO. 799-3 🔔
OVERLAND EMIGRANT TRAIL

Over a hundred years ago, this trail resounded to creaking wheels of pioneer wagons and the cries of hardy travelers on their way to the gold fields. It is estimated that over thirty thousand people used this trail in 1849. About a mile and a quarter east of this site is Johnson's Crossing, the last stop on the Overland Emigrant Trail and first settlement west of the Sierra. It was used by pioneers, miners, trappers, herdsmen, and adventurers; rescuers of the Donner Party assembled here to begin their mission on February 5, 1847.

On Spencerville Rd, 3.9 mi E of State Hwy 65, Wheatland

NO. 889 🔔

BOK KAI TEMPLE

Dedicated March 21, 1880, this building replaced the first temple built nearby in the early 1850s. It has been a Chinese community project since 1866, serving as a meeting hall, court, school, and place of worship. In this "Palace of Many Saints," Bok Eye, the water god, is the central deity and has been celebrated in Marysville on Bomb Day since Chinese settled here.

SW corner of First and D Sts, Marysville

NO. 934

TEMPORARY DETENTION CAMPS FOR JAPANESE AMERICANS–MARYSVILLE ASSEMBLY CENTER

The temporary detention camps (also known as "assembly centers") represent the first phase of the mass incarceration of 97,785 Californians of Japanese ancestry during World War II. Pursuant to Executive Order 9066 signed by President Franklin D. Roosevelt on February 19, 1942, thirteen makeshift detention facilities were constructed at various California racetracks, fairgrounds, and labor camps. These facilities were intended to confine Japanese Americans until more permanent concentration camps, such as those at Manzanar and Tule Lake in California, could be built in isolated areas of the country. Beginning on March 30, 1942, all native-born Americans and long-time legal residents of Japanese ancestry living in California were ordered to surrender themselves for detention.

Yuba County Fairgrounds, Marysville

NO. 1003 ☐

SITE OF THE WHEATLAND HOP RIOT OF 1913

The Wheatland Hop Riot was one of the most important and well-known events in California labor history. A bloody clash occurred at the Durst Ranch on August 3, 1913, climaxing growing tensions brought about by the difficult conditions farm laborers at the ranch endured. The riot resulted in four deaths and many injuries. It focused public opinion for the first time on the plight of California's agricultural laborers, and resulted in new state legislation to regulate labor camp conditions. A new State Commission on Immigration and Housing was created to help improve working conditions. Beyond that, the Wheatland Hop Riot was the first major farm labor confrontation in California and the harbinger of decades of attempts to organize or control agricultural labor.

Intersection of S "A" St and 6th St, Wheatland

California Historical Landmarks
Alphabetical Index

Full Name	County	Landmark #
Adams and Company Building	Sacramento	607
Adamson House at Malibu Lagoon State Beach	Los Angeles	966
Administration and Veteran's Memorial Building	San Luis Obispo	958
Adobe Chapel of the Immaculate Conception	San Diego	49
Adobe de Palomares	Los Angeles	372
Agua Fria	Mariposa	518
Agua Mansa	San Bernardino	121
Ah Louis Store (Site)	San Luis Obispo	862
A.K. Smiley Public Library	San Bernardino	994
Alameda Terminal of the First Transcontinental Railroad	Alameda	440
Almaden Vineyards	Santa Clara	505
Alpha Hydraulic Diggings	Nevada	628
Altaville	Calaveras	288
Alvarado Adobe	Contra Costa	512
Anaheim Landing	Orange	219
Angeles National Forest	Los Angeles & San Bernardino	717
Angel Island	Marin	529
Angels Camp	Calaveras	287
Angels Hotel	Calaveras	734
Anza Expedition Camp No. 94 Burlingame	San Mateo	48
Anza Expedition Camp No. 96 San Mateo Creek	San Mateo	47
Applegate-Lassen Emigrant Trail (Fandango Pass)	Modoc	546
Arcata and Mad River Railroad Company	Humboldt	842
Argonaut and Kennedy Mines	Amador	786
Armistice Oak Tree	Santa Clara	260
Arrowhead	San Bernardino	977
Arroyo de Cantua	Fresno	344
Arroyo de San Joseph Cupertino	Santa Clara	800
Asistencia de San Antonio	San Diego	243
Atascadero Administration and Veteran's Memorial Building	San Luis Obispo	958
Ávila Adobe	Los Angeles	145
E.J. Baldwin's Queen Anne Cottage	Los Angeles	367
Balboa Pavilion	Orange	959
Ballast Point Whaling Station Site	San Diego	50
Bancroft Ranch House	San Diego	626
Banning Park	Los Angeles	147
Barton Mound	Orange	218
Bass Hill	Shasta	148
Battle of Bloody Island	Lake	427

Battle of Land's Ranch-1872	Modoc	108
Battery Point Lighthouse	Del Norte	951
Battle Rock	Shasta	116
Beale's Cut Stagecoach Pass	Los Angeles	1006
Bealville	Kern	741
Bear Flag Monument	Sonoma	7
Bear Valley	Mariposa	331
Beckwourth Pass	Plumas	336
Bella Union Hotel Site	Los Angeles	656
Bell's Bridge	Shasta	519
Benicia Arsenal	Solano	176
Benicia Capitol	Solano	153
Benicia Seminary	Solano	795
Bennett-Arcane Long Camp	Inyo	444
Benson's Ferry	San Joaquin	149
Beringer Brothers Winery	Napa	814
Berkeley City Club	Alameda	908
B.F. Hastings Building	Sacramento	606
Bidwell's Bar	Butte	330
Big Bar	Amador & Calaveras	41
Big Basin Redwoods State Park	Santa Cruz	827
Big Oak Flat	Tuolumne	406
Birthplace of Archie Stevenot	Calaveras	769
Birthplace of "Silicon Valley"	Santa Clara	976
Birthplace of the United Nations, War Memorial Complex	San Francisco	964
Bishop Creek Battleground	Inyo	811
Black Star Canyon Indian Village Site	Orange	217
Bloody Point	Modoc	8
Blue Wing Inn	Sonoma	17
Bodega Bay and Harbor	Sonoma	833
Bodie	Mono	341
Bok Kai Temple	Yuba	889
Bonner Grade	Modoc	15
Box Canyon	San Diego	472
Brand Park (Memory Garden)	Los Angeles	150
Bridgeport Covered Bridge	Nevada	390
Broderick-Terry Dueling Place	San Mateo	19
Brother Jonathan Cemetery	Del Norte	541
Buck's Lake	Plumas	197
Buena Vista Refinery	Kern	504
Buena Vista Winery & Vineyards	Sonoma	392
Burial Place of John Brown ("Juan Flaco")	San Joaquin	513
Burlingame Railroad Station	San Mateo	846
Burned Wagons Point	Inyo	441
Burton Mound	Santa Barbara	306
Butte Store	Amador	39
Butterfield Overland Mail Route	San Diego	647
Butterfield Stage Route	Tulare	471

Casa de Carrillo	San Diego	74
Casa de Estudillo	San Diego	53
Casa de Governor Pío Pico	Los Angeles	127
Casa de la Guerra	Santa Barbara	307
Casa de López	San Diego	60
Casa de Machado	San Diego	71
Casa de Oro	Monterey	532
Casa de Pedrorena	San Diego	70
Casa de Rancho San Antonio (Henry Gage Mansion)	Los Angeles	984
Casa de San Pedro	Los Angeles	920
Casa de Stewart	San Diego	73
Casa de Tableta	San Mateo	825
Cascades, The	Los Angeles	653
Castillo de San Joaquín	San Francisco	82
Castro Home	Contra Costa	356
Castro House	San Benito	179
Catalina Adobe	Los Angeles	637
Cecil B. DeMille Studio Barn	Los Angeles	554
Centerville Beach Cross	Humboldt	173
Centinela Springs	Los Angeles	363
Chapel of San Ramon	Santa Barbara	877
Chapel of Santa Ysabel (Site of)	San Diego	369
Charles Copeland Morse Residence	Santa Clara	904
Charles Krug Winery	Napa	563
Charley's World of Lost Art	Imperial	939
Charter Oak or Election Tree	Tulare	410
Chatsworth Calera Site	Los Angeles	911
Chautauqua Hall	Monterey	839
Chawse Roundhouse	Amador	1001
Cherokee	Tuolumne	445
Chevra Kaddisha (Home of Peace Cemetery)	Sacramento	654-1
Chico Forestry Station and Nursery	Butte	840-2
Chili Gulch	Calaveras	265
Chiles Mill	Napa	547
Chimney Rock	Modoc	109
Chimney Rock	San Bernardino	737
China Camp	Marin	924
Chinese Camp	Tuolumne	423
Chinese Temple	Butte	770
Christmas Tree Lane	Los Angeles	990
Church of St. James, The Apostle	Alameda	694
City of Auburn	Placer	404
City of Eureka	Humboldt	477
City of Fresno	Fresno	488
City of Paris	San Francisco	876
City of Saratoga	Santa Clara	435
Clear Creek	Shasta	78
Clinton	Amador	37

Discovery Site of the Last Yahi Indian	Butte	809
Discovery Well of the Kern River Oil Field	Kern	290
Dog Town	Mono	792
Dogtown Nugget Discovery Site	Butte	771
Dominguez Ranch House	Los Angeles	152
Don Bernardo Yorba Ranch House Site	Orange	226
Don Fernando Pacheco Adobe	Contra Costa	455
Don Salvio Pacheco Adobe	Contra Costa	515
Donner Monument (or) Pioneer Monument	Nevada	134
Double Springs	Calaveras	264
Douglas Flat	Calaveras	272
Drum Barracks	Los Angeles	169
Drytown	Amador	31
Eadweard Muybridge & Development of Motion Pictures	Santa Clara	834
Eagle Theatre	Sacramento	595
Eastern Terminus of Clay Street Hill Railroad Company	San Francisco	500
Ebbetts Pass Route	Alpine	318
Ebner's Hotel	Sacramento	602
Eichbaum Toll Road	Inyo	848
El Adobe De Los Robles Rancho	Kings	206
El Camino Real	San Diego to San Francisco	784
El Campo Santo	San Diego	68
El Dorado	Calaveras	282
El Dorado (Mud Springs)	El Dorado	486
El Dorado-Nevada House (Mud Springs) Overland Pony Express Route in California	El Dorado	700
"El Dorado" Parker House, "Dennison's Exchange"	San Francisco	192
Elizabethtown	Plumas	231
El Monte—First Southern California Settlement by Immigrants from the U. S.	Los Angeles	975
El Vado	San Diego	634
Emigrant Gap	Placer	403
Emigrant Trail Crossing of Present Highway	Siskiyou	517
Empire City	Stanislaus	418
Empire Mine	Nevada	298
Entrance of the San Carlos into San Francisco Bay	San Francisco	236
Estrella Adobe Church	San Luis Obispo	542
Estudillo Home	Alameda	279
Evans & Bailey Fight-1861	Modoc	125
Exchange Hotel	San Diego	491
Fages-Zalvidea Crossing	Kern	291
Farnsworth's Green Street Lab	San Francisco	941
Farley's Olancha Mill Site	Inyo	796
Father Rinaldi's Foundation of 1896	Shasta	483
Felton Covered Bridge	Santa Cruz	583
Ferndale	Humboldt	883
Fifteen-Mile House—Overland Pony Express Route in California	Sacramento	698
Filoli	San Mateo	907

Fort Janesville	Lassen	758
Fort Miller	Fresno	584
Fort Reading	Shasta	379
Fort Rosecrans	San Diego	62
Fort Rosecrans National Cemetery	San Diego	55
Fort Ross	Sonoma	5
Fort Stockton	San Diego	54
Fort Tejón	Kern	129
Fort Ter-Wer	Del Norte	544
Fort Yuma	Imperial	806
Fountain Springs	Tulare	648
Fourth Crossing	Calaveras	258
Francisco Solano Alviso Adobe	Alameda	510
Frank Lloyd Wright Textile Block House		
(Freeman House, Ennis House)	Los Angeles	1011
Freeman Junction	Kern	766
Fremont Peak	San Benito	181
Frémont's Camp 1846	Modoc	6
French Camp	San Joaquin	668
French Gulch	Shasta	166
Fresno City	Fresno	488
Friday's Station, Overland Pony Express Route in California	El Dorado	728
Furnace of the Owens Lake Silver-Lead Company	Inyo	752
Gable Mansion	Yolo	864
Gamble House	Los Angeles	871
Garcés Baptismal Site	Kern	631
Garcés Circle	Kern	277
Garcés-Smith	San Bernardino	618
Gaviota Pass	Santa Barbara	248
General M. G. Vallejo's Home	Sonoma	4
George Yount Blockhouse	Napa	564
Georgetown	El Dorado	484
Giant Desert Figures Near Blythe	Riverside	101
Gilroy Yamato Hot Springs Resort	Santa Clara	1017
"The Glass House," Casa Materna of the Vallejos	Monterey	387
Glencoe (Mosquito Gulch)	Calaveras	280
Glendora Bougainvillea	Los Angeles	912
Glennville Adobe	Kern	495
Glenwood	Santa Cruz	449
Golden Gate Bridge	San Francisco	974
Gold Discovery Site	El Dorado	530
Gordon's Ferry on the Kern River	Kern	137
Governor Stoneman Adobe, "Los Robles"	Los Angeles	669
Governor's Mansion	Sacramento	823
Grandma Prisbey's Bottle Village	Ventura	939
Granville P. Swift Adobe	Glenn	345
Grave of Alexander Hamilton Willard	Sacramento	657
Grave of 1872 Earthquake Victims	Inyo	507

Hula Ville Hesperia	San Bernardino	939
Icaria-Speranza Commune	Sonoma	981
I.O.O.F. Hall, Mokelumne	Calaveras	256
Indian Military Post—Nomi Lackee Indian Reservation	Tehama	357
Indian Wells	Kern	457
Infernal Caves Battleground, 1867	Modoc	16
Iowa Hill	Placer	401
Irishtown	Amador	38
Italian Swiss Colony	Sonoma	621
Jack London State Historic Park	Sonoma	743
Jacksonville	Tuolumne	419
Jackson Gate	Amador	118
Jacoby Building	Humboldt	783
Jamestown	Tuolumne	431
Jamison City, Eureka Mills, Johnstown		
& the Famous Eureka Mines	Plumas	196
Jenny Lind	Calaveras	266
Jesus Maria	Calaveras	284
Joaquin Miller Home	Alameda	107
Joaquín Moraga Adobe	Contra Costa	509
John Adams Squire House	Santa Clara	857
John Medica's Garden	Sonoma	939
John Muir Home	Contra Costa	312
Johnson's Ranch	Yuba	493
José Eusebio Boronda Adobe Casa	Monterey	870
Juana Briones de Miranda Adobe on		
Rancho Purísima Concepción (Site of)	Santa Clara	524
Julian	San Diego	412
Kaweah Post Office, Kaweah Colony	Tulare	389
Kern River Slough Station	Kern	588
Kernville	Kern	132
Keysville	Kern	98
Kimberly Crest	San Bernardino	1019
Kingston	Kings	270
Kirkwood's	Amador	40
Kit Carson Marker	Alpine	315
Knight Foundry	Amador	1007
Knight's Ferry	Stanislaus	347
Kotani-En	Santa Clara	903
La Cañada de los Coches Rancho	San Diego	425
La Casa de Carrión	Los Angeles	386
La Christianita	San Diego	562
La Grange Mine (Hydraulic)	Trinity	778
La Grange (Town)	Stanislaus	414
La Mesa Battlefield	Los Angeles	167
La Punta de los Muertos (Dead Men's Point)	San Diego	57
La Purísima Concepción Mission Site	Imperial	350
Lady Adams Building	Sacramento	603

Oak Creek Pass	Kern	97
Oak Grove Stage Station	San Diego	502
Oak of the Golden Dream	Los Angeles	168
O'Byrne Ferry	Calaveras	281
Office of the Star Newspaper	San Francisco	85
Old Adobe Women's Club	Santa Clara	249
Old Arrow Tree	Humboldt	164
Old Bale Mill	Napa	359
Old Bear Valley Dam	San Bernardino	725
Old California-Oregon Road	Shasta	58
Old Customs House, Monterey	Monterey	1
Old Dry Diggins, Old Hangtown Placerville	El Dorado	475
Old Emigrant Road	Alpine	661
Old Emigrant Road	Amador	662
Old Emigrant Trail	Modoc	111
Old Folsom Powerhouse	Sacramento	633
Old Folsom Powerhouse—Sacramento Station A	Sacramento	633A
Old Harmony Borax Works	Inyo	773
"The Old Homestead"	Contra Costa	731
Old Indian Village of Tsurai	Humboldt	838
Old La Playa	San Diego	61
Old Lake County Courthouse	Lake	897
Old Landing	Orange	198
"Old Landing" Site of El Desembarcadero	San Diego	64
Old Lobero Theater	Santa Barbara	361
Old Maizeland School (Rivera School)	Orange	729
Old Mill	Los Angeles	302
Old Mining Camp of Brownsville	Calaveras	465
Old Mission Reservoir	Ventura	114
Old Pacific House	Monterey	354
Old Pioneer Hall	Amador	34
Old Plaza Fire House	Los Angeles	730
Old Point Loma Lighthouse	San Diego	51
Old Post Office	Santa Clara	854
Old Rómulo Pico Adobe (Ranchito Rómulo)	Los Angeles	362
Old Sacramento	Sacramento	812
Old Salt Lake	Los Angeles	373
Old Santa Ana	Orange	204
Old Santa Monica Forestry Station	Los Angeles	840
"Old Short Cut"	Los Angeles	632
Old Sites of Mission Santa Clara de Asis & Old Spanish Bridge	Santa Clara	250
Old Spanish Cemetery	San Diego	68
Old Spanish Lighthouse	San Diego	51
Old Store at La Honda	San Diego	343
Old Stovepipe Wells	Inyo	826
Old Suspension Bridge	Butte	314
Old Temescal Road	Riverside	638

Peter Lassen Marker (Site of Lassen Trading Post)	Plumas	184
Petrified Forest	Sonoma	915
Picacho Mines	Imperial	193
Pico House (Hotel)	Los Angeles	159
Piedmont Way	Alameda	986
Pigeon Point Lighthouse	San Mateo	930
Pioneer Baby's Grave	Shasta	377
Pioneer Cemetery	Calaveras	271
Pioneer Electronics Research Laboratory	Santa Clara	836
Pioneer Express Trail	Placer	585
Pioneer Grave (Grizzly Creek)	Plumas	212
Pioneer Hall	Amador	34
Pioneer House of the Mother Colony	Orange	201
Pioneer Mutual Volunteer Firehouse	Sacramento	612
Pioneer Oil Refinery—Restored	Los Angeles	172
Pioneer Paper Mill at Samuel P. Taylor State Park	Marin	552
Pioneer Schoolhouse	Plumas	625
Pioneer Ski Area of America—Plumas Eureka State Park	Plumas	723
Pioneer Ski Area of America— Squaw Valley	Placer	724
Pioneer Telegraph Station (formerly known as Terminal of the Pony Express Site)	Sacramento	366
Place Where Francisco Garcés Crossed the Kern River	Kern	278
Placerville, Overland Pony Express Route in California	El Dorado	701
Plank Road	Imperial	845
Plaza Hotel	San Benito	180
Plaza, San Diego Viejo ("Washington Square")	San Diego	63
Pleasant Grove House, Overland Pony Express Route in California	El Dorado	703
Plum Valley House	Sierra	695
Plummer Park and Oldest House in Hollywood	Los Angeles	160
Plymouth Trading Post	Amador	470
Point Dume	Los Angeles	965
Point on the Jedediah Smith Trial	Kern	660
Pomona Water Power Plant	Los Angeles	514
Pony Express Remount Station at Woodfords	Alpine	805
Portolá Expedition Camp near Gazos Creek	San Mateo	23
Portolá Expedition Camp (El Rincón de las Almejas")	San Mateo	25
Portolá Expedition Camp at Lagoon	San Mateo	27
Portolá Expedition Camp at Martini's Creek	San Mateo	25
Portolá Expedition Camp No. 8	San Mateo	94
Portolá Expedition at Pedro Grove	San Mateo	24
Portolá Expedition Camp Near Pilarcitos Creek	San Mateo	21
Portolá Expedition Camp on Purísima Creek	San Mateo	22
Portolá Expedition Camp Across San Fransquito Creek (Journey's End)	San Mateo	2
Portolá Expedition at Camp San Gregorio Creek	San Mateo	26
Portolá Expedition Camp at Woodside	San Mateo	92
Portolá Expedition Campsite	Ventura	727

Site of the First Flight of the Gossamer Condor	Kern	923
Site of First Grange Hall in California	El Dorado	551
Site of First Jewish Religious Services in San Francisco	San Francisco	462
Site of First Jewish Synagogue Owned by a Congregation on the Pacific Coast	Sacramento	654
Site of the First Junior College in California	Fresno	803
Site of the First Meeting of Freemasons Held in California	San Francisco	408
Site of First Posted Water Notice by Will S. Green	Glenn	831
Site of First Public School in Castro Valley	Alameda	776
Site of First School in Fall River Valley	Shasta	759
Site of First United States Mint in California	San Francisco	87
Site of First Water to Water Flight	Orange	775
Site of Former Benicia Barracks	Solano	177
Site of Former Village of Searsville	San Mateo	474
Site of Fort Guijarros	San Diego	69
Site of Fort Jones	Siskiyou	317
Site of Fort Romualdo Pacheco	Imperial	944
Site of Fresno Free Speech Fight of the Industrial Workers of the World	Fresno	873
Site of George Yount Blockhouse	Napa	564
Site of Giant Powder Company (Point Pinole)	Contra Costa	1002-1
Site of Grist Mill Built By Jared Dixon Sheldon 1846-1847	Sacramento	439
Site of Haraszthy Villa	Sonoma	392-1
Site of Home of Diego Sepúlveda	Los Angeles	380
Site of Home of Elisha Stevens	Kern	732
Site of Home of Newton Booth	Sacramento	596
Site of Hudson Cabin, Calistoga	Napa	683
Site of Indian Village of Pochea	Riverside	104
Site of Initial U.S. Air Meet	Los Angeles	718
Site of Invention of First Commercially Practicable Integrated Circut	Santa Clara	1000
Site of Invention of the Three-Reel Bell Slot Machine	San Francisco	937
Site of Jackson's Pioneer Jewish Synagogue	Amador	865
Site of Junipero Serra's Cross	Ventura	113
Site of the Kate O. Sessions Nursery	San Diego	764
Site of Kelsey House, Calistoga	Napa	686
Site of the Last Home of Alexis Godey	Kern	690
Site of Laurel Hill Cemetery	San Francisco	760
Site of the Lighter Wharf at Bolinas	Marin	221
Site of Llano del Rio Cooperative Colony	Los Angeles	933
Site of the Los Angeles Star	Los Angeles	789
Site of Louis Rubidoux House	Riverside	102
Site of Mark Hopkins Institute of Art	San Francisco	754
Site of Mission San Pedro y San Pablo Bicuner	Imperial	921
Site of Mission Santa Cruz	Santa Cruz	342
Site of Mission Vieja	Los Angeles	161
Site of Mokelumne City	San Joaquin	162
Site of Mormon Stockade	San Bernardino	44

Site of Murder of Dr. John Marsh	Contra Costa	722
Site of Nation's First Successful Beet Sugar Factory	Alameda	768
Site of Old Indian Village at Pebble Beach, Crescent City	Del Norte	649
Site of Old Rubidoux Grist Mill	Riverside	303
Site of Old St. Mary's Church	San Francisco	810
Site of Old Whaling Station	Los Angeles	381
Site of the Oldest Broadcasting Station in the World	Santa Clara	952
Site of One of the First Discoveries of Quartz Gold in California	Nevada	297
Site of Original Mission Dolores Chapel and Dolores Lagoon	San Francisco	327-1
Site of Orleans Hotel	Sacramento	608
Site of Overland Emigrant Trail on Highway 49	Nevada	799
Site of Parrott Granite Block	San Francisco	89
Site of Plumas House	Plumas	480
Site of "Port Los Angeles" Long Wharf	Los Angeles	881
Site of the Propagation of the Thompson Seedless Grape	Sutter	929
Site of Putnam's Cabin	Inyo	223
Site of the Rancho Chino Adobe of Isaac Williams	San Bernardino	942
Site of Sacramento Union	Sacramento	605
Site of St. Mary's College	Alameda	676
Site of Sam Brannan House	Sacramento	604
Site of San Diego Whaling Station	San Diego	50
Site of San Joaquin City	San Joaquin	777
Site of San Mateo County's First Sawmill	San Mateo	478
Site of Santa Clara Mission	Santa Clara	338
Site of Santa Cruz Mission	Santa Cruz	342
Site of Shell Mound	Alameda	335
Site of Southern's Stage Station	Shasta	33
Site of Stage and Railroad (First)	Sacramento	598
Site of Stone and Kelsey Home	Lake	426
Site of Town of Garlock	Kern	671
Site of What Cheer House	San Francisco	650
Site of the Wheatland Hop Riot of 1913	Yuba	1003
Site of Wood's Ferry and Wood's Bridge	San Joaquin	163
Site of World's First Broadcasting Station	Santa Clara	952
Site of York's Cabin, Calistoga	Napa	682
Sloughhouse	Sacramento	575
Smartsville	Yuba	321
Snelling Courthouse	Merced	409
Soberanes Adobe	Monterey	712
Sonora-Mono Road	Tuolumne	422
Soulsbyville	Tuolumne	420
South Yuba Canal Office	Nevada	832
Southern's Stage Station	Shasta	33
Soviet Transpolar Landing Site	Riverside	989
Spanish Landing	San Diego	891
Spanish Ranch and Meadow Valley	Plumas	481
Sportsman's Hall, Overland Pony Express Route in California	El Dorado	704

Springfield	Tuolumne	432
Squaw Rock	Mendocino	549
S.S. Emidio	Del Norte	497
S.S. Catalina	Los Angeles	894
Stagecoach Inn	Ventura	659
Stanford-Lathrop Home	Sacramento	614
State Capitol Site—Vallejo	Solano	574
State Indian Museum	Sacramento	991
Steele Brothers Dairy Ranches	San Mateo	906
Stockton Developemental Center	San Joaquin	1016
Stoddard-Waite Monument	San Bernardino	578
Stone Corral	Calaveras	263
Stone House	Lake	450
Strawberry Valley House, Overland Pony Express		
Route in California	El Dorado	707
Strawberry Valley Stage Station	Siskiyou	396
Studebaker's Shop	El Dorado	142
Sulphur Bank Mine	Lake	428
Summersville	Tuolumne	407
Sun House	Mendocino	926
Superintendant's Office	Santa Cruz	860
Sutter Creek	Amador	322
Sutter's Fort	Sacramento	525
Sutter's Landing	Sacramento	591
Sutterville	Sacramento	593
Swift's Stone Corral	Colusa	238
Swiss Hotel	Sonoma	496
Sycamore Grove	San Bernardino	573
Sycamore Tree	Ventura	756
Tailholt	Tulare	413
Tapia Adobe (Site of)	San Bernardino	360
Tehachapi Loop	Kern	508
Telegraph Hill	San Francisco	91
Temelec	Sonoma	237
Temporary Detention Camps for Japanese Americans	Fresno, Inyo, Los Angeles, Merced, Monterey, Sacramento, San Joaquin, San Mateo, Stanislaus, Tulare, Yuba	934
Temple Israel Cemetery	San Joaquin	765
Temple of Kuan Ti	Mendocino	927
Terminal of California's First Passenger Railroad	Sacramento	558
Terminal of the Pony Express Site	Sacramento	36
Timbuctoo	Yuba	320
Timm's Point and Landing	Los Angeles	384
Tip of Ballast Point	San Diego	56
Top of Grapevine Pass Where Don Pedro Fages Passed in 1772	Kern	283
Town of Calico	San Bernardino	782
Town of Dutch Flat	Placer	397

Warner's Ranch	San Diego	311
Warring Park	Ventura	624
Wassama Roundhouse	Madera	1001
Watts Towers of Simon Rodia	Los Angeles	993
Weaverville Joss House	Trinity	709
Weber Point and Site of Capt. Chas. M. Weber House	San Joaquin	165
Webster's (Sugar Loaf House), Overland Pony Express Route in California	El Dorado	706
Well Alamitos 1	Los Angeles	580
Well No. "2-6"	Kern	581
Well No. "CSO" (Pico" #4)	Los Angeles	516
Well No. "Hill" 4	Santa Barbara	582
Wells Fargo Express Company Building	Tuolumne	140
Wente Brothers Winery	Alameda	957
West Miner Street— Third Street Historic District	Yreka	901
West Point	Calaveras	268
Western Business Headquarters of Russell, Majors, and Waddell—Founders, Owners and Operators of Pony Express	San Francisco	696
Western Hotel	Los Angeles	658
Western Hotel	Sacramento	601
Whaley House	San Diego	65
What Cheer House	Sacramento	597
Whiskeytown	Shasta	131
Willms Ranch	Stanislaus	415
Willow Springs	Kern	130
Winchester House	Santa Clara	868
Woodbridge	San Joaquin	358
Woodland Opera House	Yolo	851
Woodside Store	San Mateo	93
Woodward's Gardens	San Francisco	454
Workman Home and Family Cemetery	Los Angeles	874
World's First Long Distance Telephone Line	Nevada	247
Yankee Jim's	Placer	398
Yank's Station, Overland Pony Express Route in California	El Dorado	708
Yorba Slaughter Adobe	San Bernardino	191
Yosemite Valley	Mariposa	790
Yucaipa Adobe	San Bernardino	528
Yucaipa Rancheria	San Bernardino	620
Yuha Well	Imperial	1008
Zanja	San Bernardino	43

Numerical Listing of Historical Landmarks

Landmark No. 514

58	Shasta	106	Monterey	153	Solano
59	San Diego	107	Alameda	154	Humboldt
60	San Diego	108	Modoc	155	San Joaquin
61	San Diego	109	Modoc	156	Los Angeles
62	San Diego	110	Siskiyou	157	Los Angeles
63	San Diego	111	Modoc	158	Los Angeles
64	San Diego	112	Orange	159	Los Angeles
65	San Diego	113	Ventura	160	Los Angeles
66	San Diego	114	Ventura	161	Los Angeles
67	San Diego	114-1	Ventura	162	San Joaquin
68	San Diego	115	Ventura	163	San Joaquin
69	San Diego	116	Shasta	164	Humboldt
70	San Diego	117	Tehama	165	San Joaquin
71	San Diego	118	Amador	166	Shasta
72	San Diego	119	San Francisco	167	Los Angeles
73	San Diego	120	Shasta	168	Los Angeles
74	San Diego	121	San Bernardino	169	Los Angeles
75	San Diego	122	Tuolumne	170	Los Angeles
76	Lassen	123	Tuolumne	171	Los Angeles
77	Shasta	124	Tuolumne	172	Los Angeles
78	Shasta	125	Modoc	173	Humboldt
79	San Francisco	126	Monterey	174	Solano
80	San Francisco	127	Los Angeles	175	Solano
81	San Francisco	128	Monterey	176	Solano
82	San Francisco	129	Kern	177	Solano
83	San Francisco	130	Kern	178	San Joaquin
84	San Francisco	131	Shasta	179	San Benito
85	San Francisco	132	Kern	180	San Benito
86	San Francisco	133	Kern	181	San Benito
87	San Francisco	134	Nevada	182	Imperial
88	San Francisco	135	Monterey	183	Tehama
89	San Francisco	136	Monterey	184	Plumas
90	San Francisco	137	Kern	185	Riverside
91	San Francisco	138	Tuolumne	186	Riverside
92	San Mateo	139	Tuolumne	187	Riverside
93	San Mateo	140	Tuolumne	188	Riverside
94	San Mateo	141	El Dorado	189	Orange
95	San Bernardino	142	El Dorado	190	Riverside
96	San Bernardino	143	El Dorado	191	San Bernardino
97	Kern	144	Los Angeles	192	San Francisco
98	Kern	145	Los Angeles	193	Imperial
99	Kern	146	Humboldt	194	Imperial
100	Kern	147	Los Angeles	195	San Benito
101	Riverside	148	Shasta	196	Plumas
102	Riverside	149	San Joaquin	197	Plumas
103	Riverside	150	Los Angeles	198	Orange
104	Riverside	151	Los Angeles	199	Orange
105	Monterey	152	Los Angeles	200	Orange

201	Orange	249	Santa Clara	297	Nevada
202	Orange	250	Santa Clara	298	Nevada
203	Orange	251	Calaveras	299	Alameda
204	Orange	252	Calaveras	300	Kern
205	Orange	253	Calaveras	301	Los Angeles
206	Kings	254	Calaveras	302	Los Angeles
207	Marin	255	Calaveras	303	Riverside
208	Inyo	256	Calaveras	304	San Diego
209	Inyo	257	Calaveras	305	Santa Barbara
210	Marin	258	Calaveras	306	Santa Barbara
211	Inyo	259	Santa Clara	307	Santa Barbara
212	Plumas	260	Santa Clara	308	Santa Barbara
213	Plumas	261	Calaveras	309	Santa Barbara
214	San Joaquin	262	Calaveras	310	Ventura
215	Humboldt	263	Calaveras	311	San Diego
216	Humboldt	264	Calaveras	312	Contra Costa
217	Orange	265	Calaveras	313	Butte
218	Orange	266	Calaveras	314	Butte
219	Orange	267	Calaveras	315	Alpine
220	Marin	268	Calaveras	316	Sonoma
221	Marin	269	Calaveras	317	Siskiyou
222	Marin	270	Kings	318	Alpine
223	Inyo	271	Calaveras	319	El Dorado
224	Riverside	272	Calaveras	320	Yuba
225	Orange	273	Calaveras	321	Yuba
226	Orange	274	Calaveras	322	Amador
227	Orange	275	Calaveras	323	Mariposa
228	Orange	276	Calaveras	324	San Benito
229	Inyo	277	Kern	325	San Luis Obispo
230	Inyo	278	Kern	326	San Luis Obispo
231	Plumas	279	Alameda	327	San Francisco
232	Monterey	280	Calaveras	327-1	San Francisco
233	Monterey	281	Calaveras	328	San Francisco
234	Sonoma	282	Calaveras	329	Butte
235	Los Angeles	283	Kern	330	Butte
236	San Francisco	284	Calaveras	331	Mariposa
237	Sonoma	285	Alameda	332	Mariposa
238	Colusa	286	Calaveras	333	Mariposa
239	San Diego	287	Calaveras	334	Alameda
240	Alpine	288	Calaveras	335	Alameda
241	Alameda	289	Los Angeles	336	Plumas
242	San Diego	290	Kern	337	Plumas
243	San Diego	291	Kern	338	Santa Clara
244	San Diego	292	Nevada	339	Santa Clara
245	Kings	293	Nevada	339-1	Santa Clara
246	Alameda	294	Nevada	340	Santa 'Barbara
247	Nevada	295	Calaveras	341	Mono
248	Santa Barbara	296	Calaveras	342	Santa Cruz

343	San Mateo	391	San Mateo	438	Tuolumne
344	Fresno	392	Sonoma	439	Sacramento
345	Glenn	392-1	Sonoma	440	Alameda
346	Sutter	393	San Mateo	441	Inyo
347	Stanislaus	394	San Mateo	442	Inyo
348	Monterey	395	Tuolumne	443	Inyo
349	Inyo	396	Siskiyou	444	Inyo
350	Imperial	397	Placer	445	Tuolumne
351	Monterey	398	Placer	446	Tuolumne
352	Monterey	399	Placer	447	Santa Clara
353	Monterey	400	Placer	448	Santa Clara
354	Monterey	401	Placer	449	Santa Cruz
355	Shasta	402	Placer	450	Lake
356	Contra Costa	403	Placer	451	Los Angeles
357	Tehama	404	Placer	452	San Diego
358	San Joaquin	405	Placer	453	San Francisco
359	Napa	406	Tuolumne	454	San Francisco
360	San Bernardino	407	Tuolumne	455	Contra Costa
361	Santa Barbara	408	San Francisco	456	El Dorado
362	Los Angeles	409	Merced	457	Kern
363	Los Angeles	410	Tulare	458	Santa Clara
364	San Luis Obispo	411	San Diego	459	San Francisco
365	San Joaquin	412	San Diego	460	Tuolumne
366	Sacramento	413	Tulare	461	Santa Clara
367	Los Angeles	414	Stanislaus	462	San Francisco
368	Los Angeles	415	Stanislaus	463	Placer
369	San Diego	416	Santa Clara	464	Sacramento
370	Calaveras	417	Santa Clara	465	Calaveras
371	Kern	418	Stanislaus	466	Calaveras
372	Los Angeles	419	Tuolumne	467	Lake
373	Los Angeles	420	Tuolumne	468	Sacramento
374	Kern	421	Sierra	469	Santa Cruz
375	San Mateo	422	Tuolumne	470	Amador
376	Kern	423	Tuolumne	471	Tulare
377	Shasta	424	Tuolumne	472	San Diego
378	Alpine	425	San Diego	473	Tulare
379	Shasta	426	Lake	474	San Mateo
380	Los Angeles	427	Lake	475	El Dorado
381	Los Angeles	A28	Lake	476	Kern
382	Kern	429	Lake	477	Humboldt
383	Los Angeles	430	Modoc	478	San Mateo
384	Los Angeles	431	Tuolumne	479	Plumas
385	Los Angeles	432	Tuolumne	480	Plumas
386	Los Angeles	433	Santa Clara	481	Plumas
387	Monterey	434	Santa Clara	482	San Diego
388	Tulare	435	Santa Clara	483	Shasta
389	Tulare	436	San Joaquin	484	El Dorado
390	Nevada	437	San Joaquin	485	Kern

486	El Dorado	533	San Diego	581	Kern
487	El Dorado	534	Solano	582	Santa Barbara
488	Fresno	535	Santa Barbara	583	Santa Cruz
489	Santa Clara	536	Los Angeles	584	Fresno
490	San Bernardino	537	Inyo	585	Placer
491	San Diego	538	San Diego	586	Alameda
492	Kern	539	Kern	587	San Francisco
493	Yuba	540	Kern	588	Kern
494	Monterey	541	Del Norte	589	Kern
495	Kern	542	San Luis Obispo	590	Los Angeles
496	Sonoma	543	Humboldt	591	Sacramento
497	Del Norte	544	Del Norte	592	Sacramento
498	Kern	545	Del Norte	593	Sacramento
499	Calaveras	546	Modoc	594	Sacramento
500	San Francisco	547	Napa	595	Sacramento
501	Sonoma	548	Merced	596	Sacramento
502	San Diego	549	Mendocino	597	Sacramento
503	Alameda	550	Merced	598	Sacramento
504	Kern	551	El Dorado	599	Sacramento
505	Santa Clara	552	Marin	600	Sacramento
506	Amador	553	Ventura	601	Sacramento
507	Inyo	554	Los Angeles	602	Sacramento
508	Kern	555	Shasta	603	Sacramento
509	Contra Costa	556	Los Angeles	604	Sacramento
510	Alameda	557	Riverside	605	Sacramento
511	Contra Costa	558	Sacramento	606	Sacramento
512	Contra Costa	559	Santa Barbara	607	Sacramento
513	San Joaquin	560	Monterey	608	Sacramento
514	Los Angeles	561	Napa	609	Sacramento
515	Contra Costa	562	San Diego	610	Sacramento
516	Los Angeles	563	Napa	611	Sacramento
516-2	Los Angeles	564	Napa	612	Sacramento
517	Siskiyou	565	Lassen	613	Sacramento
518	Mariposa	566	Sacramento	614	Sacramento
519	Shasta	567	Los Angeles	615	Mendocino
520	San Joaquin	568	Imperial	616	San Diego
521	El Dorado	569	El Dorado	617	San Bernardino
522	Los Angeles	570	El Dorado	618	San Bernardino
523	San Diego	571	El Dorado	619	San Bernardino
524	Santa Clara	572	El Dorado	620	San Bernardino
525	Sacramento	573	San Bernardino	621	Sonoma
526	Sacramento	574	Solano	622	San Bernardino
527	Mariposa	575	Sacramento	623	San Francisco
528	San Bernardino	576	San Bernardino	624	Ventura
529	Marin	577	San Bernardino	625	Plumas
530	El Dorado	578	San Bernardino	626	San Diego
531	Los Angeles	579	San Bernardino	627	Sonoma
532	Monterey	580	Los Angeles	628	Nevada

629	Nevada	675	Lassen	722	Contra Costa
630	Marin	676	Alameda	723	Plumas
631	Kern	677	Lassen	724	Placer
632	Los Angeles	678	Lassen	725	San Bernardino
633	Sacramento	679	Marin	726	San Luis Obispo
633-2	Sacramento	680	Sacramento	727	Ventura
634	San Diego	681	Los Angeles	728	El Dorado
635	San Diego	682	Napa	729	Orange
636	Santa Barbara	683	Napa	730	Los Angeles
637	Los Angeles	684	Napa	731	Contra Costa
638	Riverside	685	Napa	732	Kern
639	San Diego	686	Napa	733	Santa Clara
640	San Luis Obispo	687	Napa	734	Calaveras
641	Alameda	688	Los Angeles	735	Calaveras
642	Alameda	689	Los Angeles	736	Colusa
643	Kern	690	Kern	737	San Bernardino
644	Santa Clara	691	San Francisco	738	Riverside
645	Del Norte	692	Sonoma	739	Sonoma
646	Los Angeles	693	Napa	740	San Joaquin
647	San Diego	694	Alameda	741	Kern
648	Tulare	695	Sierra	742	Kern
649	Del Norte	696	San Francisco	743	Sonoma
650	San Francisco	697	Sacramento	744	Los Angeles
651	Monterey	698	Sacramento	745	Sacramento
652	Kern	699	El Dorado	746	Sacramento
653	Los Angeles	700	El Dorado	747	El Dorado
654	Sacramento	701	El Dorado	748	El Dorado
654-1	Sacramento	702	Sacramento	749	Riverside
655	Los Angeles	703	El Dorado	750	San Diego
656	Los Angeles	704	El Dorado	751	Solano
657	Sacramento	705	El Dorado	752	Inyo
658	Los Angeles	706	El Dorado	753	Los Angeles
659	Ventura	707	El Dorado	754	San Francisco
660	Kern	708	El Dorado	755	San Joaquin
661	Alpine	709	Trinity	756	Ventura
662	Amador	710	Napa	757	Kern
663	Calaveras	711	San Diego	758	Lassen
664	Los Angeles	712	Monterey	759	Shasta
665	Los Angeles	713	Monterey	760	San Francisco
666	Sacramento	714	Mendocino	761	Riverside
667	Sonoma	715	Amador	762	Amador
668	San Joaquin	716	Los Angeles	763	Lassen
669	Los Angeles	717	San Bernardino	764	San Diego
670	Mariposa	"	Los Angeles	765	San Joaquin
671	Kern	718	Los Angeles	766	Kern
672	Kern	719	Sacramento	767	El Dorado
673	San Diego	720	San Luis Obispo	768	Alameda
674	Mendocino	721	Santa Barbara	769	Calaveras

770	Butte	807	Butte	853	Contra Costa
771	Butte	808	Imperial	854	Santa Clara
772	San Francisco	809	Butte	855	Nevada
773	Inyo	810	San Francisco	856	San Mateo
774	San Bernardino	811	Inyo	857	Santa Clara
775	Orange	812	Sacramento	858	San Diego
776	Alameda	813	Santa Clara	859	San Bernardino
777	San Joaquin	814	Napa	860	Santa Cruz
778	Trinity	815	El Dorado	861	San Francisco
779	Solano	816	San Mateo	862	Solano
780	Sacramento	817	Sacramento	863	Nevada
780-1	Placer	818	San Diego	864	Yolo
780-2	Placer	819	San Francisco	865	Amador
780-3	Placer	820	Sonoma	866	Santa Clara
780-4	Placer	821	San Luis Obispo	867	Amador
780-5	Placer	822	Los Angeles	868	Santa Clara
780-6	Nevada	823	Sacramento	869	Sacramento
780-7	San Joaquin	824	Alameda	870	Monterey
780-8	Sacramento	825	San Mateo	871	Los Angeles
781	San Bernardino	826	Inyo	872	Sacramento
782	San Bernardino	827	Santa Cruz	873	Fresno
783	Humboldt	828	Napa	874	Los Angeles
784	San Francisco	829	Merced	875	San Francisco
784	San Diego	830	San Diego	876	San Francisco
785	San Diego	831	Glenn	877	Santa Barbara
786	Amador	832	Nevada	878	Napa
787	Riverside	833	Sonoma	879	Sonoma
788	Amador	834	Santa Clara	880	Solano
789	Los Angeles	835	Sonoma	881	Los Angeles
790	Mariposa	836	Santa Clara	882	Humboldt
791	San Francisco	837	Orange	883	Humboldt
792	Mono	838	Humboldt	884	Alameda
793	San Diego	839	Monterey	885	Placer
794	Orange	840	Los Angeles	886	San Mateo
795	Solano	840-2	Butte	887	Los Angeles
796	Inyo	841	San Francisco	888	Santa Clara
797	Placer	842	Humboldt	889	Yuba
798	San Diego	843	Nevada	890	Colusa
799	Nevada	844	San Diego	891	San Diego
799-2	Placer	845	Imperial	892	San Bernardino
799-3	Yuba	846	San Mateo	893	Sonoma
800	Santa Clara	847	Ventura	894	Los Angeles
801	San Joaquin	848	Inyo	895	Santa Clara
802	San Luis Obispo	849	Alameda	896	Alameda
803	Fresno	850	Inyo	897	Lake
804	Solano	850-2	Modoc	898	Santa Clara
805	Alpine	851	Yolo	899	Nevada
806	Imperial	852	Nevada	900	Sacramento

901	Siskiyou	939	Napa	976	Santa Clara
902	Santa Clara	"	San Mateo	977	San Bernardino
903	Santa Clara	"	San Luis Obispo	978	Los Angeles
904	Santa Clara	"	Ventura	979	Ventura
905	Contra Costa	"	Los Angeles	980	Mendocino
906	San Mateo	"	San Bernardino	981	Sonoma
907	San Mateo	"	Imperial	982	San Diego
908	Alameda	"	Sonoma	983	Santa Cruz
909	San Mateo	940	San Diego	984	Los Angeles
910	Santa Clara	941	San Francisco	985	Imperial
911	Los Angeles	942	San Bernardino	"	Riverside
912	Los Angeles	943	Riverside	"	San Bernardino
913	Santa Clara	944	Imperial	986	Alameda
914	Nevada	945	Santa Clara	987	San Francisco
915	Sonoma	946	Alameda	988	Los Angeles
916	Fresno	947	Los Angeles	989	Riverside
917	Marin	948	Riverside	990	Los Angeles
918	Orange	949	San Mateo	991	Sacramento
919	Los Angeles	950	San Bernardino	992	Riverside
920	Los Angeles	951	Del Norte	993	Los Angeles
921	Imperial	"	Contra Costa	994	San Bernardino
922	Marin	"	Monterey	995	San Joaquin
923	Kern	952	Santa Clara	996	Ventura
924	Marin	953	Inyo	997	Los Angeles
925	Alameda	954	Alameda	998	Santa Cruz
926	Mendocino	955	San Mateo	999	Marin
927	Mendocino	956	Calaveras	1000	Santa Clara
928	Santa Barbara	957	Alameda	1001	Madera
929	Sutter	958	San Luis Obispo	"	Amador
930	San Mateo	959	Orange	1002	San Francisco
931	San Joaquin	960	Los Angeles	1003	Yuba
932	Contra Costa	961	Los Angeles	1004	Orange
933	Los Angeles	962	Alameda	1005	Riverside
934	Fresno	963	Los Angeles	1006	Los Angeles
"	Inyo	963-1	San Bernardino	1007	Amador
"	Los Angeles	964	San Francisco	1008	Imperial
"	Merced	965	Los Angeles	1009	Riverside
"	Monterey	966	Los Angeles	1010	San Francisco
"	Sacramento	967	Sacramento	1011	Los Angeles
"	San Joaquin	968	Alameda	1012	Nevada
"	San Mateo	969	Santa Clara	1013	Sacramento
"	Stanislaus	970	Alameda	1014	Los Angeles
"	Tulare	971	Sierra	1015	Orange
"	Yuba	972	Los Angeles	1016	San Joaquin
935	San Joaquin	973	Solano	1017	Santa Clara
936	San Luis Obispo	974	Marin	1018	Los Angeles
937	San Francisco	"	San Francisco	1019	San Bernardino
938	Kern	975	Los Angeles	1020	San Diego

Notes

Notes

Notes

Notes

Notes

Notes